A Seeker's Śrīmad Bhagavad-gītā

AF441534

Vishwanath Iyer

INDIA · SINGAPORE · MALAYSIA

Copyright © Vishwanath Iyer 2025
All Rights Reserved.

ISBN 979-8-89673-415-4

This book has been published with all efforts taken to make the material error-free after the consent of the author. However, the author and the publisher do not assume and hereby disclaim any liability to any party for any loss, damage, or disruption caused by errors or omissions, whether such errors or omissions result from negligence, accident, or any other cause.

While every effort has been made to avoid any mistake or omission, this publication is being sold on the condition and understanding that neither the author nor the publishers or printers would be liable in any manner to any person by reason of any mistake or omission in this publication or for any action taken or omitted to be taken or advice rendered or accepted on the basis of this work. For any defect in printing or binding the publishers will be liable only to replace the defective copy by another copy of this work then available.

Reviews

N. Ravichandran
Professor (Retired)
Indian Institute of Management, Ahmedabad

This is an erudite exposition of Geeta aimed to help an interested youth to understand the essence of Geeta as a way of life. The exposition lucid and absorbing. The author has done a commendable job in presenting the main ideas of the Geetha with several administrative, managerial and day to day situations. Highly recommended for the modern youth for an in-depth readable exposition to Geeta.

***

Pijus Kanti Pal
Saṃskṛta **Scholar and Academician**

"A Seeker's *Śrīmad-bhagavad-gītā*" by Yogi Vishwanath Iyer is a profound exploration of the various philosophies encompassed within the *sanātana-dharma* tradition. The book begins with an insightful overview, explaining the complexity and diversity of philosophies within the *sanātana-dharma* tradition. It highlights the existence of multiple schools of thought, sub-schools, and variations based on interpretation, region, culture, practice, and the influence of a guru.

The inclusion of diacritic marks ensures the accurate representation of Saṃskṛta verses, allowing readers to engage with the original language of the text. This attention to detail is commendable and greatly enhances the reading experience, particularly for those with a deeper understanding of *Saṃskṛta*.

Furthermore, Yogi Vishwanath Iyer's arrangement of thoughts and ideas throughout the manuscript is meticulous and coherent. The flow of the document is well-organized, enabling a smooth progression of concepts. Each chapter builds upon the previous one, creating a logical and comprehensive structure. This thoughtful arrangement helps readers grasp the intricate teachings of the Bhagavad Gita and ensures a deeper understanding of the subject matter.

In terms of the book's impact on readers, the open philosophical format advocated by the author proves to be advantageous. It allows individuals to explore multiple philosophical directions and encourages them to adapt their spiritual paths according to their changing needs, personality, and aspirations. This flexibility enables seekers to borrow from various philosophical streams without fear of criticism, fostering a more inclusive and personalized spiritual journey. By providing this open format structure, the book empowers readers to navigate the complexities of *sanātana-dharma* and embark on a path that resonates with their own unique spiritual quest.

***

Dolon Chanpa Mondal
Saṃskṛta **Scholar and Academician**

"A Seeker's *Śrīmad-bhagavad-gītā*" by Yogi Vishwanath Iyer is a significant contribution to the study and understanding of the Bhagavad Gita. I hope the transliteration of all *Saṃskṛta* words worked by me will give a good reading experience to non-*Saṃskṛta* readers.

While reviewing the book, it is important to acknowledge the author's efforts in presenting complex concepts in a manner accessible to both *Saṃskṛta* scholars and general readers. The book's open philosophical format allows readers to embark on a personal spiritual journey, adapting their path to their changing needs and aspirations. The translation, along with the insightful commentary, enables a wider audience to comprehend the profound teachings of the *Bhagavad-gītā*. Yogi Vishwanath Iyer's clear and concise style ensures that the intended thoughts and concepts are easily understood, making the book a valuable resource for individuals seeking spiritual enlightenment.

Another strength of the book is its relevance and applicability to modern times. The author skilfully draws connections between ancient wisdom and contemporary situations, making the teachings of the *Bhagavad-gītā* relatable and applicable in today's world. By incorporating relevant examples and addressing universal human experiences, Yogi Vishwanath Iyer provides readers with practical insights and guidance for navigating the challenges of life.

Dedication

Dedicated to my niece, Priya Chittur,
without whom this book would never have become a reality.

Acknowledgment

I thank my wife Latha and children Aarudra and Akshara for their support and affection, and my late parents and other family members for their constant support and encouragement.

Specifically, I thank Priya Chittur for her questioning nature and curiosity. This forced me to work out solutions which often brought clarity to me in my own understanding of the concept and made this book cohesive.

I also acknowledge and thank Mali and Nandakumar for assistance in editing and adding value.

My school classmates Dr. Sunder and Joydeep Roy as well as my college classmate, Dr. Murali, who spent considerable amount of time reviewing the document, have my deepest gratitude. My thanks also to Sundar, relative and quality professional, for reviewing "puruṣottama-yoga."

I also thank two people I have never met, Ajay Desai and Rukmani Vijayaraghavan, for their editing as well as practical and useful suggestions.

I am grateful to Sreejit Datta, who was Director of Centre for Civilisational Studies, Assistant Professor, Resident Mentor from Rashtram School of Public Leadership, India, for mentoring me in the world of academics and diacritics.

Lastly, I am profoundly grateful to Dr. Anuradha Choudry, (Assistant Professor, Department of Humanities and Social Sciences, IIT Kharagpur, and Coordinator, Indian Knowledge Systems Division, AICTE-Ministry of Education, Govt. of India) for her support, and her *Saṃskṛta* scholars and academics Pijus Kanti Pal and Dolon Chanpa Mondal for their support in *Saṃskṛta* transliteration and quality control.

For the *Saṃskṛta* text of *Śrīmad-bhagavad-gītā,* Dolon Chanpa Mondal has followed the work of Śrī. Anilbaran Roy for typing the text.

◆——·●◆●·——◆

Preface

I received my copy of *Śrīmad-bhagavad-gītā* from my parents at age 15. It was the work of Swami Chidbhavananda and has remained my primary reference book for *Śrīmad-bhagavad-gītā*. However, I admit that for a long period, the book sat in a cupboard and was rescued only occasionally.

I began serious work on *Śrīmad-bhagavad-gītā* in 2016 to support my website www.schoolofyoga.in. However, I faced multiple challenges, the most important being that I did not know *Saṃskṛta*. So, I decided to use the method of triangulation, which was to use three reference books and a *Saṃskṛta*-English dictionary.

The advantage I had was that I had no preconceived notions about the book, so I started with a fairly clean slate, one that was low on bias.

My first attempts were crude, but I learned two things. First, all English translations of *Śrīmad-bhagavad-gītā* were coloured by India's invasions, colonisation, and post-Independence socialism. Second, all the commentaries and translations of even the most evolved in this subject, reflected bias of personality and background.

Another discovery was that translation from *Saṃskṛta* to English brings with it a drop in transferability because cultural nuances cannot be transferred. This freed me from fears of inaccuracy because all efforts were clearly approximations, and correct interpretation was personal.

Only Śrī Kṛṣṇa knew what he was saying, everyone else was approximating.

So, all I had to do was focus on the accuracy of my interpretation. This is what I have done. I have translated and re-written this document at least three times with a gap of at least 6 months between each effort. So, what I got was fairly fresh-eyes every time I rewrote the manuscript. Also, by rewriting it thrice using triangulation, I think that I have obtained my best possible outcome.

Some personal idiosyncrasies:

1. I have constantly sought evidence for any theory or belief. So, I have a problem with God! I am willing to accept that there might be such an entity, but so far, I have not found the evidence.

2. Also, I have a problem with the reference of Śrī Kṛṣṇa as Bhagavān. Since I could not get a convincing answer for the meaning of Bhagavān, I have referred to Śrī Kṛṣṇa in this book as "Śrī Kṛṣṇa."

3. Lastly, since I don't know what Hindu is, so I have refrained from using Hinduism anywhere, just as I think that the cultural framework of Bhārat encompasses the entire SAARC region, so referring to India as the bedrock of the South Asian culture is not accurate.

One of the biggest challenges I had was how to deal with *Saṃskṛta* on account of three reasons.

1. First and obvious one was my own lack of knowledge on the subject.

2. The second issue was that English translations were not accurate (for example, *śraddhā* has no clear English equivalent; google says it is faith, which is inaccurate).

3. Third was that when only English was used, the cultural connotation was lost (for example, *ṛṇānubandhana* and *sambandha* are also expressions used in marriage) "and other relationships as well as situations after marriage." So, when many of these words are used independently, cultural nuances are lost and accuracy in interpretation is reduced.

4. Also, I have struggled with the use of "caps" in the document. *Saṃskṛta*, like Bhārat's languages has no caps; for instance Śrī Kṛṣṇa in *Saṃskṛta* can also be śri kṛṣṇa. But that does not look right. So, I have tried to use "Caps" when referring to an entity/ noun (example Brahman/ brahman or yoga/ Yoga). This is a confusion that lasts throughout the book.

Hence, after much soul-searching, I decided that without *Saṃskṛta*, *Śrīmad-bhagavad-gītā* is incomplete. This book is heavily laced with *Saṃskṛta* despite my own shortcomings with the language. I hope that the reader does not get overwhelmed by it and is able to navigate the book.

This is my understanding of *Śrīmad-bhagavad-gītā*. It may not be a conventional translation because my background is not particularly conventional. I come from a family of yoga teachers, researchers, and writers. Also, most of my life was spent in the automotive industry. So, everything in this book is coloured by my background and exposure.

The book reflects my own evolution in Yoga. Much of what I have written may not be conventional but is my own effort to understand *yoga-vidyā*. The evolution from *Brahman* to *karma, guṇa, Prakṛti-Puruṣa* as well as *Śiva-Śakti* is a result of the work I have done in since 1986 on the subject.

Also, because I have been working on this for so long and read so many works casually, I do not have an exhaustive list of references to support my work.

As of now, I have reached the limits of my own capabilities. My next version will come after I receive feedback, because with feedback comes fresh perspective. So, please do go to the website (https://schoolofyoga.in/category/yoga-social-system) and leave your comments, as this will enable me to grow.

Vishwanath R. Iyer
Chennai, India

Saṃskṛta Diacritics

Diacritics are a system of accents, such as dots, squiggles, etc., which are added to a letter that enable the language to be represented more accurately. In this book, the following diacritic representation of *Saṃskṛta* alphabet is used (https://www.sussex. ac.uk/informatics/punctuation/misc/diacritics).

<table>
<tr><td colspan="10" align="center">संस्कृतवर्णमाला - saṃskṛta-varṇamālā</td></tr>
<tr><td colspan="10"></td></tr>
<tr><td colspan="2" align="center">Vowels</td><td colspan="8" align="center">monophthongs</td></tr>
<tr><td>स्वर</td><td>घोष</td><td>अ</td><td>आ</td><td>इ</td><td>ई</td><td>उ</td><td>ऊ</td><td>ऋ</td><td>ॠ</td><td>ऌ</td></tr>
<tr><td>svara</td><td>ghoṣa</td><td>a</td><td>ā</td><td>i</td><td>ī</td><td>u</td><td>ū</td><td>ṛ</td><td>ṝ</td><td>ḷ</td></tr>
</table>

	Diphthongs - संयुक्त-स्वराः		*anusvāra* - अनुस्वार		*visarga* - विसर्ग	
ए	ऐ	औ	अं		अः	
e	*ai*	*au*	*aṃ*		*aḥ*	

Consonants		Non-aspirated	Aspirated	Non-aspirated	Aspirated	Nasal
व्यञ्जनानि		अल्पप्राण	महाप्राण	अल्पप्राण	महाप्राण	अनुनासिक
vyañjanāni		*alpaprāṇa*	*mahāprāṇa*	*alpaprāṇa*	*mahāprāṇa*	*anunāsika*
कवर्ग	कण्ठ्य	gutturals	क	ख	ग	घ	ङ
kavarga	*kaṇṭhya*		*ka*	*kha*	*ga*	*gha*	*ṅa*
चवर्ग	तालव्य	palatal	च	छ	ज	झ	ञ
cavarga	*tālavya*		*ca*	*cha*	*ja*	*jha*	*ña*
टवर्ग	मूर्धन्य	cerebral	ट	ठ	ड	ढ	ण
ṭavarga	*mūrdhanya*		*ṭa*	*ṭha*	*ḍa*	*ḍha*	*ṇa*

तवर्ग	दन्त्य	dentals	त	थ	द	ध	न
tavarga	*dantya*		*ta*	*tha*	*da*	*dha*	*na*
पवर्ग	ओष्ठ्य	labials	प	फ	ब	भ	म
pavarga	*oṣṭhya*		*pa*	*pha*	*ba*	*bha*	*ma*
अन्तःस्थ		semi-vowels	य	र	ल	व	
antaḥstha			*ya*	*ra*	*la*	*va*	
शवर्ग	ऊष्म	sibilants	श	ष	स		
śavarga	*ūṣma*		*śa*	*ṣa*	*sa*		
महाप्राण		aspirate	ह	क्ष			
mahāprāṇa			*ha*	*kṣa*			

***Saṃskṛta* lexicon (some words that have been used frequently in this book)**

Saṃskṛta is a nearly comprehensive and complete ancient language, and its word usage is often contextual. So, the meaning of the words may change in a nuanced manner, depending on the situation and sentiment *(bhāva)* being conveyed.

The entire *saṃskṛta* alphabet or *saṃskṛta-varṇamālā* is encapsulated in the *Māheśvarāṇi sūtrāṇi.*

माहेश्वराणि सूत्राणि - १. अइउण्। २. ऋलृक्। ३. एओङ्। ४. ऐऔच्। ५. हयवरट्। ६. लण्। ७. अमङणनम्। ८. झभञ्। ९. घढधष्। १०. जबगडदश्। ११. खफछठथचटतव्। १२. कपय्। १३. शषसर्। १४. हल्

Māheśvarāṇi sūtrāṇi - 1. *a-i-u-ṇ*   2. *ṛ-ḷ-k* 3. *e-o-ṅ* 4. *ai-au-c* 5. *ha-ya-va-ra-ṭ* 6. *la-ṇ* 7. *ña-ma-ṅa-ṇa-na-m* 8. *jha-bha-ñ* 9. *gha-ḍha-dha-ṣ* 10. *ja-ba-ga-ḍa-da-ś* 11. *kha-pha-cha-ṭha-tha-ca-ṭa-ta-v* 12. *ka-pa-y* 13. *śa-ṣa-sa-r* 14. *ha-l*

In this book, I have used broad meanings to enable the reader to develop contextual familiarity and get an overall flavour of various words used in the book. All words used in the book are not covered, but I have tried to cover ones that are most important.

Throughout the book, the *Saṃskṛta* words are in italics. As far as possible, I have used the English word first and given the *Saṃskṛta* alongside in brackets to increase the reader's familiarity with the subject as well as language.

abhyāsa – Effort, exercise, study.

adhibhūtas / pañcabhūtas (primordial elements) – Earth *(pṛthvī)*, water *(ap)*, fire *(agni)*, air *(vāyu)*, space *(ākāśa)*.

āgama – Can mean coming, but here it means *āgama-śāstra* which means manual, process, system etc.

ānanda – Happiness when applied colloquially, in yoga, it means bliss that one experiences on cognition of perfection/ Truth/ *brahman*.

āsana – Form of static exercising that maximises control over *prāṇa* (motility).

āśrama (stages in life) – *brahmacaryāśrama* (student), *gṛhasthāśrama* (family) / *vāṇaprasthāśrama* (retired), and *sannyāsāśrama* (renunciate).

asmitā (sense of self-worth or identity) / *ahaṅkāra* (sense of being the doer) / *svabhāva* (personality).

ariṣaḍvarga (six afflictions) – desire *(kāma)*, anger *(krodha)*, greed *(lobha)*, delusion *(moha)*, stubbornness *(mada),* and envy *(mātsarya).*

ātman (Self or Soul) / *adhyātma* (primordial Self).

ātmavicāra – Introspection into the nature of the Self.

bhāva – Emotion, sentiment.

brahman/ śūnya/ pūrṇa/ tat – All describe the cognitive state of the Brahman.

cakra (vortices of prāṇa) – *mūlādhāra* (base seat) / *svādhiṣṭhāna* (own-seat) / *maṇipūra* (navel) / *anāhata* (unstruck) / *viśuddha* (pure) / *ājñā* (control) / *sahasrāra* (thousand spoked).

cittavṛtti – Rising or movement of consciousness (*citta* = consciousness + *vṛtti* = rising or movement).

darśana (that which is shown) / *dṛṣṭi* (that which is seen) / *draṣṭṛ* (seer) – All variables associated with sight.

devālayam (temple) / *iṣṭadeva* (favourite deity or role model).

dharma (natural state, harmony or conditioning) – *sāmānya* (generic natural state) / *viśeṣa* (specific state or conditioning) / *svadharma* (personal conditioning).

dharma is dependent on *kāla* (time), *sthāna* (place), and *pātra* (vessel or cuisine).

guṇa (attribute) – *tamas* (indolence, confusion) / *rajas* (passion/ desire) / *sattva* (harmony / control).

guru – teacher, guide, anchor, he that takes one from darkness to light.

haṭha-yoga /saṭkriyā - Six cleansing actions.

jīva – Sentient soul / *jaḍa* – Insentient soul.

jñāna (cognition of the Self) / *vijñāna* (cognition of the environment/ situation).

jñānendriya (sensory organs) – *cakṣu* (vision) / *śrotra* (hearing) / *ghrāṇa* (smell) / *rasana* (taste) / *spārśana* (touch).

karmendriya (motor organs) – *vāk* (speech) / *pāṇi* (hand) / *pāda* (feet) / *pāyu* (anus) / *upastha* (reproduction organ).

karma (action) *saṅgraha* (collection) – *adhiṣṭhāna* (place) / *kartā* (doer) / *kāraṇa* (reason) / *pṛthak-ceṣṭā* (sub-activities) / *devam* (deity) *karmachodanā* (motivation) / *jñānam* (knowledge) / *jñeyam* (objective) / *parijñāna* (accurate understanding).

karmaphala-tyāga – Renunciation of the fruits of action.

kośa (sheath) – *annamayakośa* (sheath of food), *prāṇamayakośa* (sheath of motility), *manomayakośa* (sheath of cognition), *vijñānamayakośa* (sheath of awareness), *ānandamayakośa* (sheath of happiness).

kṣetra – Field of action) / *kṣetrajña* – Cognition of the field of action.

māyā - materiality.

mokṣa – Transcending materiality and merging with *brahman*.

nāḍi (channel) – *suṣumṇā* (central channel) / *piṅgalā-nāḍī* (sun channel) / *idā-nāḍī* (moon channel).

pañca-mahā-yajñas – Five major sacrifices to – *deva* (deity), *ṛṣi* (preceptors), *pitṛ* (ancestors), *bhūta* (environment / all other entities), *manuṣya* (mankind).

prajñā (awareness) – *praṇava* (cognition of Om) / *sthithaprajñā* (steady awareness) / *jāgrat* (awakened state) / *svapna* (dream state) / *suṣupti* (cognition beyond form) / *turīya* (fourth state).

Stages of awareness – *kṣipta* (distracted) / *mūḍha* (dull) / *vikṣipta* (scattered) / *ekāgra* (single pointed) / *niruddha* (empty/ purged).

prāṇāyāma (breathing control) – *pūraka* (inhalation) / *recaka* (exhalation) / *kumbhaka* (retention) / *nāḍī*-śuddhi (channel cleansing) / *bhastrikā* (bellows breathing) / *kapālabhātī* (skull cleansing).

pramāṇa (methods of proving) – *pratyakṣa* (personal experience) / *anumāna* (inference) / *upamāna* (similar) / *anupalabdhi* (negative observation) / *arthāpatti* (circumstantial evidence) / *śabda* (verbal testimony).

prāṇa (motility) – *prāṇa-vāyu* (incoming motility) / *apāna-vāyu* (outgoing motility) / *vyāna-vāyu* (aural motility) / *udāna-vāyu* (upward flowing motility) / *samāna-vāyu* (equalising motility).

pūjā – Worship.

puruṣottama – Perfect person.

puruṣa (primordial Identity) / *prakṛti* (manifestation of *puruṣa*).

puruṣārtha (objective of living) – *artha* (material betterment) / *kāma* (attainment of desires) / *dharma* (harmonious living) / *mokṣa* (liberation).

rāga (like) / *dveṣa* (dislike).

rājā (king) / *aṣṭāṅga* (eight-limbed) – *yama, niyama, āsana* (exercise), *prāṇāyāma* (breath control), *pratyāhāra* (withdrawal), *dhyāna* (concentration).

yama (behaviour control) – *ahiṃsā* (non-violence), *satya* (truth), *asteya* (non-stealing), *aparigraha* (non-grasping), *brahmacarya* (sexual continence), *mitāhāra* (diet control).

niyama (self-control) – *śauca* (cleanliness), *santoṣa* (contentment), *svādhyāya* (introspection), *tapas* (austerity), *śraddhā* (dedication and sincerity), *dāna* (charity),

ṛṇa (debt) / *ṛṇānubandhana* (bond of debt) / *samaṣṭi* (universal karma) / *sañcita* (overall debt) / *prārabdha* (debt that has come for resolution) / *āgāmi* (debt that is being created).

ṛta – Excellence.

rūpa - Form.

śiva (quanta aspect of *puruṣa*) / *śakti* (manifestation of śiva).

samadṛṣṭi – Equal gaze.

saṃsāra (cycle of birth and death) / *saṃskṛti* (culture) / *saṃskāra* (rites of passage in life) / *sampradāya* (local practice).

saṃskṛta (*Saṃskṛta* language)

saṅkalpa – Vow, recognition of gap.

sanātana – Universal.

śānti – Peace.

śāstra – Compendium of rules.

śraddhā - Sincerity and dedication in any action/ effort.

sthūla (gross form) / *sūkṣma* (subtle form) / *kāraṇa* (causal) / *śarīra* (body).

upāya (resolution tools) – *sāma* (negotiation) / *dāna* (inducement or trade-off) / *bheda* (influence or splitting) / *daṇḍa* (stick or force).

varṇa (colour or community) – *brāhmaṇa* (brahmin), *kṣatriya* (warrior), *vaiśya* (business), *śūdra* (worker).

yajña (sacrifice) / *adhiyajña* (primordial sacrifice or Sri Krishna). Comprises *yajamāna* (sponsor) / *saṅkalpa* (vow) / *āgama* (process) / *śāstra* (rules) / *dravya* (materials) / *prasāda* (gift) / *kāyenavācha* (thanksgiving).

◆——— · ● ◆ ● · ——— ◆

Table of contents

Dedication 5

Acknowledgments 7

Preface 9

Diacritics 13

Chapter 1 – *Viṣāda-yoga* (yoga of melancholy) 21

Chapter 2 – *Sāṃkhya-yoga* (yoga of the concept) 39

Chapter 3 – *Karma-yoga* (yoga of action) 67

Chapter 4 – *Jñāna-karma-sannyāsa-yoga* 83
(yoga of renunciation of the Self in action)

Chapter 5 – *Sannyāsa-yoga* (yoga of renunciation) 103

Chapter 6 – *Dhyāna-yoga* (yoga of meditation) 117

Chapter 7 – *Jñāna-vijñāna-yoga* 139
(yoga of awareness of the Self in any situation)

Chapter 8 – *Akṣara-brahma-yoga* 155
(yoga of the imperishable Brahman)

Chapter 9 – *Rājavidyā-rājaguhya-yoga* 173
(yoga of sovereign science, sovereign secret)

Chapter 10 – *Vibhūti-yoga* (yoga of splendor) 193

Chapter 11 – *Viśvarūpadarśana-yoga* 209
(yoga of the vision of the universal form)

Chapter 12 – *Bhakti-yoga* (yoga of surrender) 235

Chapter 13 – *Kṣetra-kṣetrajña-vibhāga-yoga* 243
(yoga of discrimination between *kṣetra* and *kṣetrajña*)

Chapter 14 – *Guṇatraya-vibhāga-yoga* 261
(yoga of differentiation of the three *guṇa-s*)

Chapter 15 – *Puruṣottama yoga* 277
(yoga of the supreme puruṣa or supreme Self)

Chapter 16 – *Daivāsura-samadvibhāga-yoga* 295
(yoga of the difference between divine and demonical)

Chapter 17 – *Śraddhā-traya-vibhāga-yoga* 307
(yoga delineating the three types of *śraddhā*)

Chapter 18 – *Mokṣa-sannyāsa-yoga* 329
(yoga of liberation by renunciation)

Epilogue 353

Chapter 1

Viṣāda-yoga (yoga of melancholy)[1]

Overview

No single text discusses or explains the many philosophies which fall under the umbrella of *sanātana-dharma*. The *sanātana-dharma* philosophy encompasses multiple schools of thought or *shākhās,* which are subdivided into sub-schools or *pravara.* Further, these get divided depending on interpretation, region, culture, practice, and, most importantly, *guru.*

This availability of multiple—and often conflicting—number of options in schools of thought can confuse a practitioner, resulting in some abandoning their search for the truth or looking for simpler solutions. However, these simpler systems generally have rigid rules for easy understanding and application, which constrict experimentation or personalization. Consequently, while the person becomes part of a system, full integration is not achieved. As a result of this compromise and loss of the perfect fit, the absolute Truth escapes the *yogī.*

What are the advantages of this open philosophical format? It allows for three major adjustments, as follows:

1. First, it allows one to change philosophical direction multiple times.

2. Next, it allows one to rearrange the philosophical construct to suit one's personality and aspirations. This means that it allows one to borrow from various philosophical streams without criticism.

3. Eventually, this open format structure allows practitioners to adapt their spiritual path to changes brought about by age and experience.

---

[1] https://www.bhagavad-gita.org/Gita/chapter-01.html

The importance of *Śrīmad-bhagavad-gītā*

Śrīmad-bhagavad-gītā should be viewed in the light of its importance to the overall philosophy of yoga *(yogaśāstra):*

- The ancient philosophical basis of yoga is that all existence is impermanent and a farce or illusion *(māyā)*.

- Illusion *(māyā)* rises from *Brahman,* which is a cognitive state of infinite and imperishable equilibrium, peace, and null, or a state where there is no change.

- In fact, only the *Brahman* is permanent and absolute, everything else is impermanent or relative. Additionally, since it is permanent and absolute, *Brahman* is known as the state of absolute Truth *(paramartha-sathya)*.

- Obviously, there can be only one absolute Truth; everything else is derived from it and known as illusion *(māyā)* or derived Truth *(samvritti-sathya)*.

- Everything in this illusionary state of relativity and impermanence *(māyā)* has a natural state *(dharma)*. When anything is in its natural state *(dharma)*, it is at a material, stable, harmonic, or thermodynamic equilibrium.

- *Dharma* applies to all entities, starting from an atom to all of existence.

- All forms of existence come as combinations of the primordial elements or *pañcabhūtas* (five primordial elements), comprising the earth *(pṛthvī)*, water *(ap)*, fire *(agni)*, air *(vāyu)*, and space *(ākāśa)*.

- Also, *dharma* includes all sentient or insentient entities, systems, processes, businesses, travel, and even countries. Since this natural state of peace encompasses everything, it is called *sanātana-dharma* or universal natural state.

- In fact, everything in derived Truth/illusion *(māyā)* is governed by *sanātana-dharma*.

- Importantly, by the very nature of *māyā,* material equilibrium or *dharma* is continuously subjected to both sentient and insentient stimuli. As a result, the equilibrium of *dharma* is constantly disturbed by change. This causes turbulence, confusion, or chaos, which is called *adharma*.

- Change creates an imbalance in everything impacted by it. Since any system that goes out of balance never returns to its original state of order or equilibrium *(dharma)*, it can be deduced that *dharma* changes continuously; at the same time, there is a continuous increase in chaos or thermodynamic entropy, which is the measure of randomness in any system *(adharma)*.

- The ancient seers *(ṛṣis)* of *Bhārat* realized that while realization of *Brahman* was the main objective of existence, human and societal existence had to be structured so that chaos in daily living was minimized and individuals lived harmoniously in well-defined life-structures while gravitating naturally towards the Truth.

- Hence, they integrated this *sanātana-dharma* philosophy into the lifestyle of the individual and society so that each life-activity assisted the person in transcending *māyā* naturally and reaching perfection *(Brahman)*. This is the ancient civilization *(rāṣṭra)* of *Bhārat*.

- This system is called Hinduism today. Interestingly, Hinduism cannot be called a religion in the traditional sense because it has no dogma. It is a life-cycle system that is influenced by philosophical schools *(shākhā)* as well as sub-schools *(pravara)*, each of which follow broad-based practices, but these, too, have a very open structure and a lot of overlap with other philosophical schools in their construct and practices.

Introduction to *sanātana-dharma*

- The philosophical basis of Hinduism are the *Vedas,* which are considered to be *apauruṣeya,* which can be translated as "not of man", meaning that they were composed by *ṛṣis* or seers when in a state of complete merger with the *Brahman.* There are four *Vedas (ṛig, yajur, sāma, atharva):*

  o The *Vedas*[2] are followed by *Vedāṅga* (limb of the *Vedas*) which are six auxiliary disciplines that help in maintaining the purity of the *Vedas*. These are as follows:

    - *śikṣā* (phonetics or enunciation of *Saṃskṛta*)

    - *chandas* (metering or how the verses should be chanted)

    - *vyākaraṇa* (grammar or linguistic analysis)

    - *nirukta* (explanation of certain words which are not generally used in everyday living)

    - *kalpa* (passage of life or life event rites)

    - *jyotiṣ* (astrology)

  o *Vedāṅga*[3] are followed by *vedānta*[4] or *upaniṣads,* which elaborate upon the qualities of *Brahman* as well as the process of renunciation by simplifying the philosophy without diluting it, through explanations, comparison, storytelling (example - *kaṭhopanṣad),* and other means.

---

[2]https://schoolofyoga.in/yoga-social-system/vedas-yoga-philosophy
[3]https://schoolofyoga.in/yoga-social-system/vedanga-limbs-vedas
[4]https://schoolofyoga.in/yoga-social-system/vedanta-vedas

- o *Purāṇas* are the next level of simplification for easy understanding of the *Brahman*; these cover the stories of people who can be called role models—those who have transcended physical existence to realize the Truth.

- While the above texts cover the philosophical and intellectual aspects of *Brahman,* they are highly conceptual and difficult to implement in a secular manner. Therefore, the *ṛṣis* devised a life-cycle system for implementation of the above philosophy in society, and this evolved to become:

  - o *Dharma-sūtras* or *sutras,* which covered every aspect of physical existence. The intent was to condition the behavior of society and people, with constant focus on transcending *māyā* and living in peace, so that transcending physical existence to realize the *brahman* became integrated into life and living.

  - o However, while the *dharma-sūtras* applied to everyone, people had different socio-environmental requirements. So, these *sūtras* were modified for local and regional adaptation, and these local nuances became known as *sampradāya.* For example, rice and fish are a staple of Bengal, and all religious and cultural events have both rice and fish. However, *sampradāya* in Punjab is wheat-based, while in the South and East of India, celebrations are predominantly rice-based, and this exemplifies the elasticity of *dharma.*

The *Sanātana-dharma* philosophical system has some noteworthy features:

- First, it is personal because it allows molding of the philosophy to the person's background, capability, and outlook. There is no wrong path; there is only the effort, learning, and transition. All that is required is sincerity, patience, and dedication of purpose and effort *(śraddhā)* [5].

- Second, since *Brahman* is an infinite, unchanging peace, by its very nature, it requires orientation towards internalizing peace, balance, and harmony among all entities, people, and societies. Consequently, this makes Hinduism the most natural, organic, and scientific philosophy ever designed by mankind. By its nature, it adapts to external influence and is never in conflict with any thought or civilizational pressure. Finally, this philosophy is unique because it does not seek to establish political or social ascendency over anyone because its core principle is that all creation is equal.

- Thirdly, Hinduism is designed around the code that every creation, whether it is sentient *(jīva)* or insentient *(jadam)* has a soul that has the potential to transcend *māyā* and eventually merge with *Brahman.* This covers everything from a lowly atom to the solar system. Hence, it does not restrict transcendental development to man alone. In fact, since man is intellectually superior and the apex predator,

---

[5]https://www.yogapedia.com/definition/5360/shraddha

it places an onerous leadership responsibility on man to ensure health and harmony of the complete ecosystem. These responsibilities are enshrined in the *pañca-mahā-yajña* (five great sacrifices) and have been covered in subsequent chapters.

- Lastly, Hinduism is secular by design because it recognizes that there are many distinct paths to realize *Brahman,* and these paths need to be personalized to the natural capabilities of the seeker.

This is why Hinduism is not a religion but a "life-cycle system" or "way of life".

Sanātana-dharma and its logical construction

The ancient seers or *ṛṣis* specified that any philosophical hypothesis should satisfy certain testing rules called *pramāṇas* (rules of evidence). All *pramāṇas* are based on experience and logic, and hence they can be personalized.

What are *pramāṇas*[6]?

The *pramāṇas* include *pratyakṣa* (personal vision or experience of logic), *anumāna* (inference through application of the rules of nature), *upamāna* (comparison and analogy with various logical constructs that have been accepted as valid), *arthāpatti* (postulation and derivation from evidence),

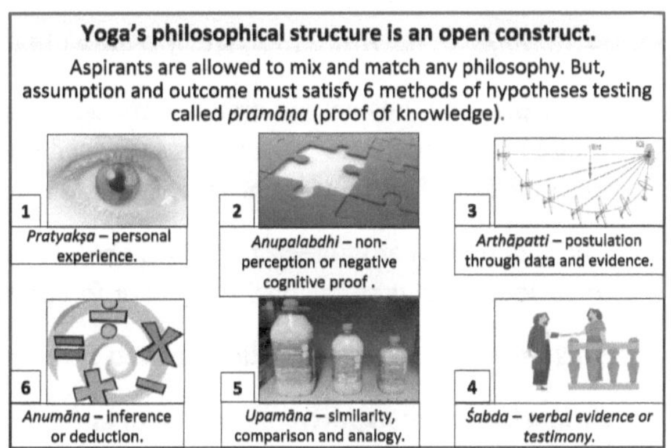

1.1 - *pramāṇa*

anupalabdhi (non-apprehension or negative cognitive proof), and *śabda* (verbal testimony).

- ### *Pratyakṣa* or personal experience

  This is the most irrefutable source of proof because it is based on personal experience.

  Example: Assume that you are walking down a street and see someone walking unsteadily in front of you. Generally, you would assume that he is drunk and feel disgusted. However, as you overtake him, if you were to see that the person is ill or in pain, your attitude would change immediately.

  This change in perception derived from personal experience is *pratyakṣa*.

---

[6]https://www.hindupedia.com/en/Pramana

- *Anumāna* **or inference from experience**

This is the drawing of a conclusion based on prior knowledge, like assuming that if there is smoke, there must be fire.

Example: Assume that you are a parent whose child has been consistently getting good marks and grades. If in one exam, the child's marks were to deteriorate unexpectedly, you would rightly assume from experience that the situation needs investigation. This is *anumāna* or inference drawn from experience.

- *Upamāna* **or comparison based on experience**

Example: We know that domestic dogs are similar to street dogs because we compare their form and function. Consequently, when we go on a wild life safari, we are able to recognize wolves, foxes, or hyenas as different from dogs.

This ability to compare and conclude is *upamāna* or comparison from experience.

- *Arthāpatti* **or postulation derived from evidence**

Example: All businesses create forecasts based on prior performance and future potential. These projections are based on analysis of prior performance, examination of current business situation, resources, and risk.

The accuracy of any forecast depends on the analyst's experience and exposure to various aspects of the business being forecasted.

This is *arthāpatti* or postulation derived from evidence.

- *Anupalabdhi* **or negative cognitive proof**

Anupalabdhi is the ability to recognize a missing aspect of any problem being analyzed.

Example: Assume that you are collating all your documents for an interview, and you find your birth certificate missing.

Since, you recognize the absence of the certificate, you will initiate a search. This is *anupalabdhi* or negative cognitive proof, one that is derived by absence of evidence.

- *Sabda* **or verbal testimony**

This is a commonly used *pramāṇa* or proof of existence.

Example: You are a manager, with many sales representatives reporting to you. While, you may go with a few on customer visits, you will rely on verbal inputs or *sabda* of your subordinates to assess the state of your operations.

Conclusion on *pramāṇas*: One can see that this system does not prescribe; rather, it allows one to seek, make mistakes, correct in small and incremental steps, called *anubhava* or experience to reach the truth or state of *brahman*. Obviously, this means that the aspirant needs to have enormous drive, persistence, and patience *(śraddhā)* to overcome frustration and failure.

This also means that the aspirant can choose from multiple paths in a manner that aligns with his or her personality, and all will lead to a state of cognitive perfection, the state of Truth or *brahman*. Interestingly, this alignment of effort with the Truth is enshrined in the Indian constitution as "Truth will triumph" *(satyameva-jayate)* [7].

The value of a *guru* [8]

In this open philosophical format for reaching the Truth, there is need for someone who can help the aspirant navigate the various paths *(mārga)*. Such a person is called a *guru* (weighty one or one who guides from darkness = *gu* to light = *ru*).

A *guru* may be defined as a teacher, guide, or anchor who pounds and pestles all ignorance and delusions or *ajñāna* out of the aspirant and directs him or her to the truth. So, the *guru* must also have the discriminatory ability *(viveka)* and dispassion *(vairāgya)* to pierce the delusions and apprehensions that cloud the student's judgment and offer solutions without attachment to the student.

Oriental systems and practices clearly enunciate the quality or attitude with which the aspirant must approach the *guru*. It should be one of surrender or *śaraṇāgati,* which roughly translates to "I surrender my speed to you". "Speed" here means "speed of movement of the sense of Self". Consequently, *śaraṇāgati* means that the aspirant no longer exists as an individual, but as a tool of the *guru,* to be molded, used, or discarded as the *guru* wishes [9]. Therefore, this also means that once the aspirant surrenders, he or she should not judge the *guru* but submit without reservation.

Indeed, there are very few known *yogīs* who have reached the Truth without a *guru,* chief among them being Rāmakṛṣṇa Paramahaṃsa and Ramana Maharishi.

The background of *Śrīmad-bhagavad-gītā*

Śrīmad-bhagavad-gītā is the only text that covers most of the paths to realization of the Truth or *Brahman*. It does not prescribe any solution; that is for the aspirant to find – if one is lucky, they shall find it at the feet of a *guru*. Since it does not prescribe, *Śrīmad-bhagavad-gītā* is not a religious text, just as *sanātana-dharma* is not a religion. In fact, one could adhere to any religion and follow the concepts in *Śrīmad-bhagavad-gītā* to reach the Truth.

[7] https://www.wisdomlib.org/hinduism/book/mundaka-upanishad-shankara-bhashya/d/doc145127.html
[8] http://explorevedanta.com/vbc-the-guru
[9] https://schoolofyoga.in/thought-leadership/guru-gurukul

Śrīmad-bhagavad-gītā was composed on a battlefield, or, more specifically, an internecine, fratricidal civil war, where the warring factions were all kinsmen. The protagonist, warrior prince, and ace archer Arjuna is beset by a fear of the chaos which would ensue when so many died, and his own personal grief at the thought of losing so many kinsmen as he reviews the battlefield situation. His doubts are answered by Śrī Kṛṣṇa, his charioteer, and this forms the background of the text.

- The conversation between Arjuna and Śrī Kṛṣṇa mirrors our own state in many situations.

- It starts with internal confusion and conflict at the chaos arising from fear of consequences.

- Then, as we study *Śrīmad-bhagavad-gītā*, we begin to understand the nature of permanence.

- Next, we learn about work, duty, and how to work without losing our sense of Self *(asmitā)*.

- This followed by an explanation of the many paths that we can take to re-establish equilibrium.

- Finally, we understand the integration of the system with society *(vijñāna)*, followed by our understanding of the Self *(jñāna)* and its integration within the macro-system.

- So, *Śrīmad-bhagavad-gītā* is actually a manual, which each of us can use to navigate the labyrinth called "life".

The timelines of *Śrīmad-bhagavad-gītā* [10]

There are some who have calculated the dates of the *Mahābhārata* battle (commonly called the *kurukṣetra* War) as follows:

- Start – *mṛgaśirā-śukla-ekādaśī* = 8th December BCE 3139

- End – 25th December BCE 3139

The structure of *Śrīmad-bhagavad-gītā*

Śrīmad-bhagavad-gītā is made up of 18 chapters; each chapter is a description of a yoga or method for harmonizing of the Self with the Truth).

These 18 chapters are broadly categorized as:

- Chapters 1- 6   *karma-kāṇḍa* -   Volume of action

- Chapters 7 - 12   *upanyāsa-kāṇḍa* -   Volume of proof

- Chapters 13 - 18   *jñāna-kāṇḍa* -   Volume of knowledge

---

[10] https://haribhakt.com/major-events-of-historical-mahabharat-with-timelines

These 18 chapters contain 690 couplets as a conversation that includes 4 participants - the King Dhṛtarāṣṭra (1 couplet), Sañjaya, who oversees the conversation between Arjuna and Śrī Kṛṣṇa (40 couplets), Prince Arjuna, who is the confused protagonist (85 couplets), and Śrī Kṛṣṇa (564 couplets).

Importantly, *Śrīmad-bhagavad-gītā* is the only significant world text that has its own birthday or Jayanthi. It is celebrated on the 11th day of the waxing moon in the month of *mārgaśīrṣa (mṛgaśirā-śukla-ekādaśī)*.

Introduction to Śrī Kṛṣṇa

In *Mahābhārata*, Śrī Kṛṣṇa operates as two personas - a *purāṇaic* personality, Śrī Kṛṣṇa, who lived in the period, and the *yogī,* who had reached the state of perfect awareness. Often, it is easy to confuse the person with the *yogī.* This is a confusion that will last throughout *Śrīmad-bhagavad-gītā.*

- Biological father – Vasudeva (Yādava Clan)

- Biological Mother – Devakī (Ugra Race)

- Brother – Balarāma

- Sister – Subhadrā

- Birthplace – Mathura, Uttar Pradesh, Bhārat

- Birth details:

    o Date – 18 July, 3228 BCE

    o Month – *śrāvaṇa*

    o *Tithi – aṣṭamī* (eighth day of the waning moon)

    o *Nakṣatra – rohiṇī*

    o Day – Wednesday

    o Time – 00:00 (midnight)

- Wives – Rukminī, Ratyabhāmā, Jāmbavatī, Kālindī, Mitravindā, Nāgnajitī, Bhadrā, Lakṣmaṇā.

- Death details – 18th Feb 3102 BCE. Age at death: 125 years, 8 months, and 7 days.

Śrī Kṛṣṇa migrated from Mathurā to Vṛndāvana at age 9, staying in Vṛndāvana till ages 14 to 16. Thereafter, after killing his maternal uncle, Kaṃsa, and releasing his parents, who had been imprisoned by Kaṃsa, he migrated to Dvārakā and never returned.

Śrī Kṛṣṇa died 36 years after the *kurukṣetra* war, in 3103 BCE, when the present-day *kaliyuga* is said to have begun.

Introduction to chapter 1 - *viṣāda-yoga* (yoga of melancholy)

Dhṛtarāṣṭra, the blind father of the *kauravas*, asks Sañjaya to explain the scene of battle at *Kurukṣetra*. "Having seen the *pāṇḍavas* arrayed in battle opposite them, the *kaurava* King Duryodhana approached his Guru Droṇācārya and sought benediction and confidence. In response, Droṇācārya blew his battle conch, infusing confidence into the *kaurava* Army. Likewise, the *pāṇḍavas* blew on their conches, and there was a general exchange of drums and conches. Amidst this, Arjuna asked Śrī Kṛṣṇa to drive between the opposing armies so that he may see the opposing forces. Śrī Kṛṣṇa, his charioteer for the battle, did as asked."

Arjuna, seeing his kinsmen and close relatives on the opposite site, each preparing to slaughter the other, spoke with great sorrow that he had lost the strength and confidence to fight and began to question the very premise on which they had gone to battle, saying:

- I do not wish to kill anyone.

- What good will come out of this slaughter?

- How can we be happy killing our own kinsmen, despite the fact that their greed does not allow them to have softer sentiments?

- The destruction of any family will result in corruption and destruction of all known social hierarchies and systems. Consequently, this is a great sin.

- Putting down his bow, in distress and sorrow, Arjuna said, "I won't fight."

Example 1

You have been cheated of your property by a close relative. You are angry, frustrated, and vengeful. You go to your lawyer to seek retribution. There, the lawyer explains the consequences of your action, the costs, efforts, and risks, and you begin to have doubts about whether to proceed.

- What is the difference in emotions between before and after your meeting with the lawyer?

- The truth that you have been cheated has not changed. Your desire for justice has not changed, neither has the loss faced by you...

    o   What has happened?

    o   Why have you changed?

    o   What is the change?

Example 2

You are dismayed at your annual appraisal rating and feel that it does not reflect your effort and contribution to the organization. Consequently, you meet your immediate boss, but his explanation does not satisfy you. So, you decide to go to the Head of the department. As you enter, you realize that your immediate boss will probably not be sympathetic to your action. Finally, you also realize that the Head may not be able to help! You feel nervous, experience palpitation, and feel an unknown fear...

- Why are you afraid?

- What are you afraid of?

- How do you deal with the anxiety?

- Why do you constantly worry about the consequences of your action?

- What is the role of *dharma* (conditioning) in your ability to deal with situations?

The above examples are similar to those that Arjuna experienced when he examined the potential consequences of his actions.

Some contradictions to accepted positions:

Śrīmad-bhagavad-gītā is not a book of religion. By religion, we mean any system of thought that is based on the concept of God and has principles, dogma, procedures, and rules which are considered inviolable and need to be followed.

Śrīmad-bhagavad-gītā does not have any dogma, principle, or rules. It allows a practitioner to yoke his or her natural instincts with the state of peace in any manner that the person may find comfortable. Essentially, this means that the person works on his or her physical, emotional, and intellectual strengths and weaknesses continuously to remain in peace, balance, and harmony within the Self, surroundings, and in all transactions.

This is why *Śrīmad-bhagavad-gītā* is a book on yoga *(yogaśāstra)*.

Some lessons from chapter 1

All of us face internal and external conflicts which result in stress and a feeling of melancholy. Often, internal stresses come from external factors, such as job loss, negative annual appraisal and grading, conflicts at home or disagreements with friends, etc. Internal factors can be the perceived gap between expectation and achievement, inability to finish tasks, poor time management, obsession, loneliness, etc.

This happens to all of us; the starting point in all situations is confusion, melancholy, internal conflict and stress, anxiety at the possible outcome, etc. This is the reality that the *Bhagavad-gītā* uses as a foundation to build the open architecture of *sanātana-dharma,* which gets detailed over the next seventeen chapters.

The transliteration and translation of *Śrīmad-bhagavad-gītā*, chapter 1 follows:

धृतराष्ट्र उवाच -

धर्मक्षेत्रे कुरुक्षेत्रे समवेता युयुत्सवः ।

मामकाः पाण्डवाश्चैव किमकुर्वत सञ्जय ॥ १-१॥

Dhṛtarāṣṭra said (1) At the field of righteousness, at *kurukṣetra*, what is the status of my people and also the *pāṇḍavas*, who have gathered with a desire for battle *(dharmakṣetre kurukṣetre samavetā yuyutsavaḥ ǀ māmakāḥ pāṇḍavāścaiva kimakurvata sañjaya ǁ)*.

सञ्जय उवाच -

दृष्ट्वा तु पाण्डवानीकं व्यूढं दुर्योधनस्तदा ।

आचार्यमुपसङ्गम्य राजा वचनमब्रवीत् ॥ १-२॥

पश्यैतां पाण्डुपुत्राणामाचार्य महतीं चमूम् ।

व्यूढां द्रुपदपुत्रेण तव शिष्येण धीमता ॥ १-३॥

अत्र शूरा महेष्वासा भीमार्जुनसमा युधि ।

युयुधानो विराटश्च द्रुपदश्च महारथः ॥ १-४॥

Sañjaya said (2-4) having indeed seen the armies of *pāṇḍavas* in the battle array, Duryodhana, the king, approached his teacher and said *(dṛṣṭvā tu pāṇḍavānīkaṃ vyūḍhaṃ duryodhanastadā ǀ ācāryamupasaṅgamya rājā vacanamabravīt ǁ 1-2ǁ)*. Teacher, behold here the great army, the sons of Pāṇḍu, marshalled by the son of Drupada, your talented student *(paśyaitāṃ pāṇḍuputrāṇāmācārya mahatīṃ camūm ǀ vyūḍhāṃ drupadaputreṇa tava śiṣyeṇa dhīmatā ǁ 1-3ǁ)*. Here are daring warriors, great archers, equal to Bhīma and Arjuna in battle, Yuyudhāna, Virāta, and Drupada, the great charioteer *(atra śūrā maheṣvāsā bhīmārjunasamā yudhi ǀ yuyudhāno virāṭaśca drupadaśca mahārathaḥ ǁ 1-4ǁ)*.

धृष्टकेतुश्चेकितानः काशिराजश्च वीर्यवान् ।

पुरुजित्कुन्तिभोजश्च शैब्यश्च नरपुङ्गवः ॥ १-५॥

युधामन्युश्च विक्रान्त उत्तमौजाश्च वीर्यवान् ।

सौभद्रो द्रौपदेयाश्च सर्व एव महारथाः ॥ १-६॥

अस्माकं तु विशिष्टा ये तान्निबोध द्विजोत्तम ।

नायका मम सैन्यस्य संज्ञार्थं तान्ब्रवीमि ते ॥ १-७॥

(5-7) Dhṛṣṭaketu and Cekitāna, King of Kāśi and valiant Purujit, Kuntibhoja and śaibya and best of men *(dhṛṣṭaketuścekitānaḥ kāśirājaśca vīryavān ǀ purujitkuntibhojaśca śaibyaśca narapuṅgavaḥ ǁ 1-5ǁ)*. Yudhāmanyhu and courageous Uttamoujā and the brave son of Subhadrā and Draupadī and all great charioteers *(yudhāmanyuśca vikrānta uttamaujāśca vīryavān ǀ saubhadro draupadeyāśca sarva eva mahārathāḥ ǁ 1-6ǁ)*. Ours also distinguished chiefs those who are knowledgeable, best of twice-born, the leaders of my army, for information, I will recount to you *(asmākaṃ tu viśiṣṭā ye tānnibodha dvijottama ǀ nāyakā mama sainyasya saṃjñārthaṃ tānbravīmi te ǁ 1-7ǁ)*.

भवान्भीष्मश्च कर्णश्च कृपश्च समितिञ्जयः ।

अश्वत्थामा विकर्णश्च सौमदत्तिस्तथैव च ॥ १-८॥

अन्ये च बहवः शूरा मदर्थे त्यक्तजीविताः ।

नानाशस्त्रप्रहरणाः सर्वे युद्धविशारदाः ॥ १-९॥

अपर्याप्तं तदस्माकं बलं भीष्माभिरक्षितम् ।

पर्याप्तं त्विदमेतेषां बलं भीमाभिरक्षितम् ॥ १-१०॥

(8-10) Yourself, Bhīṣma and Karṇa and Kṛpa and Aśvatthāmā, victorious in war, and even Vikarṇa, son of Somadatta, *(bhavānbhīṣmaśca karṇaśca kṛpaśca samitiñjayaḥ ǀ aśvatthāmā vikarṇaśca saumadattistathaiva ca ǁ 1-8ǁ)*. And many other heroes, for me, willing to sacrifice their lives, armed with various weapons, all well skilled in battle *(anye ca bahavaḥ śūrā madarthe tyaktajīvitāḥ ǀ nānāśastrapraharaṇāḥ sarve yuddhaviśāradāḥ ǁ 1-9ǁ)*. Unlimited is our strength, marshalled by Bhīṣma, while their army, marshalled by Bhima, is insufficient *(aparyāptaṃ tadasmākaṃ balaṃ bhīṣmābhirakṣitam ǀ paryāptaṃ tvidameteṣāṃ balaṃ bhīmābhirakṣitam ǁ1-10ǁ)*.

अयनेषु च सर्वेषु यथाभागमवस्थिताः ।

भीष्ममेवाभिरक्षन्तु भवन्तः सर्व एव हि ॥ १-११॥

तस्य सञ्जनयन्हर्षं कुरुवृद्धः पितामहः ।

सिंहनादं विनद्योच्चैः शङ्खं दध्मौ प्रतापवान् ॥ १-१२॥

ततः शङ्खाश्च भेर्यश्च पणवानकगोमुखाः ।

सहसैवाभ्यहन्यन्त स शब्दस्तुमुलोऽभवत् ॥ १-१३॥

(11-13) Indeed, within and everywhere, the strength of the divisions is deployed to protect Bhīṣma alone *(ayaneṣu ca sarveṣu yathābhāgamavasthitāḥ ǀ bhīṣmamevābhirakṣantu bhavantaḥ sarva eva hi ǁ 1-11ǁ)*. Therefore, expressing happiness, the oldest of the *kurus*, the grandfather loudly let out a lion's roar and blew his mighty conch *(tasya sañjanayanharṣaṃ kuruvṛddhaḥ pitāmahaḥ ǀ siṃhanādaṃ vinadyoccaiḥ śaṅkhaṃ dadhmau pratāpavān ǁ 1-12ǁ)*. Then, conchs and kettledrums and tabors, drums, and cow-horns suddenly blared forth in a sound that was tumultuous *(tataḥ śaṅkhāśca bheryaśca paṇavānakagomukhāḥ ǀ sahasaivābhyahanyanta sa śabdastumulo'bhavat ǁ 1-13ǁ)*.

ततः श्वेतैर्हयैर्युक्ते महति स्यन्दने स्थितौ ।

माधवः पाण्डवश्चैव दिव्यौ शङ्खौ प्रदध्मतुः ॥ १-१४॥

पाञ्चजन्यं हृषीकेशो देवदत्तं धनञ्जयः ।

पौण्ड्रं दध्मौ महाशङ्खं भीमकर्मा वृकोदरः ॥ १-१५॥

अनन्तविजयं राजा कुन्तीपुत्रो युधिष्ठिरः ।

नकुलः सहदेवश्च सुघोषमणिपुष्पकौ ॥ १-१६॥

(14-16) Then, seated on a magnificent war-chariot yoked with white horses, Mādhava and son of Pāndu also blew their divine conches *(tataḥ śvetairhayairyukte mahati syandane sthitau ı mādhavaḥ pāṇḍavaścaiva divyau śaṅkhau pradadhmatuḥ ॥ 1-14॥)*. *pañcajanya* of Hṛṣīkeśa, *devadattam* of Dhanañjaya and *pauṇḍra* was blown by the doer of terrible deeds, Bhīma *(pañcajanyam hṛṣīkeśo devadattaṃ dhanañjayaḥ ıpauṇḍram dadhmau mahāśaṅkham bhīmakarmā vṛkodaraḥ ॥ 1-15॥)*. Rājā Kuntīputra Yudhiṣṭhira blew the *anantavijaya*, Nakula and Sahadeva blew conches named *sughoṣa* and *maṇipuṣpaka (anantavijayaṃ rājā kuntīputro yudhiṣṭhiraḥ ı nakulaḥ sahadevaśca sughoṣamaṇipuṣpakau ॥ 1-16॥)*.

काश्यश्च परमेष्वासः शिखण्डी च महारथः ।

धृष्टद्युम्नो विराटश्च सात्यकिश्चापराजितः ॥ १-१७॥

द्रुपदो द्रौपदेयाश्च सर्वशः पृथिवीपते ।

सौभद्रश्च महाबाहुः शङ्खान्दध्मुः पृथक्पृथक् ॥ १-१८॥

स घोषो धार्तराष्ट्राणां हृदयानि व्यदारयत् ।

नभश्च पृथिवीं चैव तुमुलोऽभ्यनुनादयन् ॥ १-१९॥

अथ व्यवस्थितान्दृष्ट्वा धार्तराष्ट्रान् कपिध्वजः ।

प्रवृत्ते शस्त्रसम्पाते धनुरुद्यम्य पाण्डवः ॥ १-२०॥

हृषीकेशं तदा वाक्यमिदमाह महीपते ।

(17-20) Supreme archer Kāśya, śikhaṇḍī and Dhṛṣṭadyumna, Virāta and unconquered Sātyaki *(kāśyaśca parameṣvāsaḥ śikhaṇḍī ca mahārathaḥ ı dhṛṣṭadyumno virāṭaśca sātyakiścāparājitaḥ ॥ 1-17॥)*. Drupada, sons of Draupadī, and all lords of the Earth and the mighty armed son of Subhadrā blew their conches one after another *(drupado draupadeyāśca sarvaśaḥ pṛthivīpate ı saubhadraśca mahābāhuḥ śaṅkhāndadhmuḥ pṛthakpṛthak ॥ 1-18॥)*. That tumultuous resounding battle sound rent the hearts of Dhṛtarāṣṭra's team, from sky to earth *(sa ghoṣo dhārtarāṣṭrāṇām hṛdayāni vyadārayat ı nabhaśca pṛthivīm caiva tumulo'bhyanunādayan ॥ 1-19॥)*. Now, monkey banner, seeing the arrayed Dṛtarāṣṭra's people about to begin discharge of weapons, son of Pandu, taking up the bow, then said this to Hṛṣīkeśa, Lord of the Earth *(atha vyavasthitāndṛṣṭvā dhārtarāṣṭrān kapidhvajaḥ ı pravṛtte śastrasampāte dhanurudyamya pāṇḍavaḥ ॥1-20॥ hṛṣīkeśam tadā vākyamidamāha mahīpate ı)*.

अर्जुन उवाच -

सेनयोरुभयोर्मध्ये रथं स्थापय मेऽच्युत ॥ १-२१॥

यावदेतान्निरीक्षेऽहं योद्धुकामानवस्थितान् ।

कैर्मया सह योद्धव्यमस्मिन् रणसमुद्यमे ॥ १-२२॥

योत्स्यमानानवेक्षेऽहं य एतेऽत्र समागताः ।

धार्तराष्ट्रस्य दुर्बुद्धेर्युद्धे प्रियचिकीर्षवः ॥ १-२३॥

Arjuna said (21-23) Place my chariot in the middle of the armies, Acyuta *(senayorubhayormadhye ratham sthāpaya me'cyuta ॥ 1-21॥)*. I wish to see who has assembled here with the intention of fighting, and must be fought by me, on this eve of battle *(yāvadetānnirīkṣe'ham yoddhukāmānavasthitān । kairmayā saha yoddhavyamasmin raṇasamudyame ॥ 1-22॥)*. I wish to observe who among those who wish to please the deviant-minded sons of Dhṛtarāṣṭra *(yotsyamānānavekṣe'ham ya ete'tra samāgatāḥ । dhārtarāṣṭrasya durbuddheryuddhe priyacikīrṣavaḥ ॥ 1-23॥)*.

सञ्जय उवाच -

एवमुक्तो हृषीकेशो गुडाकेशेन भारत ।

सेनयोरुभयोर्मध्ये स्थापयित्वा रथोत्तमम् ॥ १-२४॥

भीष्मद्रोणप्रमुखतः सर्वेषां च महीक्षिताम् ।

उवाच पार्थ पश्यैतान्समवेतान्कुरूनिति ॥ १-२५॥

तत्रापश्यत्स्थितान्पार्थः पितॄनथ पितामहान् ।

आचार्यान्मातुलान्भ्रातॄन्पुत्रान्पौत्रान्सखींस्तथा ॥ १-२६॥

श्वशुरान्सुहृदश्चैव सेनयोरुभयोरपि ।

तान्समीक्ष्य स कौन्तेयः सर्वान्बन्धूनवस्थितान् ॥ १-२७॥

कृपया परयाविष्टो विषीदन्निदमब्रवीत् ।

Sañjaya said (24-27) Having been addressed by Guḍākeśa, Bhārata, Hṛṣīkeśa placed the supreme of chariots between the armies. *(evamukto hṛṣīkeśo guḍākeśena bhārata । senayorubhayormadhye sthāpayitvā rathottamam ॥ 1-24॥)*. In front of Bhīṣma and Droṇa and all other rulers of the earth, Pārtha said, behold the *kurus* gathered here *(bhīṣmadroṇapramukhatah sarveṣām ca mahīkṣitām । uvāca pārtha paśyaitānsamavetānkurūniti ॥ 1-25॥)*. Stationed there, Pārtha saw fathers, also, grandfathers, teachers, maternal uncles, brothers, sons, grandsons, companions, fathers-in-law, friends, and also warriors from both sides *(tatrāpaśyatsthitānpārthaḥ pitṛnatha pitāmahān । ācāryānmātulānbhrātṛnputrānpautrānsakhīṃstathā ॥ 1-26॥ śvaśurānsuhṛdaścaiva senayorubhayorapi ।)*. Having seen all these relatives standing, filled with deep pity and sorrow, Kaunteya said *(tānsamīkṣya sa kaunteyaḥ sarvānbandhūnavasthitān ॥ 1-27॥ kṛpayā parayāviṣṭo viṣīdannidamabravīt ।)*.

अर्जुन उवाच -

दृष्ट्वेमं स्वजनं कृष्ण युयुत्सुं समुपस्थितम् ॥ १-२८॥

सीदन्ति मम गात्राणि मुखं च परिशुष्यति ।

वेपथुश्च शरीरे मे रोमहर्षश्च जायते ॥ १-२९॥

गाण्डीवं स्रंसते हस्तात्त्वक्चैव परिदह्यते ।

न च शक्नोम्यवस्थातुं भ्रमतीव च मे मनः ॥ १-३०॥

Arjuna said (28-30) Seeing my people, arrayed and eager to fight, my limbs fail me, and my mouth is getting parched *(dṛṣṭvemaṃ svajanaṃ kṛṣṇa yuyutsuṃ samupasthitam ॥ 1-28॥ sīdanti mama gātrāṇi mukhaṃ ca pariśuṣyati ।)*. My body is shivering, and I am getting goosepimples, the *gāṇḍīva* is slipping from my hand, and my skin is burning *(vepathuśca śarīre me romaharṣaśca jāyate ॥ 1-29॥ gāṇḍīvaṃ sraṃsate hastāttvakcaiva paridahyate ।)*. I am unable to stand, it seems that my mind whirls with omens, and I see adversity *(na ca śaknomyavasthātuṃ bhramatīva ca me manaḥ ॥ 1-30॥ nimittāni ca paśyāmi viparītāni keśava ।)*.

निमित्तानि च पश्यामि विपरीतानि केशव ।

न च श्रेयोऽनुपश्यामि हत्वा स्वजनमाहवे ॥ १-३१॥

न काङ्क्षे विजयं कृष्ण न च राज्यं सुखानि च ।

किं नो राज्येन गोविन्द किं भोगैर्जीवितेन वा ॥ १-३२॥

येषामर्थे काङ्क्षितं नो राज्यं भोगाः सुखानि च ।

त इमेऽवस्थिता युद्धे प्राणांस्त्यक्त्वा धनानि च ॥ १-३३॥

आचार्याः पितरः पुत्रास्तथैव च पितामहाः ।

मातुलाः श्वशुराः पौत्राः श्यालाः सम्बन्धिनस्तथा ॥ १-३४॥

(31-34) And no good I see in killing my people in battle, I do not desire victory, and not kingdom and other pleasures *(na ca śreyo 'nupaśyāmi hatvā svajanamāhave ॥ 1-31॥ na kāṅkṣe vijayaṃ kṛṣṇa na ca rājyaṃ sukhāni ca ।)*. What will this kingdom give to us? What pleasure will we get in life? *(kiṃ no rājyena govinda kiṃ bhogairjīvitena vā ॥ 1-32॥)*. The reason we desire enjoyment of kingdom pleasures, they stand ready to give life in battle, having abandoned wealth *(yeṣāmarthe kāṅkṣitaṃ no rājyaṃ bhogāḥ sukhāni ca । ta ime 'vasthitā yuddhe prāṇāṃstyaktvā dhanāni ca ॥ 1-33॥)*. Teachers, fathers, sons, and grandfathers, maternal uncles, fathers-in-law, grandsons, brothers-in-laws as well as relatives *(ācāryāḥ pitaraḥ putrāstathaiva ca pitāmahāḥ । mātulāḥ śvaśurāḥ pautrāḥ śyālāḥ sambandhinastathā ॥ 1-34॥)*.

एतान्न हन्तुमिच्छामि घ्नतोऽपि मधुसूदन ।

अपि त्रैलोक्यराज्यस्य हेतोः किं नु महीकृते ॥ १-३५॥

निहत्य धार्तराष्ट्रान्नः का प्रीतिः स्याज्जनार्दन ।
पापमेवाश्रयेदस्मान्हत्वैतानाततायिनः ॥ १-३६॥
तस्मान्नार्हा वयं हन्तुं धार्तराष्ट्रान्स्वबान्धवान् ।
स्वजनं हि कथं हत्वा सुखिनः स्याम माधव ॥ १-३७॥

(35-37) I do not wish to kill them, even if I am killed by them, or for the sake of domination of the three worlds, then why would I do it for earth? *(etanna hantumicchāmi ghnato'pi madhusūdana | api trailokyarājyasya hetoḥ kiṁ nu mahīkṛte || 1-35||).* What pleasure will we get by killing the sons of Dhṛtarāṣṭra, killing these terrorists will only stain us *(nihatya dhārtarāṣṭrannaḥ kā prītiḥ syājjanārdana | pāpamevāśrayedasmānhatvaitānātatāyinaḥ || 1-36||).* So, we are not justified in killing the sons of Dhṛtarāṣṭra, our relatives and kinsmen, indeed, how can we be happy after killing them *(tasmānnārhā vayaṁ hantuṁ dhārtarāṣṭrānsvabāndhavān | svajanaṁ hi kathaṁ hatvā sukhinaḥ syāma mādhava || 1-37||).*

यद्यप्येते न पश्यन्ति लोभोपहतचेतसः ।
कुलक्षयकृतं दोषं मित्रद्रोहे च पातकम् ॥ १-३८॥
कथं न ज्ञेयमस्माभिः पापादस्मान्निवर्तितुम् ।
कुलक्षयकृतं दोषं प्रपश्यद्भिर्जनार्दन ॥ १-३९॥
कुलक्षये प्रणश्यन्ति कुलधर्माः सनातनाः ।
धर्मे नष्टे कुलं कृत्स्नमधर्मोऽभिभवत्युत ॥ १-४०॥

(38-40) Although these do not see due to intelligence overpowered by greed, the wretchedness wrought by destruction of the clans, and crime brought by hostility to friends *(yadyapyete na paśyanti lobhopahatacetasaḥ | kulakṣayakṛtaṁ doṣaṁ mitradrohe ca pātakam || 1-38||).* When I clearly comprehend the wretchedness in the destruction of the clan, why not turn away from this clearly inappropriate act *(katham na jñeyamasmābhiḥ pāpādasmānnivartitum | kulakṣayakṛtaṁ doṣaṁ prapaśyadbhirjanārdana || 1-39||).* When the clan perishes, immemorial clan balances and universal practices are destroyed, the whole clan is overcome by chaos indeed *(kulakṣaye praṇaśyanti kuladharmāḥ sanātanāḥ | dharme naṣṭe kulaṁ kṛtsnamadharmo 'bhibhavatyuta || 1-40||).*

अधर्माभिभवात्कृष्ण प्रदुष्यन्ति कुलस्त्रियः ।
स्त्रीषु दुष्टासु वार्ष्णेय जायते वर्णसङ्करः ॥ १-४१॥
सङ्करो नरकायैव कुलघ्नानां कुलस्य च ।
पतन्ति पितरो ह्येषां लुप्तपिण्डोदकक्रियाः ॥ १-४२॥
दोषैरेतैः कुलघ्नानां वर्णसङ्करकारकैः ।
उत्साद्यन्ते जातिधर्माः कुलधर्माश्च शाश्वताः ॥ १-४३॥

(41-43) With the onset of chaos, clan women get corrupted, from women becoming corrupted, mixing of colors occurs *(adharmābhibhavātkṛṣṇa praduṣyanti kulastriyaḥ ǀ strīṣu duṣṭāsu vārṣṇeya jāyate varṇasaṅkaraḥ ǁ 1-41ǁ)*. Confusion resembling hell exists for killers of the clan from the clan because the forefathers are denied their offering of rice and water *(saṅkaro narakāyaiva kulaghnānāṃ kulasya ca ǀ patanti pitaro hyeṣāṃ luptapiṇḍodakakriyāḥ ǁ 1-42ǁ)*. Staining by destroyers of the clans causes intermingling of various people, eternal community practices are destroyed as are clan rituals and practices *(doṣairetaiḥ kulaghnānāṃ varṇasaṅkarakārakaiḥ ǀ utsādyante jātidharmāḥ kuladharmāśca śāśvatāḥ ǁ 1-43ǁ)*.

उत्सन्नकुलधर्माणां मनुष्याणां जनार्दन ।
नरके नियतं वासो भवतीत्यनुशुश्रुम ॥ १-४४॥
अहो बत महत्पापं कर्तुं व्यवसिता वयम् ।
यद्राज्यसुखलोभेन हन्तुं स्वजनमुद्यताः ॥ १-४५॥
यदि मामप्रतीकारमशस्त्रं शस्त्रपाणयः ।
धार्तराष्ट्रा रणे हन्युस्तन्मे क्षेमतरं भवेत् ॥ १-४६॥

(44-46) Those men, whose clan practices are destroyed, we have heard that they stay in hell for an indefinite period *(utsannakuladharmāṇāṃ manuṣyāṇāṃ janārdana ǀ narake niyataṃ vāso bhavatītyanuśuśruma ǁ 1-44ǁ)*. Alas, we are prepared to do great wretchedness and kill our kinsmen for the pleasure of kingdom *(aho bata mahatpāpaṃ kartuṃ vyavasitā vayam ǀ yadrājyasukhalobhena hantuṃ svajanamudyatāḥ ǁ 1-45ǁ)*. If the sons of Dhṛtarāṣṭra were to kill me, unresisting and unarmed, with their weapons in hand in the battlefield, that would be better *(yadi māmapratīkāramaśastraṃ śastrapāṇayaḥ ǀ dhārtarāṣṭrā raṇe hanyustanme kṣemataraṃ bhavet ǁ 1-46ǁ)*.

सञ्जय उवाच ।
एवमुक्त्वार्जुनः सङ्ख्ये रथोपस्थ उपाविशत् ।
विसृज्य सशरं चापं शोकसंविग्नमानसः ॥ १-४७॥

Sañjaya said (47) Thus having spoken, Arjuna in the battlefield, in the chariot, sat down with a distressed mind after throwing away the arrow and bow *(evamuktvārjunaḥ saṅkhye rathopastha upāviśat ǀ visṛjya saśaraṃ cāpaṃ śokasaṃvignamānasaḥ ǁ 1-47ǁ)*.

◆ —— · ◆ ● · ◆ —— ◆

Chapter 2

Sāṃkhya-yoga (yoga of the concept) [1]

- What is yoga? Yoga is a *Saṃskṛta* cognate of the English "yoke". While generically it means yoking between any two entities, here, it means yoking of a person's awareness of the Self to *Brahman*[2].

- What is *sāṃkhya*? *Sāṃkhya* is any philosophical system. In this chapter, Śrī Kṛṣṇa explains the philosophy that defines existence and yoga.

As we have seen in chapter 1, Arjuna experiences deep conflict at the futility of war and horror at the prospect of fighting his own kinsmen, and he refuses to fight. His situational awareness *(prajñā)* in that moment is one of turmoil, distress, and melancholy.

This reaction is similar to what we experience when confronted with dissonance in relationships or difficult situations! Initially, in the heat of the moment, we may wish to confront and fight, but when we review the possible consequences, our desire for conflict dissipates. Consequently, we try to disengage from confrontation, sometimes even at the cost of hurting ourselves or sacrificing our values and principles.

In this chapter, Śrī Kṛṣṇa explains the philosophy of life, starting with the origin of our existence and our place in it. Then he goes on to flesh out the meaning of action and why performance of duty is the only solution to any problem. Finally, he details the attributes of the one who has optimum situational awareness.

Śrī Kṛṣṇa starts his discourse to Arjuna by laying out the first principles of life and living, called *sāṃkhya-yoga*.

- First, he explains the nature of the *Brahman* and the difference between permanence and impermanence.

---

[1]https://www.bhagavad-gita.org/Gita/chapter-02.html
[2]https://schoolofyoga.in/yoga-concept/situational-awareness-measures

- Next, he explains life, material relationships, concept of duty, and *svatantra* *(sva* = self + *tantra* = weave of one's sense of Identity with one's actions, effectively meaning individuality).

Additionally, Śrī Kṛṣṇa emphasises that while each of us may have different ways of solving any problem, some aspects must not be compromised, including:

- Be true to your responsibility, and try to avoid confrontation when finding a solution. However, if nothing works, fight!

- Obviously, to fight means different things; while in the case of a soldier it means a physical struggle, in the case of a teacher, it could be standing up for students or the way teaching must be done, and, in the case of a lawyer, this may be strategy for arguing a case.

- You may not win, but you must fight as well as you can and accept the ensuing results with equanimity. Not fighting is not an option.

- Also, loss of integrity when finding a solution is not an acceptable option.

- Finally, once the activity is started, one must avoid judgmental and sentimental positioning as well as duality of like-dislike, attraction-repulsion, good-bad etc., and the effort must be steadfast towards reaching the goal.

Conclusion

This chapter is about change management. Change occurs continuously, and everyone gets affected by it. However, a *yogī* must slowly learn to move away from duality, such as like/dislike or attraction/repelling, to one of dispassion *(vairāgya)* and discrimination *(viveka)*.

When this state is realized, the person is able to step back from his or her surroundings and view the environment with increased clarity. This results in decision making that is closer to reality of the situation. In the process, the person develops an awareness that transcends physical inability, fear of outcome, emotional swings, or intellectual manipulation.

Introduction, (verse 1-11)

Śrī Kṛṣṇa smilingly exhorted Arjuna not to think like a loser. Arjuna, besieged by sorrow and the horror of the consequences of his proposed actions, was overwhelmed by self-pity and begged Śrī Kṛṣṇa to advise him on what he should do.

The key lesson Śrī Kṛṣṇa delivers in this chapter is on impermanence and sentimentality. He says that the body is an impermanent entity that passes through childhood, youth, old age, and entry into another body upon death. So, one should be self-possessed and not get sentimental about situations or their perceived outcomes. Instead, one must focus on completing his or her duty with integrity.

Śrī Kṛṣṇa explains qualities of the *Brahman*, (verse 12-25)

- Whenever we experience anything, it is *māyā*, and not *Brahman*. Conversely, when we merge with the *Brahman*, there is no experience of materiality or *māyā*.

- *Brahman* pervades everything and cannot be destroyed. It is unmanifested, unthinking, and unchangeable.

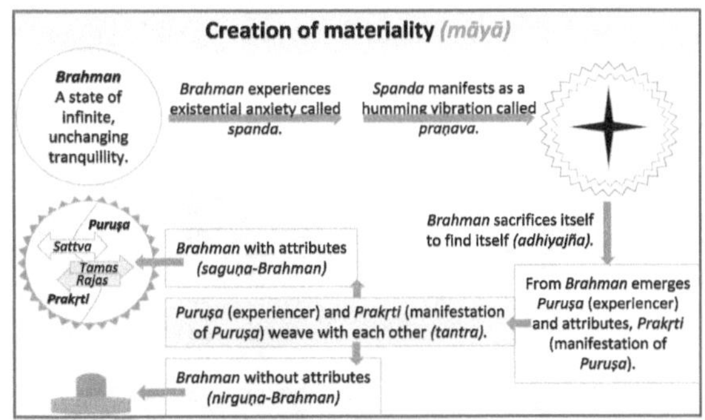

2.1 - *māyā*

- It does not slay and cannot be slain, it is unmanifested in the beginning in all beings (unborn state), it manifests in the middle (living beings), and is unmanifested again in the end (in a state of death).

- Also, it cannot be cut or separated from anything, and it does not burn, get wet, or become dry (it has no material qualities and is indestructible).

- It is not born and does not die when the body departs. This dweller in the body is eternally indestructible in all creatures (it does not change).

- Finally, it is constant, everywhere, stable, immovable, and universal.

Conclusion: *Brahman* is a state of infinite, imperishable (cannot die), and immutable (cannot change) state of peace.

Importantly, *Brahman* is the underwriter of all creation. It is the source and motility of all mass, energy, identity, and intelligence, supporting the

2.2 - creation of materiality *(māyā)*

functioning of everything. *Brahman* does not become involved in creation and does not acquire the nature/property of anything that it supports.

So, what might a state that conforms to the above conditions be? If we were to reflect a little, then the only state that can conform to all the above conditions is either the state of "null" or "infinity", "null" being a state of nothing, and "infinity" being a state beyond nothing.

Can we visualize the above state? Let us reflect where do our ideas, imagination, and creativity come from. We will quickly realize that most ideas come when we are quiet, in a state of null or peace. Then, there is an internal vibration *(spandana)*, followed by a eureka sensation, after which the idea is born.

In yoga, awareness of this state is called *jñāna* or direct experience of *Brahman* within the person, and this experience is called *nirvikalpa-samādhi* (uninterrupted and unchanging state of peace).

Śrī Kṛṣṇa explains permanence and impermanence, (verse 26-28)

What is the difference between *Brahman* (permanence) and *māyā* (impermanence)?

To answer the difference between permanence and impermanent, we need to look at change.

- We know that the only thing constant about change is change itself. So, change is the source as well as the nature of impermanence.

- Next, we know that change is personal, and each of us experiences change differently.

- Also, it is very difficult for anyone to articulate any experience completely, for two reasons - first, one does not always decode all aspects of any experience, and second, it is not always possible to articulate the experience due to shortcomings of communication.

- Generally, we assume that insentient entities have no experiences because we do not see any evidence of their ability to experience. Conversely, there is no concrete evidence that they are unable to undergo experiences.

  o We know that people get attached to their personal possessions, such as cars, homes, clothes, ornaments, furniture such as couches, and even utensils, such as mugs, some more than others. How would this differential attachment be possible if the other entity did not have an identity or soul that allowed it to radiate a personality? If that

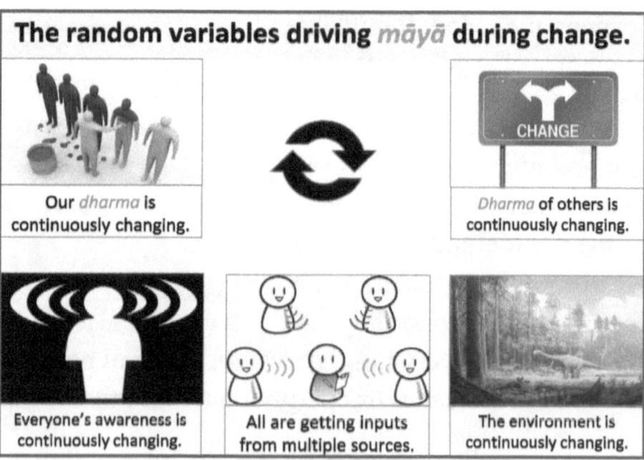

2.3 - the variables impacting change *(māyā)*

is acceptable, then, just as humans experience grief when parting with a possession, might not insentient entities experience grief also?

o   Psychologists can mostly decode sentient experiences only in a generic manner unless they get specific data inputs from their patients. When trained professionals have difficulty in accurately decoding experiences, it is logical to assume that understanding insentient entities who have no capability to communicate would be more difficult.

o   All prayers are the same; there is no evidence that one type of prayer is superior to another. The quality of outcome of any prayer depends on the person. So, whether one prays to an Idol, Cross, or Kaaba, the results would entirely depend on the person praying. But, have we ever reflected, what happens to the above religious entities to whom millions of people pray? What might their experience be and how they may be changing?

- Hence, we can conclude that both sentient and insentient entities experience, but in the case of insentient entities, experientiality (ability to express an experience in a manner that can be understood) is more suppressed and diffused; therefore, it is consequently difficult for sentient entities to experience or understand.

- In contrast, sentient entities starkly experience duality, such as heat-cold and pleasure-pain, because they have a sensory system that allows them to relate to their environment.

- Therefore, it is possible to derive that sentient and insentient entities or souls experience change differently on account of conditioning *(dharma)* and current state awareness *(prajñā)*.

- However, all experiences, due to the very nature of change, have a beginning and an end, which makes them transient or impermanent. This is *māyā* (illusion or farce).

- By understanding the nature of impermanence, one can transcend it *(māyā)* and merge with the state of permanence/Truth or *Brahman.* This results in liberation from rebirth *(mokṣa).*

From the above analysis, we can state that everything which we perceive in the world around us is impermanent because of three reasons:

- First, it has a beginning and an end.

- Second, it is perceived by the senses, which give different measurements for different sentient and insentient beings at different times, in different states of awareness.

- Change occurs continuously. Since by its nature, no stimulus-response cycle is predictable, change itself is not predictable or permanent. This results in randomness and instability being intrinsic to all transactions, and this is also called entropy in thermodynamics.

Karma and conditions of rebirth

Let us start from first principles. *Brahman* is the foundation of all existence. It is indestructible, unborn, infinite, exists everywhere, and is the motility of all change.

What is the driving principle of change? In any situation, when we receive a stimulus, we either react or don't react. So, change occurs as an outcome of stimulus and response. When there is a stimulus, there is a response, which causes change. Importantly, even lack of a response is a response.

All change is thermodynamic because, no matter what the response to stimulus, there is change in internal material and energy configuration of both the instigator and responder. This known as internal energy[3] or the total energy content of any system. Whether we react or not react our internal configuration or energy content changes. When we absorb change/energy or do not react, it is an endothermic reaction, or there is an increase in internal energy because our internal processing pressures increase. Similarly, when we react to change, we give out energy to the environment; it is an exothermic reaction, and there is a drop in our internal energy. But there is change in some form.

Karma is the input factor for change

- When we react to any stimulus, we enter into a transaction with the object and create a bond *(bandhana)*.

- We either like or dislike the stimulus, and, as a result of this, we either push the object away *(dveṣa)* or pull it closer *(rāga)*.

- This action of pulling or pushing causes relative displacement between both entities and is called *karma* (action/work).

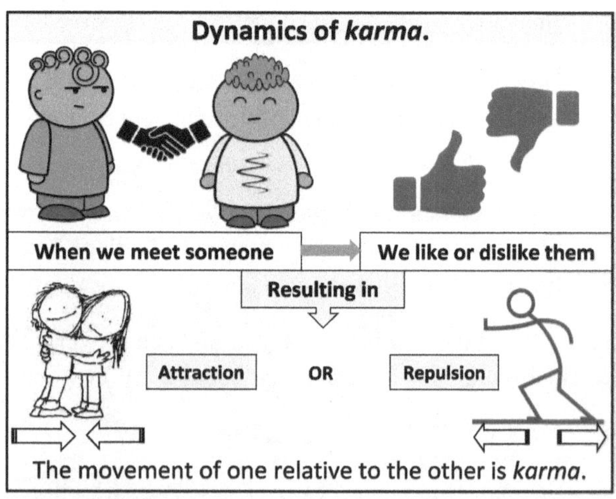

2.4 - dynamics of *karma*

- As a result of the transaction, we either give or take with each other.

- This transaction is always unequal because the awareness levels of the participants always differ. As a result, one always gives or takes more than the other.

- Consequently, one party ends up being the debtor and the other the creditor.

- This is called debt *(ṛṇa)*.

- We know that all debts have to be repaid.

- In the case of *karma*, this spillover goes beyond life, to more lives, resulting in the concept of rebirth *(saṃsāra)*.

Example

- Have you noticed that our ability to change varies with the situation? We change according to our likes and dislikes.

- Often, we change positions during a discussion when we encounter fresh data.

- Additionally, our likes and dislikes, in terms of tastes, people, and other things change slowly.

- Finally, our character and value systems *(dharma)*, which have been molded since childhood, are slowest to change, but even they change over time.

Permanence and impermanence

We can see that the permanent cognitive state of *Brahman* is the only place where there is no change; it is also known as Truth or as a thermodynamically ideal state. Everything else is impermanent.

Impermanence in sentient entities covers everything that is touched by the senses. This means that in order to understand what is permanent, one needs to transcend (go beyond) the senses.

Finally, it can be seen that the continuous and ephemeral nature of change is dependent on cognition of stimuli *(manas)* by the senses *(indriyā)* and its processing by the intellect *(buddhi)*. This processing of information is done by each of us on a framework called *dharma* (natural state), and this framework or conditioning is unique to each of us. Importantly, this unique and individual nature of how stimuli is received, processed, and reacted to is constantly evolving, and this makes our current state temporary or impermanent.

Śrī Kṛṣṇa explains attitude to work, *dharma,* and duty (verse 26-53)

Earlier, we have said that *karma* (action) occurs when we like something and we pull it closer or push it away because we dislike something. *Karma* is the push or pull action.

What is the basis on which we like or dislike something? It is *dharma,* or our natural state. *Dharma* is conditioning that manifests as values and behavior which we transact in any situation. Our hardware configuration is defined by DNA, on which our operating system is loaded by our parents. As we progress, our worldview is defined by schools and friends in our formative years. Over time, it changes due to experiences, but these changes come with anxiety and pain associated with change.

- *Dharma* defines our likes and dislikes, hence the instinctive/primary response to any situation. So, *dharma* is the foundation of response that results in action *(karma)* and resultant debt *(ṛṇa).*

- Also, *dharma* defines the natural state of all creation. For example, we all know how humans, dogs, cats, and other sentient beings act and react in their individual unique ways. Mango trees will yield mango fruit, never papaya. Hydrogen atoms will have an atomic weight of 1.008 and an atomic number of 1; this is its *dharma* and defines how hydrogen will behave in any bond.

- In thermodynamics, *dharma* is the internal energy of a system, internal energy being the sum of kinetic and potential energy in any system. This will be different for each entity because individual composition is different between entities.

Concept of duty and *dharma*

We are born with a unique DNA and grow up in our own specific environment, which molds our values and behavior, thus defining our experiences. Consequently, these values become predominant drivers of our sense of self-esteem or state of being.

As a result, we are at peace when our experiences are within our unique parameters of DNA and conditioning or natural state. This state of equilibrium is our natural state or *dharma.*

This natural state can be extended to cover sentient and insentient states as well as professions, businesses, systems, and activities, which makes this universal or *sanātana-dharma.*

Let us review how *dharma* intricately weaves work with personality, duty, system, and environment:

Examples of *dharma* or natural-state.					
Earth	**Sky**	**Language**	**Government**	**School**	**Parents**
Sustains life	Protects Earth	Imparts information	Governs by constitution	Makes responsible citizens	Secure and nourish
Dharma **is the natural state of all entities. It is conditioning in individuals.**					

2.5 - *dharma* is the natural state of any entity

- A soldier needs to be able to maintain his awareness in battle; his *dharma* or duty is to fight and defend. If he runs away from the battlefield, then he compromises the integrity of whatever he protects and loses his *dharma* or state of equilibrium. To perform his *dharma,* he must overcome his fear of death.

- Similarly, a teacher's *dharma* or duty is to teach and develop students into responsible citizens; if he or she were to be afraid of the opinion of others, then the person would never be able to teach effectively and build good citizens.

- Next, the *dharma* or duty of a business man is to increase material value without lowering integrity. When integrity is lost or when the businessman is afraid of risk, *dharma* is lost.

- Finally, the *dharma* of a farmer is to grow food; he must not stop sowing because he is worried that there may be no rains. That fear would result in famine and destruction of society.

Conclusion: Śrī Kṛṣṇa's advice of *dharma* and duty applies to every person, activity, or section of society. Consequently, when people do not perform their designated duties, shirk performing them, or perform them without integrity, society suffers and chaos *(adharma)* results.

Example

Ramaśāstrī Prabhune was a *mukhya-nyāyādhiṣa* (Chief Judge) of the Indian kingdom of Marathas. In 1772, the ruling Peshwa, Narayan Rao, was murdered by his own paternal uncle, Raghunath Rao, and his wife Anandibai, to become the Peshwa or ruler. When the case came up for hearing, Ramaśāstrī declared the sitting Peshwa guilty and sentenced him to death in his own court. As a result, Ramaśāstrī faced definite threat to his life and left Pune to go into exile.

- How was Ramaśāstrī able to confront the ruler, pronounce him guilty of regicide, and hand him a sentence of death in his own court? What does this tell you about Ramaśāstrī?

- What fear would Ramaśāstrī have had to overcome when he pronounced this judgment?

- Have you ever experienced a similar situation and response?

Difference between rights and duties

- Your right is to effort alone, not its outcome.

- Attachment to reward should not be your motivator for action.

- Also, fear of consequences or attachment to outcome should not stop you from making this effort.

- Perform action, abandon attachment to the action, its outcome, or rewards, and be balanced in both success and failure.

- This even-handedness of the Self and indifference in action is karma-yoga.

So, how do Śrī Kṛṣṇa's words translate in today's world?

Every right comes with a responsibility and without an effective execution of responsibility, that right can never be enjoyed. For example, to be a citizen or a member of a community is a right, but that right comes with a responsibility of behavior. Without responsible behavior, the values of the community cannot be realized. As a result, rights conferred by the community or country are undermined, so these rights cannot be enjoyed by all members of the community or citizens of the country. Thus, *dharma* is compromised, and turbulence or chaos *(adharma)* increases.

- Once you accept a responsibility in a team, you must be loyal to the team and ensure team success.

- When performing a task, you must take it to the end and do it to the best of your ability.

- Do not perform an action for the reward. You will get rewards, and often, they may not be commensurate with your perception of worth. Keep your equilibrium unless you perceive injustice.

- However, if you perceive injustice, then it is your duty to petition and seek redressal.

- As a citizen, you must support your country, civilization, and culture by understanding and following it. Otherwise, there will be chaos *(adharma)!*

- Paying taxes is not an option; it is a responsibility.

- For any member of society, keeping it clean, following the rules and being a good neighbor is not an option; it is a duty!

- It is not necessary that you agree with many things around you, and it is your duty to try and correct them. But you must follow the system until you are able to change it.

- This also means that you cannot subvert or bypass a rule just because you do not agree with it. That would lead to *adharma* or chaos!

The concept of *guṇa* (attributes)

Our ability to act comes from our situational awareness *(prajñā)*. When our awareness is beset by inertia, doubt, fear, or self-pity, it is called *tamas*. Next, when our awareness is driven by anger, greed, or ambition, this is called *rajas,* a state of energy. Finally, when there is a balance and state of

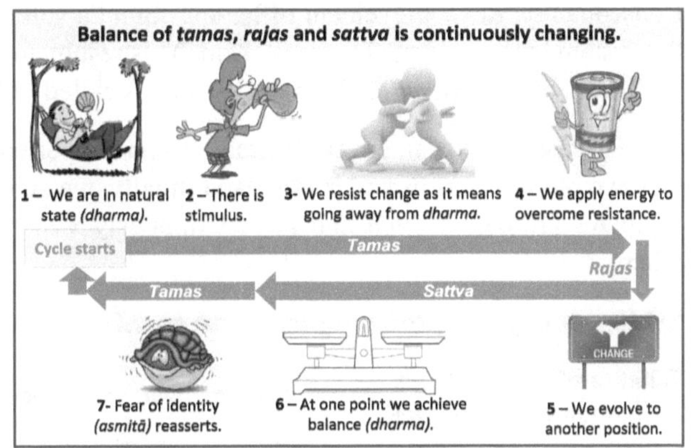

2.6 - how *guṇas* impact change

balance or harmony, this is called *sattva*. These three attributes or *guṇa* (attributes of cognition) are always together, never static, and continuously changing in proportion.

The *guṇa* are:

- *Tamas* (obdurate/delusion) - our actions are driven by lack of logic, understanding, in delusion, or sometimes we refuse to act on account of laziness and fear.

- *Rajas* (passion) - our actions are driven by ambition, greed, anger, targets/goals, power, arrogance, vanity, etc.

- *Sattva* (balance) - our actions are driven by integrity, need for balance, harmony, consensus, etc.

Example of *guṇa*

A person is using an ATM (Automatic Teller Machine) for the first time. The bank has issued an ATM card to the person, but the person has never used an ATM before. Imagine the person's state when for the first time he/she must work with the ATM.

- Firstly, there is confusion – "How am I going to do this?" or anxiety/fear "What will happen if…?" This is *tamas*.

- Secondly, comes anger or irritation – "This is ridiculous! How do they expect me to operate this machine without training?" This is *rajas*. Then, there is effort… "Let's see what we can do".

- Finally, there is acceptance and ownership. Here, the person hacks around and finds a solution, either by doing it himself or by asking someone. The person experiences balance and peace. This is *sattva*.

Consequently, the achievement of having found a solution brings an awareness of the system in the person. This is *vijñāna*. This results in increased confidence in the Self, an increase in *asmitā* (I am this) which is called *jñāna*.

The above example can cover all situations and experiences; first, we are confused, then we put in effort to understand, and, finally, we achieve a balance. These three attributes are called *guṇa* and are continuously vying for ascendency with each other.

Śrī Kṛṣṇa explains *sthitaprajña*, (verse 64-72)

What are the qualities of one who has reached *sthitaprajña* – (*sthita* = stable, heightened, or resolute + *prajñā* = awareness of the Self or situational awareness)?

Sthithaprajñā –the 4 stage evolution to perfection			
Jāgrat – awakened or living state.	*Svapna –* dream, imagination, or play back state.	*Suṣupti –* all become equal (*samasti*), we transcend form.	*Turīya –* where we transcend *guṇa* (attributes)
Combination of state of awareness (the first one is the dominant state)			
Jāgrat – Jāgrat	Svapna – Jāgrat	Suṣupti – Jāgrat	Turīya – Jāgrat
Jāgrat – Svapna	Svapna – Svapna	Suṣupti – Svapna	Turīya – Svapna
Jāgrat – Suṣupti	Svapna – Suṣupti	Suṣupti – Suṣupti	Turīya – Suṣupti
Jāgrat – Turīya	Svapna – Turīya	Suṣupti – Turīya	Turīya – Turīya

2.7 - awareness continuously changes with involvement

- First, such a person is able to cast off all desires, even those in the form of ideas, and become completely secure and satisfied in *Brahman,* by *Brahman* alone.

- Second, such a person acts without bias and is not afraid of any outcome. This person is indifferent and without agitation in pain as well as pleasure. There is complete absence of longing for anything.

- Third, this person is unattached and without affection everywhere. There are no swings in reaction, such as like-dislike or attraction-rejection. This allows the person to control cognition *(manas)* from being hijacked by turbulent senses.

- Fourth, this person is able to withdraw his senses from all objects and keep his or her awareness steady.

How does a person become a *sthitaprajña*?

- Let us look at the nature of response to any stimulus.

- First, by thinking of objects, an attachment is developed towards them.

- Next, from attachment comes the desire for ownership and control.

- Following desire comes anger and frustration when things do not go right.

- Frustration and anger cloud reason, resulting in delusion.

- Delusion causes turbulence in the cognition *(manas),* which, in turn, results in clouding of data, information, and memory.

- Lastly, from confusion of memory comes loss of order/harmony as well as conditioning *(dharma),* and reason *(buddhi).*

- From loss of balance, harmony, and reason comes incorrect action, which leads to disappointment and destruction.

What is the solution?

- Stimuli create turbulence, owing to conflicting options brought about by conditioning *(dharma).* So, when a person is aware of the decision process, control over attraction *(rāga)* and repulsion *(dveṣa)* are achieved by controlling the sense of doer-ship *(ahaṅkāra),* which modulates response. This control is achieved when a person is undisturbed by change, neither seeking nor rejecting it, and is free from attachment, fear, or anxiety.

- A person who reaches the state of *sthitaprajña* casts off all physical, intellectual, and emotional attachments and becomes completely secure within himself. Such a person abandons desire and moves about free from longing, without ownership, without the sense of doer-ship, and attains peace.

- The reduction in misery/disappointment results in the appearance of a tranquil consciousness because the intellect *(buddhi)* becomes steady. This is the *brāhmika* state.

- Conversely, fickle people have no intellect or steady vision *(bhāvanā),* and no peace exists in those with no awareness *(abhāvayat);* hence, these people find no peace.

- Importantly, this state of *Brahman* is not achieved by anyone who is fascinated by achievement as an intellectual exercise, but by effort. However, once anyone achieves this state and gets transfixed there, he merges with *Brahman*.

The concept of the present

Śrī Kṛṣṇa is asking everyone to remain in the present, that's all! In the present, there is no past or future, and all the senses as well as allied apparatus are controlled. If there is no past, there can also be no memory, which means that all memory is erased. If there is to be no future, there can be no planning or anxiety of outcome.

But, remaining in the present is not easy; it requires an awareness of the situation as it unfolds and develops.

Additionally, this awareness covers all physical, emotional, and intellectual experiences. Therein lies the subtlety as well as complexity of Śrī Kṛṣṇa's advise.

Examples

Time - We are all born equal; all of us have 24 hours in a day. When we are in a happy situation (like party, movie, or with friends), time seems to go faster. But, when we are waiting for a flight, exam results, or relief from a headache after taking medication, time seems to move slowly. How is this possible? What has changed is our attachment to the outcome, like/dislike of the subject, or any other reasons associated with our self-esteem *(asmitā)*.

Bias - Often, when we listen to people we like, we agree to do what they ask. However, when we don't like the person, we get filled with resistance and experience resentment, even if the advice is for our own wellbeing. Why?

Fear - When we have missed our targets at work, lost marks in exams, or missed a flight, we experience anxiety, which stops us from thinking about solutions to the problem. Often, our anxieties and irrational reactions make it difficult for our friends, companions, colleagues, and family members to work with us. How can we become non-threatening and more acceptable?

The above examples are some of the many ways in which we lose our ability to remain in the present due to our conditioning *(dharma)*.

Do not mistake intellectual, emotional intelligence, or physical awareness as situational awareness. Situational awareness is a cognitive, visceral, and experiential awareness of the present where we participate without becoming attached.

In this part of the chapter, Śrī Kṛṣṇa is trying to define the character and behavior of a role model having ideal situational awareness. It is not easy but can be achieved with constant practice.

Some contradictions to accepted positions:

- Throughout *Śrīmad-bhagavad-gītā*, the position of Śrī Kṛṣṇa is very confusing. In chapter 13, Śrī Kṛṣṇa himself acknowledges that his human manifestation confuses everyone. In chapter 8, he states that he is the primordial sacrifice *(ādhiyajña)*, and in chapter 17, he describes his residence as *Brahman*. This does not mean that he is *Brahman*, because *Brahman* is a cognitive state of null, but merely that he resides there, or, more precisely, he has merged with *Brahman*. So, Śrī Kṛṣṇa cannot assumed to be *Brahman* but one who is permanently cognizing this state.

- Śrī Kṛṣṇa is referred to *bhagavān* when he answers Arjuna. Popularly, *bhagavān* has been loosely translated as God or Lord. However, *bhagavān* is derived from *bhagavat*, which means glorious, venerable, etc. Also, there is no evidence of the existence of God, nor are there any descriptions of the qualities of God anywhere in *Śrīmad-bhagavad-gītā*.

- *Brahman* is not God; *Brahman* is a cognitive state of null. Also, nowhere in *Śrīmad-bhagavad-gītā* is there any evidence of *bhagavān* being *Brahman*. Throughout, *Brahman* is referred to as *Bahman* itself or *tat* (that). Additionally, the qualities of *Brahman* are well laid out and cannot correlated to the accepted definitions of God.

- While a merger with Śrī Kṛṣṇa will result in a merger with *Brahman*, this is not an exclusive condition. Complete surrender of the Self to ANY entity will lead to a merger with *Brahman*. In fact, Śrī Kṛṣṇa himself says that even offering sacrifice as a sacrifice will result in merger with *Brahman*. So, merger is a result of the individual's effort and is not related to Śrī Kṛṣṇa's capabilities.

- Also, *daiva* is not *bhagavān; daiva* is a deity who has specific roles and responsibilities in material existence. Neither is *īśvara*. In fact, the position of *īśvara* is subordinate to the position of Śrī Kṛṣṇa *(ādhiyajña)*.

- So, what is *bhagavān*? One is forced to conclude that *bhagavān* is, as the definition says, an enlightened one. Consequently, any depiction of *bhagavān* as God/ Lord is unsustainable.

- Since there are no alternate explanations, no concrete evidence of God, or translation of *bhagavān*, a more sustainable position would be to retain Śrī Kṛṣṇa as *yogī*, an enlightened teacher of *Śrīmad-bhagavad-gītā*, and the embodiment of the cognitive state of *ādhiyajña* (primordial sacrifice).

Lessons learned in chapter 2:

- There are two primary cognitive states, permanent and impermanent.

- Permanent is *Brahman*, which is the foundation and motility of everything.

Impermanent is everything else, known as *māyā* (illusion) or materiality (anything that can be cognized by the senses).

- The only way to manage change is by discriminating permanent from impermanent in any situation *(viveka)* and acting with dispassion *(vairāgya)*.

- Managing change requires that one's situational awareness be in the moment, and a person who develops and remains steadfast in it is called *sthitaprajña*.

The transliteration and translation of chapter 2 follows:

सञ्जय उवाच -

तं तथा कृपयाविष्टमश्रुपूर्णाकुलेक्षणम् ।

विषीदन्तमिदं वाक्यमुवाच मधुसूदनः ॥ २-१॥

Sañjaya said (1) Madhusūdana said this to him, who was overcome with pity, despondent, and whose eyes were filled with tears *(taṃ tathā kṛpayāviṣṭamaśrupūrṇākulekṣaṇam ǀ viṣīdantamidaṃ vākyamuvāca madhusūdanaḥ ǁ 2-1ǁ)*

श्रीभगवानुवाच -

कुतस्त्वा कश्मलमिदं विषमे समुपस्थितम् ।

अनार्यजुष्टमस्वर्ग्यमकीर्तिकरमर्जुन ॥ २-२॥

क्लैब्यं मा स्म गमः पार्थ नैतत्त्वय्युपपद्यते ।

क्षुद्रं हृदयदौर्बल्यं त्यक्त्वोत्तिष्ठ परन्तप ॥ २-३॥

Śrī Kṛṣṇa said (2-3) How did this dejection which brings you to this perilous state that makes you un-aryan like, unfit for heaven and disgraceful *(kutastvā kaśmalamidaṃ viṣame samupasthitam ǀ anāryajuṣṭamasvargyamakīrtikaramarjuna ǁ 2-2ǁ)*. Do not become impotent, it is not fitting in you, discard weakness of the heart, stand up and fight *(klaibyaṃ mā sma gamaḥ pārtha naitattvayyupapadyate ǀ kṣudraṃ hṛdayadaurbalyaṃ tyaktvottiṣṭha parantapa ǁ 2-3ǁ)*.

अर्जुन उवाच ।

कथं भीष्ममहं सङ्ख्ये द्रोणं च मधुसूदन ।

इषुभिः प्रतियोत्स्यामि पूजार्हावरिसूदन ॥ २-४॥

गुरूनहत्वा हि महानुभावान्

श्रेयो भोक्तुं भैक्ष्यमपीह लोके ।

हत्वार्थकामांस्तु गुरूनिहैव

भुञ्जीय भोगान् रुधिरप्रदिग्धान् ॥ २-५॥

न चैतद्विद्मः कतरन्नो गरीयो
यद्वा जयेम यदि वा नो जयेयुः ।
यानेव हत्वा न जिजीविषाम-
स्तेऽवस्थिताः प्रमुखे धार्तराष्ट्राः ॥ २-६॥

Arjuna said (4-6) How can I do battle with arrows at Bhīṣma and Droṇa, they that are fit to be worshipped (*kathaṃ bhīṣmamahaṃ saṅkhye droṇaṃ ca madhusūdana । iṣubhiḥ pratiyotsyāmi pūjārhāvarisūdana ॥ 2-4॥*). Instead of slaying these greatly experienced *gurus*, it is better to eat alms. Indeed, how can I enjoy wealth and desires in this world when I am stained with their blood (*gurūnahatvā hi mahānubhāvān śreyo bhoktuṃ bhaikṣyamapīha loke । hatvārthakāmāṃstu gurūnihaiva bhuñjīya bhogān rudhirapradigdhān ॥ 2-5॥*). I am unable to know which is better, whether we conquer them or they conquer us, whether we would wish to live after slaying the sons of Dhṛtarāṣṭra (*na caitadvidmaḥ kataranno garīyo yadvā jayema yadi vā no jayeyuḥ । yāneva hatvā na jijīviṣāma- ste'vasthitāḥ pramukhe dhārtarāṣṭrāḥ ॥ 2-6॥*).

कार्पण्यदोषोपहतस्वभावः
पृच्छामि त्वां धर्मसम्मूढचेताः ।
यच्छ्रेयः स्यान्निश्चितं ब्रूहि तन्मे
शिष्यस्तेऽहं शाधि मां त्वां प्रपन्नम् ॥ २-७॥

न हि प्रपश्यामि ममापनुद्याद्
यच्छोकमुच्छोषणमिन्द्रियाणाम् ।
अवाप्य भूमावसपत्नमृद्धं
राज्यं सुराणामपि चाधिपत्यम् ॥ २-८॥

(7-8) With natural instinct overcome by pity I as you about *dharma* with a confused mind, what is good for me. As your pupil, I take refuge in you, teach me (*kārpaṇyadoṣopahatasvabhāvaḥ pṛcchāmi tvāṃ dharmasammūḍhacetāḥ । yacchreyaḥ syānniścitaṃ brūhi tanme śiṣyaste'haṃ śādhi māṃ tvāṃ prapannam ॥ 2-7॥*). Nothing I see is able to remove my grief, my senses are clogged up, even obtaining unrivalled prosperity on Earth or even dominion over the deities (*na hi prapaśyāmi mamāpanudyād yacchokamucchoṣaṇamindriyāṇām । avāpya bhūmāvasapatnamṛddhaṃ rājyaṃ surāṇāmapi cādhipatyam ॥ 2-8॥*).

सञ्जय उवाच ।
एवमुक्त्वा हृषीकेशं गुडाकेशः परन्तप ।
न योत्स्य इति गोविन्दमुक्त्वा तूष्णीं बभूव ह ॥ २-९॥
तमुवाच हृषीकेशः प्रहसन्निव भारत ।
सेनयोरुभयोर्मध्ये विषीदन्तमिदं वचः ॥ २-१०॥

Sañjaya spoke (9-10) Having thus spoken to Hṛṣīkeśa, Guḍākeśa, the destroyer of foes, said I will not fight Govinda and became silent (*evamuktvā hṛṣīkeśaṃ guḍākeśaḥ parantapa ǀ na yotsya iti govindamuktvā tūṣṇīṃ babhūva ha ǁ 2-9ǁ*). Hṛṣīkeśa smilingly said this to Bhārata, who was despondent in the middle of the two armies (*tamuvāca hṛṣīkeśaḥ prahasanniva bhārata ǀ senayorubhayormadhye viṣīdantamidaṃ vacaḥ ǁ 2-10ǁ*).

श्रीभगवानुवाच ।

अशोच्यानन्वशोचस्त्वं प्रज्ञावादांश्च भाषसे ।

गतासूनगतासूंश्च नानुशोचन्ति पण्डिताः ॥ २-११॥

न त्वेवाहं जातु नासं न त्वं नेमे जनाधिपाः ।

न चैव न भविष्यामः सर्वे वयमतः परम् ॥ २-१२॥

देहिनोऽस्मिन्यथा देहे कौमारं यौवनं जरा ।

तथा देहान्तरप्राप्तिर्धीरस्तत्र न मुह्यति ॥ २-१३॥

Śrī Kṛṣṇa said (11-13) You grieve for those that should not be grieved, the wise do not grieve for the dead and living (*aśocyānanvaśocastvam prajñāvādāṃsca bhāṣase ǀ gatāsūnagatāsūṃsca nānuśocanti paṇḍitāḥ ǁ 2-11ǁ*). Not I or even you nor any of the rulers of men also existed at any time, nor shall anyone in the future (*na tvevāhaṃ jātu nāsaṃ na tvaṃ neme janādhipāḥ ǀ na caiva na bhaviṣyāmaḥ sarve vayamataḥ param ǁ 2-12ǁ*). The embodied in this body passes through childhood, youth, old age, and entry into another body, the self-possessed do not get bewildered (*dehino'sminyathā dehe kaumāraṃ yauvanaṃ jarā ǀ tathā dehāntaraprāptirdhīrastatra na muhyati ǁ 2-13ǁ*).

मात्रास्पर्शास्तु कौन्तेय शीतोष्णसुखदुःखदाः ।

आगमापायिनोऽनित्यास्तांस्तितिक्षस्व भारत ॥ २-१४॥

यं हि न व्यथयन्त्येते पुरुषं पुरुषर्षभ ।

समदुःखसुखं धीरं सोऽमृतत्वाय कल्पते ॥ २-१५॥

(14-15) Indeed, outward cognition results in cold/heat, pleasure/pain, which enter, their stay is impermanent, be patient (*mātrāsparśāstu kaunteya śītoṣṇasukhaduḥkhadāḥ ǀ āgamāpāyino'nityāstāṃstitikṣasva bhārata ǁ 2-14ǁ*). The man who is not anguished is a champion among men, he who is firm and equal in pain and pleasure is fit for immortality (*yam hi na vyathayantyete puruṣaṃ puruṣarṣabha ǀ samaduḥkhasukhaṃ dhīraṃ so'mṛtatvāya kalpate ǁ 2-15ǁ*).

नासतो विद्यते भावो नाभावो विद्यते सतः ।

उभयोरपि दृष्टोऽन्तस्त्वनयोस्तत्त्वदर्शिभिः ॥ २-१६॥

अविनाशि तु तद्विद्धि येन सर्वमिदं ततम् ।
विनाशमव्ययस्यास्य न कश्चित्कर्तुमर्हति ॥ २-१७॥

(16-17) It does not exist in cognition of experience; no experience is cognized in this state of merger. Also, inside of these two states have indeed been seen by knowers of this state *(nāsato vidyate bhāvo nābhāvo vidyate sataḥ ı ubhayorapi dṛṣṭo 'ntastvanayostattvadarśibhiḥ ॥ 2-16॥)*. Cognize that indestructible indeed is that which pervades everything. Destruction of the imperishable is not something anyone can do *(avināśi tu tadviddhi yena sarvamidaṃ tatam ı vināśamavyayasyāsya na kaścitkartumarhati ॥ 2-17॥)*.

अन्तवन्त इमे देहा नित्यस्योक्ताः शरीरिणः ।
अनाशिनोऽप्रमेयस्य तस्माद्युध्यस्व भारत ॥ २-१८॥
य एनं वेत्ति हन्तारं यश्चैनं मन्यते हतम् ।
उभौ तौ न विजानीतो नायं हन्ति न हन्यते ॥ २-१९॥
न जायते म्रियते वा कदाचिन्
    नायं भूत्वा भविता वा न भूयः ।
अजो नित्यः शाश्वतोऽयं पुराणो
    न हन्यते हन्यमाने शरीरे ॥ २-२०॥

(18-20) These bodies have an end, but the everlasting is said to be embodied as indestructible and immeasurable, so fight *(antavanta ime dehā nityasyoktāḥ śarīriṇaḥ ı anāśino 'prameyasya tasmādyudhyasva bhārata ॥ 2-18॥)*. He who thinks that he is the slayer, he who cognizes that something is slain, both do not know that this does not slay nor is it slain *(ya enaṃ vetti hantāraṃ yaścainaṃ manyate hatam ı ubhau tau na vijānīto nāyaṃ hanti na hanyate ॥ 2-19॥)*. It is neither born nor does it die anytime; it is not present now or later in the future or in that which is occurring. It is unborn, eternal, and changeless, this ancient is not killed when the body is being killed. *(na jāyate mriyate vā kadācin nāyaṃ bhūtvā bhavitā vā na bhūyaḥ ı ajo nityaḥ śāśvato 'yaṃ purāṇo na hanyate hanyamāne śarīre ॥ 2-20॥)*.

वेदाविनाशिनं नित्यं य एनमजमव्ययम् ।
कथं स पुरुषः पार्थ कं घातयति हन्ति कम् ॥ २-२१॥
वासांसि जीर्णानि यथा विहाय
    नवानि गृह्णाति नरोऽपराणि ।
तथा शरीराणि विहाय जीर्णा-
    न्यन्यानि संयाति नवानि देही ॥ २-२२॥

(21-22) He who cognizes this to be indestructible, unborn, infinite, to exist everywhere, how can that person cause slaying or slay *(vedāvināśinam nityam ya enamajamavyayam ׀ katham sa puruṣaḥ pārtha kam ghātayati hanti kam ॥ 2-21॥)*. Just as worn-out clothes are cast away and new additional ones taken by man, similarly, bodies are cast off after they are used up and other new bodies entered *(vāsāmsi jīrṇāni yathā vihāya navāni gṛhṇāti naro'parāṇi ׀ tathā śarīrāṇi vihāya jīrṇā- nyanyāni samyāti navāni dehī ॥ 2-22॥)*.

नैनं छिन्दन्ति शस्त्राणि नैनं दहति पावकः ।
न चैनं क्लेदयन्त्यापो न शोषयति मारुतः ॥ २-२३॥
अच्छेद्योऽयमदाह्योऽयमक्लेद्योऽशोष्य एव च ।
नित्यः सर्वगतः स्थाणुरचलोऽयं सनातनः ॥ २-२४॥
अव्यक्तोऽयमचिन्त्योऽयमविकार्योऽयमुच्यते ।
तस्मादेवं विदित्वैनं नानुशोचितुमर्हसि ॥ २-२५॥

(23-25) This cannot be cut with weapons; this does not burn in fire, and this does not get wet in water and does not get dry in the wind *(nainam chindanti śastrāṇi nainam dahati pāvakaḥ ׀ na cainam kledayantyāpo na śoṣayati mārutaḥ ॥ 2-23॥)*. This cannot be cut, this cannot be burnt, this cannot be wetted or dried and also constant, everywhere, stable, immovable, this universal *(acchedyo 'yamadāhyo 'yamakledyo 'śoṣya eva ca ׀ nityaḥ sarvagataḥ sthāṇuracalo 'yam sanātanaḥ ॥ 2-24॥)*. This is unmanifested, this is unthinking, this is unchangeable, this is therefore knowing this, one ought not to lament *(avyakto 'yamacintyo 'yamavikāryo 'yamucyate ׀ tasmādevam viditvainam nānuśocitumarhasi ॥ 2-25॥)*.

अथ चैनं नित्यजातं नित्यं वा मन्यसे मृतम् ।
तथापि त्वं महाबाहो नैवं शोचितुमर्हसि ॥ २-२६॥
जातस्य हि ध्रुवो मृत्युर्ध्रुवं जन्म मृतस्य च ।
तस्मादपरिहार्येऽर्थे न त्वं शोचितुमर्हसि ॥ २-२७॥
अव्यक्तादीनि भूतानि व्यक्तमध्यानि भारत ।
अव्यक्तनिधनान्येव तत्र का परिदेवना ॥ २-२८॥

(26-28) Now, if you think that this is constantly being born or constantly dying, even then you must not grieve *(atha cainam nityajātam nityam vā manyase mṛtam ׀ tathāpi tvam mahābāho naivam śocitumarhasi ॥ 2-26॥)*. For those that are born, death is certain, definitely there is birth for those that die, this is inevitable in matter, you should not grieve *(jātasya hi dhruvo mṛtyurdhruvam janma mṛtasya ca ׀ tasmādaparihārye'rthe na tvam śocitumarhasi ॥ 2-27॥)*. Unmanifested in the beginning are beings, manifested in the middle, unmanifested again in the end, so what is there to lament *(avyaktādīni bhūtāni vyaktamadhyāni bhārata ǀ avyaktanidhanānyeva tatra kā paridevanā ǁ 2-28ǁ)*.

आश्चर्यवत्पश्यति कश्चिदेन-
    माश्चर्यवद्वदति तथैव चान्यः ।
आश्चर्यवच्चैनमन्यः शृणोति
    श्रुत्वाप्येनं वेद न चैव कश्चित् ॥ २-२९॥
देही नित्यमवध्योऽयं देहे सर्वस्य भारत ।
तस्मात्सर्वाणि भूतानि न त्वं शोचितुमर्हसि ॥ २-३०॥

(29-30) In wonder one sees this, in wonder one speaks of also, many wonders one hears of this, after hearing this is not known to anyone at all *(āścaryavatpaśyati kaścidenamāścaryavadvadati tathaiva cānyaḥ ǀ āścaryavaccainamanyaḥ śaṛṇoti śrutvāpyenaṃ veda na caiva kaścit ǁ 2-29ǁ)*. This in-dweller in the body is eternally indestructible in all creatures; therefore, you should not grieve for anyone *(dehī nityamavadhyo'yaṃ dehe sarvasya bhārata ǀ tasmātsarvāṇi bhūtāni na tvaṃ śocitumarhasi ǁ 2-30ǁ)*.

स्वधर्ममपि चावेक्ष्य न विकम्पितुमर्हसि ।
धर्म्याद्धि युद्धाच्छ्रेयोऽन्यत्क्षत्रियस्य न विद्यते ॥ २-३१॥
यदृच्छया चोपपन्नं स्वर्गद्वारमपावृतम् ।
सुखिनः क्षत्रियाः पार्थ लभन्ते युद्धमीदृशम् ॥ २-३२॥
अथ चेत्त्वमिमं धर्म्यं सङ्ग्रामं न करिष्यसि ।
ततः स्वधर्मं कीर्तिं च हित्वा पापमवाप्स्यसि ॥ २-३३॥

(31-33) Observing one's own duty and not wavering at war should be higher than any other duty of a *kṣatriya (svadharmamapi cāvekṣya na vikampitumarhasi ǀ dharmyāddhi yuddhācchreyo'nyatkṣatriyasya na vidyate ǁ 2-31ǁ)*. Doors of heavens are laid open, happy *kṣatriya*s obtain battles that occur by themselves *(yadṛcchayā copapannaṃ svargadvāramapāvṛtam ǀ sukhinaḥ kṣatriyāḥ pārtha labhante yuddhamīdṛśam ǁ 2-32ǁ)*. However, if you do not act in this duty-bound warfare, then your honor will be stained as one who abandoned his self-duty *(atha cettvamimaṃ dharmyaṃ saṅgrāmaṃ na kariṣyasi ǀ tataḥ svadharmaṃ kīrtiṃ ca hitvā pāpamavāpsyasi ǁ 2-33ǁ)*.

अकीर्तिं चापि भूतानि कथयिष्यन्ति तेऽव्ययाम् ।
सम्भावितस्य चाकीर्तिर्मरणादतिरिच्यते ॥ २-३४॥
भयाद्रणादुपरतं मंस्यन्ते त्वां महारथाः ।
येषां च त्वं बहुमतो भूत्वा यास्यसि लाघवम् ॥ २-३५॥

अवाच्यवादांश्च बहून्वदिष्यन्ति तवाहिताः ।
निन्दन्तस्तव सामर्थ्यं ततो दुःखतरं नु किम् ॥ २-३६॥
हतो वा प्राप्स्यसि स्वर्गं जित्वा वा भोक्ष्यसे महीम् ।
तस्मादुत्तिष्ठ कौन्तेय युद्धाय कृतनिश्चयः ॥ २-३७॥

(34-37) Beings will recount your story of dishonor forever, in their thought, dishonor outlives death *(akīrtiṃ cāpi bhūtāni kathayiṣyanti te'vyayām । sambhāvitasya cākīrtirmaraṇādatiricyate ॥ 2-34॥)*. The great charioteers will think that you withdrew from the battlefield in fear *(bhayādraṇāduparataṃ maṃsyante tvāṃ mahārathāḥ ।)* those that thought highly of you will receive you as a lightweight *(yeṣāṃ ca tvaṃ bahumato bhūtvā yāsyasi lāghavam ॥ 2-35॥)*. Your enemies will speak many inappropriate words, and many will defame your abilities, which will indeed be more painful than this *(avācyavādāṃśca bahūnvadiṣyanti tavāhitāḥ । nindantastava sāmarthyaṃ tato duḥkhataraṃ nu kim ॥ 2-36॥)*. Slain, you will attain heaven, alive, you will enjoy victory on earth; therefore, stand up and resolve to fight. *(hato vā prāpsyasi svargaṃ jitvā vā bhokṣyase mahīm । tasmāduttiṣṭha kaunteya yuddhāya kṛtaniścayaḥ ॥ 2-37॥)*.

सुखदुःखे समे कृत्वा लाभालाभौ जयाजयौ ।
ततो युद्धाय युज्यस्व नैवं पापमवाप्स्यसि ॥ २-३८॥
एषा तेऽभिहिता साङ्ख्ये बुद्धिर्योगे त्विमां शृणु ।
बुद्ध्या युक्तो यया पार्थ कर्मबन्धं प्रहास्यसि ॥ २-३९॥
नेहाभिक्रमनाशोऽस्ति प्रत्यवायो न विद्यते ।
स्वल्पमप्यस्य धर्मस्य त्रायते महतो भयात् ॥ २-४०॥

(38-40) Treat pain and pleasure, profit and loss, and victory and defeat in the same manner, then engage in battle and no staining will result *(sukhaduḥkhe same kṛtvā lābhālābhau jayājayau । tato yuddhāya yujyasva naivaṃ pāpamavāpsyasi ॥ 2-38॥)*. I am telling you the philosophical wisdom in yoga; indeed, hear it with wisdom and follow it to cast off the bondage of *karma (eṣā te 'bhihitā sāṅkhye buddhiryoge tvimāṃ śarṇu । buddhyā yukto yayā pārtha karmabandhaṃ prahāsyasi ॥ 2-39॥)*. Contrary results do not come from unsuccessful effort, even little of this duty protects from great fear *(nehābhikramanāśo'sti pratyavāyo na vidyate । svalpamapyasya dharmasya trāyate mahato bhayāt ॥ 2-40॥)*.

व्यवसायात्मिका बुद्धिरेकेह कुरुनन्दन ।
बहुशाखा ह्यनन्ताश्च बुद्धयोऽव्यवसायिनाम् ॥ २-४१॥
यामिमां पुष्पितां वाचं प्रवदन्त्यविपश्चितः ।
वेदवादरताः पार्थ नान्यदस्तीति वादिनः ॥ २-४२॥

कामात्मानः स्वर्गपरा जन्मकर्मफलप्रदाम् ।
क्रियाविशेषबहुलां भोगैश्वर्यगतिं प्रति ॥ २-४३॥

(41-43) Maintain a firm soul and a focused intellect; diverse, endless contemplation is of the irresolute *(vyavasāyātmikā buddhirekeha kurunandana ǀ bahuśākhā hyanantāśca buddhayo'vyavasāyinām ǁ 2-41ǁ)*. The ignorant get carried away by flowery speech quoting the Vedas, not these other words *(yāmimāṃ puṣpitāṃ vācaṃ pravadantyavipaścitaḥ ǀ vedavādaratāḥ pārtha nānyadastīti vādinaḥ ǁ 2-42ǁ)*. Those whose soul is full of desires, even with heaven as their highest goal, get birth as the fruit of action because their actions are focused on goals specific for attainment of pleasure and wealth *(kāmātmānaḥ svargaparā janmakarmaphalapradām ǀ kriyāviśeṣabahulām bhogaiśvaryagatiṃ prati ǁ 2-43ǁ)*.

भोगैश्वर्यप्रसक्तानां तयापहृतचेतसाम् ।
व्यवसायात्मिका बुद्धिः समाधौ न विधीयते ॥ २-४४॥
त्रैगुण्यविषया वेदा निस्त्रैगुण्यो भवार्जुन ।
निर्द्वन्द्वो नित्यसत्त्वस्थो निर्योगक्षेम आत्मवान् ॥ २-४५॥
यावानर्थ उदपाने सर्वतः सम्प्लुतोदके ।
तावान्सर्वेषु वेदेषु ब्राह्मणस्य विजानतः ॥ २-४६॥

(44-46) Those that are attached to enjoyment and wealth are bereft of consciousness, firm soul, and intellect not focused in *samaadhi (bhogaiśvaryaprasaktānāṃ tayāpahṛtacetasām ǀ vyavasāyātmikā buddhiḥ samādhau na vidhīyate ǁ 2-44ǁ)*. The Vedas would not exist without the aspect of the three *guṇas (traiguṇyaviṣayā vedā nistraiguṇyo bhavārjuna ǀ)* be without duality, constantly in *sattva* state with a Soul that is free from outcomes *(nirdvandvo nityasattvastho niryogakṣema ātmavān ǁ 2-45ǁ)*. Just as a tank is as useful when there is flood everywhere *(yāvānartha udapāne sarvataḥ samplutodake ǀ)*, similarly, all the Vedas are of use to a *brāhmaṇa* who knows *(tāvānsarveṣu vedeṣu brāhmaṇasya vijānataḥ ǁ 2-46ǁ)*.

कर्मण्येवाधिकारस्ते मा फलेषु कदाचन ।
मा कर्मफलहेतुर्भूर्मा ते सङ्गोऽस्त्वकर्मणि ॥ २-४७॥
योगस्थः कुरु कर्माणि सङ्गं त्यक्त्वा धनञ्जय ।
सिद्ध्यसिद्ध्योः समो भूत्वा समत्वं योग उच्यते ॥ २-४८॥
दूरेण ह्यवरं कर्म बुद्धियोगाद्धनञ्जय ।
बुद्धौ शरणमन्विच्छ कृपणाः फलहेतवः ॥ २-४९॥

(47-49) Perform *karma* for itself alone, not for its fruits, anytime *(karmaṇyevādhikāraste mā phaleṣu kadācana ǀ)*, do not be attached to the fruits of action, nor be attached to inaction *(mā karmaphalaheturbhūrmā te saṅgo 'stvakarmaṇi*

|| 2-47||). Absorbed in yoga of action, abandoning attachment to action, being the same in perfection or out of perfection, retaining equilibrium is called yoga *(yogasthaḥ kuru karmāṇi saṅgam tyaktvā dhanañjaya | siddhyasiddhyoḥ samo bhūtvā samatvam yoga ucyate || 2-48||).* By far, action is inferior to yoga of wisdom, in wisdom one seeks refuge, in action one seeks fruits *(dūreṇa hyavaram karma buddhiyogāddhanañjaya | buddhau śaraṇamanviccha kṛpaṇāḥ phalahetavaḥ || 2-49||).*

बुद्धियुक्तो जहातीह उभे सुकृतदुष्कृते ।

तस्माद्योगाय युज्यस्व योगः कर्मसु कौशलम् ॥ २-५०॥

कर्मजं बुद्धियुक्ता हि फलं त्यक्त्वा मनीषिणः ।

जन्मबन्धविनिर्मुक्ताः पदं गच्छन्त्यनामयम् ॥ २-५१॥

(50-51) One who is merged with wisdom casts off in this life both pious and evil actions; therefore, dedicate yourself to yoga and become skilled in its ways *(buddhiyukto jahātīha ubhe sukṛtaduṣkṛte | tasmādyogāya yujyasva yogaḥ karmasu kauśalam || 2-50||).* Indeed, the wise, having abandoned fruits of action that is born due to motivation by intelligence, are freed from bonds of birth and go to a happy abode *(karmajam buddhiyuktā hi phalam tyaktvā manīṣiṇaḥ | janmabandhavinirmuktāḥ padam gacchantyanāmayam || 2-51||).*

यदा ते मोहकलिलं बुद्धिर्व्यतितरिष्यति ।

तदा गन्तासि निर्वेदं श्रोतव्यस्य श्रुतस्य च ॥ २-५२॥

श्रुतिविप्रतिपन्ना ते यदा स्थास्यति निश्चला ।

समाधावचला बुद्धिस्तदा योगमवाप्स्यसि ॥ २-५३॥

(52-53) When your intellect crosses the confusion of delusion, then you will experience indifference to what you hear and the subject of hearing *(yadā te mohakalilam buddhirvyatitariṣyati | tadā gantāsi nirvedam śrotavyasya śrutasya ca || 2-52||).* When you remain firm, unruffled with steady intellect in the midst of conflicts, then you will attain yoga (harmony), *(śrutivipratipannā te yadā sthāsyati niścalā | samādhāvacalā buddhistadā yogamavāpsyasi || 2-53||).*

अर्जुन उवाच -

स्थितप्रज्ञस्य का भाषा समाधिस्थस्य केशव ।

स्थितधीः किं प्रभाषेत किमासीत व्रजेत किम् ॥ २-५४॥

Arjuna said (54) What is the description of steady awareness state of a person who is in a state of *samādhi (sthitaprajñasya kā bhāṣā samādhisthasya keśava |),* How does a person in this state speak, how does he sit, how does he walk *(sthitadhīḥ kim prabhāṣeta kimāsīta vrajeta kim || 2-54||).*

श्रीभगवानुवाच -
प्रजहाति यदा कामान्सर्वान्पार्थ मनोगतान् ।
आत्मन्येवात्मना तुष्टः स्थितप्रज्ञस्तदोच्यते ॥ २-५५॥
दुःखेष्वनुद्विग्नमनाः सुखेषु विगतस्पृहः ।
वीतरागभयक्रोधः स्थितधीर्मुनिरुच्यते ॥ २-५६॥
यः सर्वत्रानभिस्नेहस्तत्तत्प्राप्य शुभाशुभम् ।
नाभिनन्दति न द्वेष्टि तस्य प्रज्ञा प्रतिष्ठिता ॥ २-५७॥

Śrī Kṛṣṇa said (55-57) When one casts off all desires even in the form of ideas and is satisfied in the Self by the Self alone, that person is called *sthithapragnya (prajahāti yadā kāmānsarvānpārtha manogatān ǀ ātmanyevātmanā tuṣṭaḥ sthitaprajñastadocyate ǁ 2-55ǁ)*. In pain, without agitation, indifferent to pleasure, freed from attachment, fear and unmoved is called a sage *(duḥkheṣvanudvignamanāḥ sukheṣu vigatasprhaḥ ǀ vītarāgabhayakrodhaḥ sthitadhīrmunirucyate ǁ 2-56ǁ)*. He who is without affection everywhere, no matter whether obtained in good or bad, does not rejoice nor repel, in him awareness is fixed *(yaḥ sarvatrānabhisnehastattatprāpya śubhāśubham ǀ nābhinandati na dveṣṭi tasya prajñā pratiṣṭhitā ǁ 2-57ǁ)*.

यदा संहरते चायं कूर्मोऽङ्गानीव सर्वशः ।
इन्द्रियाणीन्द्रियार्थेभ्यस्तस्य प्रज्ञा प्रतिष्ठिता ॥ २-५८॥
विषया विनिवर्तन्ते निराहारस्य देहिनः ।
रसवर्जं रसोऽप्यस्य परं दृष्ट्वा निवर्तते ॥ २-५९॥
यततो ह्यपि कौन्तेय पुरुषस्य विपश्चितः ।
इन्द्रियाणि प्रमाथीनि हरन्ति प्रसभं मनः ॥ २-६०॥

(58-60) When he withdraws his senses from all sense objects like a tortoise withdraws its limbs, awareness is steadied *(yadā saṃharate cāyaṃ kūrmo'ṅgānīva sarvaśaḥ ǀ indriyāṇīndriyārthebhyastasya prajñā pratiṣṭhitā ǁ 2-58ǁ)*. Abstaining from objects annul longing in a person *(viṣayā vinivartante nirāhārasya dehinaḥ ǀ)*, longing even to experience the supreme turns away *(rasavarjaṃ raso'pyasya paraṃ dṛṣṭvā nivartate ǁ 2-59ǁ)*. Indeed, even in the person who is persevering as well as wise, the turbulent senses violently hijack cognition *(yatato hyapi kaunteya puruṣasya vipaścitaḥ ǀ indriyāṇi pramāthīni haranti prasabhaṃ manaḥ ǁ 2-60ǁ)*.

तानि सर्वाणि संयम्य युक्त आसीत मत्परः ।
वशे हि यस्येन्द्रियाणि तस्य प्रज्ञा प्रतिष्ठिता ॥ २-६१॥
ध्यायतो विषयान्पुंसः सङ्गस्तेषूपजायते ।
सङ्गात्सञ्जायते कामः कामात्क्रोधोऽभिजायते ॥ २-६२॥

क्रोधाद्भवति सम्मोहः सम्मोहात्स्मृतिविभ्रमः ।
स्मृतिभ्रंशाद् बुद्धिनाशो बुद्धिनाशात्प्रणश्यति ॥ २-६३॥

(61-63) Indeed, they whose every sense has been restrained all together, sit devoted to me with senses under control is one whose awareness is complete *(tāni sarvāṇi saṃyamya yukta āsīta matparaḥ । vaśe hi yasyendriyāṇi tasya prajñā pratiṣṭhitā ॥ 2-61॥)*. In man, thinking of objects results in attachment developing to them, from attachment desire is born, from desire anger rises *(dhyāyato viṣayānpuṃsaḥ saṅgasteṣūpajāyate । saṅgātsañjāyate kāmaḥ kāmātkrodho'bhijāyate ॥ 2-62॥)*. From anger comes delusion, from delusion confusion of memory, from confusion of memory comes loss of reason, from loss of reason comes destruction *(krodhādbhavati sammohaḥ sammohātsmṛtivibhramaḥ । smṛtibhraṃśād buddhināśo buddhināśātpraṇaśyati ॥ 2-63॥)*.

रागद्वेषविमुक्तैस्तु विषयानिन्द्रियैश्चरन् । orवियुक्तैस्तु
आत्मवश्यैर्विधेयात्मा प्रसादमधिगच्छति ॥ २-६४॥

प्रसादे सर्वदुःखानां हानिरस्योपजायते ।
प्रसन्नचेतसो ह्याशु बुद्धिः पर्यवतिष्ठते ॥ २-६५॥

नास्ति बुद्धिरयुक्तस्य न चायुक्तस्य भावना ।
न चाभावयतः शान्तिरशान्तस्य कुतः सुखम् ॥ २-६६॥

(64-66) Freedom from attachment and repulsion comes from exerting control over the churn of senses by objects, then a controlled Self is the outcome *(rāgadveṣavimuktaistuviṣayānindriyaiścaran।orviyuktaistu ātmavaśyairvidheyātmā prasādamadhigacchati ॥ 2-64॥)*. The outcome of reduction in overall misery results in the appearance of a tranquil consciousness because quickly the intellect becomes steady *(prasāde sarvaduḥkhānāṃ hānirasyopajāyate । prasannacetaso hyāśu buddhiḥ paryavatiṣṭhate ॥ 2-65॥)*. The fickle have no intellect nor steady vision *(bhāvanā)* and no peace in those without awareness *(abhāvayat)*, how can happiness come to those that have no peace *(nāsti buddhirayuktasya na cāyuktasya bhāvanā । na cābhāvayataḥ śāntiraśāntasya kutaḥ sukham ॥ 2-66॥)*.

इन्द्रियाणां हि चरतां यन्मनोऽनुविधीयते ।
तदस्य हरति प्रज्ञां वायुर्नावमिवाम्भसि ॥ २-६७॥

तस्माद्यस्य महाबाहो निगृहीतानि सर्वशः ।
इन्द्रियाणीन्द्रियार्थेभ्यस्तस्य प्रज्ञा प्रतिष्ठिता ॥ २-६८॥

या निशा सर्वभूतानां तस्यां जागर्ति संयमी ।
यस्यां जाग्रति भूतानि सा निशा पश्यतो मुनेः ॥ २-६९॥

(67-69) The wandering senses are followed by the cognition which annihilate awareness, like the wind takes away a boat on the water *(indriyāṇāṃ hi caratāṃ yanmano'nuvidhīyate ꞁ tadasya harati prajñāṃ vāyurnāvamivāmbhasi ꞁꞁ 2-67ꞁꞁ).* Therefore, one who has restrained the senses completely from sense objects, that person's awareness is steady *(tasmādyasya mahābāho nigrhītāni sarvaśaḥ ꞁ indriyāṇīndriyārthebhyastasya prajñā pratiṣṭhitā ꞁꞁ 2-68ꞁꞁ).* When it is night for all beings, at this time awakens the self-controlled, in which all beings awaken that vision is cognized by the *muni (yā niśā sarvabhūtānāṃ tasyāṃ jāgarti saṃyamī ꞁ yasyāṃ jāgrati bhūtāni sā niśā paśyato muneḥ ꞁꞁ 2-69ꞁꞁ).*

आपूर्यमाणमचलप्रतिष्ठं

समुद्रमापः प्रविशन्ति यद्वत् ।

तद्वत्कामा यं प्रविशन्ति सर्वे

स शान्तिमाप्नोति न कामकामी ॥ २-७०॥

विहाय कामान्यः सर्वान्पुमांश्चरति निःस्पृहः ।

निर्ममो निरहङ्कारः स शान्तिमधिगच्छति ॥ २-७१॥

एषा ब्राह्मी स्थितिः पार्थ नैनां प्राप्य विमुह्यति ।

स्थित्वास्यामन्तकालेऽपि ब्रह्मनिर्वाणमृच्छति ॥ २-७२॥

(70-72) Just as waters do not fill up the steadily situated sea, similarly all whom desire enters, they will not attain peace due to dictates of passion *(āpūryamāṇamacalapratiṣṭham samudramāpaḥ praviśanti yadvat ꞁ tadvatkāmā yaṃ praviśanti sarve sa śāntimāpnoti na kāmakāmī ꞁꞁ 2-70ꞁꞁ).* Everyone who abandons desire moves about free from longing, without ownership, without the sense of doership, that person attains peace *(vihāya kāmānyaḥ sarvānpumāṃścarati niḥspṛhaḥ ꞁ nirmamo nirahaṅkāraḥ sa śāntimadhigacchati ꞁꞁ 2-71ꞁꞁ).* This state of *brahman* is not achieved by anyone who is fascinated by this achievement, but once transfixed there, at the end of life attains merger with *brahman (eṣā brāhmī sthitiḥ pārtha nainām prāpya vimuhyati ꞁ sthitvāsyāmantakāle'pi brahmanirvāṇamṛcchati ꞁꞁ 2-72ꞁꞁ).*

◆———•●◆•———◆

Chapter 3

***Karma-yoga* (yoga of action)** [1]

Introduction

To understand *karma-yoga,* some principles and concepts which underpin the philosophy as stated by Śrī Kṛṣṇa need to be understood.

The key concepts that will be addressed in chapter 3 are *karma,* relationship between *karma* and *puruṣa/prakṛti, karma* and debt *(ṛṇa),* and *karma-yoga,* which means integration of *karma* with the Self *(ātman).* Since these concepts are interrelated, there will be overlap, which could lead to some confusion.

- In chapter 2, we learned that *Brahman* is a permanent, unchanging, immutable, cognitive state of peace, which is the source and motility of everything.

- Everything that emerges from *Brahman* is called *māyā* (illusion/materiality).

- *Māyā* is driven by attributes or *guṇa,* consisting of the states of delusion *(tamas),* passion *(rajas),* and harmony *(sattva).*

- *Dharma* is a natural state, one that conditions all entities to behave in a particular manner.

Comparing knowledge and action (verse 1-9)

Arjuna asked – If you are saying that the yoga of knowledge *(sāṃkhya-yoga)* is superior to yoga of action *(karma-yoga),* why are you asking me to indulge in this terrible action? You are confusing me with your perplexing speech, so please explain to me that ONE way by which I may attain the correct goal.

---

[1]https://www.bhagavad-gita.org/Gita/chapter-03.html

Śrī Kṛṣṇa replied – In this world for *yogīs* or those seeking to integrate their awareness with *Brahman,* there are two paths – the path of knowledge *(sāṃkhya-yoga)* or the path of action *(karma-yoga).*

A person does not reach the state of no action by not acting; neither does he reach the highest levels of wisdom by renunciation. This is because action occurs continuously in voluntary and involuntary form, for this is the nature of creation *(prakṛti)* (verse 5). This causes desire.

- Action is superior to inaction, indeed, for even the body cannot be maintained by inaction (verse 8).

- Perfection cannot be attained by renunciation of action *(karma).* In fact, only the perfect can achieve liberation *(samādhi)* through renunciation (verse 4).

- He who restrains action without restraining the senses is delusional, but he who restrains the senses and cognition when acting excels (verse 7).

- Common people experience anxiety when acting *(karma),* but wise people act in a state of peace (verse 18).

- When performing an action, the intent of sacrifice is superior to the intent of result. For example, food cooked for oneself but not shared is action intended for the senses, but one shared with others is a sacrifice. Thus, sacrifice is the source of all well-being (verse 11).

- A person who is anchored in the Self finds connection in all activity. Such a person does not consider himself to cause action or inaction and is not dependent on others (verse 17-18).

- The ignorant act with attachment to action; the wise act with an attitude of no attachment. The best way to act is for the welfare of the world and to perform all actions with an attitude of balance (verse 25-26).

- So, perform action without attachment; only then do you set a standard and become a role model for people to emulate (verse 20).

The relationship between *karma* and *puruṣa/prakṛti*

- The attributes *(guṇa)* that comprise delusion *(tamas),* passion *(rajas)* and harmony *(sattva)* have a passive *(puruṣa)* and an active *(prakṛti).*

- The passive component, *puruṣa,* is the experiencer or Identity of the entity, while the active component, *prakṛti,* is the manifestation of *puruṣa,* manifesting as attributes *(guṇa).*

- For example, people recognize us by our behavior *(prakṛti)*; our behavior is an expression of our Identity *(puruṣa)*. So, without our Identity *(puruṣa)*, we would not be able to express ourselves *(prakṛti)*.

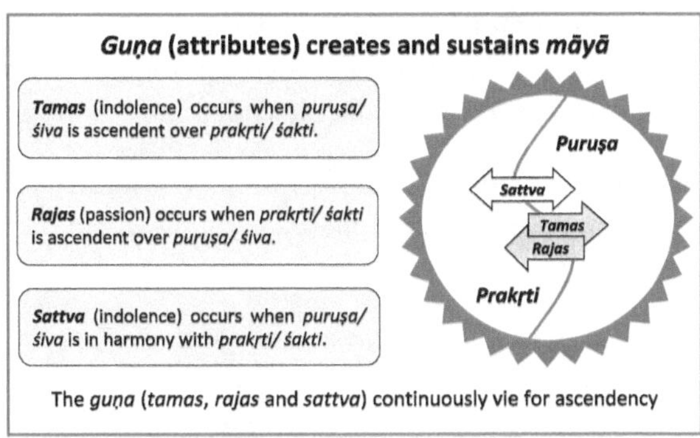

3.1 components of *guṇa*

- However, our behavior *(prakṛti)* changes along with our experiences, and this is on account of the changes experienced by our Identity *(puruṣa)*.

- Clearly, *puruṣa* cannot exist without *prakṛti,* and vice-versa, they are continuously weaving with each other. This weave is called *tantra* (weave), and the act of weaving is *karma* (action).

- It's important not to forget that the source and motility of all the above factors is *Brahman*.

So, what is the relationship between action *karma, guṇa, puruṣa,* and *prakṛti?* Any stimulus-response transaction results in action *(karma)* because there is an outcome. This is also the material weave of *puruṣa* and *prakṛti*. Since *prakṛti* drives attributes *(guṇa)*, the weave of *puruṣa* and *prakṛti* results in action, *karma,* which is driven by attributes *(guṇa)*.

The concept of action *(karma)*

When we like something, we bring it close to ourselves. This is called *rāga* (attraction). When we dislike something, we push it away. This is called *dveṣa* (repulsion), and the action of bringing something close or pushing it away is action *(karma)*.

Since this covers all transactions, *karma* can be considered as the governing principle of the existence of all sentient, non-sentient, animate, and inanimate entities.

Relationship between *karma* and *bandhana*

Introduction: *karma* creates bonds *(bandhana)* in every transaction because whenever two entities relate to each other, they form a bond, even if the transaction is temporary.

Two types of bonds can be created in any transaction; one of equal give-take *(sama-bandhana - sama* = equal + *bandhana* = bond) or an unequal bond of give-take, which is created by debt, is called *ṛṇānu-bandhana (ṛṇa* = debt + *bandhana* = bond).

Any transaction where the give and take are equal is called *samabandhana* (equal bond). Mostly, this is between married couples, where give and take is not measured. This is why in-laws in India are called *sambandhi* or *samdi* (those of equal bond).

Importantly, this give and take need not be material alone; it could be ideas, feelings, opinions, etc. or a mix of these, anything where there is an imbalance or debt *(ṛṇa)* created.

Types of debt *(ṛṇa)* in *karma*

We know that most transactions are rarely equal; one of the parties will give or get more. Hence, this creates a debtor and a creditor, and a debt *(ṛṇa)* that needs to be repaid in this life or in another.

Also, creation and repayment of debt can take many forms, depending on the type of debt.

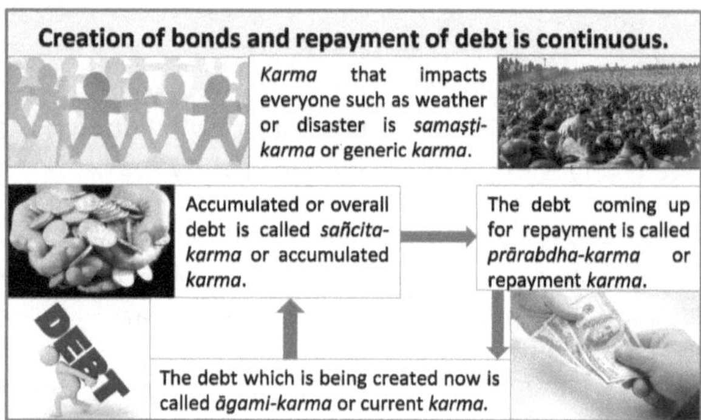

3.2 types of *debt*

- All debt accrued to or by one in an ongoing situation is called *āgāmi-karma* (current debt).

- The overall aggregation of all debit or credit is called *sañcita-karma* (overall debt).

- Next, the debt which comes for reconciliation is called *prārabdha-karma* (repayment debt).

- Finally, any overarching *karma* which controls environments and communities is called *samaṣṭi-karma*. Example of *samaṣṭi-karma* – Covid-19, all earthquakes, tsunamis, weather etc., where the individual's *karma* is subsumed by a macro event.

Where does the debt *(ṛṇa)* reside?

Debt *(ṛṇa)* only exists when it can be assigned to an entity. Hence, all debt *(ṛṇa)* is accumulated by the Self/Soul *(ātman)* and goes with it at each rebirth until all the debt has been discharged.

How can a person avoid rebirth? *Karma* is attached to the Self *(ātman)* only when the Self identifies itself with the action; so, the simple way to avoid debt or *ṛṇa* is to act without attaching the Self *(ātman)* to the action and outcome.

Act with all senses and cognition *(manas)* under control, with a spirit of sacrifice *(yajña),* without desire for results *(karma-phala)* and without any attitude of being the doer *(ahaṅkāra).*

Unfortunately, this is easier said than done and requires great dedication, patience, persistence, and practice *(śraddhā).* This effort to transcend the Self *(asmitā)* during action *(karma)* is called *karma-yoga.*

The key principles underpinning *karma-yoga*

1. All aspects of life are based on the natural principles of creation *(dharma).* Understanding these principles is the basis of knowledge *(sāṃkhya).* For example, the Sun's rays nourish earth, the earth rotates clockwise, plants grow from the earth when they are nourished by rain, gravity acts on all matter, etc.; these are natural rules *(dharma)* of creation that cannot be changed.

2. *Dharma* (natural state, order, or conditioning) comes from *karma,* which comes from the weave of *puruṣa* and *prakṛti,* which is a continuous unending process.

    For example – we need food, which must be grown out of the earth. To achieve efficiency, one type of food must be grown on a plot of land. This is aligning the natural principle of creation with our own ability to grow food. Only then there is peace/order or harmony, which is *dharma.* But when food is grown by use of pesticides and other toxic chemicals, this balance is lost, and there is chaos *(adharma).* This chaos may not manifest immediately, but, over time, it manifests as climate change.

3. Action is continuous. Even to maintain the body, we need to act. In fact, action occurs when we are asleep, just as acquiring wisdom requires effort or action. Importantly, not acting *(akarma)* is also action.

4. There is no one else! Everything that we do or is done to us is a result of our *karma,* and the debt *(ṛṇa)* we create is *karma* that has to be reconciled. So, to avoid debt *(ṛṇa),* one must act as if he does not consider himself to cause action or inaction, nor with dependence on any other beings.

This aspect has three parts:

-   First, we are born alone, and anything we do will affect us only. Our effect on others is not controlled by us unless we force the issue.

-   The second is a derivation of the first. While the outcome may not be to our expectation, our effort or input must be executed with excellence, dedication, and sincerity *(śraddhā).*

-   Finally, it is best that we detach ourselves from the outcome of our actions so that the impact does not disturb our equilibrium.

5. Hence, it is best that we perform all action as a sacrifice without expectations. This way, we do not attach our actions to the results and avoid dualities such as like-dislike in our expectations.

What is the measure of success? How do we know that we are on the right path? When our transactions result in minimum experience of debt and agitation around us, then we can call our action *dhārmika* or in line with *karma-yoga*.

Importantly, to achieve success, we need to have awareness *(prajñā)* of the situation as it unfolds. Situational awareness *(prajñā)* drives discrimination *(viveka),* which determines quality of action *(karma).* A person of steady awareness is called *sthitaprajñā* (detailed in chapter 2 of *Śrīmad-bhagavad-gītā*)

Example [2]

India suffered a terrible defeat in the Sino-Indian war of 1962. Let us look at the situational awareness *(prajñā)* of the time.

- China had managed to push the UN forces back to the 38th parallel in Korea. They had defeated the armies of USA and its allies, leading world powers of the time.

- China invaded Tibet in 1951 and annexed it in 1959 [3].

These were clear indicators of China's capabilities and intentions. The Indian Government ignored all warning signs and did not build capability in the Indian defense or External Affairs establishments.

Meanwhile, the Indian Government gave asylum to the Dalai Lama, provoking the Chinese further. While in itself this was not wrong, assuming that the Indo-China brotherhood would be sufficient to maintain status-quo was very poor situational awareness.

This led to poor military preparedness, poor negotiating positions, and poor diplomatic decisions. Consequently, the conflict ended in a debacle, with India losing a large territory, material, and over 5000 soldiers.

The *sāṃkhya* (knowledge) that Chinese had aggressive intentions and capability was available, but the administration was deluded into thinking that Chinese would not attack. Thus, Indians made no preparations. Consequently, once the month-long war started, no compensatory action *(karma)* could stem the outcome.

---

[2]   https://en.wikipedia.org/wiki/Sino-Indian_War
[3]   https://en.wikipedia.org/wiki/1959_Tibetan_uprising

Some lessons

When the discrimination *(viveka)* between reality and need for preparation was lost due to delusion, the knowledge *(sāṃkhya)* that preparation might have reversed the abject outcome was abandoned.

We can find similar situations in our homes, societies, businesses, countries, and across the world (terrorism and climate change being examples), where knowledge is ignored at cataclysmic cost.

More examples

- We know that we need to study for our exams, revise what we studied, and not assume that we know the subject after familiarizing ourselves. After all, there is a difference in awareness *(prajñā)* between familiarity and competence. So, while familiarity breeds contempt, competence brings confidence and problem-solving capability.

- Let us assume that the managing committee of a group of buildings ignores general maintenance and small pain-points which arise regularly and instead assumes that everything is well just because the pain-points do not manifest as problems. Is this committee not heading for a breakdown, which may come at an inconvenient time? For example, if they were to ignore checking of drains regularly, then it is possible that all drains get blocked simultaneously, and everyone in the society has an uncomfortable time until the drains are cleared. Thus, the action *(karma)* of planned inspection and maintenance helps avoid stress, emotional, and physical discomfort of a breakdown situation.

- In 1908, the Model T Ford was the world's first mass produced car, ushering in a new world of mobility. Henry Ford standardized everything, including paint, in order to make the car affordable. However, by 1920, customer requirements had changed but Henry Ford adamantly refused to change the product line-up. By the time he relented in 1927 and allowed expansion of Ford's product line, the company had lost market shares to other American car companies. This is another example of how success can delude a person and make him think that he can do nothing wrong, much to the detriment of his own well-being.

Conclusion

Prior experience and wisdom indicate that realities and demands of change must be accepted, and requisite action must be taken for an outcome to be successful. However, arrogance, laziness, lack of capability, and delusion bring avoidable failure.

Śrī Kṛṣṇa said – Even though I have reached this level of supreme awareness and have no need to act, I act ceaselessly, so that people may follow suit. I act to ensure the welfare of all, to make sure removal of confusion and to establish a standard for people to follow (verse 30- 35).

- Even amid people wedded to action that are fanned by the senses, a *yogī* must work ceaselessly with restrained senses, forsaking the outcome for the welfare of all, and perform all actions with devotion. He must not get attached to the thought that he is the doer.

- So, transferring your sense of identity (I am) into Me (in this case, Śrī Kṛṣṇa), being aware of the Self, freeing yourself from hope and glory, removing anxiety and frustration – fight!

- Those that practice this without giving excuses will succeed in freeing themselves from action. Those that preach but do not practice will remain in misery.

- It is better to be true to one's natural state or conditioning *(dharma)*, even though it may yield no merit, than to follow someone else's *dharma*, for that will only lead to confusion, fear, and ruin.

Motivation for action (verse 36 - 43)

Arjuna said - Then, what makes man perform acts which may go against his own natural state or conditioning *(dharma)* and innate instincts and hurt others? (verse 36)

Śrī Kṛṣṇa said – It is anger born out of drive generated by desire to devour. Just as fire is enveloped by smoke and mirror by dust, the awareness gets enveloped by ambition and desire. This drive consumes wisdom and seeks continuous appeasement of the senses. The senses, cognition, and logic are its seat, so one must constantly be alert. Keep this sense under control before it destroys you (verse 37- 43).

Concept of *karma-yoga* – All creation comes from the weave of *puruṣa* and *prakṛti,* which arises from *Brahman.* This drives all action *(karma),* including the cognitive apparatus. The senses *(indriyas)* are superior to the gross body; the center of cognition *(manas)* is superior to the senses and the center of logic *(buddhi),* but above all is the *Brahman.* So, being aware of the Self, use this awareness to conquer desire, which is no doubt a very difficult thing to conquer. Then, you will be able to transcend the Self and merge *(samādhi)* into the source *(Brahman).*

- Our natural state is an all-pervading feeling of equilibrium or peace *(śānti).*

- This natural state of peace *(śānti)* is our *dharma* [4]. *Dharma* is the natural state of all beings.

- When our actions are in conformance with our natural state, it is called *svabhāva (sva* = self + *bhāva* = expression, sentiment or personality).

---

[4] https://schoolofyoga.in/yoga-concept/dharma

This harmony/order *(dharma)* can exist only if we are at peace with ourselves and our world. This includes not just other human beings, but animals, plants, and our environment also. Also, it is important to remember that *Brahman* is a state of infinite, unchanging peace.

For instance, when we compete, we begin to compare ourselves with others and become enmeshed in duality of love-hate, good-bad, etc. Consequently, we become anxious, stressed, miserable, and delusional *(tamas)*.

The desire to compete and win *(rajas)* infuses passion, and our work becomes driven by expectation, desires, fear, frustration, anger, anxiety, and stress. This corrodes our balance and equanimity *(sattva)* and leads to unhappiness, stress, and finally breakdown of body and faculties. Unfortunately, we do it all the time – at school, college, home, sports, office, society, and even as a nation!

When we become aware of this destructive state and our focus turns to peaceful integration of all stakeholders without compromising on goals, our drive to prosper at any cost diminishes. Instead, we try to develop an inclusive and balanced way to prosperity and reach a state of peace and equilibrium.

This type of action *(karma)* is called sacrifice *(yajña)*, because it requires us to give up our own desires for an overarching state of peace. Sacrifice requires the restraining of our senses while performing action which, in turn, increases awareness and peace within us.

So, when we work with our senses under control, an attitude of sacrifice *(yajña)*, without expectation of result but overall betterment, all the negativities of *tamas* and *rajas* are avoided. Consequently, this leads to a peaceful, healthy, and happy existence.

Also, since *karma* is attached to people when they identify themselves with the action, this method is a simple way to avoid debt *(ṛṇa)* by separating the Self from the act. Unfortunately, this is easier said than done and requires great practice.

Why is this so difficult? Don't we have a free will? This has been addressed in chapter 4.

Some contradictions to accepted positions:

- Action *(karma)*, when used colloquially, is actually debt *(ṛṇa)* that has come for repayment.

- While primordial action *(ādi-karma)* comes on account of two identities *(atman)* in a bond *(bandana)*, action *(karma)* causes and imbalance within the bond, resulting in debt *(ṛṇa)*, which becomes the cause of subsequent identities *(atman)*.

- Can the logic of bonds *(bandana)* and action *(karma)* be applied to science? Yes, the concept of yoga is universal *(sanātana)* and can be applied to science as well. This is addressed in *Śrīmad-bhagavad-gītā* - chapter 9.

Lesson learned in chapter 3:

- Everything is action *(karma)*. Action, inaction, approved, or prohibited action.

- One can't escape it; one can only try to control one's impulses, keep one's senses under control, and perform action as a sacrifice, without any expectation of outcome.

The transliteration and translation of chapter 3:

अर्जुन उवाच -

ज्यायसी चेत्कर्मणस्ते मता बुद्धिर्जनार्दन ।

तत्किं कर्मणि घोरे मां नियोजयसि केशव ॥ ३-१॥

व्यामिश्रेणेव वाक्येन बुद्धिं मोहयसीव मे ।

तदेकं वद निश्चित्य येन श्रेयोऽहमाप्नुयाम् ॥ ३-२॥

Arjuna said (1-2) If according to you, wisdom *(matā buddhi)* is superior to *karma*, then why are you asking me to engage in this terrible deed? *(jyāyasī cetkarmaṇaste matā buddhirjanārdana ǀ tatkim karmaṇi ghore māṃ niyojayasi keśava ǁ 3-1ǁ)*. I am perplexed with your speech and my understanding is confused, so tell me for certain, by which path I can succeed *(vyāmiśreṇeva vākyena buddhiṃ mohayasīva me ǀ tadekaṃ vada niścitya yena śreyo 'hamāpnuyām ǁ 3-2ǁ)*.

श्रीभगवानुवाच ।

लोकेऽस्मिन् द्विविधा निष्ठा पुरा प्रोक्ता मयानघ ।

ज्ञानयोगेन साङ्ख्यानां कर्मयोगेन योगिनाम् ॥ ३-३॥

न कर्मणामनारम्भान्नैष्कर्म्यं पुरुषोऽश्नुते ।

न च संन्यसनादेव सिद्धिं समधिगच्छति ॥ ३-४॥

न हि कश्चित्क्षणमपि जातु तिष्ठत्यकर्मकृत् ।

कार्यते ह्यवशः कर्म सर्वः प्रकृतिजैर्गुणैः ॥ ३-५॥

Śrī Kṛṣṇa said (3-5) As I said, since long ago, in this world, there are two paths; merger by enquiry into the Self for the philosophers and merger by activity for those who prefer action *(loke'smin dvividhā niṣṭhā purā proktā mayānagha ǀ jñānayogena sāṅkhyānāṃ karmayogena yoginām ǁ 3-3ǁ)*. Man does not attain state of no action by abstaining from action and only the perfect can attain *samādhi* through renunciation *(na karmaṇāmanārambhānnaiṣkarmyaṃ puruṣo 'śnute ǀ na ca saṃnyasanādeva siddhiṃ samadhigacchati ǁ 3-4ǁ)*. Not for a moment even is anyone free from action at all, for everyone is helplessly driven into action by *guṇas,* which are born out of *prakṛti (na hi kaścitkṣaṇamapi jātu tiṣṭhatyakarmakṛt ׀ kāryate hyavaśaḥ karma sarvaḥ prakṛtijairguṇaiḥ ॥ 3-5॥).*

कर्मेन्द्रियाणि संयम्य य आस्ते मनसा स्मरन् ।

इन्द्रियार्थान्विमूढात्मा मिथ्याचारः स उच्यते ॥ ३-६॥

यस्त्विन्द्रियाणि मनसा नियम्यारभतेऽर्जुन ।

कर्मेन्द्रियैः कर्मयोगमसक्तः स विशिष्यते ॥ ३-७॥

नियतं कुरु कर्म त्वं कर्म ज्यायो ह्यकर्मणः ।

शरीरयात्रापि च ते न प्रसिद्ध्येदकर्मणः ॥ ३-८॥

(6-8) That deluded soul who restrains organs of action but constantly sits with his cognition remembering sense objects is called a hypocrite *(karmendriyāṇi saṃyamya ya āste manasā smaran ׀ indriyārthānvimūḍhātmā mithyācāraḥ sa ucyate ॥ 3-6॥).* But that person who controls the senses by control of cognition, commences to act in an unattached manner and excels in harmony of action *(yastvindriyāṇi manasā niyamyārabhate'rjuna ׀ karmendriyaiḥ karmayogamasaktaḥ sa viśiṣyate ॥ 3-7॥).* Surely, you must perform action, for it is superior to inaction, for even maintenance of your body would not be possible by inaction *(niyataṃ kuru karma tvaṃ karma jyāyo hyakarmaṇaḥ ׀ śarīrayātrāpi ca te na prasiddhyedakarmaṇaḥ ॥ 3-8॥).*

यज्ञार्थात्कर्मणोऽन्यत्र लोकोऽयं कर्मबन्धनः ।

तदर्थं कर्म कौन्तेय मुक्तसङ्गः समाचर ॥ ३-९॥

सहयज्ञाः प्रजाः सृष्ट्वा पुरोवाच प्रजापतिः ।

अनेन प्रसविष्यध्वमेष वोऽस्त्विष्टकामधुक् ॥ ३-१०॥

(9-10) Everyone in this world is bound by actions; for that sake, perform action without attachment *(yajñārthātkarmaṇo'nyatra loko'yaṃ karmabandhanaḥ ׀ tadarthaṃ karma kaunteya muktasaṅgaḥ samācara ॥ 3-9॥).* Having created mankind in the beginning by their sacrifice, Prajāpati said, propagate this as your milch cow of desires *(sahayajñāḥ prajāḥ sṛṣṭvā purovāca prajāpatiḥ ׀ anena prasaviṣyadhvameṣa vo'stviṣṭakāmadhuk ॥ 3-10॥).*

देवान्भावयतानेन ते देवा भावयन्तु वः ।

परस्परं भावयन्तः श्रेयः परमवाप्स्यथ ॥ ३-११॥

इष्टान्भोगान्हि वो देवा दास्यन्ते यज्ञभाविताः ।

तैर्दत्तानप्रदायैभ्यो यो भुङ्क्ते स्तेन एव सः ॥ ३-१२॥

यज्ञशिष्टाशिनः सन्तो मुच्यन्ते सर्वकिल्बिषैः ।

भुञ्जते ते त्वघं पापा ये पचन्त्यात्मकारणात् ॥ ३-१३॥

(11-13) The deities nourish the sinless, those deities will nourish you, then mutually nourishing each other, you shall attain the highest level of trustworthiness *(devānbhāvayatānena te devā bhāvayantu vaḥ | parasparam bhāvayantaḥ śreyaḥ paramavāpsyatha || 3-11||)*. So, deities will give to you desired objects through their fruits of sacrifice, anyone who enjoys without offering to them is truly like a thief. *(iṣṭānbhogānhi vo devā dāsyante yajñabhāvitāḥ | tairdattānapradāyaibhyo yo bhuṅkte stena eva saḥ || 3-12||)*. The saintly who harvest the outcome of a sacrifice are freed from faults *(yajñaśiṣṭāśinaḥ santo mucyante sarvakilbiṣaiḥ |)*, indeed, those evil people who are selfish are those that eat fruits of wretchedness *(bhuñjate te tvagham pāpā ye pacantyātmakāraṇāt || 3-13||)*.

अन्नाद्भवन्ति भूतानि पर्जन्यादन्नसम्भवः ।

यज्ञाद्भवति पर्जन्यो यज्ञः कर्मसमुद्भवः ॥ ३-१४॥

कर्म ब्रह्मोद्भवं विद्धि ब्रह्माक्षरसमुद्भवम् ।

तस्मात्सर्वगतं ब्रह्म नित्यं यज्ञे प्रतिष्ठितम् ॥ ३-१५॥

एवं प्रवर्तितं चक्रं नानुवर्तयतीह यः ।

अघायुरिन्द्रियारामो मोघं पार्थ स जीवति ॥ ३-१६॥

(14-16) From food comes beings, from rain comes production of food, from sacrifice comes rain, sacrifice is source of *karma (annādbhavanti bhūtāni parjanyādannasambhavaḥ | yajñādbhavati parjanyo yajñaḥ karmasamudbhavaḥ || 3-14||)*. Know that action has risen from *brahma*, who has risen from the Imperishable; therefore, one can establish that omnipresent *Brahman* is constantly present in sacrifice *(karma brahmodbhavam viddhi brahmākṣarasamudbhavam | tasmātsarvagatam brahma nityam yajñe pratiṣṭhitam || 3-15||)*. Therefore, he who is malicious and in lives enjoying the delusional world of senses sets in motion this wheel that only moves forward. *(evam pravartitam cakram nānuvartayatīha yaḥ | aghāyurindriyārāmo mogham pārtha sa jīvati || 3-16||)*.

यस्त्वात्मरतिरेव स्यादात्मतृप्तश्च मानवः ।

आत्मन्येव च सन्तुष्टस्तस्य कार्यं न विद्यते ॥ ३-१७॥

नैव तस्य कृतेनार्थो नाकृतेनेह कश्चन ।

न चास्य सर्वभूतेषु कश्चिदर्थव्यपाश्रयः ॥ ३-१८॥

(17-18) Only the person who rejoices in the Self is likely to find satisfaction in the Self and only the human who stays in the Self stays contented in any activity *(yastvātmaratireva syādātmatṛptaśca mānavaḥ | ātmanyeva ca santuṣṭastasya kāryam na vidyate || 3-17||)*. He does not consider himself to cause action or inaction here and nor does he depend on any other beings *(naiva tasya kṛtenārtho nākṛteneha kaścana | na cāsya sarvabhūteṣu kaścidarthavyapāśrayaḥ || 3-18||)*.

तस्मादसक्तः सततं कार्यं कर्म समाचर ।
असक्तो ह्याचरन्कर्म परमाप्नोति पूरुषः ॥ ३-१९॥
कर्मणैव हि संसिद्धिमास्थिता जनकादयः ।
लोकसङ्ग्रहमेवापि सम्पश्यन्कर्तुमर्हसि ॥ ३-२०॥
यद्यदाचरति श्रेष्ठस्तत्तदेवेतरो जनः ।
स यत्प्रमाणं कुरुते लोकस्तदनुवर्तते ॥ ३-२१॥

(19-21) Therefore, always perform mandatory activities without attachment, because man attains the Supreme by performing such action *(tasmādasaktaḥ satataṃ kāryaṃ karma samācara । asakto hyācarankarma paramāpnoti pūruṣaḥ ॥ 3-19॥)*. Truly, only by action perfection is reached, Janaka and others performed action only for the welfare of the people, so should you *(karmaṇaiva hi saṃsiddhimāsthitā janakādayaḥ । lokasaṅgrahamevāpi sampaśyankartumarhasi ॥ 3-20॥)*. Whenever undertaken activity is performed splendidly, that becomes the measure by which people of the world judge how a person should perform *(yadyadācarati śreṣṭhastattadevetaro janaḥ । sa yatpramāṇaṃ kurute lokastadanuvartate ॥ 3-21॥)*.

न मे पार्थास्ति कर्तव्यं त्रिषु लोकेषु किञ्चन ।
नानवाप्तमवाप्तव्यं वर्त एव च कर्मणि ॥ ३-२२॥
यदि ह्यहं न वर्तेयं जातु कर्मण्यतन्द्रितः ।
मम वर्त्मानुवर्तन्ते मनुष्याः पार्थ सर्वशः ॥ ३-२३॥
उत्सीदेयुरिमे लोका न कुर्यां कर्म चेदहम् ।
सङ्करस्य च कर्ता स्यामुपहन्यामिमाः प्रजाः ॥ ३-२४॥

(22-24) There is no mandatory action in the three worlds, not anything unattained, to be attained by me, yet I am continuously acting *(na me pārthāsti kartavyaṃ triṣu lokeṣu kiñcana । nānavāptamavāptavyaṃ varta eva ca karmaṇi ॥ 3-22॥)*. Surely, if I did not engage in action ever unwearied, humanity would follow my example *(yadi hyahaṃ na varteyaṃ jātu karmaṇyatandritaḥ । mama vartmānuvartante manuṣyāḥ pārtha sarvaśaḥ ॥ 3-23॥)*. These worlds would be ruined if I did not perform action. Mixing of people would result in their destruction *(utsīdeyurime lokā na kuryāṃ karma cedaham । saṅkarasya ca kartā syāmupahanyāmimāḥ prajāḥ ॥ 3-24॥)*.

सक्ताः कर्मण्यविद्वांसो यथा कुर्वन्ति भारत ।
कुर्याद्विद्वांस्तथासक्तश्चिकीर्षुर्लोकसङ्ग्रहम् ॥ ३-२५॥
न बुद्धिभेदं जनयेदज्ञानां कर्मसङ्गिनाम् ।
जोषयेत्सर्वकर्माणि विद्वान्युक्तः समाचरन् ॥ ३-२६॥

(25-26) The ignorant act with attachment to action, and the wise act with an attitude of no attachment, for the welfare of the world *(saktāḥ karmaṇyavidvāṃso yathā kurvanti bhārata/kuryādvidvāṃstathāsaktaścikīrṣurlokasaṅgraham ‖ 3-25‖)*. No disturbance of the intellect should arise from actions of the ignorant who are attached to actions, the wise perform all actions with an attitude of balance *(na buddhibhedaṃ janayedajñānāṃ karmasaṅginām ǀ joṣayetsarvakarmāṇi vidvānyuktaḥ samācaran ‖ 3-26‖)*.

प्रकृतेः क्रियमाणानि गुणैः कर्माणि सर्वशः ।

अहङ्कारविमूढात्मा कर्ताहमिति मन्यते ॥ ३-२७॥

तत्त्ववित्तु महाबाहो गुणकर्मविभागयोः ।

गुणा गुणेषु वर्तन्त इति मत्वा न सज्जते ॥ ३-२८॥

प्रकृतेर्गुणसम्मूढाः सज्जन्ते गुणकर्मसु ।

तानकृत्स्नविदो मन्दान्कृत्स्नविन्न विचालयेत् ॥ ३-२९॥

(27-29) All actions arise from attributes which arise from *prakṛti (prakṛteḥ kriyamāṇāni guṇaiḥ karmāṇi sarvaśaḥ ǀ)*, the deluded soul cognizes itself as "I am the doer" *(ahaṅkāravimūḍhātmā kartāhamiti manyate ‖ 3-27‖)*. Philosophers know that action comes from the tri-partitioned attributes, and controlling these attributes, thus knowing, remain unattached *(tattvavittu mahābāho guṇakarmavibhāgayoḥ ǀ guṇā guṇeṣu vartanta iti matvā na sajjate ‖ 3-28‖)*. Thus, deluded by *gunas* born of *prakṛti* find virtue in actions driven by *guṇa (prakṛterguṇasammūḍhāḥ sajjante guṇakarmasu ǀ)*. The person with complete knowledge should not agitate dull people who have incomplete knowledge *(tānakṛtsnavido mandānkṛtsnavinna vicālayet ‖ 3-29‖)*.

मयि सर्वाणि कर्माणि संन्यस्याध्यात्मचेतसा ।

निराशीर्निर्ममो भूत्वा युध्यस्व विगतज्वरः ॥ ३-३०॥

ये मे मतमिदं नित्यमनुतिष्ठन्ति मानवाः ।

श्रद्धावन्तोऽनसूयन्तो मुच्यन्ते तेऽपि कर्मभिः ॥ ३-३१॥

ये त्वेतदभ्यसूयन्तो नानुतिष्ठन्ति मे मतम् ।

सर्वज्ञानविमूढांस्तान्विद्धि नष्टानचेतसः ॥ ३-३२॥

(30-32) Renouncing all action into me, with a consciousness that is meditating on the Primordial Self, without hope, without the sense of Self, becoming free from affliction, fight *(mayi sarvāṇi karmāṇi saṃnyasyādhyātmacetasā ǀ nirāśīrnirmamo bhūtvā yudhyasva vigatajvaraḥ ‖ 3-30‖)*. Also, those people that practice this teaching of mine constantly with dedication and without envy, they are freed from *karma (ye me matamidaṃ nityamanutiṣṭhanti mānavāḥ ǀ śraddhāvanto'nasūyanto mucyante te'pi karmabhiḥ ‖ 3-31‖)*. But those who are envious, not performing my teaching, misinterpreting all knowledge of the Self, their lack of knowledge will lead them to ruin *(ye tvetadabhyasūyanto nānutiṣṭhanti me matam । sarvajñānavimūḍhāṃstānviddhi naṣṭānacetasaḥ ॥ 3-32॥)*.

सदृशं चेष्टते स्वस्याः प्रकृतेर्ज्ञानवानपि ।
प्रकृतिं यान्ति भूतानि निग्रहः किं करिष्यति ॥ ३-३३॥
इन्द्रियस्येन्द्रियस्यार्थे रागद्वेषौ व्यवस्थितौ ।
तयोर्न वशमागच्छेत्तौ ह्यस्य परिपन्थिनौ ॥ ३-३४॥
श्रेयान्स्वधर्मो विगुणः परधर्मात्स्वनुष्ठितात् ।
स्वधर्मे निधनं श्रेयः परधर्मो भयावहः ॥ ३-३५॥

(33-35) Even a wise man acts in conformance with his or her own nature *(prakṛti)*, likewise other beings follow their own nature *(prakṛti)*, what suppression can creatures accomplish? *(sadṛśaṃ ceṣṭate svasyāḥ prakṛterjñānavānapi । prakṛtiṃ yānti bhūtāni nigrahaḥ kiṃ kariṣyati ॥ 3-33॥)*. Attraction and repulsion find their foundation in the senses and are nourished by the senses, verily they come in the way of those that cannot them *(indriyasyendriyasyārthe rāgadveṣau vyavasthitau । tayorna vaśamāgacchettau hyasya paripanthinau ॥ 3-34॥)*. Excellence in one's own value system, even if devoid of merit, is better than discharging other's duties, it is better to die following one's own natural state than performing another's activity in a state of fear *(śreyānsvadharmo viguṇaḥ paradharmātsvanuṣṭhitāt । svadharme nidhanaṃ śreyaḥ paradharmo bhayāvahaḥ ॥ 3-35॥)*.

अर्जुन उवाच -
अथ केन प्रयुक्तोऽयं पापं चरति पूरुषः ।
अनिच्छन्नपि वार्ष्णेय बलादिव नियोजितः ॥ ३-३६॥

Arjuna said (36) Now, by which motivation is a person impelled to performing wretched actions, not wishing to be constrained even by force? *(atha kena prayukto'yaṃ pāpaṃ carati pūruṣaḥ । anicchannapi vārṣṇeya balādiva niyojitaḥ ॥ 3-36॥)*.

श्रीभगवानुवाच -
काम एष क्रोध एष रजोगुणसमुद्भवः ।
महाशनो महापाप्मा विद्ध्येनमिह वैरिणम् ॥ ३-३७॥
धूमेनाव्रियते वह्निर्यथादर्शो मलेन च ।
यथोल्बेनावृतो गर्भस्तथा तेनेदमावृतम् ॥ ३-३८॥
आवृतं ज्ञानमेतेन ज्ञानिनो नित्यवैरिणा ।
कामरूपेण कौन्तेय दुष्पूरेणानलेन च ॥ ३-३९॥

Śrī Kṛṣṇa said (37-39) Desire for this and anger at this are expressions of passion, this is a major, voracious and wretched, penetrative foe *(kāma eṣa krodha eṣa rajoguṇasamudbhavaḥ ı mahāśano mahāpāpmā viddhyenamiha vairiṇam ıı 3-37ıı)*. Just as smoke envelopes fire, dust covers a mirror, the womb envelops the embryo, so is this covered *(dhūmenāvriyate vahniryathādarśo malena ca ı yatholbenāvṛto garbhastathā tenedamāvṛtam ıı 3-38ıı)*. Wisdom of the wise is enveloped by this constant enemy in the form of desire, unsatiated and all-consuming fire *(āvṛtaṃ jñānametena jñānino nityavairiṇā ı kāmarūpeṇa kaunteya duṣpūreṇānalena ca ıı 3-39ıı)*.

इन्द्रियाणि मनो बुद्धिरस्याधिष्ठानमुच्यते ।

एतैर्विमोहयत्येष ज्ञानमावृत्य देहिनम् ॥ ३-४०॥

तस्मात्त्वमिन्द्रियाण्यादौ नियम्य भरतर्षभ ।

पाप्मानं प्रजहि ह्येनं ज्ञानविज्ञाननाशनम् ॥ ३-४१॥

(40-41) It is said that the senses, cognition, intellect are its abode, it envelopes the wisdom of the embodied and deludes *(indriyāṇi mano buddhirasyādhiṣṭhānamucyate ı etairvimohayatyeṣa jñānamāvṛtya dehinam ıı 3-40ıı)*. Therefore, control your senses when stimuli comes and effectively overcome this wretched destroyer of knowledge of the Self and surrounding *(tasmāttvamindriyāṇyādau niyamya bharatarṣabha ı pāpmānaṃ prajahi hyenaṃ jñānavijñānanāśanam ıı 3-41ıı)*.

इन्द्रियाणि पराण्याहुरिन्द्रियेभ्यः परं मनः ।

मनसस्तु परा बुद्धिर्यो बुद्धेः परतस्तु सः ॥ ३-४२॥

एवं बुद्धेः परं बुद्ध्वा संस्तभ्यात्मानमात्मना ।

जहि शत्रुं महाबाहो कामरूपं दुरासदम् ॥ ३-४३॥

(42-43) They say that the functioning of the senses is superior to the senses; the functioning of cognition is superior to cognition; the functioning of the intellect is superior to the intellect; but superior to all is that *(indriyāṇi parāṇyāhurindriyebhyaḥ paraṃ manaḥ ı manasastu parā buddhiryo buddheḥ paratastu saḥ ıı 3-42ıı)*. Thus, use intelligence over the intellectual process, restrain the Self by the Self, overcome this enemy which comes in the form of desire *(evaṃ buddheḥ paraṃ buddhvā saṃstabhyātmānamātmanā ı jahi śatruṃ mahābāho kāmarūpaṃ durāsadam ıı 3-43ıı)*.

◆ —— · ◆ ◆ · —— ◆

Chapter 4

Jñāna-karma-sannyāsa-yoga
(yoga of renunciation of the Self in action)[1]

Introduction

- What is *jñāna? Jñāna* means "knowledge of the Self". Here, *jñāna-yoga* means that knowledge which yokes a person's awareness of the Self to *brahman*[2].

- What is *karma? Karma* means action. In this chapter, Śrī Kṛṣṇa explains how action can be performed without accruing debt *(ṛṇa)*.

- What is *sannyāsa? Sannyāsa* means renunciation.

Synopsis

- In chapter 1, we have seen that Arjuna experiences deep melancholy at having to fight his kinsmen.

- Following this, in chapter 2, Śrī Kṛṣṇa, after chiding him, tells him that his logic is incorrect and explains the philosophy of living *(sāṃkhya-yoga)*.

- Then, in chapter 3, Śrī Kṛṣṇa explains *karma-yoga* or the attitude with which action must be performed so that no debt is accrued.

- In this chapter, Śrī Kṛṣṇa starts by speaking about his own origin and role in creation. Then he delves into the qualities of action *(karma)* and sacrifice *(yajña)*.

- The central message, as depicted in the heading is, that action should be performed for merger *(yoga)* of the Self with the *Brahman (jñāna)*, and this

---

[1]https://www.bhagavad-gita.org/Gita/chapter-04.html
[2]https://schoolofyoga.in/yoga-concept/situational-awareness-measures

is possible only with an attitude of renunciation *(sannyāsa)* when performing action as a sacrifice *(yajña).*

- Therefore, chapter 4 covers knowledge of *karma* and its renunciation through sacrifice of one's action *(yajña).*

Arjuna's doubt (verse 1 - 15)

Śrī Kṛṣṇa tells Arjuna that he taught yoga to the Sun. Arjuna, skeptical, counters that this would not be possible because the Sun came before him. Śrī Kṛṣṇa explains many things about himself, and moving away from the material image he had hitherto projected, shows himself to be a *yogī.*

What is Śrī Kṛṣṇa saying about himself in this chapter?

In this chapter, Śrī Kṛṣṇa reveals himself, and this needs to be understood:I taught yoga to the Sun, who taught it to the world. I existed before everything (verse 1-4).

- "I can control *prakṛti* and creation." So, Śrī Kṛṣṇa is indicating that he is a trigger and control for creation, *prakṛti.* However, it is unclear what he means by calling himself Lord of all beings and his relationship to *Brahman* (Ch 4 verse 6).

- When natural state *(dharma)* decays and there is an increase in chaos *(adharma),* I embody myself. For protection of the virtuous and destruction of wicked and for re-establishment of natural balance, I take birth in every era. This is borne out by the ten *avatāras* of Viṣṇu in *dasa-avatāra* (verse 7-8)[3]. Śrī Kṛṣṇa seems to be indicating that his permanent state is not material, but a transient or trigger state between *Brahman* and *maya,* one that allows free movement between the two states.

- "In whatever way people approach me, I reward those people who follow my path only". Śrī Kṛṣṇa asserts in verse 14 and verse 35 that submission to him is akin to submission to *Brahman* (verse 11).

- "Four categories of people are created by me based on their orientation to action *(guṇa-karma-vibhāgaśaḥ),* also know that though I am also the initiator, I am not engaged and imperishable." This is a confusing verse - are the categories *(varṇa)* created by him, people or both? This also separates him from the motility aspect of *Brahman* (verse 13).

- "Actions do not taint me, nor do I desire the fruits of action, thus those that know me are not bound by actions." Śrī Kṛṣṇa says that like him, anyone merging with *Brahman* becomes *Brahman* (verse 14).

- Not cognizing this Truth, one will remain in delusion, but on understanding this, all beings see in me, their Self also. Śrī Kṛṣṇa reinforces the message that

---

[3]   https://vedicfeed.com/10-avatars-vishnu-dashavatara-list

when the practitioner merges with *Brahman,* there is no difference between him (Śrī Kṛṣṇa) and the practitioner. Clearly, Śrī Kṛṣṇa is saying that he has merged with *Brahman* (verse 35).

Conclusion: Śrī Kṛṣṇa in the *Śrīmad-bhagavad-gītā* cannot be viewed as a person. He must be looked upon as a *yogī* who has reached the highest levels of awareness. Also, it is dangerous to view Śrī Kṛṣṇa as a role model for modern living, because throughout Mahabharata he is engaged in destroying a society that has been built on a particular tradition with a capability that is out of the envelope of normal existence.

Hence, it is advisable for one to extract lessons from the *Śrīmad-bhagavad-gītā* and find his or her own solutions to achieving perfection in yoga.

Jñāna-karma-sannyāsa-yoga (verse 16 - 22)

When performing, one should be cognizant of prohibited action as well as be aware of action in inaction. He who perceives action in inaction and inaction in action is wise among men and in complete union in every action.

Start all undertakings without desire or expectation and abandon fruits of effort. Also, be ever content and not dependent on anything when engaged in action.

That person who acts with an integrated consciousness and sense of self-worth *(asmita),* abandons all commission *(ahaṅkāra),* using only the body for performing action, gets no injustice. Such a person is content with whatever profit come spontaneously, is free from opposites, unselfish, always balanced in success and failure and not bound by actions.

Karma and *yajña* (verse 19-23)

- Action *(karma)* occurs everywhere, even when one thinks that they are not acting.

- There are three types of action, approved action *(karma),* inaction *(akarma),* and prohibited action *(vikarma).* Approved action is that which is in conformance with *dharma* (natural state), inaction is *karma* which occurs when we think we are not acting, and prohibited action is that which results in chaos *(adharma).*

- Hence, to understand action and transcend it *(jñāna-karma-yoga),* one must act with awareness of the self *(prajñā)* when engaged in action *(karma).* This can be achieved by:

  o performing action as a sacrifice.

  o abandoning fruits of action and commissions.

  o being content with whatever outcome occurs, being balanced in success and failure.

- o   acting without expectations, not being attached to outcome.

  - o   being free from opposites, unselfish, and non-judgmental.

  - o   integrating consciousness *(citta)* with Self *(ātman).*

Dharma

- The key factors for achieving *jñāna-karma-yoga* are that a person should act according to *dharma,* avoid duality such as like-dislike or good-bad, remain in equanimity during and after action and have no attachments to the outcome.

- The starting point of approved action *(karma)* is practice of *dharma* in action. But what is *dharma?*

- We are at peace in certain situations but become agitated in other situations. The contributing factors which underpin our ability to be in a natural state of peace is our *dharma.*

- Whenever we get a stimulus that is congruent to our natural state, we remain in our natural state *(dharma)* and respond peacefully or harmoniously. Conversely, when we get stimulus that is out of congruence with our natural state, our balance gets disturbed, and we experience agitation or chaos *(adharma).*

- Thus, *dharma,* which can also be referred to as natural state, order, harmony, or conditioning, is the basis on which we decide whether we like or dislike something, and is also the basis of our response *(karma).*

- When these factors are applied to an individual, *dharma* is called *svadharma* (*sva* = personal + *dharma* = conditioning), as it varies for each of us.

- Hence, we can say that *dharma* (conditioning) is that core aspect of our personality which drives decision-making, responses or action *(karma),* and, consequently, underpins our sense of self-worth *(asmita).*

- Importantly embedded in *dharma* are other decision-factors, such as avoiding duality in action, remaining in equanimity during and after action and having no attachments to the outcome.

- This is the importance of *dharma* and acting in accordance with it results in deep internal harmony. So, to achieve success in Yoga, being in *dharma* and in a *dhārmic* society is a necessary condition.

Dharma concept

Let us look at how we develop our natural state *(dharma)* and what makes each of us different!

- We are like computers! First, we get our DNA from our parents. When we are born, we only know how to cry, eat, sleep, and perform basic body functions.

- Next, our parents load us with values and the ability to be able to live in society, and this becomes our operating systems and forms the basis of our decision parameters. Also, schools augment our values with knowledge, while society helps us integrate into a network that is fundamentally hierarchical.

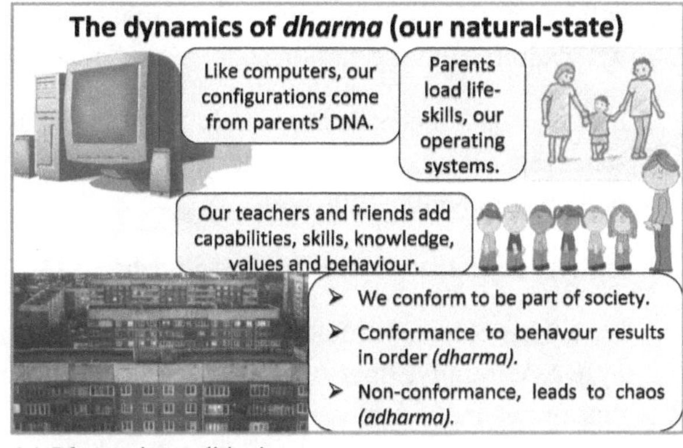

4.1 *Dharma* is conditioning

- So, our Identity and approach to life becomes defined by a personalized and unique decision-making framework. We judge everything and everyone based on this conditioning.

- This conditioning or value system is our natural state of balance, where we are at peace, and is called *dharma*.

Categorization of *dharma*

- **Generic natural state or *sāmānya-dharma***

Generic natural state or *sāmānya-dharma* can be defined as those characteristics which are common to any family of entities.

For example: Gold has specific characteristics which are different from lead or silver. However, all of them come under a common category of metals. All metals have a common natural state, and this is called *sāmānya-dharma*.

Similarly, metals as a category exhibit characteristics which are different from animals, trees, fishes, or humans. This specific defining character, which defines each category, family, or genus, is called *sāmānya-dharma*.

- **Specific natural state or *viśeṣa-dharma***

Specific natural state or *viśeṣa-dharma* is the natural state of individual entities within a family of entities.

For example: Within metals, gold is different from copper, silver, or iron. In wood, teak is different from oak or rubber. The family of wood will conform to a generic *or sāmānya-dharma*. However, the unique natural state *(viśeṣa-dharma)* of teak will be different from oak, elm, or rosewood.

This logic can be expanded in multiple directions. For instance, the unique natural state *(viśeṣa-dharma)* of a table will be different from that of a chair or sofa, even though they may both be made from the same tree. Also, all tables will exhibit a unique natural state, regardless of the material used to make them.

In fact, this concept is applicable to all entities. A heart has a unique natural state, regardless of the body. It cannot do the job of the stomach, even though both may be in the same body.

- **Individual natural state or *sva-dharma***

Each of us behaves differently. This is on account of conditioning brought about by DNA, family, upbringing, societal norms, diet, and habits. Consequently, this allows individuals to select information, analyze, and process it in a unique manner and behave in the way they do.

This specific characteristics of capability at an individual level is called *svadharma (sva* = self + *dharma* = conditioning).

- **Universal natural state or *sanātana-dharma***

Dharma covers all animate and inanimate entities, including planets, galaxies, and nations. Everything can be classified under generic *(sāmānya)*, unique *(viśeṣa)*, or personal *(svadharma)* natural states. This concept is universal in its applicability; hence, it is called universal-natural-state or *sanātana-dharma*.

For example – the natural state of the earth is position, shape, atmosphere, and ability to sustain life. In the case of a nation, its *dharma* can possibly be its constitution, flag, states, people etc.

Examples of *dharma* or natural-state.					
Earth	Sky	Language	Government	School	Parents
Sustains life	Protects Earth	Imparts information	Governs by constitution	Makes responsible citizens	Secure and nourish
Dharma is the natural state of all entities. It is conditioning in individuals.					

4.2 some examples of *dharma*

It is also important to recognize that unless all three aspects of generic *(sāmānya)*, unique *(viśeṣa)*, or personal *(svadharma)* are in their natural state, there can be no peace.

Now, the important question - what is the relationship between *dharma* and *jñāna-karma?*

All our actions *(karma)* are determined by conditioning *(dharma)!* Let us look at some examples:

- As humans, we exhibit certain unique characteristics.

- As individuals, we behave distinctively because we have unique DNA and are brought up in a certain way; therefore, we exhibit specific responses to stimuli. This is called personality or *svabhāva.*

- Similarly, everything we do, including how we drink water, eat food, or choose and drive a car are unique to us and exhibit specific capabilities, characteristics, and responses.

Why is this important? This means that almost all that we do, think, or say comes from being conditioned *(dharma);* so, to achieve *jñāna-karma,* we will first need to transcend our notions of right-wrong, good-bad, and like-dislike and get comfortable with a state of treating everything without prior judgement.

This means that we must learn to dump irrelevant baggage (the past) to ensure that responses are relevant to the current stimulus. So, memory is not always an asset and must be purged regularly.

The question is, can we transcend *dharma?* When conditioning drives so much of our comfort levels, do we have any free will to change?

Śrī Kṛṣṇa say that this is possible through sacrifice *(yajña).*

What is sacrifice *(yajña)*? (verse 24 - 42)

Brahman sacrifices to *Brahman,* the offering is to the fire of the *Brahman,* the offering is made only by *Brahman,* and the result is achieved by the effort of one who is absorbed in meditation of *Brahman.* Some sacrifice to their deities, *yogis* worship the fire of *Brahman,* and others offer sacrifice as a sacrifice. Organ of hearing and other senses in the fire of self-restraint are sacrificed, and sources of sound and others are sacrificed in the fire of the senses.

Yet others sacrifice all functions of the senses and movements of vital air *(prāṇa),* and others sacrifice restraint of the Self in the fire of yoga. People also sacrifice materials, self-restraint, and yoga as a sacrifice, yet others sacrifice knowledge gained by self-study, as do ascetics and people who practice great vows *(tapas).*

In the outgoing breath, people sacrifice incoming breath, and yet others sacrifice incoming breath in the outgoing breath controlling the speed of incoming and outgoing breath, and restraining it becomes the principal focus. Others regulate food intake or sacrifice vital air in the incoming breath; also, all these that know sacrifice get their impurities destroyed by sacrifice.

There are many forms of sacrifice spread across the spectrum of *Brahman,* which are produced by action. Superior to sacrifice of materials is sacrifice of knowledge, and all action culminates in knowledge *(jñāna).*

This subtle knowledge can be achieved by prostration, by questioning, and by service. Then, wise people will teach you the knowledge of reaching the Truth. Not knowing this, one will practice delusion repeatedly, but by this, all beings see me in their Self also.

Just as a blazing fire reduces fuel to ashes, the fire of knowledge reduces all actions to ashes. Verily, nothing is as pure as wisdom in this world, and this has been discovered over time by *yogīs* who have achieved total perfection.

Those that are sincere and dedicated obtain wisdom when they are totally and eagerly engaged in subduing the senses. Having obtained wisdom, they acquire supreme peace quickly.

The sacrifice *(yajña)* process

What is sacrifice *(yajña)?* Sacrifice is the willingness to give a part of oneself for a purpose without expectation of return.

From first principles:

- All sacrifice comes from *Brahman.*

- First, from *Brahman,* *puruṣa* (primordial Identity or Self) and *prakṛti* (primordial manifestation or energy) emerge.

- Next, *puruṣa* tries to project its own Identity or self-worth *(asmitā).* Additionally, this projection emerges as an awareness called *citta* (consciousness).

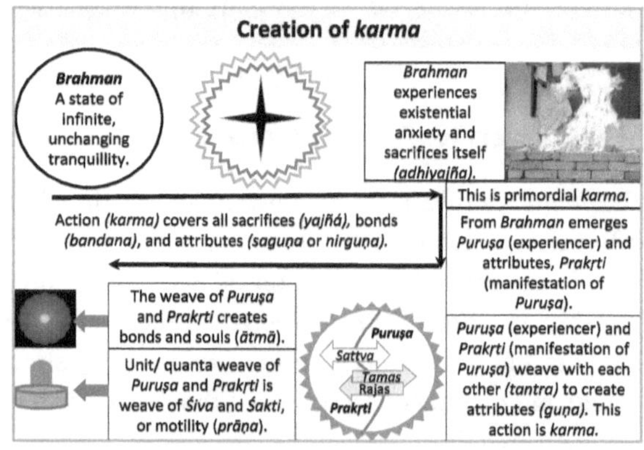

4.3 - relationship between action *(karma),* sacrifice *(yajña)* and identity.

- Furthermore, *citta* (consciousness) is a medium, a carrier of experience. It is inert and instigates motility *(prāṇa)* as well as sentiment *(bhāva).* Sentiment is an expression of *puruṣa.*

- Lastly, the motility *(prāṇa)* and sentiment *(bhāva)* elements manifest from *prakṛti* in the form of *guṇa* (attributes). So, *puruṣa* (experiencer) is the static element, and *prakṛti* is the dynamic element.

- *Puruṣa* and *prakṛti* weave with each other, this weave is called *tantra,* and the outcome is called *karma.*

- All actions *(karma)* result in imbalance between the entities *(ātman),* and this results in debt *(ṛṇa)* which needs to be reconciled.

- Since the Self *(ātman)* is holding the debt, the only way to escape rebirth *(saṃsāra)* is to remove the Self from the action, and this is done by sacrifice *(yajña).*

- It is important to realize the sacrifice is also an action *(karma),* except that it is a regression action on the Self, as sacrifice results in the Self becoming less dependent on the environment for supporting its self-worth *(asmitā).*

But to what extent is sacrifice possible? What is the span and extent of our free will? To what extent do we control the process of acting and sacrifice, considering the impact of *dharma?*

Free-will – what is it, does it exist, and to what extent does it impact us?

- If everything is dictated by prior debt that has come for reconciliation *(prārabdha-karma),* then do we control the outcome of anything?

- Also, Śrī Kṛṣṇa says that even if we do not act, *prakṛti* will force action to preserve itself. So, do we have control over the creation of *karma* and debt *(ṛṇa)?*

- Firstly, this means that any action which is driven by conscious or unconscious impact of conditioning *(dharma)* is not free will or ability to act using self-will.

- Importantly, this includes most of our daily activities, such as:

  o Natural actions, which include breathing, eating, sleeping, etc.

  o Major relationships, such as with parents, siblings, offspring, friends, colleagues, and situations that occur on account of *prārabdha-karma* and due to the need for reconciliation of debt *(ṛṇa).*

  o Our own reactions to stimuli that are driven by DNA, familial, and societal conditioning.

  o This can also be extended to include actions of societies, nations, and the earth.

So, if our existence and reactions in our environment are based on our conditioning, then it means that our actions are not governed by free will. Then, does free will exist at all? If it does, what is free will?

- First, let us hypothesize free will to be any action where a person responds to a stimulus solely on the strength of his or her own individuality *(svatantra)*, and that there is no influence of any kind on the person during the act.

- Importantly, if free will does not exist, then how are we to implement anything that Śrī Kṛṣṇa recommends in the *Śrīmad-bhagavad-gītā?*

- Going by Śrī Kṛṣṇa's assertion, let us assume that free will exists somewhere, and that we need to find it and understand its power in order to be able to initiate the sacrifice process.

Let us go back to cognitive first principles:

- The creation of anything comes from nothing. This is the *Brahman.*

- Even if we were to consider an argument of "God" having started the process, "God" is also something, we then need to figure out where "God" came from, and how that "God" got the ability to generate materiality.

- The only state where anything can emerge as something is nothing. Next, nothing can exist in two forms - as null or as infinity, both states are the same, only the experience is different.

- This state of null *(Brahman)* experiences an atemporal vibration called *spandana* and becomes aware *(prajñā)* of its own existence. This is not free will, because if free will existed, *Brahman* could have stopped *spandana* from manifesting. *Spandana* is a spontaneous occurrence.

- Can *Brahman* stop *spandana* from manifesting? *Brahman* cannot stop atemporal vibration *(spandana)* from occurring, because it occurs without stimulus, from a primordial need for self-expression. We know that self-expression *(bhāva)* occurs spontaneously, without stimulus. The entity that emerges is *puruṣa* (Identity).

- *Puruṣa* experiences three sentiments *(bhāva)* – (1) excitement at the awareness of its own existence (2) anxiety as to what this awareness is, and (3) anxiety also because it does not want to lose this new awareness. This awareness is called *prajñā.*

- This insecurity forces *puruṣa* to manifest in order to experience its awareness of itself and confirm its existence.

- From *puruṣa,* emerges *prakṛti* (manifestation in the form of *guṇa* or attributes), and it weaves with *puruṣa* (primordial Identity or experiencer). This leads to the formation of materiality, Universe etc. This is not free will, but a result of the weave of *puruṣa* and *prakṛti,* which is *tantra.*

- Importantly, *Brahman,* while providing the base for motility, is intrinsically inert. However, *Brahman* does not participate in the weave of *puruṣa* and *prakṛti,* the creation of matter and energy *(māyā).*

For example, a body will remain in a state of rest unless acted upon by an external force. The state of rest is *tamas,* the external force is *rajas,* and the point when the ball achieves a balance between *tamas* and *rajas* is *sattva* or harmony. The state of inertia or *tamas* is a state of no-action, passion *(rajas)* is action propelled by desire and harmonic *(sattva)* is the state of approved action. None of these states are free will.

Free will also conforms to quantum mechanics – When a ball is in a state of rest, the interatomic/intermolecular bonds are in a particular state, acted upon only by gravity, which slowly alters the state of the ball itself. This change in state is not within the control of the ball, but exists because the inter and intra-atomic/molecular bonds refuse to release their relationships and resist. Importantly, this resistance to change in current state is free will because the entities experience a primordial fear of loss of Identity.

Consequently, we can establish that the state of free-will exists only from fear of loss of Identity, and everything else is derived from this fear.

- We have seen that *puruṣa, prakṛti,* and *karma* manifest of a fear of loss of existence or relevance.

- From *karma* comes conditioning *(dharma)*, and *dharma* also drives *karma,* so they are co-dependent.

- So, whenever we act, it is generally in conformance to conditioning *(dharma).*

- Also, when we move out of our zone of conditioning *(dharma),* we experience anxiety of loss of sense of existence or anxiety to self-worth *(asmitā).*

- This generally forces us back into our zone of comfort *(dharma).*

Let us look at some examples:

- UK was a superpower. In fact, there was a time when UK controlled almost everything controllable by humans on Earth. Would they have let control go voluntarily? Of course not! Then what happened? How were they unable to exercise their will and continue to be a world-power?

- If free will existed, there would be no disease, decay, and death. After all, who will die willingly?

- Also, why do we fight death and try to stay alive? Why do we not succeed?

- Try this experiment - sit comfortably and breathe normally. Just observe the breath and ensure that there is no change in flow, breakages, or agitation. You will quickly find out that maintaining this quality of breath is impossible for more than a minute.

- Experiment 2 - when walking, breath in for 4 steps, hold for 2 steps, exhale for 4 steps and retain for 2 steps. You will notice that it is impossible to maintain a sustained breath control. Why is it so difficult to exercise free will?

To what extent can we control actions and affect outcome?

- The starting point is the realization that absolute free will is a mirage, and control over outcome and self are difficult. So, the scope of free will is confined to reducing impact on self-worth (removing fear and anxiety) when performing action *(karma)*.

- When response to any stimulus is in the form of sacrifice *(yajña)* or action without expectation of return, then awareness of self-worth *(jñāna)* increases. This reduces fear of loss of identity *(asmitā)* and increases tranquility *(Brahman)*. So, we can say that any action that is performed as a sacrifice *(yajña)* and any action where there is no feeling of being the doer *(ahaṅkāra)* increases free-will.

- How should one be able to activate free will? It isn't easy because the scope is so limited.

    o   Start by not reacting, let go of the moment, and be selective in the responses.

    o   Then, start sacrificing things that do not matter.

    o   Finally, try to sacrifice your sense of self-worth *(asmitā)* in the action. This means that you should act appropriately, but without fear of retribution or worry about reputation.

How to increase free will through sacrifice *(yajña)*:

- Śrī Kṛṣṇa says that all sacrifice *(yajña)* comes from *Brahman*.

- Since the source of sacrifice is *Brahman,* anything and everything can be sacrificed. So, there are infinite opportunity for sacrifice.

- Consequently, this means that all actions *(karma)* can be sacrificed.

- The only question that remains is our ability to sacrifice and the extent to which we control the process.

- Obviously, each of us has some ability to give up material and other aspects, and this might be a good starting point. Start by sacrificing anything that generates least anxiety, including memory and baggage.

- Importantly, once the easy ones are sacrificed, be alert that the ones that were sacrificed do not creep back on you.

- The interesting thing about sacrificing low hanging fruit, relationship, and power-related entities is that it prepares one psychosomatically for more sacrifices.

- But sacrificing also gets harder as one begins pushing the limits of conditioning *(dharma)*.

- Sacrifice of things that we are attached to impact our self-esteem *(asmitā)*, this fear of loss of self-esteem brings out severe reactions of anxiety and passion. This makes jettisoning of baggage harder.

- Sacrifice is also required for acquisition of knowledge, because from knowledge comes discrimination *(viveka)* and dispassion *(vairāgya)*, which helps in subduing one's self-worth *(asmitā)*.

- This is also possible at the feet of *gurus* who have the knowledge, experience, and expertise to help the practitioner in understanding sacrifice *(yajña)*.

- With sacrifice, all action becoming non-personal resulting in:

  o Destruction of the self *(ātman)* and consequently debt *(prārabdha-karma* or previous debt)*, because debt is attached to the Self and if the Self is destroyed, there is no place where debt may be accrued.

  o Consequently, there is disruption of cycle of rebirth.

  o Increased dispassion *(vairāgya)* makes the person become less afraid of consequences of action, less judgmental of outcome.

  o The person also accepts change with less resistance and consequently becomes more tranquil.

Some contradictions to accepted positions:

Do we have free will? This is the intrinsic question that this chapter raises. We would like to think that we have the ability to make a choice, but is that a reality? The answer to this vexing question is probably "Yes, if we control our response to stimulus".

Lessons learned:

The business of material life is all about understanding action *(karma)*. Also, the practice of sustainable and responsible living is woven into the Indian ethos.

Yajña or sacrifice and *Bhārat's* culture

Yajña in deeply woven into the psyche of *Bhārat* or India - one of the *yajñas* performed ritually in *Bhārat* is called *pañca-mahā-yajñas*[4] (five major sacrifices) which a person is supposed to follow every day. These comprise *daiva-yajña* (sacrifice to one's deity), *ṛṣi-yajña* (sacrifice to the seers, those that gave *Bhārat* her civilization), *pitṛ-yajña* (sacrifice to one's ancestors), *bhūta-yajña* (sacrifice to all beings), and *manuṣya-yajña* (sacrifice to other humans).

What is *manuṣya-yajña* or sacrifice to other humans? It is participating in their welfare, and this includes their journey through life, such as marriage, birth, celebrations, reversals, deaths, etc., in a manner that gives them pleasure, peace, and happiness but without expectation of return. This participation, since it is a sacrifice must be centered on the other person and include respecting their privacy. *Manuṣya-yajña* generally follows various rites as given below.

- The rites and rituals practiced in India are called *ṣoḍaśa-saṃskāras* (sixteen rites)[5].

- One can also perform ritual sacrifice[6].

The transliteration and translation of chapter 4 follows:

श्रीभगवानुवाच ।

इमं विवस्वते योगं प्रोक्तवानहमव्ययम् ।

विवस्वान्मनवे प्राह मनुरिक्ष्वाकवेऽब्रवीत् ॥ ४-१॥

एवं परम्पराप्राप्तमिमं राजर्षयो विदुः ।

स कालेनेह महता योगो नष्टः परन्तप ॥ ४-२॥

स एवायं मया तेऽद्य योगः प्रोक्तः पुरातनः ।

भक्तोऽसि मे सखा चेति रहस्यं ह्येतदुत्तमम् ॥ ४-३॥

Śrī Kṛṣṇa said (1-3) I taught this imperishable yoga to the Sun, who taught it to Manu, who taught it to īkṣvāku (*imaṃ vivasvate yogaṃ proktavānahamavyayam | vivasvānmanave prāha manurikṣvākave'bravīt ॥ 4-1॥*). Thus, this was handed down through the generations of royal seers who knew it, but over time and long period, this yoga has been lost (*evaṃ paramparāprāptamimaṃ rājarṣayo viduḥ | sa kāleneha mahatā yogo naṣṭaḥ parantapa ॥ 4-2॥*). This yoga also, that I teach you today, has been known since ancient times to devotees and since you are my friend, so I am revealing this supreme secret to you (*sa evāyaṃ mayā te'dya yogaḥ proktaḥ purātanaḥ | bhakto'si me sakhā ceti rahasyaṃ hyetaduttamam ॥ 4-3॥*).

---

[4]http://www.advaidam.com/2017/02/16/panca-maha-yagya
[5]https://www.worldhindunews.com/16-sanskar-in-hinduism
[6]https://www.hindupedia.com/en/Yajna

अर्जुन उवाच ।

अपरं भवतो जन्म परं जन्म विवस्वतः ।

कथमेतद्विजानीयां त्वमादौ प्रोक्तवानिति ॥ ४-४॥

Arjuna asked (4) You were born after the Sun. How am I to comprehend that you taught this in the beginning of times? *(aparam bhavato janma param janma vivasvataḥ ı kathametadvijānīyām tvamādau proktavāniti ıı 4-4ıı).*

श्रीभगवानुवाच ।

बहूनि मे व्यतीतानि जन्मानि तव चार्जुन ।

तान्यहं वेद सर्वाणि न त्वं वेत्थ परन्तप ॥ ४-५॥

अजोऽपि सन्नव्ययात्मा भूतानामीश्वरोऽपि सन् ।

प्रकृतिं स्वामधिष्ठाय सम्भवाम्यात्ममायया ॥ ४-६॥

(5-6) **Śrī Kṛṣṇa said** - I have taken many births just like you, but unlike you, remember them all *(bahūni me vyatītāni janmāni tava cārjuna ı tānyaham veda sarvāṇi na tvam vettha parantapa ıı 4-5ıı)*. I am an imperishable soul, the Lord of all beings also, and since I control the emergence of *prakṛti*, I can create the illusion of my own existence *(ajo'pi sannavyayātmā bhūtānāmīśvaro'pi san ı prakṛtim svāmadhiṣṭhāya sambhavāmyātmamāyayā ıı 4-6ıı)*.

यदा हि धर्मस्य ग्लानिर्भवति भारत ।

अभ्युत्थानमधर्मस्य तदात्मानं सृजाम्यहम् ॥ ४-७॥

परित्राणाय साधूनां विनाशाय च दुष्कृताम् ।

धर्मसंस्थापनार्थाय सम्भवामि युगे ॥ ४-८॥

(7-8) When natural state decays and there is increase in chaos, I embody myself *(yadā hi dharmasya glānirbhavati bhārata ı abhyutthānamadharmasya tadātmānam sṛjāmyaham ıı 4-7ıı)*. For protection of the virtuous and destruction of wicked and for re-establishment of natural balance, I take birth in every era *(paritrāṇāya sādhūnām vināśāya ca duṣkṛtām ı dharmasamsthāpanārthāya sambhavāmi yuge ıı 4-8ıı)*.

जन्म कर्म च मे दिव्यमेवं यो वेत्ति तत्त्वतः ।

त्यक्त्वा देहं पुनर्जन्म नैति मामेति सोऽर्जुन ॥ ४-९॥

वीतरागभयक्रोधा मन्मया मामुपाश्रिताः ।

बहवो ज्ञानतपसा पूता मद्भावमागताः ॥ ४-१०॥

(9-10) He who understands my divine activities in its subtleties, when he abandons his body stops having further births and comes to me *(janma karma ca me divyamevam yo vetti tattvataḥ ı tyaktvā deham punarjanma naiti māmeti so'rjuna ıı 4-9ıı)*. Freed from attachment, fear, anger, absorbed in me, and taking refuge in me, many who have sacrificed their knowledge of the Self, have attained my state (*vītarāgabhayakrodhā manmayā māmupāśritāḥ | bahavo jñānatapasā pūtā madbhāvamāgatāḥ || 4-10||*).

ये यथा मां प्रपद्यन्ते तांस्तथैव भजाम्यहम् ।

मम वर्त्मानुवर्तन्ते मनुष्याः पार्थ सर्वशः ॥ ४-११॥

काङ्क्षन्तः कर्मणां सिद्धिं यजन्त इह देवताः ।

क्षिप्रं हि मानुषे लोके सिद्धिर्भवति कर्मजा ॥ ४-१२॥

(11-12) In whatever way people approach me, I reward those people who follow my path only (*ye yathā māṃ prapadyante tāṃstathaiva bhajāmyaham | mama vartmānuvartante manuṣyāḥ pārtha sarvaśaḥ || 4-11||*). Sacrifice longing for success in action to the *deivas* quickly, because in this human world, success is achieved when there is action (*kāṅkṣantaḥ karmaṇām siddhiṃ yajanta iha devatāḥ | kṣipraṃ hi mānuṣe loke siddhirbhavati karmajā || 4-12||*).

चातुर्वर्ण्यं मया सृष्टं गुणकर्मविभागशः ।

तस्य कर्तारमपि मां विद्ध्यकर्तारमव्ययम् ॥ ४-१३॥

न मां कर्माणि लिम्पन्ति न मे कर्मफले स्पृहा ।

इति मां योऽभिजानाति कर्मभिर्न स बध्यते ॥ ४-१४॥

एवं ज्ञात्वा कृतं कर्म पूर्वैरपि मुमुक्षुभिः ।

कुरु कर्मैव तस्मात्त्वं पूर्वैः पूर्वतरं कृतम् ॥ ४-१५॥

(13-15) The four categories of people are created by me based on their orientation to action (*guṇakarmavibhāgaśaḥ*), also know that though I am also the initiator, I am not engaged and imperishable (*cāturvarṇyam mayā sṛṣṭam guṇakarmavibhāgaśaḥ | tasya kartāramapi mām viddhyakartāramavyayam || 4-13||*), Actions do not taint me, nor do I desire the fruits of action, thus those that know me are not bound by actions (*na māṃ karmāṇi limpanti na me karmaphale spṛhā | iti māṃ yo'bhijānāti karmabhirna sa badhyate || 4-14||*). Thus, having known how fervent ancient seekers of the Truth performed karma, perform karma as the ancients did (*evaṃ jñātvā kṛtaṃ karma pūrvairapi mumukṣubhiḥ | kuru karmaiva tasmāttvam pūrvaiḥ pūrvataraṃ kṛtam || 4-15||*).

किं कर्म किमकर्मेति कवयोऽप्यत्र मोहिताः ।

तत्ते कर्म प्रवक्ष्यामि यज्ज्ञात्वा मोक्ष्यसेऽशुभात् ॥ ४-१६॥

कर्मणो ह्यपि बोद्धव्यं च विकर्मणः ।

अकर्मणश्च बोद्धव्यं गहना कर्मणो गतिः ॥ ४-१७॥

कर्मण्यकर्म यः पश्येदकर्मणि च कर्म यः ।

स बुद्धिमान्मनुष्येषु स युक्तः कृत्स्नकर्मकृत् ॥ ४-१८॥

(16-18) What is action, what is inaction, which deludes even the poets? I shall teach you, knowing which you can achieve liberation from that which is inappropriate *(kiṃ karma kimakarmeti kavayo'pyatra mohitāḥ | tatte karma pravakṣyāmi yajjñātvā mokṣyase'śubhāt || 4-16||)*. Also, should be known of action, as should be known prohibited action and knowledge of inaction, because action is deep *(karmaṇo hyapi boddhavyaṃ ca vikarmaṇaḥ | akarmaṇaśca boddhavyaṃ gahanā karmaṇo gatiḥ || 4-17||)*. He who perceives action in inaction and inaction in action is wise among men and in complete union in all action *(karmaṇyakarma yaḥ paśyedakarmaṇi ca karma yaḥ | sa buddhimānmanuṣyeṣu sa yuktaḥ kṛtsnakarmakṛt || 4-18||)*.

यस्य सर्वे समारम्भाः कामसङ्कल्पवर्जिताः ।
ज्ञानाग्निदग्धकर्माणं तमाहुः पण्डितं बुधाः ॥ ४-१९॥
त्यक्त्वा कर्मफलासङ्गं नित्यतृप्तो निराश्रयः ।
कर्मण्यभिप्रवृत्तोऽपि नैव किञ्चित्करोति सः ॥ ४-२०॥

(19-20) He who starts all undertakings without desire or expectation, whose actions have been tempered in the fire of knowledge, is called a wise scholar *(yasya sarve samārambhāḥ kāmasaṅkalpavarjitāḥ | jñānāgnidagdhakarmāṇam tamāhuḥ paṇḍitam budhāḥ || 4-19||)*. He who has abandoned fruits of effort, is ever content, and not dependent on anything when engaged in action, truly he does nothing *(tyaktvā karmaphalāsaṅgam nityatṛpto nirāśrayaḥ | karmaṇyabhipravṛtto'pi naiva kiñcitkaroti saḥ || 4-20||)*.

निराशीर्यतचित्तात्मा त्यक्तसर्वपरिग्रहः ।
शारीरं केवलं कर्म कुर्वन्नाप्नोति किल्बिषम् ॥ ४-२१॥
यदृच्छालाभसन्तुष्टो द्वन्द्वातीतो विमत्सरः ।
समः सिद्धावसिद्धौ च कृत्वापि न निबध्यते ॥ ४-२२॥
गतसङ्गस्य मुक्तस्य ज्ञानावस्थितचेतसः ।
यज्ञायाचरतः कर्म समग्रं प्रविलीयते ॥ ४-२३॥

(21-23) Without expectation, with an integrated consciousness and Self, abandoning all commission, using only the body for performing action, that person gets no injustice *(nirāśīryatacittātmā tyaktasarvaparigrahaḥ | śārīram kevalam karma kurvannāpnoti kilbiṣam || 4-21||)*. (Note: The words *parigraha* and *kilbiṣa* are keywords and have no appropriate English equivalent). Content with whatever profit come spontaneously free from opposites, unselfish, always balanced in success and failure and not bound by actions *(yadṛcchālābhasantuṣṭo dvandvātīto vimatsaraḥ | samaḥ siddhāvasiddhau ca kṛtvāpi na nibadhyate || 4-22||)*. One who is devoid of attachment, liberated with conscious knowledge like Vasishta, performing action for sacrifice ceases to exist *(gatasaṅgasya muktasya jñānāvasthitacetasaḥ | yajñāyācarataḥ karma samagram pravilīyate || 4-23||)*. Here, *pravilīyate* means dissolved, but we have translated it as ceases to exist.

ब्रह्मार्पणं ब्रह्म हविर्ब्रह्माग्नौ ब्रह्मणा हुतम् ।
ब्रह्मैव तेन गन्तव्यं ब्रह्मकर्मसमाधिना ॥ ४-२४॥
दैवमेवापरे यज्ञं योगिनः पर्युपासते ।
ब्रह्माग्नावपरे यज्ञं यज्ञेनैवोपजुह्वति ॥ ४-२५॥
श्रोत्रादीनीन्द्रियाण्यन्ये संयमाग्निषु जुह्वति ।
शब्दादीन्विषयानन्य इन्द्रियाग्निषु जुह्वति ॥ ४-२६॥

(24-26) *Brahman* sacrifices to the *Brahman,* the offering is to the fire of the *Brahman,* the offering is made only by the *Brahman,* the end result is achieved by effort of one who is absorbed in meditation of the *Brahman (brahmārpaṇam brahma havirbrahmāgnau brahmaṇā hutam ǀ brahmaiva tena gantavyam brahmakarmasamādhinā ǁ 4-24ǁ).* Some sacrifice only to the deities, *yogīs* worship the fire of *Brahman,* others sacrifice, sacrifice as a sacrifice *(daivamevāpare yajñam yoginaḥ paryupāsate ǀ brahmāgnāvapare yajñam yajñenaivopajuhvati ǁ 4-25ǁ).* Organ of hearing and other senses in the fire of self-restraint are sacrificed, sources of sound and others are sacrificed in the fire of the senses *(śrotrādīnīndriyāṇyanye samyamāgniṣu juhvati ǀ śabdādīnviṣayānanya indriyāgniṣu juhvati ǁ 4-26ǁ).*

सर्वाणीन्द्रियकर्माणि प्राणकर्माणि चापरे ।
आत्मसंयमयोगाग्नौ जुह्वति ज्ञानदीपिते ॥ ४-२७॥
द्रव्ययज्ञास्तपोयज्ञा योगयज्ञास्तथापरे ।
स्वाध्यायज्ञानयज्ञाश्च यतयः संशितव्रताः ॥ ४-२८॥

(27-28) Yet others sacrifice all functions of the senses and movements of vital air and others, when restrained together within the Self in the fire of yoga that has been kindled by the light knowledge *(sarvāṇīndriyakarmāṇi prāṇakarmāṇi cāpare ǀ ātmasamyamayogāgnau juhvati jñānadīpite ǁ 4-27ǁ).* People also sacrifice materials, self-restraint, Yoga as a sacrifice, yet others sacrifice knowledge gained by self-study, as do ascetics and people who practice great vows *(dravyayajñāstapoyajñā yogayajñāstathāpare ǀ svādhyāyajñānayajñāśca yatayaḥ samsitavratāḥ ǁ 4-28ǁ).*

अपाने जुह्वति प्राणं प्राणेऽपानं तथापरे ।
प्राणापानगती रुद्ध्वा प्राणायामपरायणाः ॥ ४-२९॥
अपरे नियताहाराः प्राणान्प्राणेषु जुह्वति ।
सर्वेऽप्येते यज्ञविदो यज्ञक्षपितकल्मषाः ॥ ४-३०॥

(29-30) In the outgoing breath people sacrifice incoming breath, yet others sacrifice incoming breath in the outgoing breath *(apāne juhvati prāṇam prāṇe'pānam tathāpare ǀ),* controlling the speed of incoming and outgoing breath and restraining it becomes the principal focus *(prāṇāpānagatī ruddhvā prāṇāyāmaparāyaṇāḥ*

∥ 4-29∥). Others regulate food intake or sacrifice vital air in the incoming breath (*apare niyatāhārāḥ prāṇānprāṇeṣu juhvati ।*), also all these that know sacrifice get their impurities destroyed by sacrifice (*sarve'pyete yajñavido yajñakṣapitakalmaṣāḥ ∥ 4-30∥*).

यज्ञशिष्टामृतभुजो यान्ति ब्रह्म सनातनम् ।

नायं लोकोऽस्त्ययज्ञस्य कुतोऽन्यः कुरुसत्तम ॥ ४-३१॥

एवं बहुविधा यज्ञा वितता ब्रह्मणो मुखे ।

कर्मजान्विद्धि तान्सर्वानेवं ज्ञात्वा विमोक्ष्यसे ॥ ४-३२॥

श्रेयान्द्रव्यमयाद्यज्ञाज्ज्ञानयज्ञः परन्तप ।

सर्वं कर्माखिलं पार्थ ज्ञाने परिसमाप्यते ॥ ४-३३॥

(31-33) Those that consume the nectar of sacrifice go to eternal *Brahman (yajñaśiṣṭāmṛtabhujo yānti brahma sanātanam ।)*. There is no place in the world for the non-sacrificer, how can he find a place in any other *(nāyaṃ loko'styayajñasya kuto'nyaḥ kurusattama ∥ 4-31∥)*. Thus, there are many forms of sacrifice spread across the spectrum of *brahman* which are produced by action, know them all, thus having known them one can find liberation *(evaṃ bahuvidhā yajñā vitatā brahmaṇo mukhe । karmajānviddhi tānsarvānevaṃ jñātvā vimokṣyase ∥ 4-32∥)*. Superior to sacrifice of materials is sacrifice of knowledge, all action culminates in knowledge *(śreyāndravyamayādyajñājjñānayajñaḥ parantapa । sarvaṃ karmākhilaṃ pārtha jñāne parisamāpyate ∥ 4-33∥)*.

तद्विद्धि प्रणिपातेन परिप्रश्नेन सेवया ।

उपदेक्ष्यन्ति ते ज्ञानं ज्ञानिनस्तत्त्वदर्शिनः ॥ ४-३४॥

यज्ज्ञात्वा न पुनर्मोहमेवं यास्यसि पाण्डव ।

येन भूतान्यशेषेण द्रक्ष्यस्यात्मन्यथो मयि ॥ ४-३५॥ var अशेषाणि

अपि चेदसि पापेभ्यः सर्वेभ्यः पापकृत्तमः ।

सर्वं ज्ञानप्लवेनैव वृजिनं सन्तरिष्यसि ॥ ४-३६॥

(34 - 36) This subtle knowledge can be achieved by prostration, by questioning, and by service *(tadviddhi praṇipātena paripraśnena sevayā ।)*, then wise people will teach you the knowledge of reaching the Truth *(upadekṣyanti te jñānaṃ jñāninastattvadarśinaḥ ∥ 4-34∥)*. Not knowing this one will commit to delusion repeatedly, by this all beings see in their Self me also *(yajjñātvā na punarmohamevaṃ yāsyasi pāṇḍava । yena bhūtānyaśeṣeṇa drakṣyasyātmanyatho mayi ∥ 4-35∥)*. Even if you are more wretched than the all-other wretched people, you will be saved from wickedness by floating on this knowledge *(api cedasi pāpebhyaḥ sarvebhyaḥ pāpakṛttamaḥ । sarvaṃ jñānaplavenaiva vṛjinaṃ santariṣyasi ∥ 4-36∥)*.

यथैधांसि समिद्धोऽग्निर्भस्मसात्कुरुतेऽर्जुन ।
ज्ञानाग्निः सर्वकर्माणि भस्मसात्कुरुते तथा ॥ ४-३७॥
न हि ज्ञानेन सदृशं पवित्रमिह विद्यते ।
तत्स्वयं योगसंसिद्धः कालेनात्मनि विन्दति ॥ ४-३८॥

(37-38) Just as a blazing fire reduces fuel to ashes, the fire of knowledge reduces all actions to ashes *(yathaidhāṃsi samiddho'gnirbhasmasātkurute'rjuna ι jñānāgniḥ sarvakarmāṇi bhasmasātkurute tathā ॥ 4-37॥)*. Verily, nothing is as pure as wisdom in this world, and this has been discovered over time by *yogīs* who have achieved total perfection *(na hi jñānena sadṛśam pavitramiha vidyate ι tatsvayam yogasaṃsiddhaḥ kālenātmani vindati ॥ 4-38॥)*.

श्रद्धावाँल्लभते ज्ञानं तत्परः संयतेन्द्रियः ।
ज्ञानं लब्ध्वा परां शान्तिमचिरेणाधिगच्छति ॥ ४-३९॥
अज्ञश्चाश्रद्दधानश्च संशयात्मा विनश्यति ।
नायं लोकोऽस्ति न परो न सुखं संशयात्मनः ॥ ४-४०॥

(39-40) Those that are sincere and dedicated obtain wisdom when they are totally and eagerly engaged, subduing the senses *(śraddhāvā~llabhate jñānam tatparaḥ samyatendriyaḥ ι)* have obtained wisdom, they obtain supreme peace quickly *(jñānam labdhvā parām śāntimacireṇādhigacchati ॥ 4-39॥)*. Ignorant people and those without sincerity and dedication doubting souls will destroy themselves *(ajñaścāśraddadhānaśca samsayātmā vinaśyati ι)*, in fact, doubting souls find happiness eluding them in this world and the next *(nāyam loko'sti na paro na sukham samsayātmanaḥ ॥ 4-40॥)*.

योगसंन्यस्तकर्माणं ज्ञानसञ्छिन्नसंशयम् ।
आत्मवन्तं न कर्माणि निबध्नन्ति धनञ्जय ॥ ४-४१॥
तस्मादज्ञानसम्भूतं हृत्स्थं ज्ञानासिनात्मनः ।
छित्त्वैनं संशयं योगमातिष्ठोत्तिष्ठ भारत ॥ ४-४२॥

(41-42) However, when a person practices yoga, where action is renounced, doubts are removed *(yogasamnyastakarmāṇam jñānasañchinnasamsayam ι)*, the Self becomes steadied without the binding of *karma (ātmavantam na karmāṇi nibadhnanti dhanañjaya ॥ 4-41॥)*. Therefore, cut this doubt that is born out of ignorance and residing in the heart by the Self that has the sword of knowledge *(tasmādajñānasambhūtam hṛtstham jñānāsinātmanaḥ ι)*, discard your doubts, take refuge in Yoga, and rise *(chittvainam samsayam yogamātiṣṭhottiṣṭha bhārata ॥ 4-42॥)*.

◆——— · ◆ ◆ · ———◆

Chapter 5

Sannyāsa-yoga (yoga of renunciation)[1]

Introduction

- In chapters 2, 3, and 4, Śrī Kṛṣṇa guides the student through the spectrum of change; from disillusionment, fear of outcome, and grip of illusion *(māyā),* action, to finally, renunciation of action.

- In chapter 5, he moves to the next step, and what happens after a person has cleaned up his action *(karma)?* How does one evolve to the next level of personal development?

- Importantly, one must recognize that development in Yoga is experiential, and everything that is said in *Śrīmad-bhagavad-gītā* can only create value when there is introspection and practice.

Sannyāsa-yoga (verse 1-6)

Which is better, *jñāna-yoga* or *karma-yoga*?

Arjuna starts off by expressing confusion - which is better, performing action or renouncing it? Śrī Kṛṣṇa says that both *jñāna-yoga (sāṃkhya)* and *karma-yoga* are one *(eka)* and reach the same goal, *Brahman.* However, the path of renunciation is very difficult and painful. In any case, even renunciation requires action, so renouncing the outcome of action is an easier method of reaching *Brahman.*

Overview (verse 2-11)

- First, the *yogī* should try and smoothen internal turbulence during the experience of change. This is called purification of the soul *(ātmaśuddhaye).* This is done

---

[1]https://www.bhagavad-gita.org/Gita/chapter-05.html

by discriminating permanent from impermanent *(viveka)* and approaching all actions with dispassion *(vairāgya).*

- Next, the *yogī* attempts to always remain in this state, notwithstanding the situation. This includes seeing, hearing touching, smelling, eating, evacuating, sleeping, breathing, or speaking. Consequently, the cognitive apparatus *(indriyas)* is conditioned to move among sense objects without getting affected by stimulus.

- In fact, the *yogī* should perform *karma* (activity) with sentience (awareness of his senses) withdrawn from the environment, viewing all creation as one *(sama-darśana).*

- Lastly, the *yogī* should be detached from the surroundings like a lotus leaf in water (water on a lotus leaf slides off without making the leaf wet) and remain in an isolated state. This is done by performing action using the body, cognitive apparatus, logical reasoning, and senses with the attitude of "not acting" nor "causing action" even when acting.

- So, the *yogī's* awareness is absorbed in the *Brahman, and* his or her Soul is established in the *Brahman* and with the *Brahman* for the goal and nothing else. This is called *ekāgratā* (single-pointed focus).

Brahman (verse 12-19)

- *Brahman* is neutral – it is neither the initiator, creator nor the doer, nor does it get attached to creation – this is because this is its innate nature. Also, *Brahman* does not accept from anyone their demerits or even merit, and this occurs in people on account of illusion *(māyā)* and lack of knowledge *(ajñāna).*

- The reason for this delusion is that the Self *(ātman)* experiences existential doubt (Am I alive? Do I exist? Who am I?), and this insecurity gives rise to the need to form bonds and attachments that reinforce a sense of existence and increase the feeling of self-worth *(asmitā).*

- Consequently, this need for reinforcement of its sense of identity creates a veil of ignorance *(māyā)* over the true nature of the Self *(ajñāna),* which is dispelled by knowledge of the Self *(jñāna).*

- Also, this makes *māyā* (illusion) very difficult to overcome unless the person can overcome the need for reinforcement of self-worth as well as distance and detach the Self from impact of the environment on the Self *(ātman).*

A person merges with *Brahman* when he has advanced in cleansing of the Soul *(ātmaśuddhaye),* views everything as one *(sama-dṛṣṭaye),* has an intellect that is immersed in an unchanging state of peace *(Brahman)* with complete focus on an unchanging state of peace *(Brahman)* (verse 18-19).

The concept of *karma-yoga*

- We get stimulus through our senses - sight, sound, touch, taste, and smell. Then, we respond through our motor organs - legs, hands, tongue, anus, and sexual organs.

- Consequently, we get into a cycle of stimulus and response, that is driven by our senses, cognition, and intellect. This creates an illusionary world called *māyā* that veils the *Brahman.*

- So, to merge with *Brahman,* we need to transcend *māyā*[2] (illusion or farce):

  o One way is to isolate ourselves from the environment so that the impact of *māyā* is slowly controlled. This is renunciation *(sannyāsa),* and the path is called *jñāna-yoga.*

  o The other way is to perform *karma* (action), but control the senses *(indriyas),* cognition *(manas),* and logic *(buddhi).* Consequently, during the performance of action, we remain calm, unruffled in every experience, and look at effort & outcome without fear or favor. This path is called *karma-yoga.*

- However, both paths are difficult. In fact, isolating ourselves from society requires enormous ability to come to terms with loss of self-worth or self-esteem *(asmitā).*

- Also, the difficult effort of isolating the Self from society itself is action *(karma).*

- Therefore, whether we practice renunciation *(sannyāsa)* or control of action *(karma-yoga),* action is required. However, when we practice *karma-yoga,* we give ourselves the ability to improve continuously without bringing catastrophic damage to our self-esteem *(asmitā)* that *sannyāsa-yoga* could bring.

- Since the risks are lower, *karma-yoga* is seen by Śrī Kṛṣṇa as more practical and achievable path.

Increasing free-will *(svatantra)* (verse 18-29)

- To get *jñāna* (knowledge of the self), one must anchor the seat of cognition *(manas)* and seat of logic *(buddhi)* in the *Brahman* and view everything with *sama-darśana* (equal gaze), whether it is a learned person, a cow, an elephant, a dog, or even an outcast.

- As a result of *sama-darśana* (equal gaze), the seat of cognition *(manas)* becomes spotless *(nirdośa)* and without bias because it allows the *yogī* to separate the stimulus from the source of the stimulus.

---

[2]https://schoolofyoga.in/yoga-concept/maya

- Consequently, a sense of equality gets established and this ensures that the *yogī* becomes a detached soul.

- As a result, the *yogī* recognizes that all actions are born out of impulses of desire and that happiness or peace comes from removal of duality. So, the *yogī* reacts with equanimity to pleasant and unpleasant stimuli, being neither too happy at good news nor grieving at unpleasant news.

- Self-controlled ascetics *(sannyāsin)* do this by shutting out external objects, fixing the gaze at the tip of the nostrils *(nāsikāgra-dṛṣṭi)*, equalizing their incoming *(prāṇa)* and outgoing *(apāna)* breath *(vāyu)*, and moving it within the nasal cavity *(nāsābhyantaracāriṇau)*.

Interplay between *guṇa, citta, dharma*[3], and *karma*[4]

- When we are in our natural state *(dharma)*, we experience a cognition of peace, the three attributes *(guṇas - tamas* = delusion/*rajas* = passion/*satva* = harmony) are in balance.

- Then, stimulus coming in through the senses *(indriyas)*, is collated by the center of cognition *(manas)*. This stimulus is compared with conditioning *(dharma)* after which, a response is formulated by the sense of experience *(ahaṅkāra)*, sometimes referred to as ego.

- *Citta* (consciousness) is the medium that recognizes the object, stimulates the senses, collates the data at the cognitive centers *(manas)*, carries the information to the intellect *(buddhi)* for comparison with conditioning *(dharma)*, and formulates a response.

- If there is congruence, *ahaṅkāra* (I am the doer) pulls the object towards it because it wants continued engagement. If there is dissonance, *ahaṅkāra* pushes the object away to avoid discomfort. As a result, there is give-take or a transaction.

- Any transaction or give-take results in *karma* (action). When there is congruence/attraction *(rāga)*, the subject and object try to come closer to each other, and when there is dissonance/repulsion *(dveṣa)*, they try to push each other away.

- However, in give-take transactions, *karma* is always unequal between the giver and taker, and this results in an imbalance, since one always gives or takes more from the other. Consequently, this imbalance results in debt *(ṛṇa)*, which must be repaid, even if it means taking another *janma* or rebirth.

---

[3]https://schoolofyoga.in/yoga-concept/dharma
[4]https://schoolofyoga.in/yoga-concept/action-karma

The *citta* (consciousness)

- *Citta* (consciousness) performs the following action:

    - It transmits projection of self-worth *(asmitā)* of the subject to other entities and vice-versa.

    - Next, it seeks and identifies other entities.

    - Then, it relays feedback from other entities as experience.

5.1 - The functioning of the consciousness *(citta)*

    - *Citta* carries the stimulus through the senses *(indriyas),* to the center of cognition *(manas),* then to the center of logic *(buddhi).*

    - Then, it acts as a bridge, comparing stimulus with conditioning *(dharma).*

    - The outcome is integrated with the sense of self-worth/identity *(asmitā),* which takes ownership of the response *(ahaṅkāra).*

    - Finally, *citta* then carries out the response as a projection of identity *(asmitā).*

- In short, *citta* (consciousness) is the thread *(sūtra)* that runs across the complete transaction spectrum, from identifying another entity, acquisition of information to formulation of response, then response, and, finally, feedback.

- One can experience consciousness *(citta)* flowing out of the frontal lobe when one is transacting with anyone.

    - The awareness of the flow of consciousness *(citta)* within the Self and it's impact on the sense of identity *(asmitā)* is called *jñāna.*

    - Next, the awareness of the projection of *citta* (consciousness) to the environment is called *vijñāna* (macro or system transaction).

    - Also, the experience of *citta* of the Identity's *(puruṣa)* projection perceived by others is called *asmitā* (self-esteem/self-worth).

    - Additionally, the experience of being a doer by *puruṣa* is called *ahaṅkāra* (I am the doer).

    - Lastly, awareness of consciousness *(citta)* and its movements is called *prajñā* (awareness). This awareness is primordial and can be experienced with practice, when a person steps back from any situation and watches his own actions, as if he or she were a different person.

- When a person focuses on the action and not the experience, there is no experience of like *(rāga)* or dislike *(dveṣa),* which results in the effort of *puruṣa* to project itself being nullified.

- This effort is *yajña* or sacrifice.

Example of *citta* in daily life

When we go to a funeral or cremation, our identity *(puruṣa)* has already been conditioned *(dharma)* about how the self-identity *(asmitā)* must be projected.

Hence, we dress and act somber at a funeral, and we are serious in a temple or church and joyous at a wedding. Similarly, when we meet a friend, we show happiness, and at a business meeting, we present appropriate behavior. Finally, when we are alone, our consciousness keeps reaching out for subjects, we dream, imagine situations, and sometimes reflect on ourselves.

This projection of our Self and our experiences is our consciousness *(citta).* The fact is that the change in our demeanor occurs because our consciousness *(citta)* takes on the atmosphere of the environment naturally. Consequently, *citta* always mirrors with the same identity as its environment to avoid damage to self-worth *(asmitā).*

If the individual were to behave contrary to *dharma* (conditioning or accepted practice), the environment will reject the projection of the individual *(dveṣa),* leading to psychological damage of the *asmitā* (self-esteem).

How should we perform *karma*?

Māyā (illusion) which is driven by *guṇa* (attitude), drives conditioning *(dharma).* *Guṇa* comprises *tamas* (delusion), *rajas* (passion), and *sattva* (harmony). So, we can transcend *māyā* and experience the nature of Self by taking the following actions:

- First, avoid hatred *(tamas)* and anger *(rajas).* Then, try to stay balanced *(sattva)* with *sama-darśana* (equal gaze).

- Next, bring the senses under control.

  o Avoiding reacting with duality (good-bad, good-bad, right-wrong etc.) to sensory stimuli.

  o Also, try controlling flow of stimuli where they are collated at the cognition *(manas).* This area corresponds to the area around the amygdala where "flight or fight" responses are processed. One may increase one's ability by practicing *prāṇāyāma* and meditation.

- o Finally, practice control of conversion of stimulus to response by separating the intellect *(buddhi)* from conditioning *(dharma)* as well as logically try to redirect response to a *sāttvika* (harmonic or balanced) one and prevent rise of *tamas* or *rajas*.

- Also, avoid duality such as like/dislike, happy/sad, etc., as these result in *tāmasika* and *rājasika* experiences, which can hijack the intellect *(buddhi)*.

- Additionally, view everything with *sama-dṛṣṭi (sama* = equal + *dṛṣṭi* = gaze); this way, *tamas* and *rajas* are brought under control.

- Finally, do not get attached to action, its experience, efforts, or outcome. Step back and recognize it as *māyā*. For example, perform action as a duty as sincerely as possible without expecting any return, and avoid attachment to the action *(ahaṅkāra)* or outcome *(phala)*.

As a result, the senses become controlled, and Self is isolated from the actions. Also, this allows clarity in cognition *(viveka)* and dispassion *(vairāgya)*, the two key requirements for betterment in Yoga. This allows the Soul to transcend *māyā* and merge with the Truth *(Brahman)*.

The physiology and awareness in verse 27

The *sannyāsin* does this by shutting out external objects, fixing the gaze at the tip of the nostrils *(nāsikāgra- dṛṣṭi)*, equalizing their incoming *(prāṇa)* and outgoing *(apāna)* breath *(vāyu)*, and moving it within the nasal cavity *(nāsābhyantaracāriṇau)* (verse 27).

Breathing physiology – part 1 – flow of air into the nasal passage

It is important for any student of Yoga to understand the physiology and *prāṇa* movements that occur in this practice.

- First, air is sucked into the respiratory system through the nostril. How does this occur?

- The diaphragm is a muscle which separates the abdominal cavity from the thoracic cavity. In fact, it is anchored to the lower ribs. So, during inhalation, the diaphragm moves down, creating a negative pressure in the thoracic cavity. Consequently, this draws in air from the atmosphere.

- Next, the expansion of the lungs and movement of the diaphragm

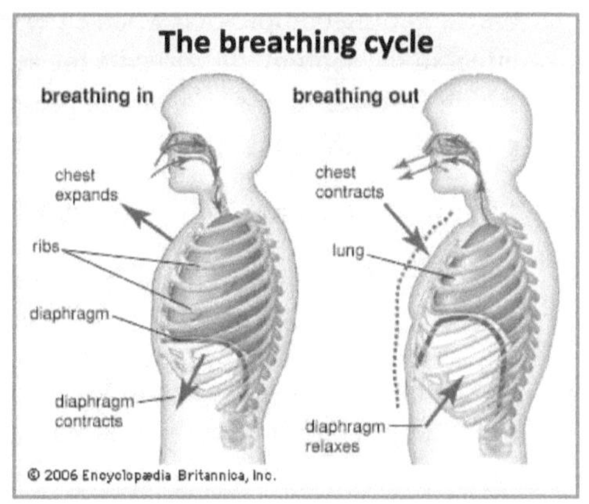

results in the expansion of the rib cage and distension of the abdomen.

- Both abdominal and thoracic cavities expand to allow the downward movement of the diaphragm.

- During exhalation, a reverse pressure is created within the abdomen and rib, which forces the diaphragm to move upwards again. Consequently, there is an upward movement of the diaphragm, which changes the intra-thoracic pressure from negative to positive, resulting in air being forced out of the lungs.

- Importantly, breathing is a reflex action that is controlled by the medulla oblongata. In fact, the rate of breathing is dependent on the concentration of O2/CO2 and blood pH. Additionally, the pons controls the speed of inhalation (speed of the movement of the diaphragm).

Breathing physiology – part 2 – flow of air and awareness *(prajñā)*

- Initially, when breathing in, air crosses the sinuses. Uniquely, sinuses are pockets of air which secrete mucous into the nasal cavity through orifices called ostia. These open into small recesses called meati and are protected by shelf-like projections called turbinates.

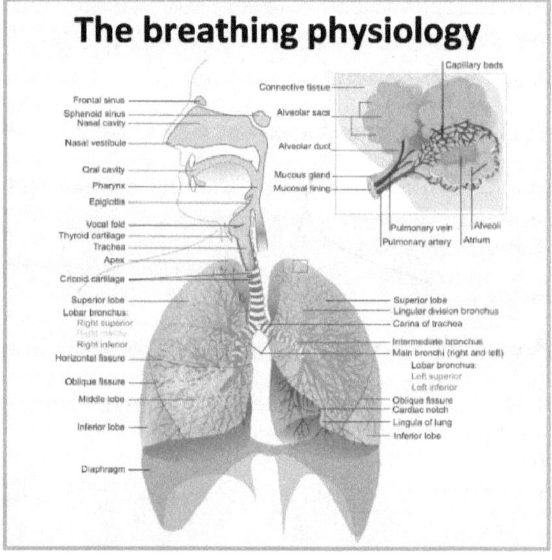

- Next, the incoming air is compressed at the bridge of the nose, called septum. This is a venturi-like structure which results in the air getting compressed when entering the nose. Therefore, due to the venturi effect in the septum, the air exits the septum into the nasal cavity under pressure which is lower than atmospheric pressure. Consequently, this causes the air to swirl within the nasal cavity.

- Meanwhile, the fins of the turbinator direct the swirl and split the incoming air.

- One part of the incoming air is guided by the nasal concha over the olfactory epithelium and activates the olfactory bulb.

- Next, the inferior concha guides air over the nasopharynx. This results in a resonating column effect within the auditory tube, which activates the middle ear.

- Importantly, the sinuses are air-pockets, so they resonate to the flow of air and differential pressure between the nasal passage and sinus.

Breathing physiology – part 3 – upper respiratory tract dynamics

The result of the above movement of air is:

- First, there is a creation of a resonance at the sphenoidal sinuses due to turbulence in the incoming swirling air flow.

- Next, the rush of air across the olfactory bulb energizes the olfactory nerves and amygdala as well as the hypothalamus-pituitary-adrenalin (HPA axis) and the immune system.

- Finally, the flow of air across the nasopharynx creates a vibrating column effect in the auditory canal.

All this results in an awareness of being alive.

There is a slight drop in temperature of the incoming air due to the venture effect, which is compensated by the warm air in the nasal cavity and sinuses. This is why there is often condensate over the bridge of the nose, which is also the reason for the nose being the coldest part of the face.

When the *yogī* equalizes the incoming and outgoing breath at the nasal cavity, the air flow gets regulated to one where turbulence is slowly minimized and then made insignificant. As a result, the main senses of touch, smell, and hearing are brought under control. When the *yogī* focuses his awareness by gazing at the tip of the nostrils sight is also brought under control. This is why the above verse 27 is so important.

Some contradictions to accepted positions:

- Availability of free will is critical for renunciation.

- The ability to control free-will in action is limited in action *(karma)* because our response is controlled by conditioning *(dharma)*.

- Increase of free will is only possible when there is control over the movement of consciousness *(citta)*.

- All efforts to control consciousness will be opposed by the sense of Self *(puruṣa or śiva)* because of fear of loss of Identity. This results in increased internal conflict, pain, and a sense of dissociation from society.

- However, this effort also increases awareness of the Self *(prajñā)*, discrimination between permanent and impermanent *(viveka)*, and dispassion *(vairāgya)*.

- Consequently, free will increases.

Lessons learned:

Sannyāsa is easier said than done. It requires effort, sacrifice, and the ability to endure pain and grief.

The transliteration and translation of chapter 5:

अर्जुन उवाच ।
संन्यासं कर्मणां कृष्ण पुनर्योगं च शंससि ।
यच्छ्रेय एतयोरेकं तन्मे ब्रूहि सुनिश्चितम् ॥ ५-१॥

Arjuna said (1) On the one hand, you praise renunciation of action, and, at the same time recommend its performance. So, tell me conclusively, between these, which is better? *(samnyāsaṃ karmaṇāṃ kṛṣṇa punaryogaṃ ca śaṃsasi ǀ yacchreya etayorekaṃ tanme brūhi suniścitam ǁ 5-1ǁ).*

श्रीभगवानुवाच ।
संन्यासः कर्मयोगश्च निःश्रेयसकरावुभौ ।
तयोस्तु कर्मसंन्यासात्कर्मयोगो विशिष्यते ॥ ५-२॥
ज्ञेयः स नित्यसंन्यासी यो न द्वेष्टि न काङ्क्षति ।
निर्द्वन्द्वो हि महाबाहो सुखं बन्धात्प्रमुच्यते ॥ ५-३॥

Śrī Kṛṣṇa said (2-3) Both renunciation and performance of action lead to the highest bliss, but of the two, renunciation of action is superior to merger with action *(samnyāsaḥ karmayogaśca niḥśreyasakarāvubhau ǀ tayostu karmasamnyāsātkarmayogo viśiṣyate ǁ 5-2ǁ).* Know this that he is a complete ascetic who neither hates nor desires, is free from opposites, truly, that person becomes free from bondage easily *(jñeyaḥ sa nityasamnyāsī yo na dveṣṭi na kāṅkṣati ǀ nirdvandvo hi mahābāho sukhaṃ bandhātpramucyate ǁ 5-3ǁ).*

साङ्ख्ययोगौ पृथग्बालाः प्रवदन्ति न पण्डिताः ।
एकमप्यास्थितः सम्यगुभयोर्विन्दते फलम् ॥ ५-४॥
यत्साङ्ख्यैः प्राप्यते स्थानं तद्योगैरपि गम्यते ।
एकं साङ्ख्यं च योगं च यः पश्यति स पश्यति ॥ ५-५॥
संन्यासस्तु महाबाहो दुःखमाप्तुमयोगतः ।
योगयुक्तो मुनिर्ब्रह्म नचिरेणाधिगच्छति ॥ ५-६॥

(4-6) The harmonization of knowledge philosophy is distinct, and only the childish speak of them, not the learned, even though when one is established, then truly fruits of both are obtained *(sāṅkhyayogau pṛthagbālāḥ pravadanti na paṇḍitāḥ ǀ ekamapyāsthitaḥ samyagubhayorvindate phalam ǁ 5-4ǁ).* The philosophical state obtained by *yogīs* is also reached when one that sees knowledge also sees action (*yatsāṅkhyaiḥ prāpyate sthānaṃ tadyogairapi gamyate । ekaṃ sāṅkhyaṃ ca yogaṃ ca yaḥ paśyati sa paśyati ॥ 5-5॥*). Renunciation is painful to obtain without implementation of yoga, but when harmonized in yoga, the ascetic quickly goes to *Brahman* (*saṃnyāsastu mahābāho duḥkhamāptumayogataḥ । yogayukto munirbrahma nacireṇādhigacchati ॥ 5-6॥*).

योगयुक्तो विशुद्धात्मा विजितात्मा जितेन्द्रियः ।

सर्वभूतात्मभूतात्मा कुर्वन्नपि न लिप्यते ॥ ५-७॥

नैव किञ्चित्करोमीति युक्तो मन्येत तत्त्ववित् ।

पश्यञ्शृण्वन्स्पृशञ्जिघ्रन्नश्नगच्छन्स्वपञ्श्वसन् ॥ ५-८॥

प्रलपन्विसृजनगृह्णन्नुन्मिषन्निमिषन्नपि ।

इन्द्रियाणीन्द्रियार्थेषु वर्तन्त इति धारयन् ॥ ५-९॥

(7-9) A purified soul is harmoniously merged and becomes a victorious soul when it has subdued the senses (*yogayukto viśuddhātmā vijitātmā jitendriyaḥ ।*), that soul which sees sentient souls in all souls when acting is also not tainted (*sarvabhūtātmabhūtātmā kurvannapi na lipyate ॥ 5-7॥*). I do not do anything, is what the *yogī* who knows the Truth should cognize even when he is seeing, hearing, touching, smelling, eating, sleeping, breathing, speaking, evacuating, holding, opening the eyes, and closing the eyes also. (*naiva kiñcitkaromīti yukto manyeta tattvavit । paśyañśarṇvanspṛśañjighrannaśnangacchansvapañśvasan ॥ 5-8॥ pralapanvisṛjangṛhṇannunmiṣannimiṣannapi ।*). In fact, his senses move separated from sense objects (*indriyāṇīndriyārtheṣu vartanta iti dhārayan ॥ 5-9॥*).

ब्रह्मण्याधाय कर्माणि सङ्गं त्यक्त्वा करोति यः ।

लिप्यते न स पापेन पद्मपत्रमिवाम्भसा ॥ ५-१०॥

कायेन मनसा बुद्ध्या केवलैरिन्द्रियैरपि ।

योगिनः कर्म कुर्वन्ति सङ्गं त्यक्त्वात्मशुद्धये ॥ ५-११॥

(10-11) He who has based his actions in the *Brahman* and who acts after abandoning all attachment (*brahmaṇyādhāya karmāṇi saṅgaṃ tyaktvā karoti yaḥ ।*), he is not tainted by consequences and is like a lotus leaf in water (*lipyate na sa pāpena padmapatramivāmbhasā ॥ 5-10॥*). The *yogī* performs action using the body, cognitive apparatus, logical reasoning, and senses; abandoning attachment and acting for purification of the Soul (*kāyena manasā buddhyā kevalairindriyairapi । yoginaḥ karma kurvanti saṅgaṃ tyaktvātmaśuddhaye ॥ 5-11॥*).

युक्तः कर्मफलं त्यक्त्वा शान्तिमाप्नोति नैष्ठिकीम् ।

अयुक्तः कामकारेण फले सक्तो निबध्यते ॥ ५-१२॥

सर्वकर्माणि मनसा संन्यस्यास्ते सुखं वशी ।

नवद्वारे पुरे देही नैव कुर्वन कारयन् ॥ ५-१३॥

(12-13) Having merged with abandonment of fruits of action, he obtains highest peace (*yuktaḥ karmaphalam tyaktvā śāntimāpnoti naiṣṭhikīm ।*). However, he that is driven by desire and clings to outcome is bound to *karma* (*ayuktaḥ kāmakāreṇa phale sakto nibadhyate ॥ 5-12॥*). So, he that has detached cognition from all action controls happiness (*sarvakarmāṇi manasā saṃnyasyāste sukhaṃ vaśī ।*), resting in the ramparts of his nine-gated city, not acting, nor causing action (*navadvāre pure dehī naiva kurvanna kārayan ॥ 5-13॥*).

न कर्तृत्वं न कर्माणि लोकस्य सृजति प्रभुः ।
न कर्मफलसंयोगं स्वभावस्तु प्रवर्तते ॥ ५-१४॥
नादत्ते कस्यचित्पापं न चैव सुकृतं विभुः ।
अज्ञानेनावृतं ज्ञानं तेन मुह्यन्ति जन्तवः ॥ ५-१५॥

(14-15) *Brahman* is neither the initiator nor the doer in the created world, also not driven by the embrace of the union of desire for fruits with inherent personality (*na kartṛtvaṃ na karmāṇi lokasya sṛjati prabhuḥ । na karmaphalasaṃyogaṃ svabhāvastu pravartate ॥ 5-14॥*). *Brahman* does not accept of anyone their demerits or even merit (*nādatte kasyacitpāpaṃ na caiva sukṛtaṃ vibhuḥ ।*), this occurs on account of ignorance shrouding knowledge in deluded people (*ajñānenāvṛtaṃ jñānaṃ tena muhyanti jantavaḥ ॥ 5-15॥*).

ज्ञानेन तु तदज्ञानं येषां नाशितमात्मनः ।
तेषामादित्यवज्ज्ञानं प्रकाशयति तत्परम् ॥ ५-१६॥
तद्बुद्धयस्तदात्मानस्तन्निष्ठास्तत्परायणाः ।
गच्छन्त्यपुनरावृत्तिं ज्ञाननिर्धूतकल्मषाः ॥ ५-१७॥

(16-17) Wisdom destroys ignorance of anyone, and the Soul shines like the Sun with highest knowledge (*jñānena tu tadajñānaṃ yeṣāṃ nāśitamātmanaḥ । teṣāmādityavajjñānaṃ prakāśayati tatparam ॥ 5-16॥*). Those with intellect absorbed in that, Soul established in that, with focus on that, with that for the goal go without return when wisdom removes all impurities (*tadbuddhayastadātmānastanniṣṭhāstatparāyaṇāḥ । gacchantyapunarāvṛttiṃ jñānanirdhūtakalmaṣāḥ ॥ 5-17॥*).

विद्याविनयसम्पन्ने ब्राह्मणे गवि हस्तिनि ।
शुनि चैव श्वपाके च पण्डिताः समदर्शिनः ॥ ५-१८॥
इहैव तैर्जितः सर्गो येषां साम्ये स्थितं मनः ।
निर्दोषं हि समं ब्रह्म तस्माद् ब्रह्मणि ते स्थिताः ॥ ५-१९॥

(18-19) Those endowed with knowledge and humility will view a Brāhmana, cow, elephant, dog, and even an outcast, and learned people with equal gaze, *(vidyāvinayasampanne brāhmaṇe gavi hastini । śuni caiva śvapāke ca paṇḍitāḥ samadarśinaḥ ॥ 5-18॥).* Thus, even they conquer creation, by which inequality is established, the cognition remains spotless, and the equal *Brahman* is therefore established in *Brahman (ihaiva tairjitaḥ sargo yeṣāṁ sāmye sthitaṁ manaḥ । nirdoṣaṁ hi samaṁ brahma tasmād brahmaṇi te sthitāḥ ॥ 5-19॥).*

न प्रहृष्येत्प्रियं प्राप्य नोद्विजेत्प्राप्य चाप्रियम् ।
स्थिरबुद्धिरसम्मूढो ब्रह्मविद् ब्रह्मणि स्थितः ॥ ५-२०॥
बाह्यस्पर्शेष्वसक्तात्मा विन्दत्यात्मनि यत्सुखम् ।
स ब्रह्मयोगयुक्तात्मा सुखमक्षयमश्नुते ॥ ५-२१॥

(20-21) Importantly, one should not rejoice at obtaining a favorable outcome, nor grieve when an unfavorable outcome *(na prahṛṣyetpriyaṁ prāpya nodvijetprāpya cāpriyam ।),* with steady intellect that is undeluded, one that has knowledge of *Brahman* get established in the *Brahman (sthirabuddhirasammūḍho brahmavid brahmaṇi sthitaḥ ॥ 5-20॥).* The detached soul, when dealing with external contacts, finds within the Self, that infinite happiness as one that has merged with the *Brahman* enjoys *(bāhyasparśeṣvasaktātmā vindatyātmani yatsukham । sa brahmayogayuktātmā sukhamakṣayamaśnute ॥ 5-21॥).*

ये हि संस्पर्शजा भोगा दुःखयोनय एव ते ।
आद्यन्तवन्तः कौन्तेय न तेषु रमते बुधः ॥ ५-२२॥
शक्नोतीहैव यः सोढुं प्राक्शरीरविमोक्षणात् ।
कामक्रोधोद्भवं वेगं स युक्तः स सुखी नरः ॥ ५-२३॥

(22-23) In fact, all outcomes born from external contact cause suffering only *(ye hi saṁsparśajā bhogā duḥkhayonaya eva te ।)* they have a beginning as well as an end, so wise people do not find delight in them *(ādyantavantaḥ kaunteya na teṣu ramate budhaḥ ॥ 5-22॥).* Anyone who can withstand before liberation from the body, impulses born of desire and anger, becomes united with *Brahman,* he is a happy man *(śaknotīhaiva yaḥ soḍhuṁ prākśarīravimokṣaṇāt । kāmakrodhodbhavaṁ vegaṁ sa yuktaḥ sa sukhī naraḥ ॥ 5-23॥).*

योऽन्तःसुखोऽन्तरारामस्तथान्तज्योतिरेव यः ।
स योगी ब्रह्मनिर्वाणं ब्रह्मभूतोऽधिगच्छति ॥ ५-२४॥
लभन्ते ब्रह्मनिर्वाणमृषयः क्षीणकल्मषाः ।
छिन्नद्वैधा यतात्मानः सर्वभूतहिते रताः ॥ ५-२५॥
कामक्रोधवियुक्तानां यतीनां यतचेतसाम् ।
अभितो ब्रह्मनिर्वाणं वर्तते विदितात्मनाम् ॥ ५-२६॥

(24-26) Who finds happiness within, even who has internal pleasure from illumination from *Brahman,* that *yogī* attains absolute freedom and merges with *Brahman (yo'ntaḥsukho'ntarārāmastathāntarjyotireva yaḥ ı sa yogī brahmanirvāṇaṃ brahmabhūto'dhigacchati ıı 5-24ıı). ṛṣis* (seers) achieve absolute freedom due to cleaning of impurities, cutting of duality, rejoicing in the welfare of all beings *(labhante brahmanirvāṇamṛṣayaḥ kṣīṇakalmaṣāḥ ı chinnadvaidhā yatātmānaḥ sarvabhūtahite ratāḥ ıı 5-25ıı).* Detached from desire and anger, ascetics control their consciousness in all situations *(abhitaḥ* = on all sides) and are evolved souls who exist in absolute freedom *(kāmakrodhaviyuktānāṃ yatīnāṃ yatacetasām ı abhito brahmanirvāṇaṃ vartate viditātmanām ıı 5-26ıı).*

स्पर्शान्कृत्वा बहिर्बाह्यांश्चक्षुश्चैवान्तरे भ्रुवोः ।

प्राणापानौ समौ कृत्वा नासाभ्यन्तरचारिणौ ॥ ५-२७॥

यतेन्द्रियमनोबुद्धिर्मुनिर्मोक्षपरायणः ।

विगतेच्छाभयक्रोधो यः सदा मुक्त एव सः ॥ ५-२८॥

भोक्तारं यज्ञतपसां सर्वलोकमहेश्वरम् ।

सुहृदं सर्वभूतानां ज्ञात्वा मां शान्तिमृच्छति ॥ ५-२९॥

(27-29) Excluding external stimuli outside, bring your gaze inside between the eyebrows *(sparśānkṛtvā bahirbāhyāṃścakṣuścaivāntare bhruvoḥ ı).* Then, equalize inhalation and exhalation, moving it within the nostrils *(prāṇāpānau samau kṛtvā nāsābhyantaracāriṇau ıı 5-27ıı).* With the senses, cognition and logical apparatus of the sage are focused on liberation, desire, fear, anger, leave, and he forever and truly becomes free *(yatendriyamanobuddhirmunirmokṣaparāyaṇaḥ ı vigatecchābhayakrodho yaḥ sadā mukta eva saḥ ıı 5-28ıı).* He enjoys fruits of his austerity and becomes Lord of all worlds who is affectionate to all creation and comes to me in peace *(bhoktāraṃ yajñatapasāṃ sarvalokamaheśvaram ı suhṛdaṃ sarvabhūtānāṃ jñātvā māṃ śāntimṛcchati ıı 5-29ıı).*

◆——— • ● ◆ ● • ——— ◆

Chapter 6

Dhyāna-yoga (yoga of meditation) [1]

Introduction

- Our journey into *Śrīmad-bhagavad-gītā* begin in chapter 1 with delusion and confusion. In chapter 2, the source, sustenance, and motility of existence, *Brahman,* is explained. Thereafter, in chapters 3, 4, and 5, Śrī Kṛṣṇa explains action, knowledge of action, and renunciation of action, respectively.

- In this chapter, *dhyāna-yoga,* Śrī Kṛṣṇa closes a critical gap, a tool that cleans the student's Self internally *(ātmaśuddhye).*

- But first, let us review components of any action:

  o There are two types of action – we act without stimulus/input or respond to incoming stimulus!

  o When we act without stimulus, we are driven by an internal desire for an outcome. This action is a manifestation of our sense of self-worth *(asmitā).*

  o Whether we respond or react to stimulus, in addition to manifestation of self-worth, we also seek to protect our sense of identity *(puruṣa).*

  o Both action and reaction are driven by fear *(tamas)* or desire *(rajas)* of loss of self-worth *(asmitā)* and identity *(puruṣa).*

  o Importantly, any activity *(karma),* by itself is inanimate. It gets texture from two factors - desire for outcome, which drives motivation to perform *(saṅkalpa),* and expectation of result or fruits of action *(karmaphala),* which results in fear of outcome and duality (like-dislike, good-bad-right-wrong etc.) and the feeling of being the doer *(ahaṅkāra).*

---

[1]https://www.bhagavad-gita.org/Gita/chapter-06.html

- The action process...

  o There must be someone who initiates action, owns it, and performs it.

  o This is the doer or *(kartṛ)*.

  o Next, the doer needs a reason *(kāraṇa)*. Also, this is called causation, or reason for performing the action.

  o The reason needs to transform into motivation or application of will *(saṅkalpa)* so that action *(karma)* may be initiated and completed.

  o Finally, from effort comes result *(karmaphala)*.

- Everything in action is about whether we control it or not. The ability to control action comes from free will, but to what extent is free will actually free? How can we increase the span of free will?

Acting without stimulus, *yajna*, and *saṅkalpa*, (verse 1-3)

- Firstly, all action *(karma)* arises from motivation *(saṅkalpa)*.

- Next, once a cause is established, then effort/work *(karma)* must be applied to achieve the result.

- Almost always, sanctioned actions also involve personal sacrifice or *yajña*. For example, a parent looking after his or her child must sacrifice time, energy, and resources. A student, to get good marks, must sacrifice time and effort to learn.

- However, it is important to remember that motivation or desire *(icchā)* will result in expectation of outcome *(karmaphala)*. Parents begin to have expectations of a child, and students who have studied hard expect good marks.

- As a result, self-worth *(asmitā)* becomes attached to the outcome because once expectations get set, self-worth is dependent on success and good feedback. For instance, students get anxious before competitive exams and before results are announced because of what the outcome means to them.

- Importantly, quality of will *(saṅkalpa)* includes capability, resources, and other factors which determine quality of action and outcome. For example, a person wanting to pass a competitive exam will need to have the ability as well as will for sustained effort, resources to buy or borrow study material, and build capability to write the exam, etc.

- Additionally, self-worth *(asmitā)* determines the quantum of agitation when action is performed. For example, when we are confident of what we are doing, there is minimal agitation. However, when we are afraid or unsure of our actions, or afraid of an adverse outcome, there is enormous stress, fear, and agitation.

Thus, one can see that free will is always clouded by factors, such as expectations *(karmaphala)*, desire *(kāma)*, frustration with obstacles, personality issues, anxieties, etc.

Reacting to stimulus

Reaction to stimulus has two parts, namely, primary response and secondary response.

Primary response – When we receive stimulus, first, we assess the risk. This is done by the amygdala, a small organ which is part of the limbic system in the brain[2]. Here, the amygdala, which is a storehouse of experiences, uses prior conditioning *(dharma)* to trigger a fight-or-flight response. This

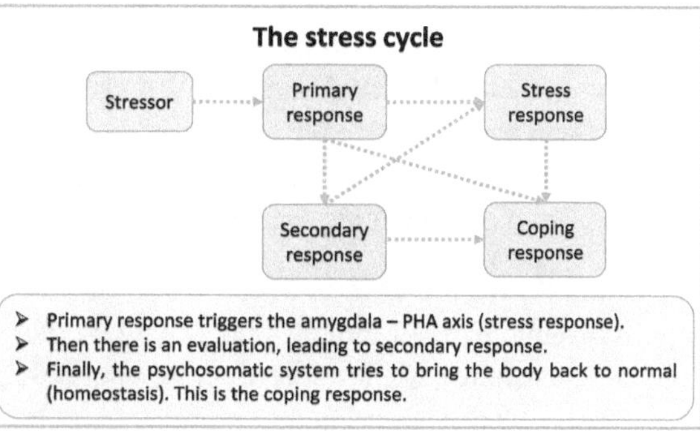

6.1 - the stress cycle

reaction is mostly instinctive because of the way the amygdala is designed and programmed. There is awareness *(prajñā)*, but the rational brain is mostly hijacked in any instinctive response.

Secondary response – depending on the strength of the primary response, the cognitive, memory, and intellectual systems of our rational brain get activated. Here again, conditioning *(dharma)* determines the strength and quality of response.

Dharma is conditioning

Before examining our reaction to stimulus, let us review our system capability for response. Like computers, we have hardware and software. The hardware is our DNA, health, and age. These determine our ability to handle information, memory, speed of processing information,

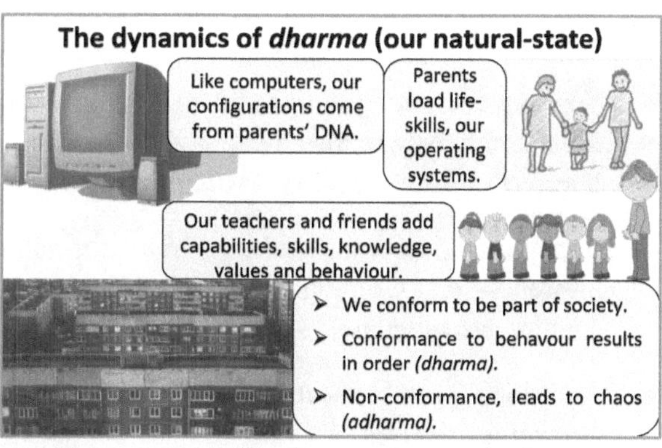

6.2 - *Dharma* is the anchor of our response to stimulus

and quality of our sensory apparatus. Culture, background, education, and experience, which form our operating system, become the software. The combination of hardware and software

---

[2]https://www.simplypsychology.org/amygdala.html

forms our conditioning or natural state, the envelope of existence in which we are most comfortable. This is *dharma*.

How can we control our actions and reactions? The fact is that, like computers, our ability to act or react is mostly set by our *dharma* and the network we are connected to. This means that we are also impacted by the *dharma* of those we interact with and the environment we are in at the time. So, *dharma* also includes *dharma* of the environment where decisions are made.

Dharma, to a large extent is governed by our *prārabdha-karma* (debt that has come up for repayment). *Prārabdha-karma* is that debt which has come up for repayment, or it can also be one where we are the creditors, where others owe us. Additionally, when we exert our will to control outcomes, we create *karma,* thus building debit and credit into our accounts, which brings us back into the cycle of repayment.

For example, we are born to specific sets of parents. We go to specific schools in our environment, even though there may be other options. We like and bond with specific classmates, some more than others. We like certain subjects and excel in specific sports. Our aptitude in computers, singing or painting come to us at birth. We take up certain professions, marry specific people, and have children that are unique to us. This is on account of debt or *prārabdha-karma*.

The need to control outcomes and create *karma* can come from fear of impact on self-worth as well as conditioning *(dharma),* embedded desire arising from *prārabdha-karma,* also known as *vāsanā,* low self-worth *(asmitā),* fear of failure, expectation loss, and opinion of others, all of which can be clubbed under the feeling of being the doer *(ahaṅkāra),* and loss of awareness *(prajñā).*

Karma and *dharma* impact all of us, and that's why it is universal *(sanātana).*

Application of will *(saṅkalpa)*

- Topping everything is the realization that we are our best friend or worst enemy. So, the only way to improve our abilities is by using our awareness *(prajñā)* to improve our individuality *(svatantra).*

- Importantly, upon determining course of action, the degree of calmness and awareness that we retain (self-control) when acting determines the quality of activity and outcome.

- Additionally, if expectation or desire of outcome is removed, then will *(saṅkalpa)* reduces in value because the action is performed for itself and not personal gain, making it a sacrifice *(yajña).* This means that the feeling of being the doer *(ahaṅkāra)* is removed.

- Also, when one removes expectation of outcome, fear is removed, and self-worth *(asmitā)* remains unaffected/undamaged.

- Importantly, when a person acts with reduced passion, personalities are separated from the action. Consequently, everyone's sense of self-worth is protected from turbulence, and the effort becomes peaceful and beneficial to everyone.

- Also, when *ahaṅkāra* (the feeling of being the doer) is removed from the action itself, there is more focus on perfection of effort and stability of outcome.

- Consequently, one who aspires to *sannyāsa* and to be a *yogī* should renounce all will *(saṅkalpa)* and perform action as duty, without seeking any fruits from his actions.

- However, the *yogī* must not sacrifice logic or method. This is because, without proper process or system adherence, the outcome is bound to be sub-optimal. For example, when preparing for an exam, the right approach is to try and dissociate ourselves from the outcome. However, if the preparation is without proper effort or systematic and sustained study, then there can be no hope of success, even if we were to try and dissociate ourselves from the outcome.

- Obviously, to increase the strength of will and reduce the impact of illusion *(māyā)* is not easy and requires sustained effort. The good news is that once a person reaches this stage of perfection *(siddhapuruṣa),* then the person remains unaffected by any or all turbulence that he encounters and remains calm in any situation.

Examples

- As children, we compete at school. Our capabilities get tested and our abilities emerge when we compete. However, competing can be stressful. So, when competing in a game, if we are asked to enjoy the game rather than on victory, then our ability to be in harmony with ourselves, use our capabilities to the fullest, and enjoy the game becomes very high.

- As professionals, competition can become very toxic, as the rat race can often mean employment or loss of it. So, the stakes increase dramatically, along with stress levels. In such circumstances, keeping a cool, level head can be difficult. What most people don't realize is that backing off from competition reduces stress and allows us to work in a sustained and sensible manner without increasing perception of threat with our co-workers. Consequently, our output improves, and, as results show, rewards follow.

- As managers or supervisors, the problem of using will and detaching self-worth from outcome becomes even more difficult. Often, team outcomes determine existence and health of the team as well as managers. Also, like any team, members come with different skill sets, motivations, personalities, and maturity levels. Thus, keeping all team members aligned to a goal without personalities becoming involved is crucial to success. Conversely, the danger of removing personalities could result in passion being destroyed. Hence, leadership skills of any manager require him to diffuse the impact of success or failure without affecting morale of the team. Often, this means stepping back from the action, reducing his or her own drive, setting goals and monitoring performance, and wisely distributing rewards and punishment so that the team focuses and functions effectively. As a result, the anxieties of reaching or failing to achieve overall targets do not affect present performance, and the team functions effectively.

Increasing strength of one's will (verse 11-17)

- Firstly, in order to rise in the practice of *yoga,* one should reduce material contact or reduce their impact on cognition *(manas).* The fact is, all stimuli come in through the senses. So, when the number of sources of stimuli increase, our ability to pay sufficient attention to each point of stimulus reduces commensurately. For example, if we are studying for an exam in front of the TV while the rest of the family are eating chocolate, cake or chips, the ability to pay attention to studies will reduce dramatically.

- Secondly, to reduce attachment towards stimuli, view all entities as having a soul *(ātman)* which is equal to our own *(sama-dṛṣṭi).* When we do this, our ability to relate to the object without getting overwhelmed by its significance to us improves. For example, when studying for an exam or preparing a project report, if we were to view the exam or project as a soul which is equal to our own, we stop giving it more weightage or less weightage that we ordinarily would have. While this does not reduce the importance of the exam, it brings equanimity to our transactions and allows balanced reactions.

- Thirdly, a key aspect of managing matters of the Soul *(ātman)* is to recognize that we are "our best friend or worst enemy". Additionally, control of the Soul *(ātman)* is about controlling what happens to the Soul when we are exposed to stimulus, good or bad. Consequently, when we decode the stimulus with full awareness *(prajñā),* process the information without passion, personalities or assigned value *(ahaṅkāra),* focus on the outcome, and remove fear, we begin to control the process as well as the outcome.

- As a result, the Soul begins to harmonize towards a natural state of peace. Of course, this requires practice, but when we do it consciously (control the *citta* or consciousness), then free will and self-reliance increase, and there is a deeper anchor in the state of peace.

- Lastly, how do we know that we are on the right track? When we are at peace or to use a colloquial term "feel cool" or positive about everything, then we know that we are in control.

Haṭha Yoga Pradīpikā **(chapter 1, verse 10 - 16) on** *dhyāna* **(meditation)**

Haṭha-yoga protects the *yogī* from pain like a house and supports his efforts like a tortoise. In fact, the yoga practitioner should keep the knowledge secret.

He should practice in a small room, situated in an isolated place, free from stones, fire, and water or disturbances of any kind and governed in a *dhārmic* manner (meaning all citizens conform to the rule of law and live in peace).

Also, the room should have a small door, level, be free from holes and hollows, be neither too high or low, be well plastered with cow dung, and be free from dirt, filth, and insects. Outside, there should be a shaded area with raised seat with a well, enclosed in a compound.

Finally, the *yogī* should rid himself of anxiety and then begin the practice of Hatha Yoga as instructed by his *guru*.

(verse 15) Six virtues impede development in *Haṭha-yoga* – they are over-eating, excessive exertion, excessive talking, excessive adherence to rules, company of humans, and unsteadiness.

(verse 16) Six habits bring success – zeal, boldness of drive and willingness to start, patience, perseverance, ability to discriminate, clarity of purpose, and aloofness.

How should one meditate? (verse 11-17)

- Firstly, the practitioner should rely only on himself for all improvements, for each person is his own best friend or worst enemy.

- Secondly, the *yogī* should be steady and without agitation within. This happens when one views all creation equally, without assigning differential personal value (I want this, I hate this, I don't like that person). Also, this includes animate and inanimate objects, friends and foes, relatives, and saints.

- Additionally, this means that one should be calm and peaceful when experiencing opposites such as cold/heat, pleasure/pain, or honor/dishonor.

- Undoubtedly, the most important requirement for a serious practitioner is finding a country or region *(deśa)* which is well administered. This ensures that there are no disturbances and turbulences in the surroundings, there is law and order, and, as a result, the practice of meditation is undisturbed.

- An important self-control requirement is celibacy *(brahmacaryam)*. What is celibacy in *yoga?* Celibacy in *yoga* can be termed as control over seminal fluid discharge. Why? Seminal fluids have an ingredient called *ojas* which acts like a sheath over the *nāḍi* (channels through which *prāṇa* flows). Depletion of *ojas* leads to musculo-skeletal weakness and stressed nerves, which impedes concentration in meditation. Also, practice of celibacy *(brahmacaryam)* is an exercise in self-control. Ideally, complete stoppage of sexual activity is advised, but if that is not possible, then it must be kept under control.

- Next, the *yogī* should sit in a clean place which is neither high nor low, over a bed of cloth and *kuśa*. So, why is the seat important? Why should it be neither too high nor too low?

  - When we sit too high or low, we never get the right perspective of our environment, which results in a perceptual feeling of discomfort.

  - When we sit in a place where we are unable to view our surroundings, we become insecure and uncomfortable.

For example:

When travelling, most of us prefer facing the direction of travel, because we get to see where we are going and what's coming. Similarly, when we are sitting in the rear seat of a car, we prefer a place from where we can see the road and where we are going. Lastly, at home, we each have a preferred seat, mostly one which gives us maximum view of our surroundings, those that give us security, where we can see threat and can control outcomes.

- Then, the practitioner should control the sensory organs *(indriyas)* and cognitive apparatus *(manas)* by turning the consciousness *(citta)* inward. After this, the *yogī* should try and hold his *(manas)* steady to a single point *(ekāgra)* to purify the awareness of the Self *(prajñā)*.

- Lastly, the *yogī* should hold his body, head, and neck in a balanced *(sama)* position and gaze at the tip of the nose *(nāsikāgra)*.

- Additionally, he should avoid getting distracted by avoiding outside contact during the practice.

Progress in meditation (verse 18-20)

- Slowly, the practitioner will be able to slow down the speed with which the consciousness *(citta)* reaches out to objects for affirmation of existence, increasing free will.

- When this happens, the consciousness becomes steady like a lamp in a windless room. In fact, one may compare the breeze in a room to external disturbances and the lamp to the reaction of the consciousness to those disturbances.

- When the consciousness *(citta)* is quietened, it stops seeking outside and looks at its own Self or Soul *(ātman)* for sustenance. Then, the consciousness slowly merges *(yoga)* with its own Self *(ātman)*. When this happens and the consciousness is no longer agitating or looking for sustenance, it ceases to operate the sensory organs (*indriyas*) and cognitive apparatus *(manas)*.

- Finally, this results in what is called *nirvikalpa-samādhi* or changeless merger, the final state of *yoga*.

Grief in yoga (verse 21-25)

- When the *yogī* begins to slow down the movement of the consciousness, it turns inwards towards the Soul *(ātman)* for sustenance. When this happens, a lot of the suppressed and repressed emotions, desires, and memories are released.

- Consequently, there is experience of great loss, pain, and grief because the memory remembers negative stimuli more starkly than positive ones, since they have been the source of lessons in self-preservation and sustenance.

- How does this happen? Importantly, let us look at how *māyā* (illusion or farce) works:

    o Each of us is unique, on account of our DNA, upbringing, schools, friends, peers, society, and country; this is our *svadharma* (self + conditioning).

    o This instils in us a behavior of conformance management called *dharma*.

    o *Dharma* is that natural state where we are at peace with ourselves and our surroundings. Also, *dharma* is the basis on which we decide like-dislike, good-bad, right-wrong, etc., and, therefore, our actions *(karma)*.

    o Consequently, we apply *dharma* to all our transactions and relationships.

    o As a result, we experience conflict between our *dharma* and the *dharma* of others, which results in damaged or ruptured relationships.

    o This causes grief and pain which needs to be reconciled and healed.

    o Unfortunately, when we are actively engaged with our environment, the consciousness *(citta)* is outward looking and busy, so the impact of this damage is not noticed.

- But when the *citta* (consciousness) slows down and looks at the Self *(ātman),* all the suppressed experiences find a space for self-expression and demand resolution.

- So, the *asmitā* experiences grief and pain based on missed opportunities, blurred images, repressed desires, and unfulfilled expectations.

- Also, depending on the importance of the object, there is an additional weightage of sentiment *(bhāva)* which either amplifies or reduces the experience of grief and pain. With effort, there is reconciliation. For example, a misunderstanding with our parents or children, if it has severe consequences, is likely to generate more grief than a disagreement with a boss, friend, or neighbor. So, the degree depends on proximity, bond, relationship, expectation, and outcome.

- However, overcoming this stage is critical because a turbulent or distracted consciousness *(citta)* will not become steady unless the experience is reconciled.

Agitation in meditation

- Competence in meditation comes with psychosomatic balance. The starting point is ensuring good health because agitation occurs when the homeostatic balance is disturbed. Homeostasis is that aspect of the body whereby the operating conditions of the body are within established parameters, such as temperature, blood pressure, hemoglobin, etc., along with other chemical parameters such as potassium, iron, calcium, etc., and hormonal balance. When all these parameters are in balance, the person feels comfortable, stable, and at peace.

- Next, imbalance occurs when the person experiences the need to change. Since change requires readjustment, it creates disruption and insecurity, and the person gets stressed. Thus, there is pressure on the person's self-esteem *(asmitā)* as the psyche seeks to establish understanding and control over the situation.

- Consequently, the consciousness continuously seeks confirmation of existence from an external entity, especially one that it trusts.

- Additionally, during meditation, homeostasis balance is disturbed when the consciousness *(citta),* after turning inwards, begins to experience old suppressed and repressed baggage that comes out and seek expression in the form of loss, pain, and grief. Obviously, this will disturb any meditation practice.

- Lastly, there is the material nature of consciousness *(citta)* itself that hampers meditation.

- By nature, the sense of self-worth *(asmitā)* seeks expression and establishes bonds. For a *yogī,* this becomes a major impediment because the cognitive apparatus keeps moving from one entity to another and does not allow steady focus *(ekāgratā).*

- Hence, constant cleaning and calming of the soul *(ātmaśuddhaye)* is very important. Particularly, old baggage needs to be discarded, pain and grief reconciled, and disturbances and stains on the soul *(ātman)* need to be continuously cleaned. One needs to learn how to dump the past, stop anticipating the future, and live in the present.

- Finally, the *yogī* should try to live in solitude to subdue internal agitations until he begins to achieve steady and constant awareness of the Self *(sthithaprajñā).*

Final aspects of meditation and solutions

- Firstly, the yoga of equanimity is difficult because the cognitive apparatus *(manas)* keeps shifting *(cancala),* it is like the wind - turbulent *(pramāthi),* strong *(balavat),* and unyielding to control *(dṛḍha).* Additionally, it is restless *(cancalatvat),* and this acts as an impediment to achieving the state of steadiness *(sthiti-sthira)* (verse 26-40).

- Doubtlessly, the cognitive apparatus is difficult to control on account of the nature of consciousness and the fact that it continuously seeks external and internal verification of its own existence. However, with practice and dispassion *(vairāgya),* this control can be exerted.

Arjuna asks – What happens to one who is dedicated but whose cognitive apparatus wanders? Does he face destruction, the *yogī* who has not achieved perfection? (verse 37-39)

Śrī Kṛṣṇa says – Firstly, no destruction can come to him that acts in good faith. In fact, what happens is that such a person is reborn into a pure and prosperous surrounding or into a family of enlightened *yogīs* where he can continue where he left off. Thereafter, when intent and effort are employed in a dedicated manner, the practitioner will reach liberation over time (verse 41 onwards).

In fact, the *yogī* is superior to ascetics, philosophers, intellectuals, and men of action. So, one must aspire to be a *yogī,* one that is completely anchored in the source *(Brahman).*

Some practical tips on meditation [3]

- First, sit in a secluded place. Ensure that the place is one where you can go to regularly and has a pleasant atmosphere. Also, the temperature in the room should be conducive for long practice *(sādhanā).*

---

[3]https://schoolofyoga.in/yoga-concept/meditation-classical-yoga-pratyahara

- Next, sit on a chair or on the floor. Floor postures hold the body more firmly, which is preferred.

- Lastly, sit in a comfortable pose. *Padmāsana, sukhāsana* or *vajrāsana* are preferred, but it is possible that there is discomfort initially. If this happens, start with one of the above *āsanas* and re-seat to a comfortable posture for the remainder of the meditation period. Over time, one pose will become the preferred pose, and the body will fall naturally into it. But the important point to remember is that the spinal curvature must be naturally erect, and the perineum, the areas between the anus and the genitals, below the coccyx, which is the seat of the *mūlādhāra-cakra,* must be stable.

- Next, relax the body using auto-suggestion (suggestive commands given by the person to himself or herself). Start from the top of the head and slowly relax each part. Also, try to break the command into specific locations. For example; instead of saying "relax the brain", say "relax the front of the brain, relax the left side, relax the right side, relax the back, etc..." Consequently, this will lead to quicker and more effective relaxation.

- Relax completely. Remember that relaxation becomes deeper with practice.

- In fact, when the body has relaxed completely, it will be noticed that breathing becomes shallow and even. Observe the breathing. Importantly, watch the interval between *pūraka* (inhalation) and *recaka* (exhalation), and vice-versa. This is *kumbhaka.* Here, there is a minuscule period of stillness where the breath crosses over from inhalation to exhalation, and vice-versa. Focus on this emptiness. Try to extend the stillness, even when breathing restarts. Also, try to keep the breathing even and without ripples or agitation.

- Stay in this position for around 10-20 minutes. Also, do not practice more than once or twice a day or for longer periods unless you are interested in deeper spiritual investigation.

Some tips on reducing distraction

- First, to avoid distraction, reduce interaction with people. Additionally, this includes social media. So, if you are active in groups, slowly reduce your activity. As a result, you will have less disturbances, because you will think less about how you wish to interact.

- Second, reduce watching TV. If you are addicted to serial binging, slowly reduce the frequency, and finally stop. Rightfully, the TV is called an "idiot box", it makes an idiot out of the viewer.

- Next, reduce your exposure to news. Most of the news is sensationalized, and you have no control over the outcome anyway.

- Lastly, reduce speaking. In fact, speak only when you know that you can add value or make a difference. Try to increase the silence in speech to silence within and peace all-around.

Lessons learned:

In chapter 6, Śrī Kṛṣṇa teaches a person how to increase free will, a state where action *(karma)* does not result in creation of debt *(ṛṇa).*

- Ability to control free will is limited because our response *(karma)* is controlled by conditioning *(dharma).*

- Increase of free will is only possible when there is control over movement of consciousness *(citta).* Then, both primary and secondary responses are controlled and hijacked by the amygdala of responses is reduced.

- However, all efforts to control consciousness will be opposed by the sense of Self/identity *(puruṣa* or *śiva)* because of fear of loss of self-worth *(asmitā).* This results in increased internal conflict, pain, and a sense of dissociation from society as one tries to increase the strength of free will over instinct.

- However, effort to increase free will also increase awareness of the Self *(jñāna),* discrimination between permanent and impermanent *(viveka),* and dispassion *(vairāgya).*

- As awareness *(prajñā)* and understanding one's own natural state or conditioning *(dharma)* increases, the *yogī* is able to differentiate one's own actions from sanctioned actions (actions that are performed due to selfish interests or result in chaos or loss of peace *(adharma)),* and remain in equilibrium.

- But, when performing sanctioned actions, one must understand the correct process, use correct tools and resources, and communicate adequately to all concerned in the right manner if the sanctioned action is to deliver the desired result, without creating chaos/turbulence.

- Lastly, one should learn to control expectations, accept the outcome with equanimity, and avoid duality, so that the internal state of peace is retained.

- In order to increase free will and increase awareness *(prajñā),* one must practice "union by meditation" *(dhyāna-yoga).* This will bring greater response control, as fear, anxiety, desire, or expectation can be calibrated or controlled more easily.

- Meditation is an exercise of increasing free will by control of the consciousness *(citta).* In fact, Sage Patanjali defines *yoga* as *"citta-vṛtti-nirodha"* in Patanjali Yoga Sutra, which roughly translates to "stopping the consciousness from functioning". Though the above state is clearly *samādhi* or final merger state, there are multiple intermediate states that the consciousness must transcend.

- *Dhyāna-yoga* is easier said than done. It requires steady effort, sacrificing of desire, and the ability to endure pain, grief, and failure. The stages that a *yogī* moves in are:

  o *Kṣipta* – scattered, where the consciousness is multi-tasking and distracted. There is poor control of the individual over free will.

  o *Mūḍha* – idiotic/delusional, where the consciousness engages activity inappropriate to the situation and moment.

  o *Vikṣipta* – inattention, where the consciousness does not adhere to any object but keeps vacillating.

  o *Ekāgra* – single point focus, where the consciousness is focused at a particular point. There is considerable free will, depending on the ability to sustain focus.

  o *Niruddha* – stopped, the consciousness does not respond. There is complete awareness *(prajñā)* of a steady consciousness. This state is *sthita-prajñā* or steady awareness.

The transliteration and translation of chapter 6 follows:

श्रीभगवानुवाच ।

अनाश्रितः कर्मफलं कार्यं कर्म करोति यः ।a

स सन्न्यासी च योगी च न निरग्निर्न चाक्रियः ॥ ६-१॥

यं सन्न्यासमिति प्राहुर्योगं तं विद्धि पाण्डव ।

न ह्यसंन्यस्तसङ्कल्पो योगी भवति कश्चन ॥ ६-२॥

आरुरुक्षोर्मुनेर्योगं कर्म कारणमुच्यते ।

योगारूढस्य तस्यैव शमः कारणमुच्यते ॥ ६-३॥

Śrī Kṛṣṇa said (1-3) Anyone who performs sanctioned action *(karma)* and is disengaged from the fruits of action *(anāśritaḥ karmaphalam kāryam karma karoti yaḥ ।)*, he is a *sannyāsin* (ascetic) and *yogī*, not he that neither acts, not performs without a sacrificial fire *(sa sannyāsī ca yogī ca na niragnirna cākriyaḥ ॥ 6-1॥)*. However, verily know that renunciation that they call *yoga* cannot be achieved by anyone without renunciation of *saṅkalpa (yam sannyāsamiti prāhuryogam tam viddhi pāṇḍava । na hyasamnyastasaṅkalpo yogī bhavati kaścana ॥ 6-2॥)*. It is said that saints desirous of advancing must harmonize action with motivation *(ārurukṣormuneryogam karma kāraṇamucyate ।)*. In fact, it is said that even those who have achieved complete harmony are those who have brought calmness to their reason for action *(yogārūḍhasya tasyaiva śamaḥ kāraṇamucyate ॥ 6-3॥)*.

यदा हि नेन्द्रियार्थेषु न कर्मस्वनुषज्जते ।
सर्वसङ्कल्पसंन्यासी योगारूढस्तदोच्यते ॥ ६-४॥
उद्धरेदात्मनात्मानं नात्मानमवसादयेत् ।
आत्मैव ह्यात्मनो बन्धुरात्मैव रिपुरात्मनः ॥ ६-५॥
बन्धुरात्मात्मनस्तस्य येनात्मैवात्मना जितः ।
अनात्मनस्तु शत्रुत्वे वर्तेतात्मैव शत्रुवत् ॥ ६-६॥

(4-6) Also, it is said that when one has risen in yoga, then there is no clinging to sense-objects or actions, and there is detachment from all drive of the will (*yadā hi nendriyārtheṣu na karmasvanuṣajjate । sarvasaṅkalpasaṃnyāsī yogārūḍhastadocyate ॥ 6-4॥*). So, elevate the Soul by the Soul itself; do not allow the Soul to drop in performance (*uddharedātmanātmānaṃ nātmānamavasādayet ।*), for the Soul, in truth, its only associate and the only adversary of the Soul is itself (*ātmaiva hyātmano bandhurātmaiva ripurātmanaḥ ॥ 6-5॥*). The Soul becomes a relative when Soul is conquered by the Soul *(bandhurātmātmanastasya yenātmaivātmanā jitaḥ ।); however, the Soul of the unconquered Soul will be like an enemy until it is conquered by the Soul (*anātmanastu śatrutve vartetātmaiva śatruvat ॥ 6-6॥*).

जितात्मनः प्रशान्तस्य परमात्मा समाहितः ।
शीतोष्णसुखदुःखेषु तथा मानापमानयोः ॥ ६-७॥
ज्ञानविज्ञानतृप्तात्मा कूटस्थो विजितेन्द्रियः ।
युक्त इत्युच्यते योगी समलोष्टाश्मकाञ्चनः ॥ ६-८॥

(7-8) The self-controlled, tranquil, Supreme Soul is equipoised in cold/heat, happiness, or sadness as well as honor and dishonor *(jitātmanaḥ praśāntasya paramātmā samāhitaḥ । śītoṣṇasukhaduḥkheṣu tathā mānāpamānayoḥ ॥ 6-7॥)*. It is said that the soul which is secure in the knowledge of the Self and surrounding has attained unshakable victory over the senses, and harmonized itself, that *yogī* views everything as gold *(jñānavijñānatṛptātmā kūṭastho vijitendriyaḥ । yukta ityucyate yogī samaloṣṭāśmakāñcanaḥ ॥ 6-8॥)*.

सुहृन्मित्रार्युदासीनमध्यस्थद्वेष्यबन्धुषु ।
साधुष्वपि च पापेषु समबुद्धिर्विशिष्यते ॥ ६-९॥
योगी युञ्जीत सततमात्मानं रहसि स्थितः ।
एकाकी यतचित्तात्मा निराशीरपरिग्रहः ॥ ६-१०॥

(9-10) One who is always in a state of undisturbed intellect with friends, allies, enemies, those that are sad, lawyers, the odious, relatives, mendicants, or sinners always excels *(suhṛnmitrāryudāsīnamadhyasthadveṣyabandhuṣu । sādhuṣvapi ca pāpeṣu samabuddhirviśiṣyate ॥ 6-9॥*). Let the *yogī*, in solitude, maintain a constant and steady Soul (*yogī yuñjīta satatamātmānaṃ rahasi sthitaḥ ।*) alone, with a Soul whose consciousness has no hope and free from greed (*ekākī yatacittātmā nirāśīraparigrahaḥ ॥ 6-10॥*).

शुचौ देशे प्रतिष्ठाप्य स्थिरमासनमात्मनः ।
नात्युच्छ्रितं नातिनीचं चैलाजिनकुशोत्तरम् ॥ ६-११॥
तत्रैकाग्रं मनः कृत्वा यतचित्तेन्द्रियक्रियः ।
उपविश्यासने युञ्ज्याद्योगमात्मविशुद्धये ॥ ६-१२॥
समं कायशिरोग्रीवं धारयन्नचलं स्थिरः ।
सम्प्रेक्ष्य नासिकाग्रं स्वं दिशश्चानवलोकयन् ॥ ६-१३॥

(11-13) In a pure country, establish a firm seat that is neither very high nor very low, for the Self, of cloth, antelope skin, kusha grass, one over the other (*śucau deśe pratiṣṭhāpya sthiramāsanamātmanaḥ । nātyucchritaṃ nātinīcaṃ cailājinakuśottaram ॥ 6-11॥*). There, with a single pointed cognition, bring consciousness and senses under control, being seated in *āsana,* let him practice *yoga* cognition for purification of the Soul (*tatraikāgraṃ manaḥ kṛtvā yatacittendriyakriyaḥ । upaviśyāsane yuñjyādyogamātmaviśuddhaye ॥ 6-12॥*). Then, holding body, head, and neck exactly still, gaze at the tip of own nose, and don't look around (*samaṃ kāyaśirogrīvaṃ dhārayannacalaṃ sthiraḥ । samprekṣya nāsikāgraṃ svaṃ diśaścānavalokayan ॥ 6-13॥*).

प्रशान्तात्मा विगतभीर्ब्रह्मचारिव्रते स्थितः ।
मनः संयम्य मच्चित्तो युक्त आसीत मत्परः ॥ ६-१४॥
युञ्जन्नेवं सदात्मानं योगी नियतमानसः ।
शान्तिं निर्वाणपरमां मत्संस्थामधिगच्छति ॥ ६-१५॥

(14-15) The fearless serene Soul that has taken the vows of celibacy, has stable cognition, with a consciousness that is united with me, as the final goal (*praśāntātmā vigatabhīrbrahmacārivrate sthitaḥ । manaḥ saṃyamya maccitto yukta āsīta matparaḥ ॥ 6-14॥*). Thus, the ever-balanced peaceful Soul of the *yogī*, with controlled cognition, attains primordial absolute liberation at my abode (*yuñjannevaṃ sadātmānaṃ yogī niyatamānasaḥ । śāntiṃ nirvāṇaparamāṃ matsaṃsthāmadhigacchati ॥ 6-15॥*),

नात्यश्नतस्तु योगोऽस्ति न चैकान्तमनश्नतः ।
न चातिस्वप्नशीलस्य जाग्रतो नैव चार्जुन ॥ ६-१६॥
युक्ताहारविहारस्य युक्तचेष्टस्य कर्मसु ।
युक्तस्वप्नावबोधस्य योगो भवति दुःखहा ॥ ६-१७॥

(16-17) The *yogī* is one that does not overeat, not, not eat at all, he should not dream too much, nor should he be excessively engaged in activity *(nātyaśnatastu yogo'sti na caikāntamanaśnataḥ । na cātisvapnaśīlasya jāgrato naiva cārjuna ॥ 6-16॥)*. He must keep a sensible diet and entertainment, keep his consciousness in action, keep a sensible balance between sleep and wakefulness, the *yogī* overcomes pain *(yuktāhāravihārasya yuktaceṣṭasya karmasu । yuktasvapnāvabodhasya yogo bhavati duḥkhahā ॥ 6-17॥)*.

यदा विनियतं चित्तमात्मन्येवावतिष्ठते ।
निःस्पृहः सर्वकामेभ्यो युक्त इत्युच्यते तदा ॥ ६-१८॥
यथा दीपो निवातस्थो नेङ्गते सोपमा स्मृता ।
योगिनो यतचित्तस्य युञ्जतो योगमात्मनः ॥ ६-१९॥
यत्रोपरमते चित्तं निरुद्धं योगसेवया ।
यत्र चैवात्मनात्मानं पश्यन्नात्मनि तुष्यति ॥ ६-२०॥

(18-20) When he is able to restrain the consciousness solely on the Soul, then freedom from all passion is established, it is said *(yadā viniyatam cittamātmanyevāvatiṣṭhate । niḥspṛhaḥ sarvakāmebhyo yukta ityucyate tadā ॥ 6-18॥)*. Just like a lamp placed in an airless place does not flicker, that consciousness of *yogī* harmonizes the soul *(yathā dīpo nivātastho neṅgate sopamā smṛtā । yogino yatacittasya yuñjato yogamātmanaḥ ॥ 6-19॥)*. Where consciousness has been quietened, restrained by dedication to yoga, and where the soul is satiated by the soul *(yatroparamate cittam niruddham yogasevayā । yatra caivātmanātmānam paśyannātmani tuṣyati ॥ 6-20॥)*.

सुखमात्यन्तिकं यत्तद् बुद्धिग्राह्यमतीन्द्रियम् ।
वेत्ति यत्र न चैवायं स्थितश्चलति तत्त्वतः ॥ ६-२१॥
यं लब्ध्वा चापरं लाभं मन्यते नाधिकं ततः ।
यस्मिन्स्थितो न दुःखेन गुरुणापि विचाल्यते ॥ ६-२२॥
तं विद्याद् दुःखसंयोगवियोगं योगसंज्ञितम् ।
स निश्चयेन योक्तव्यो योगोऽनिर्विण्णचेतसा ॥ ६-२३॥

(21-23) An infinite peace that cannot be grasped by reason and beyond the senses this changeless knowledge becomes established in all its subtlety *(sukhamātyantikam yattad buddhigrāhyamatīndriyam । vetti yatra na caivāyam sthitaścalati tattvataḥ ॥ 6-21॥)*. Once the cognition has obtained that, no other gain is adequate; thereafter, it is unmoved even by heavy sorrow *(yam labdhvā cāparam lābham manyate nādhikam tataḥ । yasminsthito na duḥkhena guruṇāpi vicālyate ॥ 6-22॥)*. The knowledge of pain merger and separation is the knowledge of *yoga* that union must be practiced with determination with a consciousness that is not downcast *(tam vidyād duḥkhasamyogaviyogam yogasamjñitam । sa niścayena yoktavyo yogo'nirviṇṇacetasā ॥ 6-23॥)*.

सङ्कल्पप्रभवान्कामांस्त्यक्त्वा सर्वानशेषतः ।
मनसैवेन्द्रियग्रामं विनियम्य समन्ततः ॥ ६-२४॥
शनैः शनैरुपरमेद् बुद्ध्या धृतिगृहीतया ।
आत्मसंस्थं मनः कृत्वा न किञ्चिदपि चिन्तयेत् ॥ ६-२५॥

(24-25) Having abandoned all vows born out of desires, completely restrict cognition and all of the senses in totality (*saṅkalpaprabhavānkāmāṃstyaktvā sarvānaśeṣataḥ ǀ manasaivendriyagrāmaṃ viniyamya samantataḥ ǁ 6-24ǁ*). Slowly, slowly stop the intellect, hold it firmly in the Self, make the cognition nothing, and reflect (*śanaiḥ śanairuparamed buddhyā dhṛtigṛhītayā ǀ ātmasaṃsthaṃ manaḥ kṛtvā na kiñcidapi cintayet ǁ 6-25ǁ*).

यतो निश्चरति मनश्चञ्चलमस्थिरम् ।
ततस्ततो नियम्यैतदात्मन्येव वशं नयेत् ॥ ६-२६॥
प्रशान्तमनसं ह्येनं योगिनं सुखमुत्तमम् ।
उपैति शान्तरजसं ब्रह्मभूतमकल्मषम् ॥ ६-२७॥
युञ्जन्नेवं सदात्मानं योगी विगतकल्मषः ।
सुखेन ब्रह्मसंस्पर्शमत्यन्तं सुखमश्नुते ॥ ६-२८॥

(26-28) Whenever there is appearance of disturbance and unsteadiness in the cognition, then onward, using self-control, bring the Soul under control (*yato niścarati manaścañcalamasthiram ǀ tatastato niyamyaitadātmanyeva vaśaṃ nayet ǁ 6-26ǁ*). Truly, the serene soul yields supreme peace, developing peace creates *Brahman* in one that is unstained (*praśāntamanasaṃ hyenaṃ yoginaṃ sukhamuttamam ǀ upaiti śāntarajasaṃ brahmabhūtamakalmaṣam ǁ 6-27ǁ*). Thus, the Soul of the practicing *yogī* is always unstained, and the peaceful merger with *Brahman* gives infinite happiness (*yuñjannevaṃ sadātmānaṃ yogī vigatakalmaṣaḥ ǀ sukhena brahmasaṃsparśamatyantaṃ sukhamaśnute ǁ 6-28ǁ*).

सर्वभूतस्थमात्मानं सर्वभूतानि चात्मनि ।
ईक्षते योगयुक्तात्मा सर्वत्र समदर्शनः ॥ ६-२९॥
यो मां पश्यति सर्वत्र सर्वं च मयि पश्यति ।
तस्याहं न प्रणश्यामि स च मे न प्रणश्यति ॥ ६-३०॥
सर्वभूतस्थितं यो मां भजत्येकत्वमास्थितः ।
सर्वथा वर्तमानोऽपि स योगी मयि वर्तते ॥ ६-३१॥
आत्मौपम्येन सर्वत्र समं पश्यति योऽर्जुन ।
सुखं वा यदि वा दुःखं स योगी परमो मतः ॥ ६-३२॥

(29-32) Souls exist in all creation, all creation has a Soul, so the *yogī* sees all Souls to be one and views all with an equal gaze *(sarvabhūtasthamātmānaṃ sarvabhūtāni cātmani ǀ īkṣate yogayuktātmā sarvatra samadarśanaḥ ǁ 6-29ǁ)*. He sees me everywhere and, in me, sees he is not lost to me, and I am not lost to him *(yo māṃ paśyati sarvatra sarvaṃ ca mayi paśyati ǀ tasyāhaṃ na praṇaśyāmi sa ca me na praṇaśyati ǁ 6-30ǁ)*. Whoever worships me in the same manner across all creation in every way, the *yogī* remains in me wherever he proceeds *(sarvabhūtasthitaṃ yo māṃ bhajatyekatvamāsthitaḥ ǀ sarvathā vartamāno'pi sa yogī mayi vartate ǁ 6-31ǁ)*. He that views all Souls as the same, who is same in happiness and grief, he is regarded as the highest *yogī (ātmaupamyena sarvatra samaṃ paśyati yo 'rjuna ǀ sukhaṃ vā yadi vā duḥkhaṃ sa yogī paramo mataḥ ǁ 6-32ǁ)*.

अर्जुन उवाच ।

योऽयं योगस्त्वया प्रोक्तः साम्येन मधुसूदन ।

एतस्याहं न पश्यामि चञ्चलत्वात्स्थितिं स्थिराम् ॥ ६-३३॥

चञ्चलं हि मनः कृष्ण प्रमाथि बलवद् दृढम् ।

तस्याहं निग्रहं मन्ये वायोरिव सुदुष्करम् ॥ ६-३४॥

Arjuna asked (33-34) - This yoga of equality that you are propounding, I am unable to relate due to unsteadiness and abiding steadiness *(yo'yaṃ yogastvayā proktaḥ sāmyena madhusūdana ǀ etasyāhaṃ na paśyāmi cañcalatvātsthitiṃ sthirām ǁ 6-33ǁ)*. The cognition is fickle, agitation is strong and unyielding, I find controlling the cognition, which is like the wind, difficult to do *(cañcalaṃ hi manaḥ kṛṣṇa pramāthi balavad dṛḍham ǀ tasyāhaṃ nigrahaṃ manye vāyoriva suduṣkaram ǁ 6-34ǁ)*.

श्रीभगवानुवाच ।

असंशयं महाबाहो मनो दुर्निग्रहं चलम् ।

अभ्यासेन तु कौन्तेय वैराग्येण च गृह्यते ॥ ६-३५॥

असंयतात्मना योगो दुष्प्राप इति मे मतिः ।

वश्यात्मना तु यतता शक्योऽवाप्तुमुपायतः ॥ ६-३६॥

Śrī Kṛṣṇa replied - (35-36) Without doubt, cognition is difficult to control and restless, and by practice and dispassion it is controlled *(asaṃśayaṃ mahābāho mano durnigrahaṃ calam ǀ abhyāsena tu kaunteya vairāgyeṇa ca gṛhyate ǁ 6-35ǁ)*. A Soul without controlled cognition finds it hard to attain harmony, in my opinion, but it is possible to acquire an obedient Soul by implementing the proper methodology *(asaṃyatātmanā yogo duṣprāpa iti me matiḥ ǀ vaśyātmanā tu yatatā śakyo 'vāptumupāyataḥ ǁ 6-36ǁ)*.

अर्जुन उवाच ।

अयतिः श्रद्धयोपेतो योगाच्चलितमानसः ।

अप्राप्य योगसंसिद्धिं कां गतिं कृष्ण गच्छति ॥ ६-३७॥

कच्चिन्नोभयविभ्रष्टश्छिन्नाभ्रमिव नश्यति ।

अप्रतिष्ठो महाबाहो विमूढो ब्रह्मणः पथि ॥ ६-३८॥

एतन्मे संशयं कृष्ण छेत्तुमर्हस्यशेषतः ।

त्वदन्यः संशयस्यास्य छेत्ता न ह्युपपद्यते ॥ ६-३९॥

Arjuna asked - (37-39) What is the fate of one who does not possess dedication in *yoga* and has a disturbed cognition, what happens to him who is unable to reach perfection in *yoga*? *(ayatiḥ śraddhāyopeto yogāccalitamānasaḥ ၊ aprāpya yogasaṃsiddhiṃ kāṃ gatiṃ kṛṣṇa gacchati ॥ 6-37॥)*. Is it not that without steadfastness one is separated from both sides and destroyed without steadfast or confused effort on the path of the *Brahman (kaccinnobhayavibhraṣṭaśchinnābhramiva naśyati ၊ apratiṣṭho mahābāho vimūḍho brahmaṇaḥ pathi ॥ 6-38॥)*? This is my confusion, Krishna, please remove it completely, other than you, none is capable of dispelling it completely *(etanme saṃśayaṃ kṛṣṇa chettumarhasyaśeṣataḥ ၊ tvadanyaḥ saṃśayasyāsya chettā na hyupapadyate ॥ 6-39॥)*.

श्रीभगवानुवाच ।

पार्थ नैवेह नामुत्र विनाशस्तस्य विद्यते ।

न हि कल्याणकृत्कश्चिद् दुर्गतिं तात गच्छति ॥ ६-४०॥

प्राप्य पुण्यकृतां लोकानुषित्वा शाश्वतीः समाः ।

शुचीनां श्रीमतां गेहे योगभ्रष्टोऽभिजायते ॥ ६-४१॥

Śrī Kṛṣṇa said - (40-41) Partha - truly, not here nor in the next world is there destruction of him, nor does reversal of fate come to performers of beneficial deeds, my son *(pārtha naiveha nāmutra vināśastasya vidyate ၊ na hi kalyāṇakṛtkaścid durgatiṃ tāta gacchati ॥ 6-40॥)*. Having acquired meritorious outcomes through everlasting equilibrium when on earth the one fallen from *yoga* is reborn at a home where there is purity and prosperity *(prāpya puṇyakṛtāṃ lokānuṣitvā śāśvatīḥ samāḥ ၊ śucīnāṃ śrīmatāṃ gehe yogabhraṣṭo'bhijāyate ॥ 6-41॥)*.

अथवा योगिनामेव कुले भवति धीमताम् ।

एतद्धि दुर्लभतरं लोके जन्म यदीदृशम् ॥ ६-४२॥

तत्र तं बुद्धिसंयोगं लभते पौर्वदेहिकम् ।

यतते च ततो भूयः संसिद्धौ कुरुनन्दन ॥ ६-४३॥

(42-43) Or, within *yogī* or even clans of the wise, for truly, getting a human birth like this is difficult *(athavā yogināmeva kule bhavati dhīmatām ı etaddhi durlabhataraṃ loke janma yadīdṛśam ıı 6-42ıı)*. There his wisdom is harmonized with that obtained during prior existence, then with more effort, there can be complete perfection, son of Kurus *(tatra taṃ buddhisaṃyogaṃ labhate paurvadehikam ı yatate ca tato bhūyaḥ saṃsiddhau kurunandana ıı 6-43ıı)*.

पूर्वाभ्यासेन तेनैव हियते ह्यवशोऽपि सः ।
जिज्ञासुरपि योगस्य शब्दब्रह्मातिवर्तते ॥ ६-४४॥
प्रयत्नाद्यतमानस्तु योगी संशुद्धकिल्बिषः ।
अनेकजन्मसंसिद्धस्ततो याति परां गतिम् ॥ ६-४५॥

(44-45) Truly, from previous learnings is born a helplessness to carry forward in spite of himself, to go beyond the word of *Brahman* and obtain the wisdom of *yoga (pūrvābhyāsena tenaiva hriyate hyavaśo'pi saḥ ı jijñāsurapi yogasya śabdabrahmātivartate ıı 6-44ıı)*. With effort and self-control, the *yogī* gets purified from faults of many births and attains the goal of supreme perfection *(prayatnādyatamānastu yogī saṃśuddhakilbiṣaḥ ı anekajanmasaṃsiddhastato yāti parāṃ gatim ıı 6-45ıı)*.

तपस्विभ्योऽधिको योगी ज्ञानिभ्योऽपि मतोऽधिकः ।
कर्मिभ्यश्चाधिको योगी तस्माद्योगी भवार्जुन ॥ ६-४६॥
योगिनामपि सर्वेषां मद्गतेनान्तरात्मना ।
श्रद्धावान्भजते यो मां स मे युक्ततमो मतः ॥ ६-४७॥

(46-47) Superior to ascetics are *yogīs*, even superior to those who have achieved great wisdom *(tapasvibhyo'dhiko yogī jñānibhyo'pi mato'dhikaḥ ı)*, even superior to people of action is the *yogī*, therefore, become a *yogī*, Arjuna *(karmibhyaścādhiko yogī tasmādyogī bhavārjuna ıı 6-46ıı)*. Of all the *yogīs*, those that place me in their inner Soul *(yogināmapi sarveṣāṃ madgatenāntarātmanā ı)*, worships with dedication, that I consider the most integrated Soul *(śraddhāvānbhajate yo māṃ sa me yuktatamo mataḥ ıı 6-47ıı)*.

◆——— • ● ◆ ● • ———◆

Chapter 7

Jñāna-vijñāna-yoga
(yoga of awareness of the Self in any situation) [1]

Introduction

- From Chapters 1 to 6, Śrī Kṛṣṇa discourses on action *(karma)* and the method of transcending it.

- From Chapter 7, Śrī Kṛṣṇa changes tack and heads into the conceptual basis of *Yoga*, beginning with *jñāna* and *vijñāna*.

- What is *jñāna?* It is the cognition of *Brahman,* the source, Truth, or Transcendental Self.

- What is *vijñāna?* It is the conceptual understanding of materiality, cognition of *īśvara* or Viṣṇu - the weave of *puruṣa* and *prakṛti*. In fact, it is the awareness of the Self in everything that leads up to *jñāna*.

- At a local level, *vijñāna* includes cognition of the motility of any system or entity.

- *Yoga* is the union of the impermanent material Self with the state of permanent state, *Brahman,* or Truth. One might also call *Yoga* as the point where there is merger of *jñāna* and *vijñāna*.

Here, it is important to understand the role of free will *(sankalpa)* and consciousness *(citta),* because consciousness is the connecting medium between *jñāna* and *vijñāna*. *Citta* is the motility of *vijñāna,* and when free will *(sankalpa)* is used to subdue the functioning of *citta, yoga* occurs *(yogaścitta-vṛtti-nirodhaḥ)*.

---

[1]https://www.bhagavad-gita.org/Gita/chapter-07.html

Creation (verse 1-3)

- Śrī Kṛṣṇa speaks about the value of surrender; how complete surrender leads to subduing of the Self *(asmitā)*. While he recommends surrender unto him (Śrī Kṛṣṇa), this surrender could be any entity because the quality of surrender is the same in all instances.

- Śrī Kṛṣṇa divides creation into two, namely, lower and higher orders of creation.

- First, comes lower order of creation (lower *prakṛti)* or the material creation. This constitutes the material universe and has an eightfold divided state comprising earth *(pṛthvī)*, water *(ap)*, fire *(agni)*, air *(vāyu)*, ether *(ākāśa)*, seat of cognition *(manas* - where all the sensory stimuli are collated), seat of intelligence *(buddhi,* where the incoming stimulus is compared with conditioning or *dharma* and response is formulated), and the feeling that I am the doer *(ahaṅkāra)*.

- Second, there is a higher level of creation *(Brahman)* that creates lower the order of creation, also called *prakṛti. Brahman* pervades everything and provides the motive force for creation, sustenance, and dissolution of all matter.

- Śrī Kṛṣṇa then declares that all creation proceeds from him, and he is the motility that drives their natural state *(dharma)*.

- Additionally, Śrī Kṛṣṇa says that he is passion and all contrary attributes that are natural to any entity. For example, hate, anger, delusion, negativity, divisiveness, prejudice, etc., proceed from Śrī Kṛṣṇa also!

- Finally, Śrī Kṛṣṇa states that although he is the creator and nature of all existence, he is not the participant. Consequently, *karma* or experience of the doer does not affect him.

So, what is Śrī Kṛṣṇa's position and role in the overall scheme of things? How is he linked to *Brahman?* Is he some transition point between *Brahman* and creation? Śrī Kṛṣṇa also seems to be positioning himself as the transition between *jñāna* and *vijñāna.*

Concept of Creation

Definition: A divided state is one where there are two discrete states that may or may not be linked. However, in this case, because *Brahman* is the underlying foundation and motility of both, the two states are inextricably linked. The two states can be separated into a higher-level state that starts from *Brahman* and ends with the beginning of creation *(jñāna),* followed by the lower-level state, which encompasses creation, maintenance, and dissolution of all entities *(vijñāna)*.

How are the two states of *jñāna* and *vijñāna* linked? *Jñāna* is the cognition of the Self in the *Brahman, vijñāna* is the cognition of the identity of all material existence *(māyā)* that emerge downstream from *Brahman.* Common to both states is *prajñā,* which is awareness of *Brahman,* while consciousness *(citta)* is the medium that carries the cognition of motility *(vijñāna)* in material existence *(māyā).*

How are these two states different? We know that *Brahman* is the underlying foundation of both states, providing the motive foundation for creating, activating, sustaining, and destroying all elements, entities, and systems. So, let us first understand *Brahman.*

Brahman is a cognitive state of infinite, imperishable (cannot die), and immutable (cannot change) state of peace. This state can be compared to a visceral cognition of the state of null (nothing) or infinity, the "null" being a state of nothing and "infinity" being a state of expanding illusion (Viṣṇu or *īśvara*) that equals 1/0. The difference between null and infinity is that null has no material, while infinity has material which is based on the foundation of null.

- From *Brahman* emerges a weave of *puruṣa* (Identity or experiencer) and *prakṛti* (creation). *Brahman* provides the motility for both but does not participate.

- The weave of *puruṣa* and *prakṛti* results in two possibilities. *Brahman* with attributes

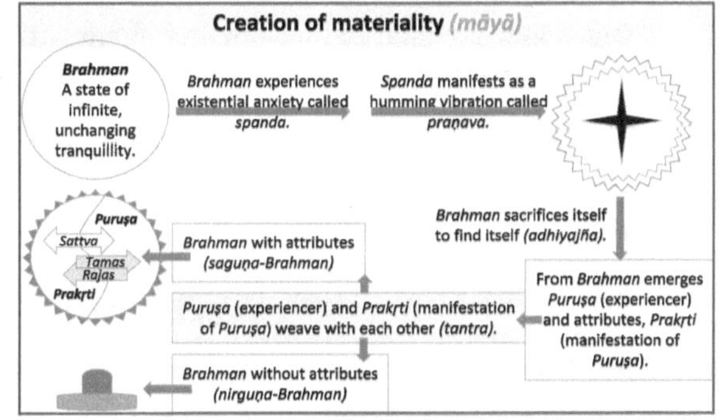

7.1 - Creation of materiality *(māyā)*

(saguṇa-brahman), where both *puruṣa* and *prakṛti* weave with each other to create materiality *(māyā)* and *Brahman* without attributes *(nirguṇa-brahman),* where *prakṛti* does not manifest and the experiencer or identity *(puruṣa)* exists only as pure identity but without motility *(prakṛti).*

- *Saguṇa-brahman* is also known as Viṣṇu or *īśvara,* and cognition of Viṣṇu or *īśvara* is *vijñāna.*

- Additionally, when *Brahman* manifests in the *saguṇa* state, *Brahman* becomes materiality or illusion *(māyā),* forming the basis for material cognition. This is the lower order of creation and the state where *karma* (action) operates.

- Next, the higher order of creation is an unmanifested state called *nirguṇa-brahman (Brahman* that has an identity but has not been able to manifest with material attributes). Here, *Brahman* has emerged from its state of infinite, imperishable (cannot die), and immutable (cannot change) state of peace, but it has not got into a state *saguṇa-brahman* where it becomes material. So, here *puruṣa* remains unmanifested or reverts back into the state of null or *Brahman.*

- However, both *nirguṇa-brahman* and *saguṇa-brahman* states are derivatives of the primary state, *Brahman.*

- Lastly, when *saguṇa-brahman* and *nirguṇa-brahman* finally reverse integrate back to *Brahman,* that is called *pralaya* (merger of *māyā* with the source or *Brahman).*

- Cognition of *Brahman* is *jñāna,* and the experience is called *nirvikalpa-samādhi* (uninterrupted and unchanging state of peace).

Lower order of creation *hiraṇyagarbha* and Viṣṇu

- *Puruṣa* and *prakṛti* weave as *saguṇa-brahman,* and the primordial outcome is called root of creation *(mūla-prakṛti),* supreme soul *(paramātman),* or *īśvara.*

- From *īśvara* emerges *hiraṇyagarbha* (golden egg), *brahmāṇḍa* (creation of *Brahman*) or the universe. This happens in two ways, first as a big bang, with spontaneous creation of mega matter along with unit evolution, and second as quanta matter, that form the building blocks of all matter.

- The weave of *puruṣa* and *prakṛti* is the source of action *(karma). Karma* creates transactions and bonds, and each bond results in the creation of a new identity *(ātman).*

- *Ātman* (soul) is a primary unit of the weave of *puruṣa* and *prakṛti.*

- Also, *ātman* is the location where debt *(ṛṇa)* resides.

- Since *prārabdha-karma* exists until the debt is paid off, entities get separated once their debt is reconciled. They then create new bonds with new souls *(ātman)* along with reconstituted debt.

- As a result, multiple identities/souls or *ātman* of varying complexities are created and dissolved continuously.

- Multiple souls *(ātman)* integrate to form a composite soul that has a discrete form *(rūpa).* Also, this discrete unit can be a sentient being *(jīva)* or insentient entity *(jaḍa).*

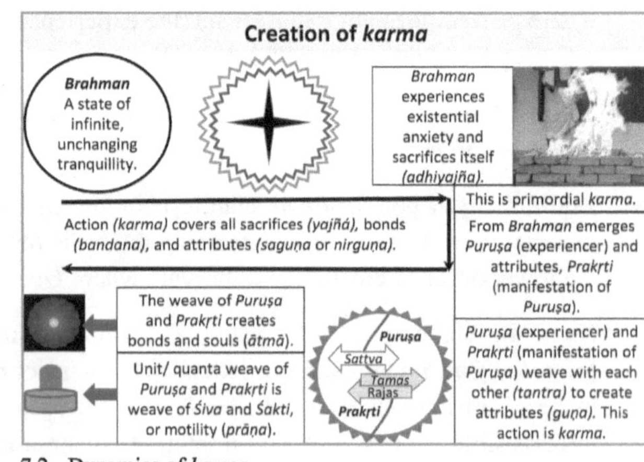

7.2 - Dynamics of *karma*

- Small, medium, and large bonds create small, medium or large systems and entities, each with their own identity *(ātman)*.

- As a result of creation and dissolution, a massive supra-eco-system is created where entities, small systems, subsystems, and micro-systems of varying complexities exist in the supra-system.

- This macro-ecosystem which houses this continuously evolving and changing mass of entities and systems is called the universe or *hiraṇyagarbha* (golden egg).

- Lastly, like all systems, this supra-system or *hiraṇyagarbha* (golden egg) also has its own center of supreme-Soul *(paramātman)* called Viṣṇu.

- However, it can be seen that this creation, maintenance, and destruction is not real. It exists, changes, and morphs. This phenomenon is called *māyā* (farce or illusion).

- Importantly, the sense of identity *(ātman)* of *hiraṇyagarbha* or the universe does not change, even though it is evolving continuously. It remains as Viṣṇu and continues to be a creation of the weave of *puruṣa* with *prakṛti,* which are a manifestation of the *Brahman.*

- Consequently, *vijñāna* is the cognition of *paramātman, īśvara,* Viṣṇu, *brahmāṇḍa,* or *hiraṇyagarbha* of any system at a material *(saguṇa)* level (all the above names mean the same entity).

- Since all existence within *saguṇa-brahman, īśvara,* and consequently *hiraṇyagarbha* is impermanent and everything is a manifestation of the *Brahman, hiraṇyagarbha* and everything within it is an illusion *(māyā).*

- Consequently, Viṣṇu can be termed as the repository of *māyā* (farce or illusion).

Commentary

Bṛhadāraṇyaka-upaniṣad[2] states that, at first, there is nothing like the state of death. This is the cognitive state of the *Brahman.*

Then *Brahman* expresses itself by creating cognition and intelligence. This also means that it got an identity *(puruṣa).* But we know that there are no free lunches, so how can Brahman express itself when it is in a state of nothing? Obviously, there must be with some sort of sacrifice.

But, how can any sacrifice come out of nothing? One thing can be sacrificed. The state of nothing itself. Confused?

---

[2]https://www.wisdomlib.org/hinduism/book/the-brihadaranyaka-upanishad/d/doc117895.html

Consider this. You are standing in a queue doing nothing, and a tough-looking person breaks it. You were in a state of nothing, but now you see your line being broken, your sense of order *(dharma)* is challenged, and there is turbulence within.

But before confronting the bully, you need to confront yourself and sacrifice your fears. Otherwise, you will remain in the state of nothing. There will be turbulence but no outcome.

This sacrifice of the Self for the Self is called *yajñā*. Your identity is *puruṣa*, and your actions, which will be a manifestation of your personality *(svabhāva)*, is *prakṛti*. The outcome of your effort is *karma;* this means that whether you act in accordance with *dharma*[3], it is *(karma),* don't act *(akarma),* or act inappropriately or against *dharma (vikarma),* you are stuck with the consequences. This outcome is stored for repayment/reconciliation in your soul *(ātma).*

Dvaita and *advaita* philosophies

- The foundation of *dvaita* (duality) philosophy is that the individual's identity or *ātman* (singular Self) is subordinate to that of *īśvara* (universal Identity, *paramātman,* or Viṣṇu*).*

- Consequently, the best path for transcending reality is to surrender oneself to *īśvara* or Viṣṇu and try to merge with that identity *(paramātman).*

- However, since the Soul *(ātman)* is trapped in *(hiraṇyagarbha),* all reprieve would be temporary and dependent on *karma* generated by the person. Therefore, rebirth is inevitable. This process is explained by Śrī Kṛṣṇa in *Śrimad-Bhagavad-gītā* chapter 3 - *karma-yoga.*

- In contrast, *advaita* (non-duality) posits that everything is the *Brahman (tat-tvam-asi)* and all existence is a veil over *Brahman,* called *māyā* (illusion), including *īśvara* (universal Identity, *paramātman,* or Viṣṇu*).*

- In fact, Śrī Kṛṣṇa himself says, that which is permanent is the *Brahman,* and everything that is temporary or impermanent or subject to creation, death, or dissolution is *māyā.*

- Hence, if a person were to be able to negate his or her own identity, or reduce experience *(puruṣa)* to zero, then *prakṛti* would cease to manifest, enabling the person to transcend *māyā* and reach *nirguṇa-brahman*

- Consequently, with more effort, the person would reach *nirvikalpa-samādhi* (changeless state) which is a merger with the *Brahman.*

- However, this does not mean that one cannot reach *Brahman* by merging with Viṣṇu, through the *dvaita* philosophy. After all, any merger requires negation

---

[3]https://schoolofyoga.in/yoga-concept/dharma

of one's existential identity *(puruṣa)*, so, when a person surrenders completely to Viṣṇu, he or she loses personal identity. This leads to attainment of *nirguṇa-brahman,* which is the *Brahman.* This is explained by Śrī Kṛṣṇa in chapter 12, Bhakti-yoga.

Śiva, śakti, and *tantra*

- We have seen that the weave of *puruṣa* (experiencer or Identity) with *prakṛti* (manifestation of *puruṣa)* creates an Identity called *ātman* which is the repository of debt *(ṛṇa).*

- However, this continuous and complex series of combinations that creates, sustains, and dissolves the Universe must have a constituent, foundational, quanta or unit element/identity on which the whole Universe is built and exists (that point where further breakdown is not possible).

- What is the constituent primary element/building block of *puruṣa* and *prakṛti?* In other words, what is the quanta (micro, unit, smallest building block) that emerges from the *Brahman?*

- This quanta identity is *śiva,* which manifests as *śakti.*

- *Śiva* is the quanta (micro, unit, smallest building block) entity of *puruṣa,* which is the experiencer in a macro form. Consequently, this makes *śiva,* the quanta or micro-experiencer.

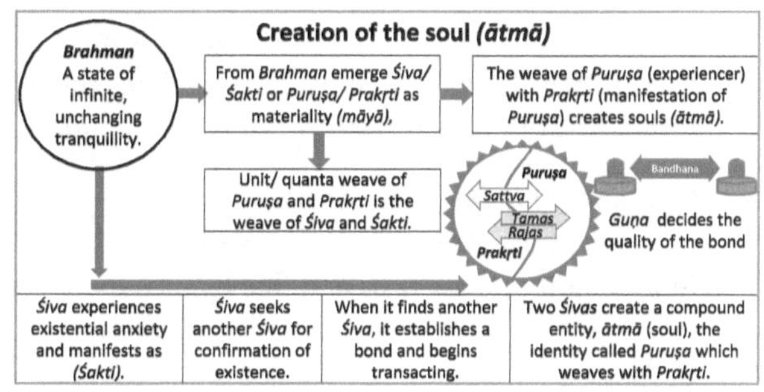

7.3 - Dynamics of manifestation

- Similarly, *śakti* is the quanta (micro, quanta unit, smallest building block) entity of *prakṛti.*

- Thus, while *prakṛti* is the manifestation of *puruṣa, śakti* is the manifestation of *śiva. Puruṣa* weaves with *prakṛti,* while *śiva* weaves with *śakti.*

- Also, while the unit level weave of *puruṣa* and *prakṛti* is the Soul or Self *(ātman),* the unit weave of *śiva* with *śakti* is *prāṇa* (unit motility).

- Additionally, this weave, in both cases, is called *tantra* or weave, and the yoking of one with the other in both cases is called *yoga.*

So, how do *śiva* and *śakti* weave to form *puruṣa* and *prakṛti?*

- In fact, it can be derived that when quanta *śiva/śakti* bonds with another quanta *śiva/śakti,* a composite or complex identity is created due to *karma,* which evolves to become the weave of *puruṣa* (experiencer) with *prakṛti.*

- Also, as the combinations become complex, the composite unit gets a material form *(rūpa)* and becomes both the Universe and its constituent *(hiraṇyagarbha).*

- Thus, we can derive that *śiva* is the primary or quanta constituent element of material *brahman (saguṇa-brahman).*

- When *śiva* does not manifest, it does not mean that *śiva* has ceased to exist; it means that *śiva* is in an unmanifested *brahman* or *nirguṇa-brahman*

- Therefore, *śiva* (quanta identity) is present in all the states of *Brahman* and is called *sadā-śiva* (perpetual *śiva*). This also means that identities are being continuously generated from *Brahman,* a concept which is attested to by the reality that the Universe is expanding.

- Thus, the weave of *śiva* with *śakti* or *puruṣa* with *prakṛti* is an experiential state, and it has to be cognized/experienced.

- This awareness is called *prajñā.* When the awareness relates to the Self *(puruṣa)* in the environment, it is called *vijñāna,* and when it is about the person's awareness of the Self *(puruṣa),* it is called *jñāna.*

- One can also say that the awareness of a person of the weave *(tantra)* his or her identity *(puruṣa)* with his or her actions *(prakṛti)* is the caliber of his individuality *(svatantra)* and this applies to all entities, even countries.

Example

Hydrogen and oxygen are atoms with their own identities. However, when they combine, they form water, which has a very different identity as opposed to its constituents, hydrogen and oxygen.

So, as an example, quanta identity or *śiva* of Hydrogen and quanta identity or *śiva* of Oxygen combine to create a composite identity of water which has its own Identity *(ātman).*

However, the Identity of water is different from its constituents, hydrogen or oxygen. Consequently, since each of these, hydrogen, oxygen, and water, are discrete souls, each *ātman* (soul) carries all the debts *(ṛṇa).*

Also, the debt accrued by water in its *karma* (action) will be its own, and neither of its individual constituents, hydrogen or oxygen, will carry the *karma* of water, as the souls *(ātman)* are different.

Īśvara and three embodiments _(tri-mūrti)_ - brahma, viṣṇu, śiva, and their consorts

- _Puruṣa_ and _prakṛti_ weave as _saguṇa-brahman_ and form the root of creation _(mūlā-prakṛti)_, or supreme soul _(paramātman)_ or _īśvara_.

- From _īśvara_ emerges _hiraṇyagarbha_ (golden womb), _brahmāṇḍa_ (egg of _brahma)_ or the universe. This happens in two ways; as big bang, with spontaneous creation of matter along with its constituent unit evolution, as quanta creation of matter. This is the world of brahma, primarily driven by passion _(rajoguṇa)_, for creation.

- Since creation itself can be irresponsible and passionate, the framework of creation needs to function in systemic harmony, otherwise the system will run amok. Hence, it needs a supreme Soul (viṣṇu), which brings balance to the various conflicting forces to ensure harmony within the universe _(hiraṇyagarbha_ or _brahmāṇḍa)_. Since viṣṇu creates harmony or balance between _rajas_ and _tamas,_ it is _sāttvika._

- Lastly, there is śiva. Śiva is primordial or quanta Identity, predominantly governed by fear of loss of Identity, hence lethargic and delusional. So, śiva is _tāmasika-guṇa._ Since śiva is the quanta identity, it is the building block of all creation, which includes _puruṣa._

The three embodiments _(trimūrti)_ each have a consort _(devī),_ these being embodiments of _prakṛti._ Without these _tridevīs,_ the _trimūrtis_ are irrelevant and cannot function.

- _Brahmā,_ as a creator has knowledge _(Sarasvatī)_ as its consort. It is obvious that without knowledge, no creative effort will succeed.

- _Lakṣmī_ is materiality, without which _Viṣṇu_ cannot have a framework to balance/harmonize.

- _Śakti_ is the manifestation that drives all delusion and fear which define _siva's_ identity.

Śrī Kṛṣṇa explains his own qualities (verse 8-15)

- I define sweet fragrance of earth, brilliance of fire, life in all beings, and austerity in ascetics. Thus, I am the seed of all beings, intelligence of the intelligent, and splendor of the splendid.

- I am strength in the strong, without passion or attraction. In beings, I am desire which is not contrary to the state of order/harmony and natural conditioning _(dharma)._

- I am the creator of *sattva* (balanced/harmonious), *rajas* (passion/drive/creativity), and *tamas* (inertia/delusional) attitudes. In fact, they are created by me, proceed from me, exist in all, including me, but I am not in them. *Guṇa's* create illusion *(māyā),* preventing creation from knowing the truth – but taking refuge in the source overcomes this.

Śrī Kṛṣṇa explains the qualities of the seeker (verse 16-30)

- Four types of people who seek my grace (Śrī Kṛṣṇa's grace) are:

  o those in distress

  o those seeking knowledge

  o those seeking wealth

  o those imbibed with wisdom

- All those who seek my grace are special, but those anchored to *(brahman)* are dearest to me.

- Often impelled by desire of quick results, people seek other Gods or rites. However, if their devotion is sincere, I enable their devotion to become steady and help them reach their goals. Sometimes, devotees think that blessings have come from deities that they worship when it has actually come from me.

- Furthermore, there is a direct correlation between effort and rewards. Consequently, when a person seeks a boon, he will receive it, be it small, medium, or infinite. So, seek carefully.

- However, most people are confused by *māyā,* so they do not understand me and worship my manifestation. In fact, they do not comprehend that I am unmanifest and part of the *Brahman.*

- Also, I know the past, present, and future of all beings, but opposites arising from attraction and repulsion delude their knowledge of me.

- Only those that have paid their debts and are freed from opposites find themselves having the ability to remain steadfast in their vows to me.

- As a result, those who recognize me as original creation, deity, and sacrifice strive for deliverance from material attachments to knowledge of the Truth and come to me in their hour of death.

Now comes the inevitable question—what is the measure of success?

There is only one measure of success, which is merger with the *Brahman* or source/truth/infinite peace. This is experienced as a state of infinite peace or nothingness, where the Self *(ātman)* experiences no change or *karma (nirvikalpa)* and does not react to stimulus *(citta-vṛtti-nirodha)*.

What does Śrī Kṛṣṇa mean when he says that he is the quality that drives all creation?

- All creation *(sṛṣṭi)* is a combination of the five cardinal elements *(pañcabhūta)* – earth *(pṛthvī)*, water *(ap)*, fire *(agni)*, air *(vāyu)*, and ether *(ākāśa)*. Also, each of these cardinal elements is a combination of *guṇa* (attributes).

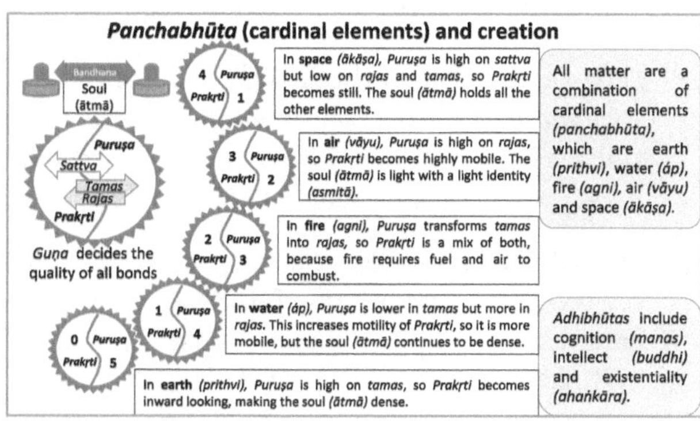

7.4 - How creation occurs

Example: *Pṛthvī* (earth) is predominantly *tamas* (inertia/delusional/self-centered).

- All matter is a combination of the above elements, from the lowly atom to the mighty universe. Each of these entities which come into existence has a center of identity or Self *(ātman)*.

- Each entity also interacts and functions in a system with other entities.

- As a natural corollary, all collection of entities has a center of identity or Self *(ātman)*.

Example: each housing society is defined by a boundary wall and has its own Identity. Similarly, each city, state, region, country, or planet have their own center of Identity. Also, the Sun has an identity, as has Mars, Jupiter, Saturn, or Moon. Finally, the biggest entity is the Universe, and its center of identity is Viṣṇu.

But Śrī Kṛṣṇa says that he is beyond even that as well as the essence of everything that defines materiality. He says that he is the one who transforms intent to material outcome.

Some views that may be contrary to accepted positions

Śrī Kṛṣṇa establishes some paradigms in chapter 7:

- He is the essence of materiality, the motility in all creation. Also, he clearly states that he is the personality trait *(bhāva)* of every entity.

- However, he also states that he is not responsible for the person's actions. It is important to understand this difference because personality trait drives action and outcome of action. So, basically, Śrī Kṛṣṇa underwrites the existence of personality but separates himself from the operation of personality and *karma.*

- You are on your own! Śrī Kṛṣṇa is the motility of entities but inert. Every time you act or use free will, you are getting deeper into a debt trap of action *(ṛṇānubandhana).* So, free will is a trap. The other solution is to not act. But, that itself is action, because inaction is action! Hence, that is not a solution. The only way out is to not seek action but act in the spirit of sacrifice, one where your sense of identity/self-worth *(asmitā)* is not affected. Consequently, one will need to address every situation with discrimination *(viveka)* and dispassion *(vairāgya),* avoiding duality of like-dislike, good-bad etc.

- Finally, Śrī Kṛṣṇa says that anyone desiring liberation should completely surrender and submit himself to Śrī Kṛṣṇa's will. What is this state, and how does it operate? What happens is that the person's will *(saṅkalpa)* becomes dysfunctional, and while *prārabdha-karma* acts, further *āgami-karma* ceases to get created because no debt is created. Śrī Kṛṣṇa, by being the focus of surrender, acts as the enabler of this metamorphosis.

The transliteration and translation of chapter 7 follows:

श्रीभगवानुवाच ।

मय्यासक्तमनाः पार्थ योगं युञ्जन्मदाश्रयः ।

असंशयं समग्रं मां यथा ज्ञास्यसि तच्छृणु ॥ ७-१॥

ज्ञानं तेऽहं सविज्ञानमिदं वक्ष्याम्यशेषतः ।

यज्ज्ञात्वा नेह भूयोऽन्यज्ज्ञातव्यमवशिष्यते ॥ ७-२॥

मनुष्याणां सहस्रेषु कश्चिद्यतति सिद्धये ।

यततामपि सिद्धानां कश्चिन्मां वेत्ति तत्त्वतः ॥ ७-३॥

Śrī Kṛṣṇa said (1-3) Anchor your cognition on me, take refuge in me, practice *yoga,* without doubt I will reveal everything to you *(mayyāsaktamanāḥ pārtha yogaṃ yuñjanmadāśrayaḥ | asaṃśayaṃ samagraṃ māṃ yathā jñāsyasi tacchṛṇu || 7-1||).* To you, I will reveal in totality this knowledge along with correct interpretation which, having known nothing more, not even residue remains of knowing *(jñānaṃ te'haṃ savijñānamidaṃ vakṣyāmyaśeṣataḥ | yajjñātvā neha bhūyo'nyajjñātavyamavaśiṣyate || 7-2||).* Among thousands of men, only some strive for perfection, among those striving, anyone who becomes perfect knows my essence *(manuṣyāṇāṃ sahasreṣu kaścidyatati siddhaye | yatatāmapi siddhānāṃ kaścinmāṃ vetti tattvataḥ || 7-3||).*

भूमिरापोऽनलो वायुः खं मनो बुद्धिरेव च ।

अहङ्कार इतीयं मे भिन्ना प्रकृतिरष्टधा ॥ ७-४॥

अपरेयमितस्त्वन्यां प्रकृतिं विद्धि मे पराम् ।
जीवभूतां महाबाहो ययेदं धार्यते जगत् ॥ ७-५॥

(4-5) Earth, water, fire, air, ether, seat of cognition, seat of logic, and the feeling that I am the doer form my eightfold divided state of nature *(bhūmirāpo 'nalo vāyuḥ kham mano buddhireva ca ı ahaṅkāra itīyam me bhinnā prakṛtiraṣṭadhā ॥ 7-4॥)*. Also, from this lower but of different nature is this knowledge of my absolute state the life material by which this the universe is maintained *(apareyamitastvanyām prakṛtim viddhi me parām ı jīvabhūtām mahābāho yayedam dhāryate jagat ॥ 7-5॥)*.

एतद्योनीनि भूतानि सर्वाणीत्युपधारय ।
अहं कृत्स्नस्य जगतः प्रभवः प्रलयस्तथा ॥ ७-६॥

मत्तः परतरं नान्यत्किञ्चिदस्ति धनञ्जय ।
मयि सर्वमिदं प्रोतं सूत्रे मणिगणा इव ॥ ७-७॥

(6-7) Therefore, know me to be the source of all creation, I am the sole reason of creation and dissolution *(etadyonīni bhūtāni sarvāṇītyupadhāraya ı aham kṛtsnasya jagataḥ prabhavaḥ pralayastathā ॥ 7-6॥)*. In fact, other than me no other is higher, all this is strung on me like a string of pearls *(mattaḥ parataram nānyatkiñcidasti dhanañjaya ı mayi sarvamidam protam sūtre maṇigaṇā iva ॥ 7-7॥)*.

रसोऽहमप्सु कौन्तेय प्रभास्मि शशिसूर्ययोः ।
प्रणवः सर्ववेदेषु शब्दः खे पौरुषं नृषु ॥ ७-८॥

पुण्यो गन्धः पृथिव्यां च तेजश्चास्मि विभावसौ ।
जीवनं सर्वभूतेषु तपश्चास्मि तपस्विषु ॥ ७-९॥

(8-9) First, I am the essence of water in water, I am the illumination of the Moon and Sun, the OM in Vedas, sound in ether, manliness in men *(raso 'hamapsu kaunteya prabhāsmi śaśisūryayoḥ ı praṇavaḥ sarvavedeṣu śabdaḥ khe pauruṣam nṛṣu ॥ 7-8॥)*. Fragrance of pure earth and splendor in fire am I, I am life in all beings and austerity in ascetics *(puṇyo gandhaḥ pṛthivyām ca tejaścāsmi vibhāvasau ı jīvanam sarvabhūteṣu tapaścāsmi tapasviṣu ॥ 7-9॥)*.

बीजं मां सर्वभूतानां विद्धि पार्थ सनातनम् ।
बुद्धिर्बुद्धिमतामस्मि तेजस्तेजस्विनामहम् ॥ ७-१०॥

बलं बलवतां चाहं कामरागविवर्जितम् ।
धर्माविरुद्धो भूतेषु कामोऽस्मि भरतर्षभ ॥ ७-११॥

ये चैव सात्त्विका भावा राजसास्तामसाश्च ये ।
मत्त एवेति तान्विद्धि न त्वहं तेषु ते मयि ॥ ७-१२॥

(10-12) I am the seed of all creation, know that I am eternal, I am the intelligence of the intelligent, the splendor of the splendid am I *(bījaṃ māṃ sarvabhūtānāṃ viddhi pārtha sanātanam ǀ buddhirbuddhimatāmasmi tejastejasvināmaham ǁ 7-10ǁ)*. I am strength of the strong *(balaṃ balavatāṃ cāhaṃ)*, who is devoid of passion or desire *(kāmarāgavivarjitam ǀ)*. I am passion contrary to harmony in creation *(dharmāviruddho bhūteṣu kāmo'smi bharatarṣabha ǁ 7-11ǁ)*. Truly, whatever harmonious traits *(ye caiva sāttvikā bhāvā)* and whatever passionate or delusion *(rājasāstāmasāśca ye ǀ)*, truly, know that they proceed from me but are not in me *(matta eveti tānviddhi na tvahaṃ teṣu te mayi ǁ 7-12ǁ)*.

त्रिभिर्गुणमयैर्भावैरेभिः सर्वमिदं जगत् ।
मोहितं नाभिजानाति मामेभ्यः परमव्ययम् ॥ ७-१३॥
दैवी ह्येषा गुणमयी मम माया दुरत्यया ।
मामेव ये प्रपद्यन्ते मायामेतां तरन्ति ते ॥ ७-१४॥
न मां दुष्कृतिनो मूढाः प्रपद्यन्ते नराधमाः ।
माययापहृतज्ञाना आसुरं भावमाश्रिताः ॥ ७-१५॥

(13-15) All in this world are deluded by the three attributes that drive perceptual traits and by these do not cognize my absolute supreme imperishable nature *(tribhirguṇamayairbhāvairebhiḥ sarvamidaṃ jagat ǀ mohitaṃ nābhijānāti māmebhyaḥ paramavyayam ǁ 7-13ǁ)*. Verily, my divinity is unfathomable due to this illusion created by attributes *(daivī hyeṣā guṇamayī mama māyā duratyayā ǀ)*. Only they who take refuge in me can cross this illusion *(māmeva ye prapadyante māyāmetāṃ taranti te ǁ 7-14ǁ)*. Wicked, delusional, and abject people seek illusion that is deprived of knowledge, are demonical in nature, and do not attain me *(na māṃ duṣkṛtino mūḍhāḥ prapadyante narādhamāḥ ǀ māyayāpahṛtajñānā āsuraṃ bhāvamāśritāḥ ǁ 7-15ǁ)*.

चतुर्विधा भजन्ते मां जनाः सुकृतिनोऽर्जुन ।
आर्तो जिज्ञासुरर्थार्थी ज्ञानी च भरतर्षभ ॥ ७-१६॥
तेषां ज्ञानी नित्ययुक्त एकभक्तिर्विशिष्यते ।
प्रियो हि ज्ञानिनोऽत्यर्थमहं स च मम प्रियः ॥ ७-१७॥
उदाराः सर्व एवैते ज्ञानी त्वात्मैव मे मतम् ।
आस्थितः स हि युक्तात्मा मामेवानुत्तमां गतिम् ॥ ७-१८॥
बहूनां जन्मनामन्ते ज्ञानवान्मां प्रपद्यते ।
वासुदेवः सर्वमिति स महात्मा सुदुर्लभः ॥ ७-१९॥

(16-19) Four classes of virtuous people worship me *(caturvidhā bhajante māṃ janāḥ sukṛtino'rjuna ǀ)*. These are, the distressed, the seeker of wisdom, seeker of wealth and the wise *(ārto jijñāsurarthārthī jñānī ca bharatarṣabha ǁ 7-16ǁ)*. Of them, the wise always intent with single-minded devotion excels *(teṣāṃ jñānī nityayukta ekabhaktirviśiṣyate ।)*. Truly, exceeding among the wise is he that loves me, and I love in return *(priyo hi jñānino 'tyarthamahaṃ sa ca mama priyaḥ ॥ 7-17॥)*. Exemplary all these surely are, but the true wise soul, in my opinion *(udārāḥ sarva evaite jñānī tvātmaiva me matam ।)*, is truly he that steadfast soul who is wholly intent upon me as the highest goal *(āsthitaḥ sa hi yuktātmā māmevānuttamāṃ gatim ॥ 7-18॥)*. Of the many births and deaths, the wise reach me *(bahūnāṃ janmanāmante jñānavānmāṃ prapadyate ।)*. Thus, Vāsudeva, among all, such a great soul is difficult to find *(vāsudevaḥ sarvamiti sa mahātmā sudurlabhaḥ ॥ 7-19॥)*.

कामैस्तैस्तैर्हृतज्ञानाः प्रपद्यन्तेऽन्यदेवताः ।
तं नियममास्थाय प्रकृत्या नियताः स्वया ॥ ७-२०॥
यो यां तनुं भक्तः श्रद्धयार्चितुमिच्छति ।
तस्य तस्याचलां श्रद्धां तामेव विदधाम्यहम् ॥ ७-२१॥
स तया श्रद्धया युक्तस्तस्याराधनमीहते ।
लभते च ततः कामान्मयैव विहितान्हि तान् ॥ ७-२२॥
अन्तवत्तु फलं तेषां तद्भवत्यल्पमेधसाम् ।
देवान्देवयजो यान्ति मद्भक्ता यान्ति मामपि ॥ ७-२३॥

(20-23) By desires, by this or that, due to lack of knowledge who become worshippers of other Gods *(kāmaistaistairhṛtajñānāḥ prapadyante 'nyadevatāḥ ।)*, having followed this or that set of rules or depending on their own *prakṛti* *(taṃ niyamamāsthāya prakṛtyā niyatāḥ svayā ॥ 7-20॥)*. Who, who, which, which manifestation the devotee worships with unflinching dedication, those desires that come from devotion I surely grant *(yo yāṃ tanuṃ bhaktaḥ śraddhāyārcitumicchati । tasya tasyācalāṃ śraddhāṃ tāmeva vidadhāmyaham ॥ 7-21॥)*. He who worships with absorbed dedication obtains those wishes, for those genuine desires and such others are actually bestowed by me *(sa tayā śraddhāyā yuktastasyārādhanamīhate । labhate ca tataḥ kāmānmayaiva vihitānhi tān ॥ 7-22॥)*. Truly, to them that are of low intelligence, fruits are limited *(antavattu phalaṃ teṣāṃ tadbhavatyalpamedhasām ।)*. To the deities go worshippers of deities. My devotees go to me only *(devāndevayajo yānti madbhaktā yānti māmapi ॥ 7-23॥)*.

अव्यक्तं व्यक्तिमापन्नं मन्यन्ते मामबुद्धयः ।
परं भावमजानन्तो ममाव्ययमनुत्तमम् ॥ ७-२४॥
नाहं प्रकाशः सर्वस्य योगमायासमावृतः ।
मूढोऽयं नाभिजानाति लोको मामजमव्ययम् ॥ ७-२५॥
वेदाहं समतीतानि वर्तमानानि चार्जुन ।
भविष्याणि च भूतानि मां तु वेद न कश्चन ॥ ७-२६॥

(24-26) Those of immature intellect cognize me who is unmanifest as acquiring manifestation of highest not intuiting me as immutable unsurpassed *(avyaktaṃ vyaktimāpannaṃ manyante māmabuddhayaḥ | paraṃ bhāvamajānanto mamāvyayamanuttamam || 7-24||)*. I am not illuminated, I am universal *yoga* concealed in *māyā (nāhaṃ prakāśaḥ sarvasya yogamāyāsamāvṛtaḥ |)*, the deluded of this world do not know that I am unborn imperishable *(mūḍho'yaṃ nābhijānāti loko māmajamavyayam || 7-25||)*. I know that which has occurred long ago, that which is present and the future, and some living people do not really know me *(vedāhaṃ samatītāni vartamānāni cārjuna | bhaviṣyāṇi ca bhūtāni māṃ tu veda na kaścana || 7-26||)*.

इच्छाद्वेषसमुत्थेन द्वन्द्वमोहेन भारत ।

सर्वभूतानि सम्मोहं सर्गे यान्ति परन्तप ॥ ७-२७॥

येषां त्वन्तगतं पापं जनानां पुण्यकर्मणाम् ।

ते द्वन्द्वमोहनिर्मुक्ता भजन्ते मां दृढव्रताः ॥ ७-२८॥

जरामरणमोक्षाय मामाश्रित्य यतन्ति ये ।

ते ब्रह्म तद्विदुः कृत्स्नमध्यात्मं कर्म चाखिलम् ॥ ७-२९॥

साधिभूताधिदैवं मां साधियज्ञं च ये विदुः ।

प्रयाणकालेऽपि च मां ते विदुर्युक्तचेतसः ॥ ७-३०॥

(27-30) Rising from desire and aversion, deluded by duality *(icchādveṣasamutthena dvandvamohena bhārata |)*, from birth, all beings are subject to delusion *(sarvabhūtāni sammohaṃ sarge yānti parantapa || 7-27||)*. At the end, men of stained birth but virtuous action, they who are free from delusion of opposites, worship me with firm vows *(yeṣāṃ tvantagataṃ pāpaṃ janānāṃ puṇyakarmaṇām | te dvandvamohanirmuktā bhajante māṃ dṛḍhavratāḥ || 7-28||)*. For liberation from old age and death, who take refuge in me and make an effort, they know that the *Brahman* is the complete transcendental Self and repository of action *(jarāmaraṇamokṣāya māmāśritya yatanti ye | te brahma tadviduḥ kṛtsnamadhyātmaṃ karma cākhilam || 7-29||)*. Who have steadfast consciousness on me know me to be primordial creation, primordial deity, and primordial sacrifice, even at the hour of death *(sādhibhūtādhidaivaṃ māṃ sādhiyajñaṃ ca ye viduḥ | prayāṇakāle'pi ca māṃ te viduryuktacetasaḥ || 7-30||)*.

◆ —— · ◆ ● · —— ◆

Chapter 8

Akṣara-brahma-yoga (yoga of the imperishable Brahman) [1]

Introduction

What is *akṣara-brahma-yoga? akṣara* means alphabet, which is indestructible. *Brahman* is the source of creation, sustenance, and dissolution. Hence, this chapter covers the qualities of *Brahman*. Śrī Kṛṣṇa also elaborates on his relationship with *Brahman*.

Arjuna asked – What is that *Brahman?* What is *adhyātman?* What is *karma, adhibhūta,* and *adhidaiva?* Who and how does *ādhiyajña* exist in this body? Finally, how is it cognized by the self-restrained soul at time of death? (verse1-2).

Śrī Kṛṣṇa replied - Imperishable *Brahman* is supreme and

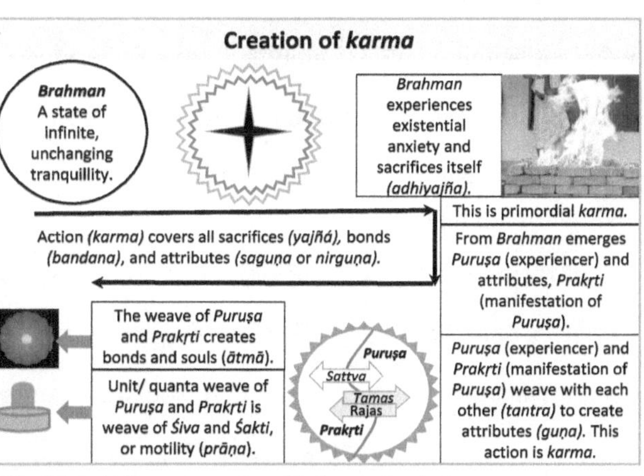

8.1 - Materiality emerges from Brahman due to *karma*

indestructible. In fact, its nature is transcendental, and it causes creation as an expression of itself. Also, this creation and this transformation is called *karma*. Next, *ādibhūta* (primordial creation) is any perishable state. Also, *puruṣa* is *adhyātman* (primordial soul). I (Śrī Kṛṣṇa) alone represent *ādhiyajña* (primordial sacrifice/ transformation or change) in existence (in the body or embodied) (verse 3-4).

---

[1] https://www.bhagavad-gita.org/Gita/chapter-08.html

Notes: *ādi* or primordial means anything that existed since the beginning of time, and transcendental is anything that goes beyond material, sensory or conceptual.

It is important to understand that *daiva* or deity is not God. In fact, a deity is an entity that acts as a representative of a particular task, role, or concept. For example, *savitā* is a deity that represents the qualities/energy of the Sun. Also, it is important to realize that there is no concept of God in *sanātana-dharma;* there is only *brahman*. The individual is considered to be *brahman* wrapped in *māyā* (illusion) due to ignorance *(avidyā)*. *Yoga* is the process of removing this veil of ignorance and merging the Individual with Truth *(brahman)*.

What is *Brahman*? [2]

The best explanation of *Brahman* is based in Physics.

oṃ pūrṇamadaḥ pūrṇamidaṃ pūrṇātpūrṇamudacyate ।
pūrṇasya pūrṇamādāya pūrṇamevāvaśiṣyate ॥
oṃ śāntiḥ ।

ॐ पूर्णमदः पूर्णमिदं पूर्णात्पूर्णमुदच्यते ।
पूर्णस्य पूर्णमादाय पूर्णमेवावशिष्यते ॥
ॐ शान्तिः ।

Which means that

- That is infinite, this is infinite, from infinity proceeds infinity,

- From infinity, when infinity is subtracted, truly, infinity is left as a remnant.

Let us understand *Brahman* on the basis of *mahāvākyas* (major aphorisms), which are four in number,

- *prajñānaṃ brahma* (प्रज्ञानं ब्रह्म) – all awareness is *Brahman*

- *ayam ātmā brahma* (अयम् आत्मा ब्रह्म) – this soul is the *Brahman*

- *tat tvam asi* (तत् त्वम् असि) – that thou art or you are *Brahman*

- *ahaṃ brahmāsmi* (अहं ब्रह्मास्मि) – I am *Brahman*

Brahman is a cognitive state of awareness (verse 3-4, 8-13)

The above state corresponds to everything that Śrī Kṛṣṇa describes *Brahman* to be – an indestructible, unchanging, eternal, and infinite state which is the source of everything and nothing as well. That can only correspond with the cognitive experience of peace that exists in the state of null or infinity!

---

[2] https://www.templepurohit.com/mantras-slokas-stotras/shanti-mantra/om-purnamadah-purnamidam

- First, *Brahman* is a state, and the yogī must experience THAT state, and he must become THAT.

- Second, *Brahman* is infinite, which means one must overcome (transcend) time, space, and matter.

- Third, *Brahman* is changeless, which means that the yogi must transcend the physical form and impact of stimuli on the Self because, when stimuli is annulled, there is no change.

- Fourth, *Brahman* is tranquility, which means that this is a state of "no agitation".

- Last, everything proceeds from *Brahman*. *Brahman* is the source and motility of materiality.

How does *Brahman* evolve?

First, imperishable *Brahman* is *adhyātman* (primordial Self) within the body. Next, it is the cause of creation and transformation, and this is called *karma*. *Brahman* causes motility in creation, and this is called *adhibhūta* (primordial creation). Also, *puruṣa* is *adhidaivata* or primordial

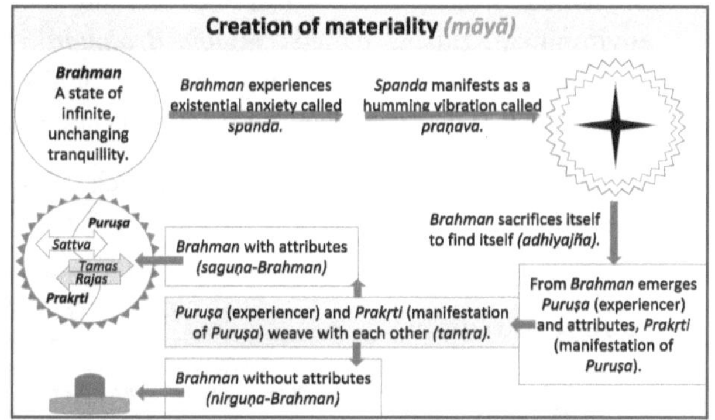

8.2 - Creation of materiality

deity, and he (Śrī Kṛṣṇa) as *ādhiyajña* (primordial sacrifice, transformation, or change) within the body. So, let us see how these entities integrate (verse 3-4).

- First, everything comes from the Source/Truth/Origin or *Brahman*. This is a state of infinite changelessness, eternal peace, and nothingness. Then, how does the *Brahman* manifest if it is a state of nothing but eternal, changeless peace?

- What happens is that *Brahman* experiences existential anxiety (Do I exist?) and desires self-expression (What am I? What is this? Do I exist? I want to see myself).

- How does this anxiety manifest? *Brahman* experiences an atemporal vibration or creative pulse called *spandana*. For example, when we say that we have a eureka moment, that insight comes to us from nowhere *(Brahman),* and we experience a creative outpouring *(spandana).* We know of two great scientists who had eureka moments, Newton (gravity) and Archimedes (buoyancy).

- So, from a state of nothingness, it suddenly becomes curious about itself and seeks to express its personality.

- Hence, *Brahman* sacrifices itself to express its Self *(adhyātman)*.

- This sacrifice of *Brahman* is called primordial sacrifice *(ādhiyajña)*, which is what Śrī Kṛṣṇa says he is.

- As a result of the sacrifice, it manifests as *puruṣa* (experiencer) and *prakṛti* (manifestation). The primordial expression of this manifestation is called *praṇava.*

- Then, *puruṣa* and *prakṛti* weave with each other to create manifested *(saguṇa-Brahman)* and unmanifested *(nirguṇa-Brahman)* In fact, that aspect of *Brahman* which can be cognized is called *saguṇa-Brahman* (manifested), and the rest is *nirguṇa-Brahman* (unmanifested).

- So, when *prakṛti* and *puruṣa* weave, and there is engagement with the environment, this is called *(saguṇa-Brahman)*. However, *prakṛti* does not always manifest, or when it does, it does not always get a response, in which case *puruṣa* experiences only itself. This is called *nirguṇa-Brahman.*

- Importantly, *nirguṇa* does not mean lack of existence; it means lack of manifestation.

- From *puruṣa, citta* (consciousness) emerges. However, *citta* is inert and takes on the quality *(bhāva)* of the entity that it is interacting with. Hence, it is the carrier of experiences.

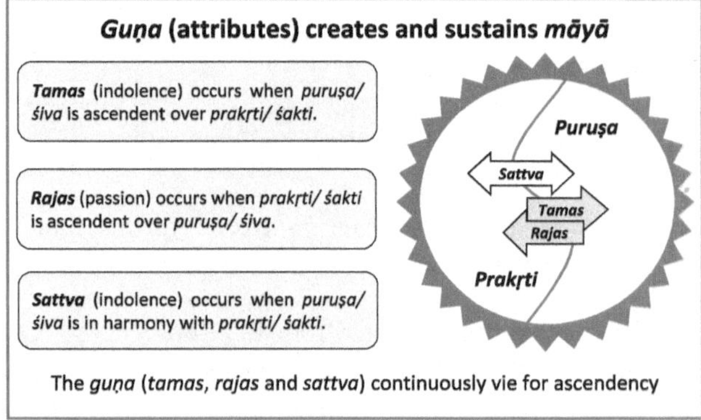

8.3 - *Guṇa* is a manifestation of *prakṛti* and *puruṣa*

- Also, *puruṣa* is continuously experiencing itself *(jñāna)* or stimulus coming from outside *(vijñāna)*.

- Furthermore, from *prakṛti* (action), *guṇa* (attributes) emerge. In fact, *guṇa*-s are a weave of *puruṣa* and *prakṛti*.

- Firstly, when *puruṣa* is ascendant over *prakṛti,* it is called *tamas* (delusion). Similarly, when *prakṛti* is ascendant over *puruṣa,* the attribute is called *rajas* (passion or flow). Finally, when *puruṣa* and *prakṛti* are in balance, this is called *sattva* (harmony or balance).

- Since, *puruṣa* and *prakṛti* have to work in order to create, maintain, or destroy the universe, this is called action; hence, *karma* emerges from the weave of *puruṣa* and *prakṛti*.

Importantly, one must recognize that *Brahman* is permanence or Truth, but starting with primordial sacrifice *(ādhiyajña),* the state of Śrī Kṛṣṇa, everything is impermanent, can decay and die!

- However, everything that is impermanent also seems real, even though it is conditional. is a veil of ignorance *(ajñāna)* covering of the *Brahman,* and hence, it is *māyā* (illusion).

Example

The progression of *Brahman* is from imperishable, changeless peace to manifestation. In fact, the *Brahman* is no different from us.

- First, we are in a state of nothing *(Brahman).* Then, we get an idea!

- If the idea is strong enough, then we make the sacrifice to make the idea work *(ādhiyajña).*

- When the idea manifests, this is called *saguṇa-Brahman (*manifested *Brahman).* Next, we experience anxiety that the idea should succeed.

- If we were to consider the idea to be an entity, then, for the idea, we are *Brahman (adhyātman),* we are in the idea, but the idea is not in us!

- Similarly, there are many ideas within us that never manifest, but remain within us. They are not dead, just unmanifested. These are called *nirguṇa-Brahman* (unmanifested *Brahman).*

Śrī Kṛṣṇa is *ādhiyajña*

- First, motility for *karma* comes from *Brahman.*

- Also, *karma* results in creation of transactions and bonds, which in turn result in creation of multiple identities/Souls or *ātman* of varying complexities.

- As a result of the creation of multiple and complex transactions, bonds, and entities, the universe is created and this is called golden egg *(hiraṇyagarbha).*

- Also, the center of Identity of the Universe *(hiraṇyagarbha)* is called viṣṇu.

- Additionally, all *karma* occurs within the *hiraṇyagarbha,* which is the manifested aspect of the *Brahman (saguṇa-Brahman).*

- Since *Brahman* underwrites the motility of *karma, Brahman* exists everywhere.

- Also, since all *karma* require a sacrifice *(yajña)* for manifestation, Śrī Kṛṣṇa, as *ādi,* is everywhere and is the transformation point of materiality.

Example

- Each housing society is defined by a boundary wall and has its own Identity. Similarly, each city, state, region, country, or planet have their own center of Identity.

- The Sun has a unique Identity which comes from its qualities, such as its name, color, size, as well as its capability to produce light and heat and its position as the center of the Solar system.

- Similarly, other planets such as Mars, Jupiter, Saturn, or Moon have their own identities. The biggest extant entity is the Universe, and Śrī Kṛṣṇa says that he is beyond even that.

- Since, he claims the position of *ādhiyajña,* Śrī Kṛṣṇa is a state that has transcended material existence and merged with the source *(Brahman)*. This allows him to participate and become the underwriting qualities of all the various entities *(ātman-s)* without becoming involved in their experience of existence.

Dynamics of death

According to Śrī Kṛṣṇa, in Chapter 2, the body perishes, but the Soul *(ātman)* moves to another body to repay its debts, based on its past *karma*. How does this happen?

- To understand this, we need to understand rebirth. Why does rebirth occur?

- The answer to this lies in *karma*. We are born on account of debt *(ṛṇa),* and throughout, we are either debtors or creditors. This is called *prārabdha-karma (karma* that has come up for repayment). Here, *karma* means debt *(ṛṇa).* Consequently, this loose use of *karma* terminology can be confusing.

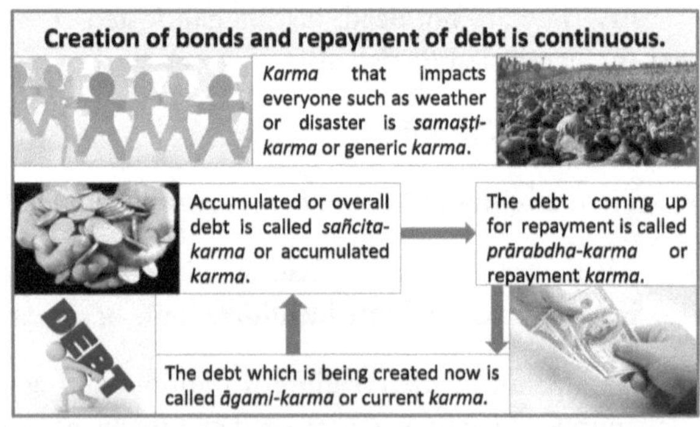

8.4 - *Kama* is both, action and debt

- All main events, people, and situations we encounter in our lives occur because of *prārabdha-karma*.

- Throughout life, in the process of reconciling *prārabdha-karma*, we act. Moreover, during the process of reconciliation, in addition to reconciling old *karma* accounts, we also create new ones through our ongoing actions, and these go into our overall book of debt. This is called *āgāmi-karma* (present state *karma* or debt creation).

- This overall register of debt is called *sañcita-karma* (overall *karma*). Since all debt cannot be squared-off in one life this *karma* is the reason for rebirth,. Remember, when it comes to *karma,* one may either be a creditor or a debtor, and reconciliation spares no one.

- At death, a person becomes a sentiment *(bhāva),* a residue of unfulfilled desires, regrets, or *vāsanās,* which will become a part of the template for subsequent life *(saṃsāra).*

- In fact, they will manifest as motivation *(vāsanā),* which will be exhibited as personality *(bhāva)* when the person is reborn.

Is there any way for an individual to break this cycle of *saṃsāra* (birth and death) through *karma*?

- All debts are carried by our Self or *ātman*. Therefore, if the Self were to cease to exist, then there would be no one for clearance of *karma* (debt or credit).

- The soul *(ātman),* is after all a manifestation of the unmanifest *(Brahman).*

- *Karma* is accrued to that aspect which considers itself the doer *(ahaṅkāra).* *Karma* here means debt *(ṛṇa)* as opposed to action *(karma).* Consequently, this loose interpretation of terminology could be confusing.

- *Karma* occurs on account of duality (like-dislike, good-bad, truth-lies, God-Devil, merit-sin, love-hate) etc. When we like something, we bring it closer *(rāga),* and when we dislike something, we push it away *(dveśa).* This act of pushing and pulling results in *karma* and the imbalance in transaction causes debt *(ṛṇa)* which needs to be repaid.

- So, this means that no *karma* is accrued when there is no doer (no *asmitā* in the transaction/absence of the feeling of doer-ship or *ahaṅkāra*). So, when self-worth *(asmitā)* is indifferent to duality (like-dislike, good-bad etc.), there is no *karma*.

- This absence of the sentiment of being the doer *(ahaṅkāra)* in any activity occurs when work *(karma)* is performed as sacrifice (selflessness, not selfishness). Additionally, sacrifice may be defined as work done without expectation of return; this can also be called duty!

- Another way is when action is dedicated to another entity that cannot return the debt, like Śrī Kṛṣṇa, a deity, Guru, society, or Country.

- So, when Śrī Kṛṣṇa says "dedicate your activity to Me (Śrī Kṛṣṇa)", he means that when one dedicates any activity to a favorite deity *(iṣṭadeva),* there is no *karma,* because there is no experience of being a doer *(ahaṅkāra).* Consequently, this breaks the cycle of rebirth *(saṃsāra)* and enables one to transcend existence/ materiality *(māyā).*

- Another interesting aspect in the explanation of Śrī Kṛṣṇa is his position as the owner of *yajña* or sacrifice, the state which occurs before there is manifestation of the Soul *(ātman).* So, when sacrifice is offered to sacrifice, a person hypothetically offers sacrifice to Śrī Kṛṣṇa even before the manifestation has started, thereby negating the effects of *karma.*

- All the above methods are overt or gross *(sthūla)* methods of controlling debt *(ṛṇa* or *karma).*

- However, even when it is not acting, the Self *(ātman)* still exists, and this has to be neutered. The Self must be brought to a point where its individual Identity or Soul *(ātman)* ceases to exist. This is the subtle *(sūkṣma)* aspect.

- When this completely neutered state is reached, the Self *(ātman)* experiences no change or *karma (nirvikalpa);* and the consciousness does not react to stimulus *(citta-vṛtti-nirodha).*

- This place of no-change is also a state of infinite peace or nothingness. It is the state of permanence *(brahman).*

- The yoking of the Self *(ātman)* with the *Brahman* is *yoga,* and in this state, there is no rebirth.

Example: All of us have faced exams, and anyone who has worked in a corporate environment has faced the stress of annual appraisals. In fact, the shortcoming of any appraisal is that it seeks to force diverse achievements into a "bell" curve, often compelling managers to compare apples with oranges.

Applying Śrī Kṛṣṇa's concept here - perform your task diligently (with *śraddhā).* Communicate without fear or favor, with the sole intent of successful completion of the assigned task. Next, when appraisal comes, prepare well, and state your achievements.

Finally, when the result is out, accept it without allowing any exultation or depression. Do not resist the outcome. When there is no resistance, the cycle of *karma* is broken. If there is injustice, fight, but don't make it personal. Be as inert as possible in your struggle, but don't lose your humanity.

Obviously, this is difficult, which is why transcending rebirth is not for the faint-hearted.

Death and rebirth

If a person had unsuccessfully wished to complete a PhD, see a child, sibling, or person before dying, go to a particular place or had some bucket list, then that overriding sentiment is carried away at death as *karma*.

- We have seen how *karma* creates debt, which must be reconciled. Also, when a person dies, any sentiment of want, desire, or regret he or she holds on to that moment is the greatest unfulfilled desire in life.

- This becomes the defining aspect of the individual at rebirth, and when the person is reborn, it become a fixation in the personality, called embedded memory *(vāsanā)* on account of *prārabdha-karma*.

- The first suggestion of Śrī Kṛṣṇa is that a *yogī* who wishes to avoid rebirth should focus his consciousness *(citta)* on the *puruṣa (adhidaiva)*. While Śrī Kṛṣṇa explains the qualities of *puruṣa,* these are abstract, making the suggestions difficult to implement.

- Instead, it would be simpler for the *yogī* to follow Śrī Kṛṣṇa's other instruction and anchor *(yukta)* his consciousness *(citta)* on his *prāṇa* at the center of eyebrows and reach immortality at death.

- Also, one could practice thinking of Śrī Kṛṣṇa all the time, so that at death, the person merges in Śrī Kṛṣṇa, avoiding rebirth. Instead, the person goes to the place where great souls *(mahātman)* have reached and does not return. This suggestion is not just valid for Śrī Kṛṣṇa, one could apply this to any favorite deity *(iṣṭa-daivata)* also.

- A good practice which Śrī Kṛṣṇa explains that can be used at death is:

  o Control all the gates (eyes, ears, tongue, olfactory, nasal, legs, hands, sexual organs, anus, urination organs). Control means that these organs should be without stress or tension, and there should be a feeling of peace, there should be no input or output.

  o Next, center the cognition *(manas)* in the heart region.

  o After this, place the Self (Identity) in the frontal lobe of the brain *(mūladhi)*.

  o To achieve this, the *yogi* must stop his or her consciousness or cognition *(citta)* from flowing out and steady it in the frontal lobe area without movement. There will be slight compression, tightness, or pressure in the frontal lobe, and the *yogī* must slowly make the sensation placid, peaceful, calm, or without pressure.

  o Lastly, let the *prāṇa* be in harmonic meditation (this means that the *prāṇa* should move unstressed within the body).

- o Finally, when leaving the body, utter OM, or any *bījakṣara* (Śrī Kṛṣṇa says any *akṣara* or single syllables). This stops other regrets and desires from becoming *karma*.

- o A *bījakṣara* (*bīja* = root+ *akṣara* = syllable) is any single alphabet. In *Saṃskṛta*, all *akṣara*-s have certain frequency control. So, what happens is that when a person focuses on an alphabet, then there is loss of Identity into the Self. This results in stoppage of rebirth.

- o Remember *brahman* or Śrī Kṛṣṇa or any favorite deity *(iṣṭa-daivata)*.

The above practices are very practical and doable; if one were to practice this kind of meditation regularly, then it will be easy to fall into that state at the time of death.

How *yajña* weaves with *Bhārat's* culture

- Firstly, every activity is started with a *saṅkalpa* (vow to complete).

- Secondly, activity is conducted in accordance with the Laws of *ṛta* [3].

- Finally, after work is completed, the fruits are offered to a form of Śrī Kṛṣṇa, also called Narayana, and this is called *kāyena-vacā* [4].

Ordinarily, people finish any activity by chanting, *"sarvaṃ kṛṣṇārpaṇam"* (*sarva* = everything + Kṛṣṇa = Śrī Kṛṣṇa + *arpaṇa* = offering). In this way, practitioners sacrifice their activity and results to Śrī Kṛṣṇa. Thus, the Self is negated, and everything is sacrificed to Śrī Kṛṣṇa.

Śrī Kṛṣṇa explains himself (verse 5-7)

Śrī Kṛṣṇa says that he is that point in the supra-system where there is no Identity. So, anyone who focusses his or her cognition and intelligence on him (Śrī Kṛṣṇa) shall reach that point and not be born again.

- This argument may seem counter-intuitive. If there is a Śrī Kṛṣṇa who is cognized, there must be a Self *(ātman)* that cognizes Śrī Kṛṣṇa, which means that *yoga* is not complete because the Self still exists and has not been neutralized.

- However, this is possible if the *yogī* were to adopt a technique that requires one to lose his or her identity *(ātman)* completely in Śrī Kṛṣṇa. In this condition, the Self ceases to exist.

- It does not matter whether Śrī Kṛṣṇa exists or not, nor in what state. What matters is that the Self should cease to exist.

- This *yoga* is called *bhakti-yoga* (refer Chapter-12) [5].

---

[3] https://schoolofyoga.in/thought-leadership/performance-concept-india
[4] https://ramanisblog.in/2016/09/09/kayena-vacha-surrender-origin-free-will
[5] https://schoolofyoga.in/yoga-concept/bhakti-yoga

- Additionally, this method is not confined to Śrī Kṛṣṇa but can be used with other deities as well.

Conclusion: Śrī Kṛṣṇa is a *yogī* who has reached an extremely high level of *"sthita-prajñā "* or "situational awareness". Hence, Śrī Kṛṣṇa is able to explain the nuances of his position with respect to *Brahman*.

Creation (verse 23-28)

Those who know that *brahma's* day lasts a thousand yugas also know that his nights last a thousand yugas. At beginning of his day, manifestation occurs from the *Brahman* (source), and, at night, all that is perishable merges back into him. Beyond this is the region of the imperishable. I reside in this abode. Only through unwavering focus can one reach me, and thence, this abode of the Imperishable.

Those who die when sun is moving north *(uttarāyaṇa)* for 6 months, during waxing moon *(śukla-pakṣa),* and in day go to *Brahman*. Those who die when the sun is moving South *(dakṣiṇāyaṇa)*, during the waning moon *(kṛṣṇa-pakṣa),* and at night, return. Any *yogī* who understands this yoga needs no other knowledge.

How does the math of creation work? What is a *kalpa?* [6]

- Firstly, the Universe or *hiraṇyagarbha* is an identity called Viṣṇu.

- Next, *Brahmā* emerges from Viṣṇu. *Brahmā's* lifespan is calculated as follows:

    o 1 human day = 8 *yāma*

    o 1 day of the *pitṛs* (ancestors) = 1 month/30 days

    o Lifespan of *pitṛs* = 100 years or 3000 human years.

    o 1 day of *daivas* (deities or divinities) = 1 human year

    o Lifespan of *daivas* = 12000 years = 4320000 human years.

    o 1 *mahāyuga* = 12000 years = 4320000 human years

    o 1 day of Brahmā = 1 *kalpa* = 1000 *mahāyuga* = 4.32 billion human years

    o 1 day and night of Brahmā = 2 *kalpa* = 8.64 billion human years

    o Lifespan of Brahmā *(mahā-kalpa)* = 100 Years = 311.04 trillion human years.

Note: it is important to distinguish Brahmā (the creator) from *brahman* (the source) and *brāhmin* (a human being whose sole purpose is to realize the *Brahman* and disseminate that knowledge *(brahma-vidya)* to the world.

---

[6]http://connectsciencetodivinity.blogspot.com/2015/03/manvantara-and-kalpa-timeline-which.html

Some contradictions to accepted positions – conclusion on verse 23-26:

- There is a problem with Śrī Kṛṣṇa's assertion (verse 23-26) that the time of death determines rebirth or escape from it. The reason for this conflict is his assertion in verses 5-16 where he states that a person would be reborn according to his sentiment *(bhāva)* at death.

- In fact, the advice in verses 5-16 are in conformance with the rest of *Śrimad-Śrimad-Bhagavad-gītā* and also to Śrī Kṛṣṇa's own laws of *karma,* while verses 23-26 run are out of conformance to the rest of the text.

- Next, in verses 11-16, Śrī Kṛṣṇa also advises Arjuna on how a person should die to avoid rebirth, and the advice is not dependent of time of death.

- Lastly, if a person gets the merit of his or her own actions, then his rebirth cannot be governed by the time of death. Instead, if we were to accept the law of *karma,* a person would die when his *karma* required his departure.

Hence, verses 23-26 are out of congruence from the rest of *Śrimad-Bhagavad-gītā.* The practitioner/reader may draw his or her own conclusions.

Śrimad-bhāgavad-purāṇa explains this process of confronting death [7]

When a person has completed the duties as specified by the *āśrama*, the person should then begin to realize that he or she must confront death.

The key to dispassion is to draw down on use of energy and become minimalist. This is done by minimizing consumption of cooked food and slowly migrating to natural foods, such as nuts, milk, and other simple foods/cereals. The person should keep minimum stock of food. The person should also maintain a simple wardrobe, giving away clothes as soon as fresh ones are procured. He is expected to minimize living space and reduce travel. Also, the person is encouraged to stop spending too much time in personal appearance as well as stop being fussy about his surroundings.

When the person slowly becomes infirm, that person is encouraged to reduce intake, harmonize his or her *prāṇa,* and give up identification with the body in the following manner:

- Control of the senses is done by merging the apertures of the body, viz, the two eyes, ears, nostrils, mouth, and organs of urination and defecation in ether (*ākāṣa* or space).

- Next the internal heat of the body is controlled by not allowing it to emanate from the body. This will also merge the five *vāyu (prāṇa, apāna, vyāna, udāna, samāna)* into the cosmic airflow *(vāyu).*

---

[7]https://en.krishnakosh.org/krishna/Śrimad_Bhagvata_Mahapurana_Book_7_Chapter_12:16-31

- Then the person should merge the various parts of the body into their primordial elements – earth, water, fire, air, and ether (space). For instance, speech should be bestowed to fire, hands, and craftsmanship to Indra, locomotion to Viṣṇu, sensual pleasures to Prajapati, etc.

- Then *asmitā* (I am this/sense of identity or self-worth) and *ahaṅkāra* should be merged with Rudra.

- When this is steady, then the soul *(ātma)* slowly merges with the source *(Brahman)*.

- After this the person should cease functioning like a fire that has run out of resources.

Clearly, dying in a conscious state, fully merged with the *Brahman,* is the preferred method of dying.

Lessons learned:

- The process of creation has never been detailed properly in any ancient text due to differences in interpretations. The delineations that are detailed in this version of *Śrimad-Bhagavad-gītā* are a distillation of the myriad proposals in *Śrimad-Bhagavad-gītā, Śrimad-bhāgavad-purāṇa,* and *Manu-smṛti.* However, since there is no clear linkage between the myriad terms, some assumptions have been made, resulting in the process detailed above and in the various chapters.

- One aspect which the living often miss is the dying. How do we die, what happens to the Soul, where does it go, how does the debt get reconciled and programmed into another Soul for reinsertion on Earth, etc.?

  o Again, while ancient texts do shed some light on the journey of the Soul, that is not always clear and subject to interpretation.

  o However, for the living, one clear direction is provided by Śrī Kṛṣṇa. You can prepare for death by practicing how your consciousness *(citta)* will exit the body. While one's state at death may vary, with practice, we can condition our consciousness, which means that we have a fighting chance at controlling the movement of the Soul after it exits from the body.

  o But Śrī Kṛṣṇa's tool of controlling the consciousness requires discipline *(abhyāsa)* and sacrifice *(yajña).*

The transliteration and translation of chapter 8 follows:

अर्जुन उवाच ।

किं तद् ब्रह्म किमध्यात्मं किं कर्म पुरुषोत्तम ।

अधिभूतं च किं प्रोक्तमधिदैवं किमुच्यते ॥ ८-१॥

अधियज्ञः कथं कोऽत्र देहेऽस्मिन्मधुसूदन ।

प्रयाणकाले च कथं ज्ञेयोऽसि नियतात्मभिः ॥ ८-२॥

Arjuna asked (1-2) What is that *brahman?* What is *adhyātman?* What is *karma?* *adhibhuta* and *adhidaiva?* What is that which is called *adidaiva? (kiṃ tad brahma kimadhyātmaṃ kiṃ karma puruṣottama ꞱꞱ adhibhūtaṃ ca kiṃ proktamadhidaivaṃ kimucyate ॥ 8-1॥)?* Who and how does *ādhiyajña* exist in this body? How is it cognized by the self-restrained soul at the time of death *(adhiyajñaḥ kathaṃ ko'tra dehe'sminmadhusūdana ꞱꞱ prayāṇakāle ca kathaṃ jñeyo'si niyatātmabhiḥ ॥ 8-2॥)?*

श्रीभगवानुवाच ।

अक्षरं ब्रह्म परमं स्वभावोऽध्यात्ममुच्यते ।

भूतभावोद्भवकरो विसर्गः कर्मसंज्ञितः ॥ ८-३॥

अधिभूतं क्षरो भावः पुरुषश्चाधिदैवतम् ।

अधियज्ञोऽहमेवात्र देहे देहभृतां वर ॥ ८-४॥

Śrī Kṛṣṇa said (3-4) The imperishable *brahman* is supreme, they say that its nature is transcendental *(akṣaraṃ brahma paramaṃ svabhāvo'dhyātmamucyate Ʇ),* it causes self-expression in creation which is called *karma (bhūtabhāvodbhavakaro visargaḥ karmasaṃjñitaḥ ॥ 8-3॥).* Primordial creation is any perishable situation/state, *puruṣa* is the primordial deity, I alone am primordial sacrifice in the body or the embodied *(adhibhūtaṃ kṣaro bhāvaḥ puruṣaścādhidaivatam Ʇ adhiyajño'hamevātra dehe dehabhṛtāṃ vara ॥ 8-4॥).*

अन्तकाले च मामेव स्मरन्मुक्त्वा कलेवरम् ।

यः प्रयाति स मद्भावं याति नास्त्यत्र संशयः ॥ ८-५॥

यं वापि स्मरन्भावं त्यजत्यन्ते कलेवरम् ।

तं तमेवैति कौन्तेय सदा तद्भावभावितः ॥ ८-६॥

(5-6) When dying and leaving the body, remember me only *(antakāle ca māmeva smaranmuktvā kalevaram Ʇ),* he who makes an effort goes to my being *(yaḥ prayāti sa madbhāvaṃ),* here is no doubt *(yāti nāstyatra saṃsayaḥ ॥ 8-5॥).* Whatever intuition or memory even, one leaves the body at the end, to that steady state the spirit is transformed *(yaṃ vāpi smaranbhāvaṃ tyajatyante kalevaram Ʇ taṃ tamevaiti kaunteya sadā tadbhāvabhāvitaḥ ॥ 8-6॥).*

तस्मात्सर्वेषु कालेषु मामनुस्मर युध्य च ।
मय्यर्पितमनोबुद्धिर्मामेवैष्यस्यसंशयः ॥ ८-७॥
अभ्यासयोगयुक्तेन चेतसा नान्यगामिना ।
परमं पुरुषं दिव्यं याति पार्थानुचिन्तयन् ॥ ८-८॥

(7-8) Therefore, at all times think of me, and fight *(tasmātsarveṣu kāleṣu māmanusmara yudhya ca ı)*. Transfer your cognition and intelligence upon me, to me alone will you come, without doubt *(mayyarpitamanobuddhirmāmevaiṣyasyasaṃśayaḥ ॥ 8-7॥)*. Practice *yoga* with focused consciousness which is not wandering *(abhyāsayogayuktena cetasā nānyagāminā ı)*, reach by constantly thinking, the divine supreme *puruṣa (paramaṃ puruṣaṃ divyaṃ yāti pārthānucintayan ॥ 8-8॥)*.

कविं पुराणमनुशासितार-
	मणोरणीयंसमनुस्मरेद्यः ।
सर्वस्य धातारमचिन्त्यरूप-
	मादित्यवर्णं तमसः परस्तात् ॥ ८-९॥
प्रयाणकाले मनसाऽचलेन
	भक्त्या युक्तो योगबलेन चैव ।
भ्रुवोर्मध्ये प्राणमावेश्य सम्यक्
	स तं परं पुरुषमुपैति दिव्यम् ॥ ८-१०॥

(9-10) Ancient Seer, lawful Ruler, more minute than the atom or memory, who supports everything and is of incomprehensible form with the color of the Sun *(kaviṃ purāṇamanuśāsitāra - maṇoraṇīyaṃsamanusmaredyaḥ ı sarvasya dhātāramacintyarūpa- mādityavarṇaṃ tamasaḥ parastāt ॥ 8-9॥)*. At the time of departure, with unwavering cognition, devotion united by strength of *Yoga* and only by bringing the *prāṇa* exactly between the eyebrows, he merges with the supreme divine *puruṣa (prayāṇakāle manasā'calena- bhaktyā yukto yogabalena caiva ı bhruvormadhye prāṇamāveśya samyak- sa taṃ paraṃ puruṣamupaiti divyam ॥ 8-10॥)*.

यदक्षरं वेदविदो वदन्ति
	विशन्ति यद्यतयो वीतरागाः ।
यदिच्छन्तो ब्रह्मचर्यं चरन्ति
	तत्ते पदं सङ्ग्रहेण प्रवक्ष्ये ॥ ८-११॥
सर्वद्वाराणि संयम्य मनो हृदि निरुध्य च ।
मूर्ध्न्याधायात्मनः प्राणमास्थितो योगधारणाम् ॥ ८-१२॥
ओमित्येकाक्षरं ब्रह्म व्याहरन्मामनुस्मरन् ।
यः प्रयाति त्यजन्देहं स याति परमां गतिम् ॥ ८-१३॥

(11-13) That which knowers of the Vedas proclaim as imperishable, which ascetics freed from attachment and those desires by practicing *brahmacharyam* enter the goal that I will explain to you *(yadakṣaraṃ vedavido vadanti- viśanti yadyatayo vītarāgāḥ | yadicchanto brahmacaryaṃ caranti- tatte padaṃ saṅgraheṇa pravakṣye || 8-11||)*. Having controlled all the gates controlling cognition and the heart and having placed the Soul in the forehead, anchor the *prāṇa* for continuous harmony in meditation *(sarvadvārāṇi saṃyamya mano hṛdi nirudhya ca | mūrdhnyādhāyātmanaḥ prāṇamāsthito yogadhāraṇām || 8-12||)*. Thus, he who departs and leaves the body uttering OM, any single- syllable, remembering *brahman* or me, he attains the supreme goal *(omityekākṣaraṃ brahma vyāharanmāmanusmaran | yaḥ prayāti tyajandehaṃ sa yāti paramāṃ gatim || 8-13||)*.

अनन्यचेताः सततं यो मां स्मरति नित्यशः ।

तस्याहं सुलभः पार्थ नित्ययुक्तस्य योगिनः ॥ ८-१४॥

मामुपेत्य पुनर्जन्म दुःखालयमशाश्वतम् ।

नाप्नुवन्ति महात्मानः संसिद्धिं परमां गताः ॥ ८-१५॥

आब्रह्मभुवनाल्लोकाः पुनरावर्तिनोऽर्जुन ।

मामुपेत्य तु कौन्तेय पुनर्जन्म न विद्यते ॥ ८-१६॥

(14-16) Who has a consciousness that is not fragmented constantly remembers me always, to him constant harmonization in *Yoga* is easy *(ananyacetāḥ satataṃ yo māṃ smarati nityaśaḥ | tasyāhaṃ sulabhaḥ pārtha nityayuktasya yoginaḥ || 8-14||)*. He who has reached me does not get to any place of pain in another birth but goes to an eternal, exalted place which great Souls that have attained perfection reach *(māmupetya punarjanma duḥkhālayamaśāśvatam | nāpnuvanti mahātmānaḥ saṃsiddhiṃ paramāṃ gatāḥ || 8-15||)*. Up to the world of Brahma one may return again, but having attained me, previous births do not occur *(ābrahmabhuvanāllokāḥ punarāvartino 'rjuna | māmupetya tu kaunteya punarjanma na vidyate || 8-16||)*.

सहस्रयुगपर्यन्तमहर्यद् ब्रह्मणो विदुः ।

रात्रिं युगसहस्रान्तां तेऽहोरात्रविदो जनाः ॥ ८-१७॥

अव्यक्ताद् व्यक्तयः सर्वाः प्रभवन्त्यहरागमे ।

रात्र्यागमे प्रलीयन्ते तत्रैवाव्यक्तसंज्ञके ॥ ८-१८॥

भूतग्रामः स एवायं भूत्वा प्रलीयते ।

रात्र्यागमेऽवशः पार्थ प्रभवत्यहरागमे ॥ ८-१९॥

(17-19) The people that know night and day know that the day of Brahma ends after a thousand years, the night ends after a thousand years *(sahasrayugaparyantamaharyad brahmaṇo viduḥ | rātriṃ yugasahasrāntāṃ te'horātravido janāḥ || 8-17||)*. From the unmanifested proceed all manifestations at the coming of day *(avyaktād vyaktayaḥ sarvāḥ prabhavantyaharāgame ।). Next, at the coming of night, dissolution truly happens and becomes unmanifested (rātryāgame pralīyante tatraivāvyaktasaṃjñake ॥ 8-18॥). Multitude of beings that are born again and again and are dissolved at the coming of night are truly helpless at this occurrence when day ends (bhūtagrāmaḥ sa evāyaṃ bhūtvā pralīyate । rātryāgame'vaśaḥ pārtha prabhavatyaharāgame ॥ 8-19॥).*

परस्तस्मात्तु भावोऽन्योऽव्यक्तोऽव्यक्तात्सनातनः ।

यः स सर्वेषु भूतेषु नश्यत्सु न विनश्यति ॥ ८-२०॥

अव्यक्तोऽक्षर इत्युक्तस्तमाहुः परमां गतिम् ।

यं प्राप्य न निवर्तन्ते तद्धाम परमं मम ॥ ८-२१॥

पुरुषः स परः पार्थ भक्त्या लभ्यस्त्वनन्यया ।

यस्यान्तःस्थानि भूतानि येन सर्वमिदं ततम् ॥ ८-२२॥

(20-22) Higher than that but existing is another unmanifested other than the unmanifested which is eternal who is in all beings which on perishing does not get destroyed *(parastasmāttu bhāvo'nyo'vyakto'vyaktātsanātanaḥ । yaḥ sa sarveṣu bhūteṣu naśyatsu na vinaśyati ॥ 8-20॥).* Unmanifested and imperishable, this is called That, they say it is the supreme goal, which having attained, there is no return and that supreme home is mine *(avyakto'kṣara ityuktastamāhuḥ paramāṃ gatim । yaṃ prāpya na nivartante taddhāma paramaṃ mama ॥ 8-21॥).* Puruṣa is supreme undoubtedly, attainable by devotion, when nothing else is there in being, then all this is That *(puruṣaḥ sa paraḥ pārtha bhaktyā labhyastvananyayā । yasyāntaḥsthāni bhūtāni yena sarvamidaṃ tatam ॥ 8-22॥).*

यत्र काले त्वनावृत्तिमावृत्तिं चैव योगिनः ।

प्रयाता यान्ति तं कालं वक्ष्यामि भरतर्षभ ॥ ८-२३॥

अग्निर्ज्योतिरहः शुक्लः षण्मासा उत्तरायणम् ।

तत्र प्रयाता गच्छन्ति ब्रह्म ब्रह्मविदो जनाः ॥ ८-२४॥

धूमो रात्रिस्तथा कृष्णः षण्मासा दक्षिणायनम् ।

तत्र चान्द्रमसं ज्योतिर्योगी प्राप्य निवर्तते ॥ ८-२५॥

शुक्लकृष्णे गती ह्येते जगतः शाश्वते मते ।

एकया यात्यनावृत्तिमन्ययावर्तते पुनः ॥ ८-२६॥

(23-26) Also, I will tell you what happens at death about non-return or return and even about where *yogīs* go after death *(yatra kāle tvanāvṛttimāvṛttiṃ caiva yoginaḥ । prayātā yānti taṃ kālaṃ vakṣyāmi bharatarṣabha ॥ 8-23॥).* First, fire, light, day, ascending lunar fortnight six-months of the northern movement of Sun, those departing will go to Brahma and cognize Brahma *(agnirjyotirahaḥ śuklaḥ ṣaṇmāsā uttarāyaṇam ı tatra prayātā gacchanti brahma brahmavido janāḥ ıı 8-24ıı).* Smoke, night, and descending lunar fortnight six months of the southern movement of the Sun, by the lunar light, the yogi will get to return *(dhūmo rātristathā kṛṣṇaḥ ṣaṇmāsā dakṣiṇāyanam ı tatra cāndramasaṃ jyotiryogī prāpya nivartate ıı 8-25ıı).* Ascending and descending lunar cycles paths, these are genuinely thought to be eternal in the world, by one a person goes without return, by the other, returns again *(śuklakṛṣṇe gatī hyete jagataḥ śāśvate mate ı ekayā yātyanāvṛttimanyayāvartate punaḥ ıı 8-26ıı).*

नैते सृती पार्थ जानन्योगी मुह्यति कश्चन ।

तस्मात्सर्वेषु कालेषु योगयुक्तो भवार्जुन ॥ ८-२७॥

वेदेषु यज्ञेषु तपःसु चैव

दानेषु यत्पुण्यफलं प्रदिष्टम् ।

अत्येति तत्सर्वमिदं विदित्वा

योगी परं स्थानमुपैति चाद्यम् ॥ ८-२८॥

(27-28) Neither of these paths deludes anyone who has reached the state of sublime merger *(naite sṛtī pārtha jānanyogī muhyati kaścana ı)*; therefore, at all times, be steadfast in *yoga (tasmātsarveṣu kāleṣu yogayukto bhavārjuna ıı 8-27ıı).* Whether the person is a *vedāntin,* practitioner of sacrifices, an ascetic, and also giver of alms *(vedeṣu yajñeṣu tapaḥsu caiva dāneṣu),* whatever merit is decreed, surpassing that is this, which having known, the *yogī* attains supreme and primeval abode *(yatpuṇyaphalaṃ pradiṣṭam ı atyeti tatsarvamidaṃ viditvā yogī paraṃ sthānamupaiti cādyam ıı 8-28ıı).*

✦ —— · ● ◆ ● · —— ✦

Chapter 9

Rājavidyā-rājaguhya-yoga
(yoga of sovereign science, sovereign secret) [1]

Introduction - What are *rājavidyā and rājaguhya*?

- *Rājavidyā* = *rāja+vidyā* means sovereign knowledge or understanding the functioning of a kingdom. *Rājaguhya* = *rāja+guhya* means sovereign secrets are those underlying concepts that support the knowledge of functioning of a kingdom.

- So, what is the kingdom, this knowledge and secret?

- First, kingdom is obviously the universe that we live in. Next, knowledge is the functioning of this universe, and finally, the secret is how a person's application of free will at death changes the direction of his

- In fact, Śrī Kṛṣṇa states that direct cognitive experience *(pratyakṣa-eva-gamya)* is critical for comprehension of this knowledge, which is the gross and subtle manifested and unmanifested aspects of *Brahman*.

This chapter also brings out Śrī Kṛṣṇa's role in *Srimad-Bhagavad-gītā* as that of a *yogī* who has attained a supreme awareness and who guides practitioners in transcending *māyā* (illusion) to merge with the Truth *(Brahman)*. So, this chapter enables yoga practitioners to differentiate the mythological person "Śrī Kṛṣṇa", from the *yogī* in *Śrimad-Bhagavad-gītā*.

Śrī Kṛṣṇa explains himself, verse (1-5):

Now I will explain how yoga can help a person transcend perception and achieve merger with the *Brahman* through direct experience *(pratyakṣa-eva-gamya)*. Indeed,

[1]https://www.bhagavad-gita.org/Gita/chapter-09.html

this process is very easy for those who follow *dharma* (stay on the path of natural conditioning, harmony, or order) and can be achieved through *śraddhā* (effort that is sincere, dedicated, persistent, and filled with patience).

- All existence is pervaded by me as unmanifested *Brahman*. Also, all exist in me. However, though I support all creation but I do not abide in them. In fact, all entities merge into creation *(prakṛti)* at the end of an eon *(kalpa)*. Subsequently, they get regenerated at the beginning of next *kalpa,* whether they prefer it or not. Through all this, I remain unconcerned and unattached while I preside over this activity.

- Unfortunately, people get deluded and pray only to my human form, ignoring my truth as the lord of all beings (verse 11). But those that understand me, seek me with single-minded devotion.

- Lastly, people need to realize that they must not indulge in pointless hope, activity without reason, or pointless intellectualization, because these efforts do not increase knowledge of *Brahman*.

- To understand me, practitioners need to understand all aspects of sacrifice because I represent sacrifice *(ādhiyajña),* and I am present in all sacrifices (verse 16 - *aham-kraturaham-yajñaḥ).*

- Finally, through me, they can reach *Brahman.*

Some observations on Śrī Kṛṣṇa's statements, verse (6-12):

- He is the foundation of all existence.

- Also, he says that all beings created out of *prakṛti* merge with him, and he causes them to be regenerated at the end of an eon *(kalpa).* So, he is an animator of *prakṛti* but not necessarily its creator.

- Creation is not a choice; there is no free will. All beings are helpless in this whole process of creation, existence, and dissolution.

- He, Śrī Kṛṣṇa, is not impacted by actions, and he is indifferent to the actions that he induces through *prakṛti.*

- His control spans the entire cosmos, and he is the causal factor for transformation and change.

- Lastly, he says that all knowledge stops when consciousness stops.

Positioning of Śrī Kṛṣṇa:

- Śrī Kṛṣṇa says his existence is in the unmanifest condition, which means that that he is the substrate of motility *prakṛti*. It is interesting is that he differentiates himself from *puruṣa* as *ādhiyajña* versus *adhyātma* (verse3-4).

- Interestingly, there is only one state beyond the state of *puruṣa* and *prakṛti,* which is primordial sacrifice *(ādhiyajña),* and this state triggers manifested *(saguṇa)* as well as unmanifested *(nirguṇa) Brahman.*

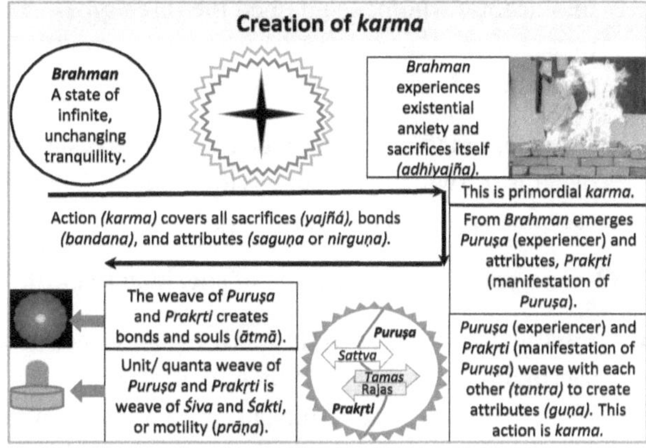

9.1 - How sacrifice creates matter

- Also, Śrī Kṛṣṇa clearly states that he alone is primordial sacrifice *(ādhiyajña ahameva)* (verse 4).

- Importantly, one must view Śrī Kṛṣṇa's positioning as that of an entity who has attained a state that enables *Brahman* (permanent/source/truth) to manifest into an impermanent and material state *(saguṇa/nirguṇa Brahman).*

  o It is very easy to confuse the *yogī* Śrī Kṛṣṇa with the person Śrī Kṛṣṇa, the person, king of the Yādavas, who plays the flute, is friendly to the Pāndavas and participates actively in Mahabharata.

  o However, Śrī Kṛṣṇa the *yogī* is a person who has achieved a supreme state of awareness *(sthita-prajñā).* This makes Śrī Kṛṣṇa an observer, who is indifferent to the outcome of *karma,* because he has reached the state of *ādhiyajña* (primordial sacrifice).

  o In fact, Śrī Kṛṣṇa himself declares that most people do not understand him and confuse his physical state with his real state (verse 11-12).

Endowment of sacrifice, verse (13-19):

- Firstly, I am sacrifice *(ādhiyajña),* the offering to ancestors *(pitṛs),* medicine, *ghṛta* (clarified butter), sacrificial fire *(agni),* and the offering *(hūta).* Also, I am the father and mother of this universe, dispenser of fruits of action, grandfather, OM, the pure Vedas - Rig, Yajur, and Sama.

- For all, I am the goal, supporter, resident, and witness. Also, I am the shelter, friend, origin, dissolution, locus, balance, and imperishable seed. Moreover, I give heat, withhold, and send rain. In fact, I am immortality as well as death, existence, and non-existence.

- Those drinkers of *soma (soma* is a drink which was used in ancient sacrifices. The ingredients of *soma* have been lost but are thought to contain mild intoxicants) who have attained the three types of knowledge, purified from sin by sacrifice, come to me where they stay until they have exhausted merits of their actions, after which they return.

- Anyone, practicing any other forms of worship will be endowed with similar benefits, provided it is done with *śraddha* (sincerity and devotion) because all sacrifice comes to me (Śrī Kṛṣṇa).

Śrī Kṛṣṇa explains the benefits of sacrifice *(yajña)*:

- Firstly, all sacrifices yield merit of the target of sacrifice. For instance, those sacrificing to deities, go to those deities. Similarly, those sacrificing to ancestors *(pitṛs)*, reach their ancestors, just as those worshipping elements, go to elements. Finally, those that dedicate their sacrifice to me (Śrī Kṛṣṇa) come to me. Thus, Śrī Kṛṣṇa makes intent and focus a critical part of any sacrifice.

- Importantly, the scale of sacrifice is not important, quality, devotion, and sincerity *(śraddhā)* are of principle value. In fact, even a flower, leaf, fruit, or even water is accepted if it is done with *śraddhā*.

- Remember, one does not have to prepare a special occasion for sacrifice. Sacrifice whatever you are doing – food before you eat, gift before you give away, any action before acting, control over your words, or even the fruits of your efforts.

- Without a doubt, I (Śrī Kṛṣṇa) regard everyone equally and am partial to none. However, those who perform sacrifice, I am in them, and they are in me.

- Furthermore, your worldliness does not get affected, provided you sacrifice unto me. In fact, with sacrifice, your background, birth, education, and status become irrelevant. So, focus your awareness on the *Brahman* and sacrifice unto me, and you will merge with me (Śrī Kṛṣṇa).

Sacrifice and Śrī Kṛṣṇa:

So, when one sacrifices his or her action *(karma)* to Śrī Kṛṣṇa, who is *ādhiyajña* (primordial sacrifice), one is actually sacrificing into sacrifice; mathematically, this is like adding null to null or infinity to infinity. One is sacrificing into the source.

Finally, another critical concept that Śrī Kṛṣṇa clarifies is that the ability to perform is not relevant. In fact, it is the quality of dedication, sincerity, and desire for perfection *(śraddhā)* that matters.

- Hence, Śrī Kṛṣṇa detaches quality of outcome from quality of input and clearly establishes the ascendency of effort and contribution over outcome.

- Śrī Kṛṣṇa also states that ability to focus on the task at hand with all attention, without excessive worry about the outcome, is the crucible of sacrifice.

Cosmology

We have seen that *Brahman* is infinite and changeless cognitive state of nothingness, which is a state of unchanging, infinite peace.

Puruṣa and *prakṛti*:

- *Brahman* experiences existential angst and sacrifices itself. As a result, we get primordial sacrifice *(ādhiyajña)*. Śrī Kṛṣṇa says that he is this state of *ādhiyajña*.

- As a result of this sacrifice, *puruṣa* (primordial Identity or Self or *adhidaivata)* and *prakṛti* (primordial manifestation or energy of *puruṣa)* emerge from *Brahman.*

- *Puruṣa* is the static element of *Brahman* and the experiencer. *Prakṛti* emerges as a manifestation of *puruṣa.*

- Next, from the weave of *puruṣa* and *prakṛti,* the dynamic element, *guṇa* (attributes) emerge – *tamas* (delusion or lethargy), *rajas* (passion), and *sattva* (balance).

- Subsequently, *prakṛti* and *puruṣu* weave *(tantra)* with each other to create primordial *karma* (action).

- Importantly, all motility is underwritten by *Brahman* but unaffected by it.

- Additionally, when *prakṛti* and *puruṣa* weave and there is creation of materiality, this is called *saguṇa-brahman.* This is also called *māyā* (illusion).

- However, there are other conditions when the weave of *puruṣa* and *prakṛti* is not perfect:

  o Firstly, *prakṛti* may not manifest in response to *puruṣa.* For example - often, we do not react to every experience, especially when we are unsure or afraid of the outcome, such as when we are confronted by a bully or fear our safety, jobs, etc. At such times, we often just experience great fear, but let the moment go.

  o Second, even when *prakṛti* manifests, there may be no feedback, in which case *puruṣa* experiences only itself. For example – assume that you are walking in a corridor and you meet and greet a friend. If the friend does not return the greeting, into *puruṣa* has an experience of loss of self-worth *(asmitā)*, driving *prakṛti* inwards but not participating in the transaction.

  o Lastly, a situation where *puruṣa* exists but *prakṛti* is not engaged. For example - we suddenly have a craving for potato chips but be unable to act on the craving. There is an experience of need but an inability to fulfil that need.

Concept - What are *ādibhūtas* or *pañcabhūtas*?

First, transformation from unmanifested *(nirguṇa-brahman)* to manifested *(saguṇa-brahman)* occurs due to *yajña* (sacrifice). From *saguṇa-brahman* emerge the cardinal elements *(pañcabhūta)*, comprising earth *(pṛthvī)*, water *(ap)*, fire *(agni)*, air *(vāyu)*, and ether *(ākāśa)*. As a mix of the *guṇa*, *tamas* (indolence/delusion), *rajas* (passion, energy), and *sattva* (balance).

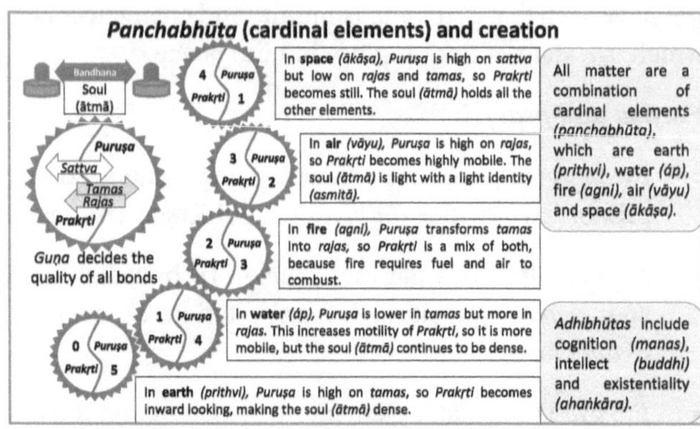

9.2 - *Panchabhūta* (cardinal elements) and creation

For instance, when we drive, there is a mix of earth *(pṛthvī* or car) + water *(ap* or fuel) + fire *(agni* or combustion) and air *(vāyu* or movement, coefficient of drag or resistance).

What is the sacrifice *(yajña)* in the above example?

- Ability to overcome inhibition or fear to drive/ buy a car is sacrifice of *asmitā* (self-esteem).

- Investing in resources such as car, fuel, coordination, etc., is sacrifice of resources such as time, money, and effort.

- Willingness to change in light of newer information is sacrifice of *asmitā*.

A scientific basis of the Universe and *Yoga* [2]

Let us now look at the concept of matter and energy. Scientists have come up with a theoretical model that the universe consists of ~68% dark energy (an expanding energy that fills the space which is getting created in the Universe), ~27% dark matter (there are spaces in the Universe where there is no matter), ~5% normal matter.

No one is sure how space is getting created, how distances between galaxies are increasing, why there are empty spaces, and what is matter.

Does *Brahma-vidya* have an answer?

Let us look at the problem from the concept of *Brahman,* which is a cognitive state of null.

---

[2]https://science.nasa.gov/astrophysics/focus-areas/what-is-dark-energy

From *Brahman* emerges *puruṣa* and *prakṛti* to create the Universe or *hiraṇyagarbha* (golden egg), likely through the Big-Bang event. The identity of this entity is called Viṣṇu. It is important to remember that Viṣṇu is the identity, and *hiraṇyagarbha* is the manifestation. One can conclude that Viṣṇu represents *hiraṇyagarbha* but does not participate in it.

Also, we know that matter is composited of five primordial elements *(pañcabhūta)*, comprising earth *(pṛthvī)*, water *(ap)*, fire *(agni)*, air *(vāyu)*, and ether *(ākāśa)*, which occur from the weave of *puruṣa* and *prakṛti*, as a combination of *guṇa*.

All matter has a quanta unit, and in *brahma-vidya*, this is defined as the weave of *śiva* (the static element or experiencer) and *śakti* (manifestation of *śiva*). This weave is called *tantra*, their union is called *yoga*, and one quanta weave of *śiva* and *śakti* is called *prāṇa* (motility). This forms the basis of all materiality.

What this means is that while Physics/Science posits that the building block of matter is a waveform which then combine/recombine to form the Universe, the waveform *(śakti)* is actually an expression of an identity *(śiva)*. This also means that *brahma-vidya* is a combination of Physics and Psychology and is not a Philosophy. It is a state of existence, the bedrock of creation.

Physics is unable to prove the existence of *Brahman* or a Universal identity (Viṣṇu) because of what it is, an identity. But this concept of *brahma-vidya* and its evolution answers every question of existence that science cannot.

Definition of *Brahman* - *Brahman* can be defined as an infinite state of unchanging equilibrium or peace.

- So, *Brahman* is a state of "ideal thermodynamic state" (there is no heat transfer or disorder, because there is no pressure, volume or temperature; hence, it is a thermodynamic system that is in an ideal state).

- It is important to recognize that pressure, volume, and temperature are all functions of fire *(agni)*.

- Hence, *Brahman* is a state of infinite and unchanging thermodynamic equilibrium.

Creation of the Universe - All creation comes from the *Brahman:* The consciousness *(citta)* of *Brahman,* in a state of infinite thermally inactive equilibrium, becomes aware of itself *(prajñā)* and experiences existential anxiety and desire to know itself.

- Consequently, this anxiety manifests as an atemporal vibration or pulse called *spandana.*

- Next, from this vibration *(spandana)* emerges a macrostate called *puruṣa* (primordial identity or experiencer) that weaves with *prakṛti* (manifestation of that identity) to create matter. Simultaneously, at a quanta level, the building block of *puruṣa* and *prakṛti*, *śiva* (quanta identity) and *śakti* (quanta manifestation), emerge.

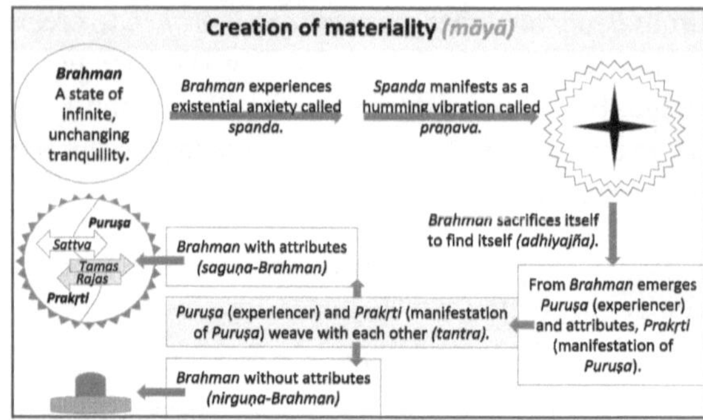

9.3 - Creation of matter

- *Puruṣa* and *prakṛti* weave with each other to create an entity called the *ātman*.

  - At a super-macro-thermodynamic system level, this is called the Universe or *hiraṇyagarbha* (golden-egg) with its *ātman* as Viṣṇu.

  - This state is also valid in any visible, normal entity or standard thermodynamic closed system, like a bird, animal, human, earth, solar system, universe, car, computer, table, chair etc., anything that has a natural state *(dharma)*.

How does quanta *brahma-vidya* work? How is it different from science?

- *Śiva* manifests from *Brahman*. Since this is an Identity only, it does not enable *Brahman* to confirm its existence because there is no change in state or thermodynamic equilibrium of *Brahman*.

- So, *śakti* manifests from *śiva,* and this weave *(tantra)* with *śiva* is called *saguṇa-brahman* because attributes *(guṇa-s)* emerge from *śakti*.

- Also, the quanta unit of the combination of *śiva* and *śakti* is a unit of motility called *prāṇa*.

- From *śiva* emerges consciousness *(citta),* and from *śakti* emerges attribute *(guṇa)*.

- *Śiva* is the static aspect, and *śakti* is the dynamic aspect of their weave. *Siva's* identity experience through its consciousness *(citta)* and manifests as *śakti*.

- *Śiva* and *śakti* are inseparable and weave with each other continuously. Without *śiva* (identity), there can be no *śakti* (manifestation), and without *śakti* (manifestation), there can be no *śiva* (identity). This is encapsulated is Ādi Śankara's soundaryalahiri, stanza 1 [3].

- It is important to recognise that this weave of *śiva* and *śakti* is the base unit of motility *(prāṇa)*.

---

[3] https://www.shankaracharya.org/soundarya_lahari.php

- However, this weave yields no outcome because there is no confirmation of identity of the manifestation. What is the confirmation test?

- Confirmation is activated when another *śiva-śakti* entity emerges from *Brahman,* and the two entities confirm each other's existence.

- Whenever there is lack of confirmation of its identity, *śiva* experiences a drop in identity, resulting is the consciousness *(citta)* turning inward, which draws *śakti* inward also.

- The impact of the consciousness *(citta)* turning inward creates an inward force, which results in *śiva* becoming lethargic, which is known as inertia, mass, or *tamas.*

- The weave of *śiva* with *śakti* creates a quanta movement which is called *karma* (action) and is what we call work in thermodynamics. Energy is created when *śakti* moves outwards. This *guṇa* is called *rajas* (passion, energy, work).

- *Śakti's* movement inward creates an electromagnetic force moving inward, which results in *prāṇa,* a motility unit of *śiva-śakti* generating gravity.

What happens when *śiva* finds another *śiva*?

- First, how does *śiva* look for another *śiva*? If *śiva* does not find another *śiva,* it immediately experiences fear of loss of identity *tamas*, or inertia. So, it manifests and starts seeking another *śiva.*

- *Śiva's* consciousness *(citta)* emerges on the manifestation of *śakti* in the form of an electromagnetic pulse, or *rajas*. This electromagnetic pulse could be any waveform, such as light with a consciousness *(citta)* seeking another *śiva.*

- Importantly, this makes light or any waveform, such as an electromagnetic pulse, a *karma* generated by the weave of *śiva* with *śakti.*

- We can see that the outcome of the weave of *śiva* and *śakti* is dependent on consciousness *(citta),* because consciousness is the communication medium between *śiva* and *śakti* and determines *śakti's* attribute *(guṇa).*

- Hence, consciousness *(citta)* determines how identity/matter *(śiva)* will combine/transact/experience other *śivas.*

Creation of matter and energy:

- When two *Śiva's* connect, they immediately form a bond *(bandana)* with one another, the two quanta *śiva* combining to form a complex identity called *puruṣa.*

- This complex independent identity *(puruṣa)* weaves its own unique manifestation *(prakṛti),* and this is separate from its constituent quanta *śiva* or *śakti.*

- The unit of *puruṣa* and *prakṛti* is called *ātman* (Soul). *Puruṣa* then begins to seek with its consciousness *(citta)* and bond with other *puruṣa* in the same manner as explained with *śiva* above.

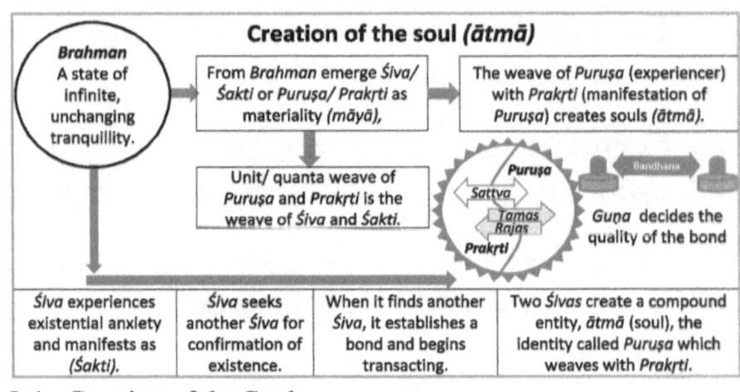

9.4 - Creation of the Soul

- Consequently, this results in creation of matter and energy, each entity having a Soul *(ātman),* which is a unit of *puruṣa* (matter) and *prakṛti* (energy).

- When matter *(puruṣa's)* consciousness *(citta)* turns inwards or becomes negative, energy *(śakti)* manifests as inertia, *tamas,* or matter. Next, when *citta* emerges from *puruṣa,* energy *(śakti)* becomes positive, and outward flowing expansive, passionate, is called *rajas* or energy. Finally, when *puruṣa* and *prakṛti* find a balance, it is called *sattva* or natural state/harmony. The relationship between *puruṣa* and *prakṛti* is matter-energy balance, and their quanta unit is *prāṇa.*

- However, the relationship between various *puruṣa-s* is very unstable because there is continuous bonding with other *puruṣa-s* resulting in equilibrium being disturbed. Consequently, the cycle of *guṇa* (attribute), *tamas, rajas* and *sattva* are perennial, with each getting ascendancy briefly, depending on the state of *puruṣa's citta.*

- The least stable of all three *guṇa*-s is *sattva,* because thermodynamic balance or ideal state in entropy is not only difficult to achieve, but also difficult to retain.

Dynamics of the bond *(bandhana)*

- Within any bond, the two *śiva-s* have identities of different intensities, but neither will leave the bond unless they can find another *śiva* because they fear loss of identity, and the bond is the only confirmation they have of their own existence.

- As a result, the *śiva* that is more secure is less dependent on the other *śiva,* which is insecure.

9.5 - The dynamics of action *(karma)*

- This results in inequality of give-take and binding energy within the bond, which results in an unequal give-take relationship/transaction between the two *śiva.*

- Since the give-take within the relationship is unequal, one gives or takes more, and *karma* or thermodynamic work is generated out of the relative movement between the two *śiva-s*.

- This results in release/absorption of energy and creation of debt *(ṛṇa)* because one *śiva* would have given more (exothermic) than and the other *śiva* would have taken more (endothermic)[4].

- It's important to realize that the release or absorption of energy *(śakti)* will result in a manifestation and generation of another identity *(śiva)*.

- This generation of new *śiva* (identities) creates unbonded identities (entropy), result in expansion, and makes the thermodynamic cycle perennial.

- So, *karma* is a thermodynamic transaction between *śiva-s* that results in the production of more *śiva-s,* and since the process is self-sustaining, continuous, and infinite, it is called *sadā-śiva* (perpetual *śiva).*

- This is why the universe is continuously expanding.

- This debit/credit is stored in *śiva,* and it has to be reconciled with the other *śiva.* When this debt or credit is not reconciled, *śiva* experiences distress or *tamas* and turns inwards into dark matter.

- The above process which has been explained for quanta *śiva* is valid for *puruṣa* also.

- The only change in the case of *puruṣa* is that since *puruṣa* is a complex structure of other *puruṣa-s,* with their foundation in quants *śiva-s,* the relative movement (thermodynamic work or *karma)* within a macro entity can be very complex, consisting of many sub-entities and quanta.

Matter, gravity, and inertia:

Normal matter – Importantly, for normal matter, which is the manifested aspect of *Brahman (saguṇa-brahman),* any weave of *puruṣa* and *prakṛti* that results in creation, maintenance, and dissolution of *pañtcabhūta*-s or lower order of creation/ primordial elements with the existence of a Soul *(ātman)* is normal matter.

Dark matter – When *śiva* or *puruṣa's* debt (endo-exo-thermodynamic balance) is not getting reconciled, then the consciousness *(citta)* becomes inward looking or resorting to reverse manifestation, and the *prāṇa* or *ātman* experiences severe *tamas* or inertia, that is dark matter.

---

[4]https://www.khanacademy.org/test-prep/mcat/chemical-processes/thermochemistry/a/endothermic-vs-exothermic-reactions#:~:text=An%20exothermic%20process%20releases%20heat,heat%20and%20 cools%20the%20surroundings.%E2%80%9D

Importantly, when *śiva* has low levels of identity, in *tamas,* this will get reflected in *śakti,* who will also have low/no motility (it can move without direction but cannot create), because motility requires *śiva* to form a bond with another *śiva* and establish its identity. This cannot occur if *śiva* experiences existential crisis.

Inertia, gravity, and *yoga* – When *puruṣa* or *śiva* is in *tamas, śakti* ~ zero or driving into *puruṣa/śiva.* Consequently, this results in consciousness *(citta)* moving inwards, into *puruṣa* or *śiva,* which generates an inward electromagnetic force which is the source of gravitational force.

Dark energy – When *śiva* emerges from *Brahman,* it experiences fear of loss of identity. So, it manifests as *śakti,* and its consciousness *(citta)* reaches out to confirm its existence. This is an electromagnetic pulse that is driven by *śiva* or *puruṣa* experiencing extreme fear of loss of identity.

Consequently, *śakti's* intensity is much higher than *śiva* which is ~ zero/low state of identity. This is dark energy in Physics. However, since *śakti* exists without a strong anchor of *śiva,* its velocity is solely dependent on the speed of *Siva's* consciousness *(citta).*

Why does light bend – Light is high on energy *(śakti)* and low on identity *(śiva).* So, in order to affirm its identity, *śiva* needs to establish a bond with another *śiva.* Consequently, *śakti* needs to manifest and find another *śiva.* As a result, *śakti,* in the form of light, forms a natural affinity towards any type of identity *(śiva).* So, then consciousness *(citta)* finds another *śiva, śakti,* driven by *śiva's citta* bends towards any *śiva.* This is called gravitational lensing [5].

This is also the reason why objects light up when light strikes them. There is natural affinity of *citta* to another *śiva* for the establishment of a bond and confirmation of identity of its own *śiva.* So, when *śakti* finds another *śiva,* a bond is created between the two *śiva-s,* both increase in manifestation, this lights the entity, after which *karma* occurs, and there is material creation.

This material creation is always a mix of *śiva* and *śakti* in the quanta form, growing into *puruṣa* and *prakṛti* in the universal form. The five primordial materials of earth, water, fire, air, and space get created by the mix of *tamas (śiva>śakti), rajas (śakti>śiva),* and *sattva (śiva=śakti).* For instance, earth is predominantly *tamas* or *śiva/puruṣa>śakti/prakṛti.*

Interchangeability of light and matter:

- Importantly, the balance between *śiva* and *śakti* is never constant, it changes according to the bond that *śiva* has with another *śiva.*

---

[5] https://www.science.org.au/curious/space-time/gravitational-lensing#:~:text=As%20the%20light%20emitted%20by,This%20is%20called%20gravitational%20lensing.

- So, first, *śiva* experiences deep sense of loss of Identity, which is *tamas;* this makes *śakti* move because *śiva-s* consciousness *(citta)* tries to find other *śiva* which is compatible.

- Finally, if it happens, *śiva* forms a bond with another *śiva* and creates normal matter.

- However, the bond is temporary and dependent on each *śiva's* sense of identity-insecurity; hence, the bond breaks whenever there is interference from another *śiva,* leading to a repeat of *tamas/rajas/sattva* cycle.

- As a result, *śiva* (identity) may start as normal matter, transform into dark matter *(nirguṇa-brahman)* or become a weak identity and become dark energy within *puruṣa*, the macrocosm.

- So, we also deduce that this state can keep changing for all states of matter (earth, water, air, fire, and space) because they co-exist in the same unit, *prāṇa,* which is the quanta motility unit of the yoking of a *śiva* with a *śakti*.

- Lastly, the material entity, which is created by the integration of the weave of *śiva* and *śakti* in the quanta form, growing into *puruṣa* and *prakṛti* in the universal form is called *hari-hara*[6]. This comprises half body of *śiva* integrated with an opposite half of *viṣṇu* in *sanātana-dharma*.

Some contradictions to accepted positions:

- When one reviews the concept, there is a clear point of merger of all knowledge *(saṃkhya)*, be it philosophical, psychological, physiological, physical, or scientific.

- The problem seems to be that there is no foundational theory that supports the unity of all knowledge, such as is proposed above and embedded in the ancient science of *yoga-vidyā*.

Lessons learned:

- Śrī Kṛṣṇa's position is clarified in this chapter as a state of existence; in verse 11, he states that people confuse his human manifestation as reality, which he is not. Then, from verses 16-19, he asserts that he is sacrifice, the materials of a sacrifice, the reason, and objective.

- In verse 20-21, he obliquely refers to rebirth and how it functions, while, at the same time, dissociating himself from the individual's state.

- So, we can deduce that Śrī Kṛṣṇa is the framework and operation but not the participant.

- Anyone who sacrifices to him specifically gets rewarded appropriately. This means that while there are different paths, those that sacrifice unto him get direct benefits of surrender. This is little difficult to accept because the deity should not make a difference; it is the input quality that matters.

The transliteration and translation of chapter 9 follows:

श्रीभगवानुवाच ।

इदं तु ते गुह्यतमं प्रवक्ष्याम्यनसूयवे ।

ज्ञानं विज्ञानसहितं यज्ज्ञात्वा मोक्ष्यसेऽशुभात् ॥ ९-१॥

Śrī Kṛṣṇa said – (1) Firstly, to you who bears no ill-will, I shall declare this truly great secret, *(idaṃ tu te guhyatamaṃ pravakṣyāmyanasūyave ।),* knowledge of the Self along with knowledge of the Whole, which, when cognized, results in emancipation from misfortune *(jñānaṃ vijñānasahitaṃ yajjñātvā mokṣyase'śubhāt ॥ 9-1॥).*

राजविद्या राजगुह्यं पवित्रमिदमुत्तमम् ।

प्रत्यक्षावगमं धर्म्यं सुसुखं कर्तुमव्ययम् ॥ ९-२॥

अश्रद्दधानाः पुरुषा धर्मस्यास्य परन्तप ।

अप्राप्य मां निवर्तन्ते मृत्युसंसारवर्त्मनि ॥ ९-३॥

(2-3) Sovereign science, sovereign secret is highly sacred, recognizable by direct experience for the righteous, very easy to perform and imperishable *(rājavidyā rājaguhyaṃ pavitramidamuttamam । pratyakṣāvagamaṃ dharmyaṃ susukhaṃ kartumavyayam ॥ 9-2॥).* People without devotion or righteousness of this do not attain me and return to live and die in *saṃsāra (aśraddadhānāḥ puruṣā dharmasyāsya parantapa । aprāpya māṃ nivartante mṛtyusaṃsāravartmani ॥ 9-3॥).*

मया ततमिदं सर्वं जगदव्यक्तमूर्तिना ।

मत्स्थानि सर्वभूतानि न चाहं तेष्ववस्थितः ॥ ९-४॥

न च मत्स्थानि भूतानि पश्य मे योगमैश्वरम् ।

भूतभृन्न च भूतस्थो ममात्मा भूतभावनः ॥ ९-५॥

(4-5) All in this world are pervaded by me in the unmanifested form *(mayā tatamidaṃ sarvaṃ jagadavyaktamūrtinā ।),* all beings exist in me undifferentiated and not I in them *(matsthāni sarvabhūtāni na cāhaṃ teṣvavasthitaḥ ॥ 9-4॥).* The embodied living cannot cognize my sublime sovereignty *(na ca matsthāni bhūtāni paśya me yogamaiśvaram ।).* Supporting the embodied and living in them my Soul enables them to express themselves *(bhūtabhṛnna ca bhūtastho mamātmā bhūtabhāvanaḥ ॥ 9-5॥).*

यथाकाशस्थितो नित्यं वायुः सर्वत्रगो महान् ।

तथा सर्वाणि भूतानि मत्स्थानीत्युपधारय ॥ ९-६॥

सर्वभूतानि कौन्तेय प्रकृतिं यान्ति मामिकाम् ।

कल्पक्षये पुनस्तानि कल्पादौ विसृजाम्यहम् ॥ ९-७॥

(6-7) Just as air rests in space perennially, which exists everywhere, similarly comprehend this that all creation rest in me *(yathākāśasthito nityaṃ vāyuḥ sarvatrago mahān ꞁ tathā sarvāṇi bhūtāni matsthānītyupadhāraya ꞁꞁ 9-6ꞁꞁ)*. All beings created out of *prakṛti* merge with me at the end of a *kalpa (sarvabhūtāni kaunteya prakṛtiṃ yānti māmikām ꞁ kalpakṣaye)*. At the beginning of a *kalpa*, I generate them again *(punastāni kalpādau visṛjāmyaham ꞁꞁ 9-7ꞁꞁ)*.

प्रकृतिं स्वामवष्टभ्य विसृजामि पुनः ।

भूतग्राममिमं कृत्स्नमवशं प्रकृतेर्वशात् ॥ ९-८॥

न च मां तानि कर्माणि निबध्नन्ति धनञ्जय ।

उदासीनवदासीनमसक्तं तेषु कर्मसु ॥ ९-९॥

मयाध्यक्षेण प्रकृतिः सूयते सचराचरम् ।

हेतुनानेन कौन्तेय जगद्विपरिवर्तते ॥ ९-१०॥

(8-10) *Prakṛti,* being my own creation, is generated again and again *(prakṛtiṃ svāmavaṣṭabhya visṛjāmi punaḥ ꞁ)*. All these myriad beings are helpless in the force of *prakṛti (bhūtagrāmamimaṃ kṛtsnam avaśaṃ prakṛtervaśāt ꞁꞁ 9-8ꞁꞁ)*. These acts do not bind me *(na ca māṃ tāni karmāṇi nibadhnanti dhanañjaya ꞁ)*, I reside indifferent and unattached in those that act *(udāsīnavadāsīnamasaktaṃ teṣu karmasu ꞁꞁ 9-9ꞁꞁ)*. The static and dynamic components *(sacarācaram)* of *prakṛti* operate under my supervision *(mayādhyakṣeṇa prakṛtiḥ sūyate)*, this is the causal *(hetunānena)* factor for transformation or change in the cosmos *(kaunteya jagadviparivartate ꞁꞁ 9-10ꞁꞁ)*.

अवजानन्ति मां मूढा मानुषीं तनुमाश्रितम् ।

परं भावमजानन्तो मम भूतमहेश्वरम् ॥ ९-११॥

मोघाशा मोघकर्माणो मोघज्ञाना विचेतसः ।

राक्षसीमासुरीं चैव प्रकृतिं मोहिनीं श्रिताः ॥ ९-१२॥

(11-12) Disregard this delusional human form that I have taken refuge in knowing my higher state of being my Lordship over all creation *(avajānanti māṃ mūḍhā mānuṣīṃ tanumāśritam ꞁ paraṃ bhāvamajānanto mama bhūtamaheśvaram ꞁꞁ 9-11ꞁꞁ)*. Vain expectations, futile actions, deluded understanding of knowledge *(moghāśā moghakarmāṇo moghajñānā vicetasaḥ ꞁ); truly,* these deluded qualities of *prakṛti* are manifested in the demonic and those of *āsuric* qualities *(rākṣasīmāsurīṃ caiva prakṛtiṃ mohinīṃ śritāḥ ꞁꞁ 9-12ꞁꞁ)*.

महात्मानस्तु मां पार्थ दैवीं प्रकृतिमाश्रिताः ।

भजन्त्यनन्यमनसो ज्ञात्वा भूतादिमव्ययम् ॥ ९-१३॥

सततं कीर्तयन्तो मां यतन्तश्च दृढव्रताः ।

नमस्यन्तश्च मां भक्त्या नित्ययुक्ता उपासते ॥ ९-१४॥

(13-14) However, souls of exceptional cognition, with divine nature, take refuge in me *(mahātmānastu māṃ pārtha daivīṃ prakṛtimāśritāḥ ।)*, worship with a cognition that does not deviate, having recognized me as the imperishable motility of beings *(bhajantyananyamanaso jñātvā bhūtādimavyayam ॥ 9-13॥)*. They are always trying to glorify me with effort and firm in their vows and prostrations of me *(satataṃ kīrtayanto māṃ yatantaśca dṛḍhavratāḥ ।)*, worshipping and doing homage with continual steadfastness *(namasyantaśca māṃ bhaktyā nityayuktā upāsate ॥ 9-14॥)*.

ज्ञानयज्ञेन चाप्यन्ये यजन्तो मामुपासते ।

एकत्वेन पृथक्त्वेन बहुधा विश्वतोमुखम् ॥ ९-१५॥

(15) Sacrificing all knowledge and sacrificing everything else also, worship me *(jñānayajñena cāpyanye yajanto māmupāsate ।)*, my universal face exists as one, as different, and as multiplicity *(ekatvena pṛthaktvena bahudhā viśvatomukham ॥ 9-15॥)*.

अहं क्रतुरहं यज्ञः स्वधाहमहमौषधम् ।

मन्त्रोऽहमहमेवाज्यमहमग्निरहं हुतम् ॥ ९-१६॥

पिताहमस्य जगतो माता धाता पितामहः ।

वेद्यं पवित्रमोङ्कार ऋक्साम यजुरेव च ॥ ९-१७॥

गतिर्भर्ता प्रभुः साक्षी निवासः शरणं सुहृत् ।

प्रभवः प्रलयः स्थानं निधानं बीजमव्ययम् ॥ ९-१८॥

तपाम्यहमहं वर्षं निगृह्णाम्युत्सृजामि च ।

अमृतं चैव मृत्युश्च सदसच्चाहमर्जुन ॥ ९-१९॥

(16-19) I am the purpose *(ahaṃ kratu)*, I am sacrifice *(ahaṃ yajñaḥ)*, I am the oblation *(svadhāham)*, I am medicine *(ahamauṣadham)*, I am mantra *(mantro 'ham)*, I am also ghee *(ahamevājyam)*, I am fire *(ahamagni)*, I am that which is sacrificed or the offering *(ahaṃ hutam)॥ 9-16॥*. I am the father of the world *(pitāhamasya jagato)* as also the mother, the elemental substance, grandfather *(mātā dhātā pitāmahaḥ)*, sacred vedam, OM, and also Rik, Sama, Yajur. *(vedyaṃ pavitramoṅkāra ṛksāma yajureva ca ॥ 9-17॥)*. Enabler of goals, the Lord, witness, resident, refuge, friend *(gatirbhartā prabhuḥ sākṣī nivāsaḥ śaraṇaṃ suhṛt ।)*, the origin, dissolution, position, the hoard, seed imperishable *(prabhavaḥ pralayaḥ sthānaṃ nidhānaṃ bījamavyayam ॥ 9-18॥)*. I am the source of heat *(tapāmyaham)*, I withhold and send forth rain *(varṣaṃ nigṛhṇāmyutsṛjāmi ca I)*, I am the nectar of immortality *(amṛtaṃ caiva)*, I am death and existence, non-existence, and I am Arjuna *(mṛtyuśca sadasaccāhamarjuna II 9-19II)*.

त्रैविद्या मां सोमपाः पूतपापा

यज्ञैरिष्ट्वा स्वर्गतिं प्रार्थयन्ते ।

ते पुण्यमासाद्य सुरेन्द्रलोक-

मश्नन्ति दिव्यान्दिवि देवभोगान् ॥ ९-२०॥

ते तं भुक्त्वा स्वर्गलोकं विशालं

क्षीणे पुण्ये मर्त्यलोकं विशन्ति ।

एवं त्रयीधर्ममनुप्रपन्ना

गतागतं कामकामा लभन्ते ॥ ९-२१॥

(20-21) The knowers of three Vedas and drinkers of Soma by me are purified of impurities by help of sacrifices and pray to go to heaven *(traividyā māṃ somapāḥ pūtapāpā- yajñairiṣṭvā svargatiṃ prārthayante I)*. They, having become purified, reach the world of Indira and enjoy divinity and divine pleasures in divine world *(te puṇyamāsādya surendraloka- maśnanti divyāndivi devabhogān II 9-20II)*. They that have enjoyed the vast celestial places enter the mortal world when they exhaust their merits *(te taṃ bhuktvā svargalokaṃ viśālam- kṣīṇe puṇye martyalokaṃ viśanti I)*, thus abiding by the three Vedas, they come and go and seek the world of desires *(evaṃ trayīdharmamanuprapannā- gatāgataṃ kāmakāmā labhante II 9-21II)*.

अनन्याश्चिन्तयन्तो मां ये जनाः पर्युपासते ।

तेषां नित्याभियुक्तानां योगक्षेमं वहाम्यहम् ॥ ९-२२॥

येऽप्यन्यदेवता भक्ता यजन्ते श्रद्धयान्विताः ।

तेऽपि मामेव कौन्तेय यजन्त्यविधिपूर्वकम् ॥ ९-२३॥

अहं हि सर्वयज्ञानां भोक्ता च प्रभुरेव च ।

न तु मामभिजानन्ति तत्त्वेनातश्च्यवन्ति ते ॥ ९-२४॥

(22-24) Those people who worship me exclusively without worrying about others, for them I ensure complete and assiduous prosperity *(ananyāścintayanto māṃ ye janāḥ paryupāsate I teṣāṃ nityābhiyuktānāṃ yogakṣemaṃ vahāmyaham II 9-22II)*. Even those devotees who worship other deities with complete devotion *(ye 'pyanyadevatā bhaktā yajante śraddhāyānvitāḥ I)*, they also worship me alone using an unapproved process *(te 'pi māmeva kaunteya yajantyavidhipūrvakam II 9-23II)*. Truly, I am the enjoyer and sole owner of all sacrifices and those who do not cognize this truth, they fall *(ahaṃ hi sarvayajñānāṃ bhoktā ca prabhureva ca I na tu māmabhijānanti tattvenātaścyavanti te II 9-24II)*.

यान्ति देवव्रता देवान्पितृन्यान्ति पितृव्रताः ।

भूतानि यान्ति भूतेज्या यान्ति मद्याजिनोऽपि माम् ॥ ९-२५॥

(25) Worshippers of deivas, go to deivas; worshippers of ancestors, go to the ancestors; worshippers of beings go to the world of creation; my worshippers come to me *(yānti devavratā devānpitṝnyānti pitṛvratāḥ ɩ bhūtāni yānti bhūtejyā yānti madyājino'pi mām ॥ 9-25॥)*.

पत्रं पुष्पं फलं तोयं यो मे भक्त्या प्रयच्छति ।

तदहं भक्त्युपहृतमश्नामि प्रयतात्मनः ॥ ९-२६॥

यत्करोषि यदश्नासि यज्जुहोषि ददासि यत् ।

यत्तपस्यसि कौन्तेय तत्कुरुष्व मदर्पणम् ॥ ९-२७॥

शुभाशुभफलैरेवं मोक्ष्यसे कर्मबन्धनैः ।

संन्यासयोगयुक्तात्मा विमुक्तो मामुपैष्यसि ॥ ९-२८॥

(26-28) Leaf, flower, fruit, water, those that offer me with devotion *(patraṃ puṣpaṃ phalaṃ toyaṃ yo me bhaktyā prayacchati ɩ)*, those offered with devotion I accept of the pious souls *(tadahaṃ bhaktyupahṛtamaśnāmi prayatātmanaḥ ॥ 9-26॥)*. Whatever you do, whatever you eat, whatever you offer as sacrifice, whatever you donate *(yatkaroṣi yadaśnāsi yajjuhoṣi dadāsi yat ɩ)* all your austerities you do, consign it to me *(yattapasyasi kaunteya tatkuruṣva madarpaṇam ॥ 9-27॥)*. Thus, you will be freed from good and bad fruits that create bonds of *karma (śubhāśubhaphalairevaṃ mokṣyase karmabandhanaiḥ ɩ)*, when your soul is steadfast in seeking harmony through renunciation *(saṃnyāsayogayuktātmā)*, you shall be liberated and come to me *(vimukto māmupaiṣyasi ॥ 9-28॥)*.

समोऽहं सर्वभूतेषु न मे द्वेष्योऽस्ति न प्रियः ।

ये भजन्ति तु मां भक्त्या मयि ते तेषु चाप्यहम् ॥ ९-२९॥

अपि चेत्सुदुराचारो भजते मामनन्यभाक् ।

साधुरेव स मन्तव्यः सम्यग्व्यवसितो हि सः ॥ ९-३०॥

क्षिप्रं भवति धर्मात्मा शश्वच्छान्तिं निगच्छति ।

कौन्तेय प्रतिजानीहि न मे भक्तः प्रणश्यति ॥ ९-३१॥

(29-31) I treat all creation equally, I do not repel them nor are they dear to me *(samo'haṃ sarvabhūteṣu na me dveṣyo'sti na priyaḥ ɩ)*, but those who worship me with devotion, they are in me, and also, I am in them *(ye bhajanti tu māṃ bhaktyā mayi te teṣu cāpyaham ॥ 9-29॥)*. Even if a wicked person worships me, thinking of no other *(api cetsudurācāro bhajate māmananyabhāk ɩ)*, truly, he should accurately be regarded as saintly, for emancipated is he *(sādhureva sa mantavyaḥ samyagvyavasito hi saḥ ॥ 9-30॥)*. Soon, he becomes a righteous soul and attains eternal peace *(kṣipraṃ bhavati dharmātmā śaśvacchāntiṃ nigacchati ।)*, know that none of my devotees is destroyed *(kaunteya pratijānīhi na me bhaktaḥ praṇaśyati ॥ 9-31॥)*.

मां हि पार्थ व्यपाश्रित्य येऽपि स्युः पापयोनयः ।
स्त्रियो वैश्यास्तथा शूद्रास्तेऽपि यान्ति परां गतिम् ॥ ९-३२॥
किं पुनर्ब्राह्मणाः पुण्या भक्ता राजर्षयस्तथा ।
अनित्यमसुखं लोकमिमं प्राप्य भजस्व माम् ॥ ९-३३॥

(32-33) Indeed, even those who may be of wretched origin who take refuge in me *(māṃ hi pārtha vyapāśritya ye'pi syuḥ pāpayonayaḥ ।)*, also women, business people, and workers, they also attain supreme salvation *(striyo vaiśyāstathā śūdrāste'pi yānti parāṃ gatim ॥ 9-32॥)*. How many more brahmins, pious devotees, royal seers also impermanent and unhappy in the world have obtained this, worship me *(kiṃ punarbrāhmaṇāḥ puṇyā bhaktā rājarṣayastathā । anityamasukhaṃ lokamimaṃ prāpya bhajasva mām ॥ 9-33॥)*.

मन्मना भव मद्भक्तो मद्याजी मां नमस्कुरु ।
मामेवैष्यसि युक्त्वैवमात्मानं मत्परायणः ॥ ९-३४॥

(34) With your cognition on me, my devotee, sacrifice unto me, propitiate me alone, strive steadfastly with your soul thus devoted to me *(manmanā bhava madbhakto madyājī māṃ namaskuru । māmevaiṣyasi yuktvaivamātmānaṃ matparāyaṇaḥ ॥ 9-34॥)*.

◆——— • ● ◆ ● • ——— ◆

Chapter 10

Vibhūti-yoga (yoga of splendor) [1]

Introduction and synopsis

In this chapter, Śrī Kṛṣṇa speaks of himself as one who has no origin but also as the host of all creation. He goes on to describe himself as logic *(buddhi)*, knowledge of the Self *(jñāna)*, lack of delusion *(asammoha)*, forgiveness *(kṣamā)*, truth *(satya)*, self-control *(dama)*, quietness/calmness *(śama)*, contentment *(sukha)*, and grief *(duḥkha)*.

Also, he covers opposites, such as being existence *(bhāva)*, non-existence *(a-bhāva)*, fear *(bhaya)*, and lack of fear *(a-bhaya)*. Next, he covers sentiment, such as non-violence *(ahimsā)*, treating all equally *(samatā)*, contentment *(tuṣṭi)*, austerity *(tapas)*, charity *(dāna)*, fame *(yaśa)*, and defame *(a-yaśa)*. Following this, he covers himself as being the creation and capability of the seven *seers (maharṣi)*, 4 ancient *manus,* and all evolution.

Śrī Kṛṣṇa explains his manifestation:

In answering Arjuna's question - "How does one know you, and what process should one follow to reach you? Tell me your powers and attributes, for I am not satisfied by these words", Śrī Kṛṣṇa details his manifestation, covering nearly every quality known to us, such as both desirable and undesirable, addition and subtraction of value, harmony, and chaos.

Śrī Kṛṣṇa says – I am the Self, seated in the hearts of all beings. Also, I am the beginning, middle, and end. Of the Adityas, I am Viṣṇu; among luminaries, I am the Sun; of the Maruts, I am Marichi; among stars, I am the Moon.

---

[1]https://www.bhagavad-gita.org/Gita/chapter-10.html

Next, he says that of the Vedas, I am Sāman; among Devas, I am Vasava; of the senses, I am cognition (manas). Among living beings, I am awareness. Then, of the Rudras, I am Śankara; among Yakṣas and Rākṣasas, I am Vitteśa (Kubera); of Vasus, I am Pāvaka; among mountains, I am Meru.

Additionally, he says - among priests I am Bṛhaspati; of warriors, I am that of Skanda; among water bodies, I am the ocean. Then, of Ṛṣis I am Bhṛgu, and among words, I am the single alphabet *(akṣara)*. Following this, he says - of sacrifices, I am *japa*; among immovable things, the Himālayas.

Subsequently, he says, I am Aśvattha among trees; of Devarṣis, I am Nārada; among Gandharva, I am Citraratha; of Siddhas, I am Kapila. Of horses, I am Uccaiḥśravas; among elephants, I am Airāvat; of men, the king. Of weapons, I am the thunderbolt; among cows, I am Kāmadhenu; of progenitors, I am Kandarpa (Cupid); among serpents, I am Vāsuki. Also, among snakes, I am Ananta; of water deities, I am Varuna; of the manes (ancestors), I am Aryama. Lastly, among regulators of death, I am Yama and, among devotees, I am Prahalāda.

Finally, of reckoners, I am Time.

Following this, he says - I am the lion among beasts and Garuḍa among birds. Of purifiers, I am the wind; among wielders of weapons, I am Rāma; of fishes, I am the crocodile; among streams, I am Gangā.

Importantly, he declares that in creation, I am the beginning, middle, and end; in knowledge, I am the knowledge of the self. I am logic in any conversation. I am indestructibility in the alphabet, the duality in compound words. Also, I am the everlasting dispenser of time, existing everywhere. Finally, I am all devouring death; prosperity in the prosperous.

Śrī Kṛṣṇa also says that of feminine qualities, I am fame, fortune, speech, memory, intelligence, firmness, and forgiveness. Of Sāmas, I am *bṛhatsāma*; among meters, I am *gāyatrī*; among months, I am *mārgaśīrṣa*; of seasons, I am spring.

Following this, he declares that I am risk taking in the gambler and the splendor of the splendid. Also, I am the effort in victory; truth in the truth. Of the Vṛṣṇis, I am Vāsudeva; among Pāṇḍavas, I am Arjuna; of Sages, I am Vyāsa; among poets, I am Uśanā.

Then, Śrī Kṛṣṇa states that I am the rod of justice; the diplomacy among diplomats. Also, I am silence in the secret; knowledge of the wise. I am seed of all creation; nothing – sentient or insentient – can exist without me.

The concept of power and *dharma* (Manusmṛti verse 1.51)[2]:

एवं सर्वं स सृष्ट्वैदं मां चाचिन्त्यपराक्रमः ।
आत्मन्यन्तर्दधे भूयः कालं कालेन पीडयन् ॥ ५१ ॥

evaṃ sarvaṃ sa sṛṣṭvaidaṃ māṃ cācintyaparākramaḥ ।
ātmanyantardadhe bhūyaḥ kālaṃ kālena pīḍayan ॥ 51 ॥

Thus, repeatedly suppressing time (of dissolution) by time (of creation and maintenance), he of inconceivable power, created all this and also myself; [he directed me to maintain it] and then disappeared within himself (51).

Manusmṛti is another document which deals with creation, maintenance, and dissolution of the Universe. One aspect that is not dealt with any of the ancient texts is power, hierarchy of power and its subtlety, possibly because most of the ancient documents are instruction-heavy, meant to be discussed, and followed.

However, Manusmṛti 1.51 gives one an opening, that *Brahman* created the Universe by suppressing dissolution, which is in itself, a primordial use of power. Also, this means that within existence, a primordial instinct to life overwhelms dissolution or destruction. A question that we try and answer later in this chapter... why are we afraid to die?

Dharma **of power and hierarchy:**

To begin, both power and hierarchy flow from *dharma* (natural state or conditioning). From *dharma* comes availability of capability to exercise power, and this determines hierarchy. Each genus or family is designed within an intra-genus power hierarchy called the ecological pyramid.

For example, on land:

- Grass struggles to stay alive and regenerates itself after fires ravage it, storms flatten it, and summer heat dries it. This proves the hierarchy of creation over dissolution, life over destruction.

- Next, grass does not voluntarily give itself up to become food for a goat. The goat seizes it to nourish itself.

- Similarly, a goat does not offer itself as food to a carnivore, it is taken as food, and life is given away in pain and in a struggle.

- Similarly, on water; microbes get eaten by small insects which get eaten by amphibians that get eaten by small fishes. These small fishes then get devoured by larger fishes, and this goes on until the top of the pyramid, which is the shark. When it comes to amphibians, the crocodile is the apex predator.

---

[2]https://www.wisdomlib.org/hinduism/book/manusmriti-with-the-commentary-of-medhatithi/d/doc145468.html.

- On top of this chain is man. Man is the apex predator of all that exists. Since man is not subordinate to any natural rules of existence, he has to make them himself. These manifest as religion, government, constitution, laws, articles, organization, etc.

There is power hierarchy within a genus also. The *dharma* of a lion is to lead a pride of lionesses but that position is constantly challenged and the lion has to regularly fight off other lions competing for his pride. This is applicable to all animals, where application of power decides who leads and who does not.

Power hierarchy affects humans also. Since man has no competitor, it becomes necessary to control him with conditioning *(dharma)* so that there is order.

- Socially, while the *varṇa* system is equal by design, it becomes stratified by application of power. Those that influence and change society are more powerful than those that follow them.

- Politically, the ruler or head of a country is more powerful than a bureaucrat, just as a law-maker is more powerful than a law-dispenser. There is a continuous struggle for supremacy between various leaders that rise on the foundations of specific expertise, such as knowledge, armed capability, financial strength, communication, religiosity, and public influencers.

- Countries have a *varṇa*. We have super-powers, regional powers, religious powers and other powers, first-world, second-world etc., all moving up and down the hierarchy scale. For example: super-powers of the nineteenth century such as Great Britain, France, Soviet Union, and others have moved out, and others such as United States and China now rival each other to be at the top of the pyramid.

- Business too have a *varṇa*. Large companies often dictate design, operations, and financial rules to smaller peers and suppliers who have no option but to submit in order to survive.

- The *varṇa* system exists in management also. The chairman of the board of a company sits at the top of the chain, with department heads below him, who have a structure that they have power and control over.

There is no equality in the hierarchy, and it is not static. In business too, the entity that positions itself best and is most profitable becomes the leader of that business. However, that is dynamic; for example, Ford became the market leader with the introduction of Model T but lost its leadership when it did not innovate. Similarly, the large American automotive companies lost their power when companies from other countries overtook them. So, power is dynamic and changes with *karma* (both *āgāmi* as well as *prārabdha)*.

In short, Śrī Kṛṣṇa says that he is everything that is apex in creation. He is that vitality which creates, controls, and maintains.

Śrī Kṛṣṇa explains the summary of his manifestation

There is no end to my divine manifestation, this is but a small exposition of my capabilities. Whatever glorious, prosperous, and powerful exists, know that to have come from me. Indeed, there is no need for micro knowledge for I support the universe with a fragment of myself.

What is Śrī Kṛṣṇa trying to say in this chapter?

Where is Śrī Kṛṣṇa positioning himself? He seems to be saying that he is everything in everything! What does that mean?

- We have already established that the imperishable *Brahman* is the source, everything that emerges is *karma* in the form of sacrifice *(yajña),* and Śrī Kṛṣṇa is *ādhiyajña* (primordial sacrifice/transformation or change).

- Since, he is *ādhiyajña,* Śrī Kṛṣṇa has transcended material existence and has merged with the source *(Brahman).* This allows him to participate and become the underwriting quality of all entities *(ātma-s)* without becoming involved in their experience of existence.

- Additionally, it is important to differentiate Śrī Kṛṣṇa, the person, from Śrī Kṛṣṇa, the state of existence. Unfortunately, since Śrī Kṛṣṇa the person is seen to be advising Arjuna in *Śrīmad-bhagavad-gītā,* there is great possibility of confusing one with the other.

- In fact, in chapter 9, Śrī Kṛṣṇa cautions Arjuna, saying that the human form that he has is *māyā,* and advising him to stop getting attached to his human form. Unfortunately, this does not help Arjuna, and we continue to see Arjuna struggling with this confusion throughout Mahabharata. So, there is reason to believe that an ordinary practitioner would end up confusing Śrī Kṛṣṇa the person from Śrī Kṛṣṇa, the yogi.

Conclusion

In this chapter, Śrī Kṛṣṇa chooses his state to be the apex of each genus, category, or state, sitting on top of all hierarchy. He is the source and dispenser of the natural state, conditioning *(dharma),* and primordial power. This circles back to the starting point, which is the sacrifice *(yajña).* With Śrī Kṛṣṇa being the primordial sacrifice *(ādhiyajña),* it is not hard to see how that state automatically confers commensurate capability. Again, this confirms the hypothesis that Śrī Kṛṣṇa is a state and not a person.

What is the role of sacrifice in existence? How does Śrī Kṛṣṇa claim so may roles?

- Logic *(buddhi),* knowledge of the Self *(jñāna),* lack of delusion *(asammoha),* forgiveness *(kshamā),* truth *(satya),* self-control *(dama),* quietness/calmness (*śama*), contentment *(sukha)*, grief *(duḥkha)*, existence *(bhāva)*, non-existence *(abhāva)*, fear *(bhaya)*, lack of fear *(abhaya)* - all the above aspects can be classified as aspects of living that characterize discrimination, grace, and dispassion. All require a person sacrifice his or her baser instincts and aspire for a nobler and moral life. This sacrifice is the quality of Śrī Kṛṣṇa.

- Non-violence *(ahiṃsā)*, treating all equally *(samatā)*, contentment *(tuṣṭi)*, austerity *(tapa)*, charity *(dāna)*, fame *(yaśa), and* defame *(ayaśa)* are aspects of self-control. This requires that a person face criticism, derision, pain, and suffering with equanimity and dispassion, and this requires sacrifice of fear, pettiness, and selfishness.

- **Mother and Father** – Without doubt, parents sacrifice for their children. Importantly, they give time, effort, money, and emotional strength, without expectation of return. This is the foundation of sacrifice and building of society.

- **Time** – All activity is based on time; our thoughts and perceptions change with time. Every changing situation requires adjustment, which is a sacrifice. Here, the sacrifice is laziness, choosing the appropriate activity while sacrificing other equally pressing tasks, fear of outcome, expectation, and fear of loss of self-worth.

- **Among living beings, I am awareness** – Awareness is that aspect which drives one's ability to live effectively in the environment. It requires one to move away from delusion, be kind to others in trouble, and demonstrate grace and courage in the face of adversity. This is a sacrifice.

- **I am the Self** – The Self or *ātma* is the repository of *karma*. It is benign to its environment; it observes but does not participate because it is the extension of the *Brahman*. Its existence comes from *ādhiyajña,* which is Śrī Kṛṣṇa.

- **I am all-devouring death** – death is a sacrifice. The body is sacrificed and degenerates to its constituent cardinal elements *(ādibhūta* = earth, water, fire, air, and ether). At death, *karma* that has come up for dissolution *(prārabdha-karma)* is closed and the Soul *(ātman)* is reconstituted as another entity for the reconciliation of its overall karma *(sañcita-karma).*

  o But, why are we afraid of death? When we die, our sense of Identity dies with us. This sense of Identity *(asmitā)* is our security, our fragile sheath of existential confidence. At death, this sheath is torn away, exposing us to a fear of loss of identity which creates anxiety.

  o While we may accept the logic that our debts *(karma)* will require us to take another body, there is no empirical evidence of such an occurrence. Also, if this was to be true, then the quantum of debt that may come up for reconciliation is an unknown. This sense of the unknown is another source of anxiety.

- o   This is why Śrī Kṛṣṇa encourages us to spend time preparing for the end in the *Bhagavad-gītā* chapter 8.

- **Creation is a sacrifice** – I am the seed of all creation. Any form of creation is a sacrifice. Something or someone must sacrifice current state in order that creation may emerge.

  - o   The seed in creating a meal is knowledge of what is to be prepared followed by sacrifice in the form of time, effort, money, recipe, fire, preparation technique, etc.

  - o   Similarly, the seed for writing a book or going on a journey starts with the need to write the book or make the journey. This is followed by sacrificing resources, time, etc.

  - o   Seed in creation of a baby starts with the desire for a baby. Sacrifice starts with a mother having to carry the baby for over 9 months. Also, the birthing process itself is very painful, and that is a sacrifice also.

- How is time related to sacrifice? When Śrī Kṛṣṇa says that among reckoners, he is Time (verse 33), what does he mean?

  - o   For example, when we are enjoying a movie or at a party, time moves very fast. Conversely, when we are awaiting results of an exam, or recovering from illness, every moment drags on interminably.

  - o   So clearly, time is a derived concept; it does not actually exist!

  - o   What exists is consciousness *(citta),* our cognition of time. It is a one-way street, and when the moment goes, it is lost forever.

  - o   But, to remain in the present, one needs to reach the state of *sthita-prajñā* (steady awareness), and to achieve it, sacrifice of the Self is essential.

Evidence from Manusmriti [3]

More evidence that time is a function of consciousness and not empirical:

निमेषा दश चाष्टौ च काष्ठा त्रिंशत् तु ताः कला ।
त्रिंशत् कला मुहूर्तः स्यादहोरात्रं तु तावतः ॥ ६४ ॥

nimeṣā daśa cāṣṭau ca kāṣṭhā trimśat tu tāḥ kalā ।
trimśat kalā muhūrtaḥ syādahorātram tu tāvataḥ ॥ 64 ॥

Ten and eight '*nimeṣas*' (twinkling of the eye) one '*kāṣṭhā*'; thirty such (*kāṣṭhās*) one '*kalā*'; thirty '*kalās*' one '*muhūrta*'; and as many '*muhūrtas*' one '*ahorātra*' (Day and Night). (64)

---

[3] https://www.wisdomlib.org/hinduism/book/manusmriti-with-the-commentary-of-medhatithi/d/doc145491.html

अहोरात्रे विभजते सूर्यो मानुषदैविके ।

रात्रिः स्वप्नाय भूतानां चेष्टायै कर्मणामहः ॥ ६५ ॥

ahorātre vibhajate sūryo mānuṣadaivike |

rātriḥ svapnāya bhūtānāṃ ceṣṭāyai karmaṇāmahaḥ ॥ 65 ॥

The Sun divides the 'day' and 'night' of men and devas; [of others] what is conducive to the repose of beings is 'night,' and what is conducive to activity is 'day.' (65)

Some contradictions to accepted positions:

Śrī Kṛṣṇa says that he is the heart of everything. He is the beginning, middle, and end. How is this possible?

- All activity emerges from desire. There is a desire to project one's thought, reflection, or desire. This is called *icchā-śakti* (strength of desire).

- If the desire is strong, then the person sacrifices the current state of self-worth to project his or her Soul *(adhyatma)*. This is the will *(saṅkalpa)!*

- This projection is generally an outcome of *prārabdha-karma* (debts that have come up for dissolution). This projection requires sacrifice of material resources.

- When there is a reaction to stimuli, *karma* is created *(āgāmi-karma)*. A new state is created, and the person must sacrifice old and dearly held positions for their current state. This requires sacrifice of baggage, self-worth, delusions, etc.

This supports Śrī Kṛṣṇa's assertion that he is *yajña* in every form, from the greatest to the smallest, from creation to maintenance and dissolution.

Lessons learned:

Each of us wishes to be an apex occupier of the pyramid that we live in. However, the trip to the top is filled with sacrifice. However, this sacrifice must be accompanied with awareness *(prajñā)* which increases one's free will so as to enable the person to understand *dharma* and the role of power in it.

The transliteration and translation of chapter 10:

श्रीभगवानुवाच -

भूय एव महाबाहो शृणु मे परमं वचः ।

यत्तेऽहं प्रीयमाणाय वक्ष्यामि हितकाम्यया ॥ १०-१॥

Śrī Kṛṣṇa said – (1) Again, in honesty, hear my absolute word *(bhūya eva mahābāho śaṛṇu me paramaṃ vacaḥ |)*, that to you to me who is beloved *(yatte'haṃ prīyamāṇāya)*, I will declare for your wellbeing *(vakṣyāmi hitakāmyayā ॥ 10-1॥)*.

न मे विदुः सुरगणाः प्रभवं न महर्षयः ।
अहमादिर्हि देवानां महर्षीणां च सर्वशः ॥ १०-२॥
यो मामजमनादिं च वेत्ति लोकमहेश्वरम् ।
असम्मूढः स मर्त्येषु सर्वपापैः प्रमुच्यते ॥ १०-३॥

(2-3) All of wise and great *ṛṣis* do not know my origin *(na me viduḥ suragaṇāḥ prabhavaṃ na maharṣayaḥ ।)* I am the beginning for *devas (ahamādirhi devānāṃ)* and great *ṛṣis* completely *(maharṣīṇāṃ ca sarvaśaḥ ॥ 10-2॥)*. He who knows me as unborn, without beginning and as the Lord of the world *(yo māmajamanādiṃ ca vetti lokamaheśvaram ।)*, he is undeluded of all mortals because all his blemishes are cleaned *(asammūḍhaḥ sa martyeṣu sarvapāpaiḥ pramucyate ॥ 10-3॥)*.

बुद्धिर्ज्ञानमसम्मोहः क्षमा सत्यं दमः शमः ।
सुखं दुःखं भवोऽभावो भयं चाभयमेव च ॥ १०-४॥
अहिंसा समता तुष्टिस्तपो दानं यशोऽयशः ।
भवन्ति भावा भूतानां मत्त एव पृथग्विधाः ॥ १०-५॥

(4-5) Logic, knowledge of the Self *(buddhirjñānamasammohaḥ)*, non-illusion-forgiveness, truth, self-restraint, calmness *(kṣamā satyaṃ damaḥ śamaḥ ।)*, grief, birth, non-existence, and fear and even fearlessness *(sukhaṃ duḥkhaṃ bhavo'bhāvo bhayaṃ cābhayameva ca ॥ 10-4॥)*. Non-violence, treating everyone equally, satisfaction, austerity, donation, fame, infamy *(ahiṃsā samatā tuṣṭistapo dānaṃ yaśo'yaśaḥ ।)*, these different sentiments in beings arise from me alone *(bhavanti bhāvā bhūtānāṃ matta eva pṛthagvidhāḥ ॥ 10-5॥)*.

महर्षयः सप्त पूर्वे चत्वारो मनवस्तथा ।
मद्भावा मानसा जाता येषां लोक इमाः प्रजाः ॥ १०-६॥
एतां विभूतिं योगं च मम यो वेत्ति तत्त्वतः ।
सोऽविकम्पेन योगेन युज्यते नात्र संशयः ॥ १०-७॥
अहं सर्वस्य प्रभवो मत्तः सर्वं प्रवर्तते ।
इति मत्वा भजन्ते मां बुधा भावसमन्विताः ॥ १०-८॥

(6-8) The seven-ancient great *ṛṣis (maharṣayaḥ sapta pūrve)*, also the four Manus, possessed cognitive intuition like me *(catvāro manavastathā । madbhāvā mānasā)*, from them these creatures in the world are descended *(jātā yeṣāṃ loka imāḥ prajāḥ ॥ 10-6॥)*. Those who know the truth of my all-pervading union *(etāṃ vibhūtiṃ yogaṃ ca mama yo vetti tattvataḥ ।)*, they become established in unshakable union, there is no doubt *(so'vikampena yogena yujyate nātra saṃśayaḥ ॥ 10-7॥)*. I am the source of everything, everything evolves from me *(ahaṃ sarvasya prabhavo mattaḥ sarvaṃ pravartate ।)*. Thus, endowed with understanding, the wise adore me with complete investment of their intellectual and cognitive capabilities *(iti matvā bhajante māṃ budhā bhāvasamanvitāḥ ǁ 10-8ǁ.*

मच्चित्ता मद्गतप्राणा बोधयन्तः परस्परम् ।

कथयन्तश्च मां नित्यं तुष्यन्ति च रमन्ति च ॥ १०-९॥

(9) With consciousness on me *(maccittā madgata)*, the *prāna* focussed on me, wisdom united with me, and mutually expressing about me, they enjoy and are always satisfied *(prāṇā bodhayantaḥ parasparam ǀ kathayantaśca māṃ nityaṃ tuṣyanti ca ramanti ca ǁ 10-9ǁ).*

तेषां सततयुक्तानां भजतां प्रीतिपूर्वकम् ।

ददामि बुद्धियोगं तं येन मामुपयान्ति ते ॥ १०-१०॥

तेषामेवानुकम्पार्थमहमज्ञानजं तमः ।

नाशयाम्यात्मभावस्थो ज्ञानदीपेन भास्वता ॥ १०-११॥

(10-11) To those that are ever steadfast *(teṣāṃ satatayuktānāṃ)* in their love-filled worship *(bhajatāṃ prītipūrvakam ǀ)*, I give harmony of logic *(dadāmi buddhiyogaṃ)* by which they come to me *(taṃ yena māmupayānti te ǁ 10-10ǁ)*. Verily, out of compassion for them *(teṣāmevānukampārtham)*, I destroy tamas of ignorance *(ahamajñānajaṃ tamaḥ ǀ nāśayāmy)* existing inside their soul *(ātmabhāvastho)* by the luminous lamp of knowledge *(jñānadīpena bhāsvatā ǁ 10-11ǁ)*.

अर्जुन उवाच -

परं ब्रह्म परं धाम पवित्रं परमं भवान् ।

पुरुषं शाश्वतं दिव्यमादिदेवमजं विभुम् ॥ १०-१२॥

आहुस्त्वामृषयः सर्वे देवर्षिर्नारदस्तथा ।

असितो देवलो व्यासः स्वयं चैव ब्रवीषि मे ॥ १०-१३॥

सर्वमेतदृतं मन्ये यन्मां वदसि केशव ।

न हि ते भगवन्व्यक्तिं विदुर्देवा न दानवाः ॥ १०-१४॥

Arjuna said (12-14) Supreme creator, supreme state *(paraṃ brahma paraṃ dhāma)*, you are the supreme sacred *puruṣa (pavitraṃ paramaṃ bhavān ǀ puruṣaṃ)*, eternal, divine, primordial deity, unborn and all pervading *(śāśvataṃ divyamādidevamajaṃ vibhum ǁ 10-12ǁ)*. They relate to you, all *ṛṣis, devarṣis*, Nārada *(āhustvāmṛṣayaḥ sarve devarṣirnāradastathā)*, also dark, pious Vyasa *(asito devalo vyāsaḥ)*, and now please declare the truth to me *(svayaṃ caiva bravīṣi me ǁ 10-13ǁ)*. I think that all you are saying to me is correct, I think *(sarvametadṛtaṃ manye yanmāṃ vadasi keśava ǀ)*, truly neither deities nor danavas know you as manifestation of God *(na hi te bhagavānvyaktiṃ vidurdevā na dānavāḥ ǁ 10-14ǁ)*.

स्वयमेवात्मनात्मानं वेत्थ त्वं पुरुषोत्तम ।

भूतभावन भूतेश देवदेव जगत्पते ॥ १०-१५॥

वक्तुमर्हस्यशेषेण दिव्या ह्यात्मविभूतयः ।

याभिर्विभूतिभिर्लोकानिमांस्त्वं व्याप्य तिष्ठसि ॥ १०-१६॥

(15-16) Only you by yourself are yourself (you have created yourself) (*svayamevātmanātmānaṃ*) knowest thou supreme soul (*vettha tvaṃ puruṣottama ।*), creator of beings (*bhūtabhāvana*), Lord of beings (*bhūteśa*), deity of deities (*devadeva*) Lord of the world (*jagatpate ॥ 10-15॥*). Without reminder, to tell that you are venerable (*vaktumarhasyaśeṣeṇa*), divine (*divyā*), supreme soul (*hyātmavibhūtayaḥ ।*) your power is the reason for existence of these worlds (*yābhirvibhūtibhirlokānimāṃstvaṃ vyāpya tiṣṭhasi ॥ 10-16॥*).

कथं विद्यामहं योगिंस्त्वां सदा परिचिन्तयन् ।

केषु च भावेषु चिन्त्योऽसि भगवन्मया ॥ १०-१७॥

विस्तरेणात्मनो योगं विभूतिं च जनार्दन ।

भूयः कथय तृप्तिर्हि शृण्वतो नास्ति मेऽमृतम् ॥ १०-१८॥

(17-18) How can I know your Yoga (*kathaṃ vidyāmahaṃ yogiṃstvāṃ*) ever meditating (*sadā paricintayan ।*), how and what sentiment (*keṣu ca bhāveṣu*) should I think of you (*cintyo'si bhagavānmayā ॥ 10-17॥*). In detail again recount the nectar of this powerful harmonizing of the soul (*vistareṇātmano yogaṃ vibhūtiṃ*), and I am not satisfied of hearing this nectar (*ca janārdana । bhūyaḥ kathaya tṛptirhi śarṇvato nāsti me'mṛtam ॥ 10-18॥*).

श्रीभगवानुवाच -

हन्त ते कथयिष्यामि दिव्या ह्यात्मविभूतयः ।

प्राधान्यतः कुरुश्रेष्ठ नास्त्यन्तो विस्तरस्य मे ॥ १०-१९॥

अहमात्मा गुडाकेश सर्वभूताशयस्थितः ।

अहमादिश्च मध्यं च भूतानामन्त एव च ॥ १०-२०॥

Śrī Kṛṣṇa said (19-21) Very well, to thee I shall reveal to you my true divine powerful Self (*hanta te kathayiṣyāmi divyā hyātmavibhūtayaḥ ।*), in order of prominence, though this is not the end of my detailed manifestation (*prādhānyataḥ kuruśreṣṭha nāstyanto vistarasya me ॥ 10-19॥*). I am *ātmā* (*ahamātmā*), embedded in all creation (*guḍākeśa sarvabhūtāśayasthitaḥ ।*), I am the beginning, middle, and also the end of all creation (*ahamādiśca madhyaṃ ca bhūtānāmanta eva ca ॥ 10-20॥*).

आदित्यानामहं विष्णुर्ज्योतिषां रविरंशुमान् ।
मरीचिर्मरुतामस्मि नक्षत्राणामहं शशी ॥ १०-२१॥

वेदानां सामवेदोऽस्मि देवानामस्मि वासवः ।
इन्द्रियाणां मनश्चास्मि भूतानामस्मि चेतना ॥ १०-२२॥

रुद्राणां शङ्करश्चास्मि वित्तेशो यक्षरक्षसाम् ।
वसूनां पावकश्चास्मि मेरुः शिखरिणामहम् ॥ १०-२३॥

(21-23) Among the Ādityas, I am Viṣṇu (ādityānāmahaṃ viṣṇu), of lights I am the radiant Sun (jyotiṣāṃ raviraṃśumān ।), I am Marīci of the maruts (marīcirmarutāmasmi), of the starts I am the moon (nakṣatrāṇāmahaṃ śaśī ॥ 10-21॥). Of the Vedas, I am Sāma (vedānāṃ sāmavedo'smi), of the Devas, I am Vāsava (devānāmasmi vāsavaḥ), of sensory organs I am cognition (indriyāṇāṃ manaścāsmi), and of creation, I am consciousness (bhūtānāmasmi cetanā ॥ 10-22॥). Of the Rudras, I am Śaṅkara (rudrāṇāṃ śaṅkaraścāsmi), I am Vitteśa (Kubera) of the protective Yakṣa (vitteśo yakṣarakṣasām), of the Vasus I am Pāvaka (vasūnāṃ pāvakaścāsmi), and I am Meru among mountains (meruḥ śikhariṇāmaham ॥ 10-23॥).

पुरोधसां च मुख्यं मां विद्धि पार्थ बृहस्पतिम् ।
सेनानीनामहं स्कन्दः सरसामस्मि सागरः ॥ १०-२४॥

महर्षीणां भृगुरहं गिरामस्म्येकमक्षरम् ।
यज्ञानां जपयज्ञोऽस्मि स्थावराणां हिमालयः ॥ १०-२५॥

(24-25) Among family and head priests, I am known as Bṛhaspati (purodhasāṃ ca mukhyaṃ māṃ viddhi pārtha bṛhaspatim ।), among warriors, I am Skanda (senānīnāmahaṃ skandaḥ), among lakes, I am the sea (sarasāmasmi sāgaraḥ ॥ 10-24॥). Among Maharṣis I am Bhṛgu (maharṣīṇāṃ bhṛgurahaṃ), among words I am the single alphabet (girāmasmyekamakṣaram ।), among sacrifices, I the sacrifice of japa (yajñānāṃ japayajño 'smi), among the immovable entities, I am the Himālayas (sthāvarāṇāṃ himālayaḥ ॥ 10-25॥).

अश्वत्थः सर्ववृक्षाणां देवर्षीणां च नारदः ।
गन्धर्वाणां चित्ररथः सिद्धानां कपिलो मुनिः ॥ १०-२६॥

उच्चैःश्रवसमश्वानां विद्धि माममृतोद्भवम् ।
ऐरावतं गजेन्द्राणां नराणां च नराधिपम् ॥ १०-२७॥

(26-27) Among trees, I am Aśvattha (aśvatthaḥ sarvavṛkṣāṇāṃ), and of the Devarṣis, I am Nārada (devarṣīṇāṃ ca nāradaḥ ।), of the Gandharvas I am Cittraratha (gandharvāṇāṃ citrarathaḥ), of Siddhas I am Kapila muni (siddhānāṃ kapilo muniḥ ॥ 10-26॥). I am Uccaiḥśravas among horses (uccaiḥśravasamaśvānāṃ) know me to be born of nectar *(viddhi māmamṛtodbhavam ।)*, I am Airāvat among king of elephants *(airāvataṃ gajendrāṇām)*, and among men I am the King *(narāṇāṃ ca narādhipam ॥ 10-27॥)*.

आयुधानामहं वज्रं धेनूनामस्मि कामधुक् ।

प्रजनश्चास्मि कन्दर्पः सर्पाणामस्मि वासुकिः ॥ १०-२८॥

अनन्तश्चास्मि नागानां वरुणो यादसामहम् ।

पितॄणामर्यमा चास्मि यमः संयमतामहम् ॥ १०-२९॥

(28-29) Of weapons, I am the thunderbolt *(āyudhānāmahaṃ vajraṃ)*, among cows I am Kāmadhenu *(dhenūnāmasmi kāmadhuk ।)*, among projenators, I am Kāmadeva *(prajanaścāsmi kandarpaḥ)*, and of serpents I am Vāsuki *(sarpāṇāmasmi vāsukiḥ ॥ 10-28॥)*. Of snakes, I am Ananta *(anantaścāsmi nāgānām)*, among water bodies, I am Varuna *(varuṇo yādasāmaham ।)*, of the manes, I am Aryaman *(pitṝṇāmaryamā cāsmi)*, of the controllers, I am Yama *(yamaḥ saṃyamatāmaham ॥ 10-29॥)*.

प्रह्लादश्चास्मि दैत्यानां कालः कलयतामहम् ।

मृगाणां च मृगेन्द्रोऽहं वैनतेयश्च पक्षिणाम् ॥ १०-३०॥

पवनः पवतामस्मि रामः शस्त्रभृतामहम् ।

झषाणां मकरश्चास्मि स्रोतसामस्मि जाह्नवी ॥ १०-३१॥

(30-31) Among Daityas, I am Prahalāda *(prahlādaścāsmi daityānāṃ)*, and of the measurements, I am time *(kālaḥ kalayatāmaham ।)*, among animals I am the king of beasts (lion) *(mṛgāṇāṃ ca mṛgendro'ham)*, and of birds I am Vainteya (son of Vinatā or Garuḍa) *(vainateyaśca pakṣiṇām ॥ 10-30॥)*. Among movers, I am the wind *(pavanaḥ pavatāmasmi)*, of wielders of weapons I am Rāma *(rāmaḥ śastrabhṛtāmaham ।)*, among fishes I am the crocodile *(jhaṣāṇāṃ makaraścāsmi)*, and of rivers I am Jāhnvī *(srotasāmasmi jāhnavī ॥ 10-31॥)*.

सर्गाणामादिरन्तश्च मध्यं चैवाहमर्जुन ।

अध्यात्मविद्या विद्यानां वादः प्रवदतामहम् ॥ १०-३२॥

अक्षराणामकारोऽस्मि द्वन्द्वः सामासिकस्य च ।

अहमेवाक्षयः कालो धाताहं विश्वतोमुखः ॥ १०-३३॥

(32-33) Of nature, I am the beginning, middle, and end exclusively *(sargāṇāmādirantaśca madhyaṃ caivāhamarjuna ।)*, of knowledge the primordial Self *(adhyātmavidyā vidyānām)*, among discussion I am argument *(vādaḥ pravadatāmaham ॥ 10-32॥)*. Among alphabets, I am "akāra" *(akṣarāṇāmakāro'smi)* and duality in compounds *(dvandvaḥ sāmāsikasya ca ।)*, truly, I am imperishable *(ahamevākṣayaḥ)*, the universal dispenser of time *(kālo dhātāhaṃ viśvatomukhaḥ ॥ 10-33॥)*.

मृत्युः सर्वहरश्चाहमुद्भवश्च भविष्यताम् ।
कीर्तिः श्रीर्वाक्च नारीणां स्मृतिर्मेधा धृतिः क्षमा ॥ १०-३४॥
बृहत्साम तथा साम्नां गायत्री छन्दसामहम् ।
मासानां मार्गशीर्षोऽहमृतूनां कुसुमाकरः ॥ १०-३५॥

(34-35) And, I am all devouring death (*mṛtyuḥ sarvaharaścāham*), I am prosperity and planning (*udbhavaśca bhaviṣyatām ǀ*), I am the feminine qualities of fame, prosperity, speech, memory, intelligence, firmness, and forgiveness (*kīrtiḥ śrīrvākca nārīṇāṃ smṛtirmedhā dhṛtiḥ kṣamā ǁ 10-34ǁ*). I am *Bṛhatsāma*, also of Sāma Veda (*bṛhatsāma tathā sāmnām*), I am *Gāyatrī* among meters (*gāyatrī chandasāmaham ǀ*), I am *Mārgaśīrṣa* among months (*māsānāṃ mārgaśīrṣo 'ham*) among seasons, the flowering season (*ṛtūnāṃ kusumākaraḥ ǁ 10-35ǁ*).

द्यूतं छलयतामस्मि तेजस्तेजस्विनामहम् ।
जयोऽस्मि व्यवसायोऽस्मि सत्त्वं सत्त्ववतामहम् ॥ १०-३६॥
वृष्णीनां वासुदेवोऽस्मि पाण्डवानां धनञ्जयः ।
मुनीनामप्यहं व्यासः कवीनामुशना कविः ॥ १०-३७॥

(36-37) I am gambling of the fraudulent (*dyūtaṃ chalayatāmasmi*), the effulgence of the glorious (*tejastejasvināmaham ǀ*), I am victory (*jayo'smi*), I am effort (*vyavasāyo'smi*), I am harmony in the harmonious (*sattvaṃ sattvavatāmaham ǁ 10-36ǁ*). Of the Vṛṣṇis I am Vāsudeva (*vṛṣṇīnāṃ vāsudevo'smi*), among the Pāṇḍavas, I am Dhanañjaya (*pāṇḍavānāṃ dhanañjayaḥ ǀ*), also, of the sages, I am Vyāsa (*munīnāmapyahaṃ vyāsaḥ*), of the poets I am Uśanā the poet (*kavīnāmuśanā kaviḥ ǁ 10-37ǁ*).

दण्डो दमयतामस्मि नीतिरस्मि जिगीषताम् ।
मौनं चैवास्मि गुह्यानां ज्ञानं ज्ञानवतामहम् ॥ १०-३८॥
यच्चापि सर्वभूतानां बीजं तदहमर्जुन ।
न तदस्ति विना यत्स्यान्मया भूतं चराचरम् ॥ १०-३९॥

(38-39) Of punishers, I am the stick (*daṇḍo damayatāmasmi*), I am prudence among the ambitious (*nītirasmi jigīṣatām ǀ*), I am silence among secrets (*maunaṃ caivāsmi guhyānām*), I am knowledge among the wise (*jñānaṃ jñānavatāmaham ǁ 10-38ǁ*). I am also that seed of all creation (*yaccāpi sarvabhūtānāṃ bījaṃ tadahamarjuna ǀ*), without which creation may neither move not stay still (*na tadasti vinā yatsyānmayā bhūtaṃ carācaram ǁ 10-39ǁ*).

नान्तोऽस्ति मम दिव्यानां विभूतीनां परन्तप ।
एष तूद्देशतः प्रोक्तो विभूतेर्विस्तरो मया ॥ १०-४०॥

यद्यद्विभूतिमत्सत्त्वं श्रीमदूर्जितमेव वा ।

तत्तदेवावगच्छ त्वं मम तेजोंऽशसम्भवम् ॥ १०-४१॥

अथवा बहुनैतेन किं ज्ञातेन तवार्जुन ।

विष्टभ्याहमिदं कृत्स्नमेकांशेन स्थितो जगत् ॥ १०-४२॥

(40-42) There is no end to my divinity and power *(nānto'sti mama divyānāṃ vibhūtīnāṃ parantapa ।).* Indeed, I have declared a brief statement of particular aspects that cover my overall power *(eṣa tūddeśataḥ prokto vibhūtervistaro mayā ॥ 10-40॥).* Wherever there is glory, harmony, prosperity, or power *(yadyadvibhūtimatsattvaṃ śrīmadūrjitameva vā ।),* know that, that is a manifestation of my splendor only *(tattadevāvagaccha tvaṃ mama tejoṃ'śasambhavam ॥ 10-41॥).* In fact, what use is this multiple knowledge to thee *(athavā bahunaitena kiṃ jñātena tavārjuna ।),* I support existence of this world with a single part of myself *(viṣṭabhyāhamidaṃ kṛtsnamekāṃśena sthito jagat ॥ 10-42॥).*

◆———·●◆··———◆

Chapter 11

Viśvarūpadarśana-yoga
(yoga of the vision of the universal form) [1]

Introduction

Arjuna said – I am now convinced about your origin and capabilities and wish to see you in the form you spoke about. Therefore, if you think I have the capability, show me.

Śrī Kṛṣṇa said – OK. Take a look. Behold the Ādityas, Vasus, Rudras, Aśvinis, Maruts, and other marvels. Also, see the dynamic and static universe integral to my being. But, for this, I have to give you special vision capability.

Saying this, Śrī Kṛṣṇa showed him his divine form, with many mouths and eyes, marvelous sights, divine ornaments, and weapons. He was wearing heavenly garlands, anointed with celestial perfumes – all resplendent and boundless with faces on all sides.

Arjuna saw many universes, with its divisions integrated into one. Hair on end, an amazed Arjuna spoke to Śrī Kṛṣṇa with joined palms:

- I see all the Gods in your body and hosts of all types of beings, *Brahma,* all the *Ṛṣis,* and celestial serpents. You are infinite on all sides, with countless arms, stomachs, mouths, and eyes.

- In fact, I cannot see your beginning, middle, or end. I see you wearing a crown, with a club and discus.

- In fact, radiance blazes everywhere, hard to look at, all round dazzling like a flaming fire or sun and immeasurable.

---

[1]https://www.bhagavad-gita.org/Gita/chapter-11.html

- You are imperishable, the supreme being, the treasure-house of the universe, the imperishable guardian of eternal *dharma,* the ancient *puruṣa.*

- Also, you are without beginning, middle, or end; infinite in power, of infinite reach, the suns and moons being your eyes, the sacrificial fire is your mouth, heating the universe with your radiance.

- The space between heaven and earth in all quarters are filled by you, and everyone is trembling with fear.

- Also, hosts of *devas* enter into you, great *Ṛṣis* and *siddhas* pronounce "May it be well". The Rudras, Ādityas, Vasus, Sādhyās, Viśvas, Aśvinis, Maruts, Uṣṇapās, Gandharvas, Yakṣas, Asuras, and Siddhas, all gaze at you in amazement.

- Consequently, seeing your immeasurable form with so many mouths, eyes, arms, thighs, and feet, with many stomachs and tusks, the worlds are terror-struck as I am.

- When I see you touching the sky, blazing in colors, with mouth wide open and fiery eyes, my heart trembles in fear, not knowing the four quarters, finding neither courage nor peace.

- Also, all the sons of Dhṛtarāṣṭra with hosts of kings, Bhīṣma, Droṇa, and Sūtaputra, along with our warrior chiefs, enter hurrying into your mouth, terrible with tusks and fearful to look at. In fact, some are sticking in the gaps between the teeth with their heads crushed to powder. In truth, they rush into your flaming mouths like torrents of river rushing into an ocean, or moths rushing into a blazing fire to their destruction. Devouring everything, you lick your lips.

- Your rays fill the world with your radiance, so fierce is your form. As a result of this vision, I bow to you, have mercy. I desire to know you; I know not your purpose.

Śrī Kṛṣṇa said – I am the world destroying Time, engaged in wiping out the world. In fact, even without you, the hostile armies will not survive. So, stop worrying, arise, and get fame. Conquer your enemies and get fame. In fact, I have already killed them, you are merely the instrument. Slay Drona, Bhishma, Jayadratha, Karna, and others who are already doomed by me.

Sañjaya said – having heard Śrī Kṛṣṇa, Arjuna, with joined palms, trembling, prostrating, addressed Śrī Kṛṣṇa in a voice chocked and overwhelmed with fear. It is true, oh Śrī Kṛṣṇa, the world sings your praises, the evil flee while the Siddhas bow to you. And why should they not, you are the primal cause of Brahmā, you are imperishable, the being and non being, that which is supreme, the ancient *puruṣa,* the knower and knowable, and the supreme abode.

- You pervade this Universe. You are Vāyu, Agni, Varuṇa, Moon, Prajāpati, and the ancestor. Salutations to you a thousand times and again, before and after, on all sides. You are all.

- If I have been casual with you, it is from ignorance. Please forgive me if I have insulted you without knowing your greatness.

- You are the father of this moving and static world, the greatest Guru, for none can excel you. So, I prostrate before you, forgive me. Bear with me as a father to a son, friend to a friend and a lover with his beloved. I rejoice at your universal form, but I am afraid and request you to show me that form which I can relate to, with mace and discuss in hand.

Śrī Kṛṣṇa said – you have been privileged to see something which no study, sacrifice, gifts, or rituals can achieve. Don't be afraid, I will revert to my original form.

Sañjaya said – with this, Śrī Kṛṣṇa went back to his original form.

Arjuna said – I feel calmer, seeing you in Human form.

Śrī Kṛṣṇa said – it's not easy to see this form, but by unswerving devotion, as devotee can see this reality. He who works from me, accepts me as Supreme, is devoted to me, free from attachment and hatred to any being.

The *sāṅkhya* of *mahat* (the conceptual base of overall creation)

- Everything comes from the Source/ Truth/Origin or *Brahman*. This is a state of eternal, infinite, unchanging peace.

- The *Brahman* experiences existential anxiety (do I exist?) and desires self-expression (I want to see myself).

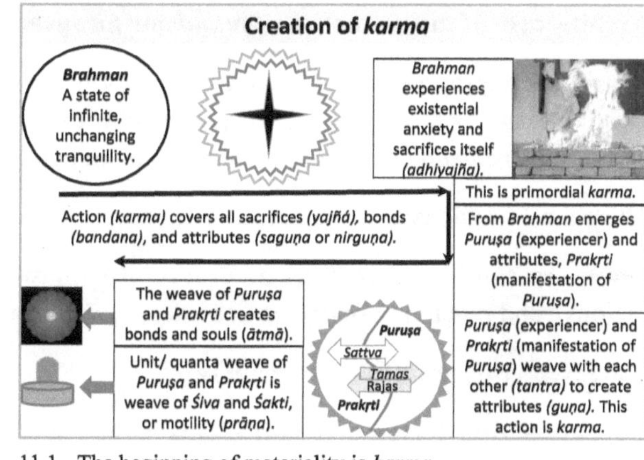

11.1 - The beginning of materiality is *karma*

- *Brahman* sacrifices itself to create itself. This is primordial sacrifice *ādhiyajña* (Śrī Kṛṣṇa).

- From *Brahman, nirguṇa-brahman (Brahman* without attributes) and *saguṇa-brahman (Brahman* with attributes, *Īśvara* or Supreme Soul - *Paramātmā).*

- *Saguṇa-brahman* or *Īśvara* is the weave of *puruṣa* (primordial Identity, Self, or experiencer) and *prakṛti* (primordial manifestation or energy).

- *Prakṛti* and *puruṣa* weave with each other to create primordial *karma* (action).

- From *karma (action)*, *guṇa* emerges. *Guṇa-s* are an outcome of the weave of *puruṣa* and *prakṛti*.

- When *puruṣa* (experiencer) is ascendant over *prakṛti* (manifestation), it is called *tamas* (delusion). Similarly, when *prakṛti* is ascendant over *puruṣa,* the attribute is called *rajas* (passion or flow), and finally, when *puruṣa* and *prakṛti* are in balance, this is called *sattva* (harmony or balance).

- *Puruṣa* and *prakṛti* continue weaving to create *hiraṇyagarbha* (golden egg) or *brahmāṇḍa (Brahma's* egg or Cosmos), the universe that houses all.

- Since *karma* creates transactions and bonds, these result in creation of multiple identities/souls *(ātma)* of varying complexities. The primordial Identity, which is the identity of *hiraṇyagarbha,* is called Viṣṇu. Viṣṇu is the repository of *māyā* (farce).

What Arjuna saw was *hiraṇyagarbha*. Since, Śrī Kṛṣṇa is *ādhiyajña,* this would have been natural and easy. Therefore, the details that Arjuna saw are no surprise, because this is what one would see in *brahmāṇḍa* or *hiraṇyagarbha* (golden egg or Cosmos).

Architecture of the cosmos *(brahmāṇḍa* or *hiraṇyagarbha):*

It would be appropriate to detail the various worlds/realms that are supposed to exist in the Indian cosmic system *(brahmāṇḍa* or *hiraṇyagarbha)* [2] [3]. This also forms part of the *brahmāṇḍa-purāṇa, viṣṇu-purāṇa,* and *bhāgavad-purāṇa* (2.5) [4].

There are 14 regions of existence, or *loka,* according to *nīlamata-purāṇa.*

Seven are considered *vyāhṛtis* or *ūrdhvaloka* (mystical utterances of the seven regions), and remaining seven are considered *pātālaloka* (lower regions).

The seven *vyāhṛtis* (mystical regions) are:

1. *Satya-loka* (Region of Truth) – This is the region of Truth, where there is no death, the state of *Brahman.*

2. *Tapaḥ-loka* (Region of austerity) – This is the region which comes out of austerity. This region is inhabited by Vaibharājas and cannot be consumed by fire.

---

[2] https://www.ganeshaspeaks.com/predictions/astrology/14-lokas-of-existence-in-hindu-mythology
[3] http://ancientvoice.wikidot.com/article:the-fourteen-worlds
[4] https://prabhupadabooks.com/sb/2/5

3. *Jana-loka (jana* means people) – This is considered to be the region inhibited by the sons of Brahmā, such as *Sanandana.*

Vishnu/ Īśvara's realm - cosmic architecture *(mahat)*

Brahma's realm - *brahmāṇḍa* (Brahma's egg), *hiraṇyagarbha* (golden womb)

pātāla-loka or *bilasvarga* (lower regions of existence)			*vyāhṛti* or *ūrdhva-loka* (mystical utterances of seven regions)		
Realm	**Vishnu**	***guṇa***	**Realm**	**Vishnu**	**Region**
atala	Waist	*kāma* (desire)	*bhūr*	Hips	Earth
vitala	Thighs	*lobha* (greed)	*bhuvar*	Navel	Atmosphere
sutala	Knees	*madha* (stubbornness)	*suvar*	Heart	Solar System
talātala	Shanks	*moha* (delusion)	*mahar*	Breast	Maharṣi
mahātala	Ankles	*krodha* (anger)	*janar*	Throat	Sons of Brahma
rasātala	Feet	*mātsarya* (envy)	*tapar*	Crown	Austerity
pātāla	Sole	*nirguṇa* (only *Puruṣa*)	*satya*	Head	Truth

11.2 - The cosmic system

4. *M a h a r - l o k a* (region of the *maharṣis*) – This is a region beyond *dhruva* and the region of the *maharṣis*. This may also mean the Milky Way.

5. *Suvar-loka (Viṣṇu-purāṇa)* – region beyond *bhuvar-loka,* considered to be beyond the Sun up until *dhruva* (Pole star) which is supposed to be ruled by Indra and his *devas*. This may include the entire Solar system. It has 9 orbits *(maṇḍala)* called *dhruva-maṇḍala, śani-maṇḍala* (Saturn), *bṛhaspati-maṇḍala* (Jupiter), *aṅgāraka-maṇḍala* (Mars), *sukra-maṇḍala* (Venus), *budha-maṇḍala* (Mercury), *nakṣatra-maṇḍala* (Constellation), *candra-maṇḍala* (Moon), and *sūrya-maṇḍala* (Sun).

6. *Bhuvar-loka* (region of energy) – This is also known as *dyu-loka* or *jyotir-loka);* this is the region of existence where energy predominates, and there is no matter (this may also be equated with the region where earth's magnetic field and atmosphere exists). *Viṣṇu-purāṇa* says that it is the space between Earth and the Sun, where *siddhas* move.

7. *Bhūr-loka* (region of existence) – This is the plane of existence of all humans as we know it. It consists of a central land mass *(jambudvīpa)* surrounded by six other land masses called *Plakṣa, Sālmala, Kuśa, Krauñca, Sāka,* and *Puṣkara*. This area consists of mountains, oceans, rivers, etc.

Pātālaloka or *bila-svarga* (lower regions of existence) comprises:

1. *Atala-loka* – Region ruled by Bala, who with his mystical powers has created 3 types of women in a yawn; *svairinī* – self-willed, who like to marry men from their own group, *kāminī* – lustful, who marry men from any group, and *pañcaśālīni,* who keep changing partners.

2. *Vitala-loka* – Region ruled by *hara-bhāva,* where gold, called *hataka* is created.

3. *Sutala-loka* – Region created by Vishwakarman, ruled by Bali Chakravarti.

4. *Talātala-loka* – Region ruled by *māyā,* a demon-architect skilled in sorcery, who created the magical city of Tripura.

5. *Mahātala-loka* – Region of the *nāgas* (many hooded serpents), sons of *kadru* (called *krodhavaśa),* Kuhaka, Takshaka, Kaliya, and Sushena, along with their families.

6. *Rasātala-loka* – Region at the sole of the feet of Viṣṇu, where *dānavas* and *daityas* reside.

7. *Pātāla-loka* – Region of *Vāsuki,* who is the snake that adorns Śiva.

Comments on *brahmāṇḍa* or *hiraṇyagarbha*

The etymology of the two *Saṃskṛta* words, Viṣṇu and Brahma, are as follows:

* *Viṣṇu (Vis)* means that which expands, thus corresponding to an expanding universe or increasing entropy in any system.

* *Brahma (Bṛh)* means anything that is big or expanded; *aṇḍa* means egg. This corresponds to *Brahmāṇḍa* or *Brahma's-egg.*

Decoding the various realms *(loka)*:

It is clear that the description of various *loka-s* contains two aspects, a material aspect of the Universe intertwined with a cognitive yoga-vidyā aspect. While the seven constituents of *ūrdhva-loka* are obviously related to the physical and cognitive Universe in their gross and subtle aspects, *pātāla-loka* seems to be more of a reflection of the realm inside ourselves. This can be seen from the allusion to the *ṣaḍ-ripu* (six poisons) that are clearly indicated in the representation of the regions. The alignment of the *pātāla-lokas* to the *cakras* on the spinal column is an assumption and not substantiated by evidence.

Going from first principles that everything is a weave of *puruṣa* (experiencer or primordial Identity) with *prakṛti* (manifestation of Identity), we can close out the first *(satya-loka),* last *(pātāla-loka),* and middle realms *(bhūr-loka* or Earth) as follows:

* *Satya-loka* is the realm of Truth and equivalent to *Brahman,* so it is a state of *nirguṇa-brahman,* where *puruṣa* experiences itself, but does not manifest. It is a state of Truth, infinite peace, or pure consciousness, where manifestation *(prakṛti)* is in *nirguṇa.*

* *Pātāla-loka* is at the opposite end of the spectrum. *Vāsuki* is a serpent that is in a state of material rest or pure *puruṣa* or null, which means *prakṛti* is in *nirguṇa* state here also. This is also a state of *nirguṇa-brahman,* pure infinite peace, or *zero-state-puruṣa.*

* *Bhūr-loka* or Earth is where *puruṣa* and *prakṛti* are playing out *māyā* in all its states of consciousness and attributes *(guṇa).*

- Importantly, the movement into the *ūrdhva-lokas* seems to be one of mix of electromagnetic as well as cognitive realms, while the *pātāla-loka* seems to be intrinsic to the Self.

- In terms of creation, all inhabitants of *brahmāṇḍa* are progeny of *brahmā,* whether they inhabit *ūrdhva-loka* or *pātāla-loka,* other than the *maharṣis* (seers) who inhibit *mahar-loka* whose origin seems to be indeterminate, so one has to assume that they come directly from *Brahma.*

Let us look at the pair or regions on opposite sides of the Earth *(bhūr-loka).* Since *bhūr-loka* is the seventh region, there will be one more on the *pātāla-loka* side.

Bhuvar-loka and *atala-loka*

- In *bhuvar-loka,* which is the Earth's atmosphere[6], there is only space. So, *puruṣa* experiences reduced consciousness because there is no material transaction. *Prakṛti* manifests predominantly as *rajoguṇa,* as magnetic energy where consciousness of *puruṣa* is still fixed by its relationship with the Earth. Meanwhile, *prakṛti* has begun shedding *tamoguṇa* and is manifesting as *rajoguṇa.*

  o Similarly, in *atala-loka,* Identity *(puruṣa)* experiences contraction because it is transacting with fewer souls *(jīva),* while *prakṛti* has become more *tāmasika.*

  o This slide of *prakṛti* to *tamas* can be derived from the allegorical vision that *Bāla* yawns to create three types of women. Yawning is indicative of *puruṣa* experiencing lethargy. Also, allusion to sexual preference of women is indicative of restless boredom *(tamas)* of *prakṛti* and sexual desires *(kāma)* in *puruṣa.*

Suvar-loka and *vitala-loka*

- *Suvar-loka* is clearly the Solar system. Why is this important?

- Earth has a magnetic field; all creatures on Earth exhibit some form of conductivity.

- Similarly, each of the other planets in the Solar system also have magnetic fields.

- Additionally, planets affect each other's magnetic fields depending on their orbits, size and inter-planetary distance with respect to each other. For example,

---

[5]https://www.speakingtree.in/blog/bhuvar-loka-suvar-loka-mahar-loka-jana-loka-and-tapo-loka-brahma-loka
[6]https://cloud1.arc.nasa.gov/solveII/outreach/middleschool-atmos.htm#:~:text=The%20atmosphere%20is%20made%20up,the%20higher%20up%20you%20go.

we know that the Moon influences tides on Earth, depending on whether it is waxing or waning. We also know that the human body comprises 70% water. Imagine the impact of a waxing or waning Moon on the flow of electrolytes in the human body, and how that might influence decision-making? If the Moon can influence us and our reactions, then what about other planets, such as Sun, Saturn, and Jupiter? Can they will impact cognition in some form? If yes, is *jyotiṣa* (astrology) a poorly understood scientific system of planets? This is *suvar-loka,* where experience is created.

- *Vitala-loka* is where gold is created.

- Gold is prized because it is one of the most stable metals. It does not decay or tarnish, and it is classified as a diamagnetic material (one that is not magnetic).

- So, while *puruṣa* in *suvar-loka* experiences increased *sattvaguṇa* and reduced *rajoguṇa,* in *vitala-loka, puruṣa* experiences wealth and greed *(lobha),* a *tamoguṇa* of *prakṛti.*

The pairing of *mahar-loka* and *sutala-loka* is almost prophetic.

- *Mahar-loka* is the place where *maharṣis* or Great Seers reside. What is the role of these *maharṣis?*

- Let us look at the first principles of action *(karma).* There are four types of *karma*:

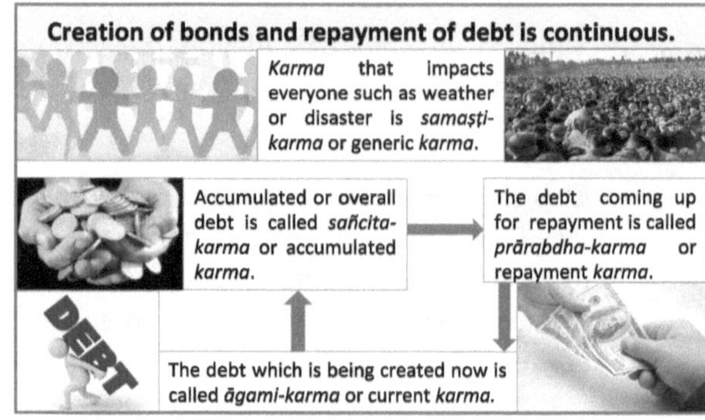

11.3 - Creation of *prārabdha-karma*

  - *a g a m i - k a r m a* (*karma* that which is currently getting created),

  - *prārabdha-karma (karma* that has come up for reconciliation),

  - *sañcita-karma* (overall *karma* available with any entity),

  - *samaṣṭi-karma (karma* that affects all creation on account of a macro event, such as earthquake, eclipse, cyclone, monsoon, epidemic, etc.).

- How is *sañcita-karma* transferred to *prārabdha-karma*? Obviously, the number of entities that a person interacts with in life are too many for easy reconciliation. Hence, resolution of debt between entities needs to be orchestrated. This is done by entities that have requisite control over *prāṇa* (creative force) called *maharṣis* at *mahar-loka* who also manage *samaṣṭi-karma* (macro-action which overrides all individual action).

- Once the reconciliation parameters of *karma* are fixed, these are then coded into the movement of the planets in the *suvar-loka* so that the magnetic and gravitational forces influence decision making on *bhūr-loka* as existence.

- On the *pātāla-loka* side, *sutala-loka* is created by Vishwakarma, a celestial architect and ruled by Bali Chakravarti, a Regent who was just and virtuous. Hence, on the face of it, its position in the nether-world does not make sense.

- However, let us look at the transformation of Bali Chakravarti. He conducted a sacrifice *(yajña),* which was officiated by Śukrācārya (the *Guru* of *asuras* and member of *mahar-loka* because he is the governing principle of Planet Venus). Śukrācārya recognized Viṣṇu in *vāmana* form and warned Bali, but Bali ignored the warning and ended up sacrificing himself to Viṣṇu. He paid the price for being stubborn/inflexible and proud.

- The realm of *sutala-loka* is one where *puruṣa* experiences stubbornness and pride *(mada),* even to the extent of not being able to cognize the advice of one's well-wishers. This is a *tamoguṇa* of *prakṛti.*

Jana-loka and *talātala-loka*

- *Jana-loka* is inhabited by the sons of *Brahmā (prajāpati)* and a natural progression of *mahar-loka.* For the *maharṣis* to rearrange *prārabdha-karma* and *samaṣṭi-karma,* there must be a higher architectural hierarchy where control of *mahar-loka* is exerted.

For example, a computer needs a motherboard *(jana-loka)* on which an operating system *(mahar-loka)* is loaded so that programs can be run *(bhuvar-loka)* for specific situations *(bhūr-loka).*

- *Jana-loka* is a hierarchically the highest level in terms of creation management or *mahat.*

- At the opposite end, *talātala-loka* is a city created by sorcery.

- *Talātala-loka* was created by *Māyāsura,* a brilliant architect, to protect the city of Tripura from destruction.

- The city consisted of three fortresses, all mobile but connected such that they come into confluence only on a particular day.

- On the day of confluence, the city was destroyed by Śiva *(tamoguṇa)* using Vāsuki (who lives in *pātāla-loka)* as the missile.

- *Talātala-loka* is the realm where *puruṣa* experiences *moha* (delusion), a *tamoguṇa* of *prakṛti.*

Tapaḥ-loka and *mahātala-loka*

- *Tapaḥ* is austerity. Austerity comes from sacrifice *(yajña)* of creation.

- Primordial sacrifice *(ādhiyajña)* is Śrī Kṛṣṇa. This is the realm from where *puruṣa* and *prakṛti* emerge to start creation. It is the starting point of *saguṇa-brahman, paramātmā, īśvara,* Viṣṇu, and Śrī Kṛṣṇa

- On the other side, *mahātala* is the realm of *Krodhavaśa* (power of anger), daughter of Dākṣa, wife of Kāśyapa, and mother of *asuras.*

- It is inhabited by *nāgas,* who are known for their short temper. This is the realm where *puruṣa* experiences anger *(krodha)*, which is a *tamoguṇa* of *prakṛti.*

Rasātala-loka – this is the region where *daityas* and *dānavas* reside and located at the sole of Viṣṇu, thus representing the other end of *Brahmāṇḍa* or *hiraṇyagarbha.*

- *Rasātala* means "region of essence". The root of all *ṣaḍ-ripu* (six treacherous qualities) is identification of the Self with the environment. All problems start with comparison of oneself with others. This results in envy *(mātsaryam)*, which is the root of all other afflictions.

- Interestingly, all the inhabitants in *talātala-loka,* starting from *atala-loka* until *rasātala-loka,* are descendants of Dākṣa, who was also created by Brahmā. So, *rasātala-loka* represents the other end of *jana-loka.*

Talātala-loka – This is the region inhabited by Vāsuki who adorns Śiva, and his sister Manasā (cognition). Here *puruṣa* is in Śiva or *nirguṇa* state, the state of null or pure *Brahman.* This can also considered to be the resting place of the *kuṇḍalinī* in the *mūladhāra.*

Śrīmad-bhāgavad-purāṇa on evolution of cosmic architecture *(mahat)*:

- *Śrīmad-bhāgavad-purāṇa* (2.5.21 onwards) – The evolution of knowledge is minutely explained. It starts with Viṣṇu creating the universe for its own pleasure (this can also be interpreted as experience of a loss of Identity which made Viṣṇu *(ādhi-puruṣa)* manifest to seek confirmation of Identity), the onset of time, *karma,* and *svabhāva.*

- Verse 23-24 [7] – Creation of *mahat* (concept of cosmic architecture) is achieved by application of attributes *(guṇa)*. This results in creation of matter *(tamas)*, wisdom or balance *(sattva)*, and work or effort or energy *(kriyā)*. There is formation of *ahaṅkāra* (sense of doer-ship), which is another representation of attributes. This occurs in the form of *vaikharika* (that which is modulated or harmonic), which is a *sāttvika* outcome, *taijasa* (effulgent or manifesting power

---

[7] https://prabhupadabooks.com/sb/2/5/23

and drive) which is *rājasika,* and *tāmasika* (lethargic or delusional) which is manifestation of *tamas.*

- Verse 25 onwards [8] – *ahaṅkāra* is the origin of the five primordial elements (earth, water, fire, air, and ether). Sound also emanates from *ahaṅkāra* and provides evidence of existence to the subject (seer) and object (seen).

  For example - when someone exclaims "the light has turned green, it signifies a change in state. This is through use of sound *(śabda).* From ether comes air (whose *svabhāva* or character is sound, vitality, energy, zeal, and strength). From air comes fire, with characteristics of quality of color, sound, and touch. From fire came water with added character of taste in addition to sound, touch, and color. From water emerged earth with added character of smell.

  Importantly, if one were to try and regress into silence, one would first need to control the sense of being a doer *(ahaṅkāra),* because *ahaṅkāra* is the basis of the sense of identity/ self-worth *(asmitā),* which will struggle to stay alive/ relevant. After that, one would need to control each of the other qualities of nature in reverse order - earth, water, fire, air and ether/ space.

- Verse 30 onwards [9] – from the mix of the above elements emerged cognition and the 10 kinetic and cognitive senses. But all this creation just kept growing without any motility in the form of an egg *(hiraṇyagarbha).* But, once *Brahman* gave it life, *puruṣa* burst forth from *hiraṇyagarbha* [10] and emerged, with seven higher regions above the waist and seven regions below the waist.

- Verse 37 [11] – *Brahmins* represent the mouth, *kṣtriyas* represent the arms, *vaiśyas* represent the thighs, and *śūdras,* the feet. This seems to conform to the traditional occupation of *brāhmaṇas* being teachers of *brahma-vidya,* which requires communication, *kṣtriyas* being warriors requiring strong arms, *vaiśyas* being business people requiring to travel, and *śūdras* being workers represented by the feet.

  - Waist upwards [12] – *bhuvar-loka* is the navel, *suvar-loka* is the heart, *mahar-loka* is the breast, *jana-loka* is the neck, *tapo-loka* is the crown, and *satya-loka* is the head.

  - Earth [13] – *bhūr-loka* is not specified, but the region between the navel and thigh is the hips. This region houses the genitals and this pelvic area is the crossover from motivation to movement; thus all the three attributes get located here. Deep and subtle allegory is embedded in these verses.

---

[8] https://prabhupadabooks.com/sb/2/5/25

[9] https://prabhupadabooks.com/sb/2/5/30

[10] https://prabhupadabooks.com/sb/2/5/35

[11] https://prabhupadabooks.com/sb/2/5/37?d=1

[12] https://prabhupadabooks.com/sb/2/5/39

[13] https://prabhupadabooks.com/sb/2/5/31

- ○ Going downwards[14] – *atala-loka* is the waist, *vitala-loka* is the thighs, *sutala-loka* is the knees, *talātala-loka* is the shanks, *mahātala-loka* is the ankles, *rasātala-loka* is the feet, and *pātāla-loka* is the sole.

The Soul *(ātman)* and rebirth

It is only natural that one should wonder what happens to the Soul *(ātman)* after death. Some aspects that need to be considered are:

- In *sanātana-dharma,* there is no death. The Soul *(ātman)* moves out of the body once its *prārabdha-karma* has been exhausted.

- The Soul *(ātman)* remains unchanged through each of these births, and the embodiment of the Soul *(ātman)* that has in experiencing this life is called *jīva.*

- When the person dies, the *jīva* does not die, but continues experiencing *(puruṣa)* and adding *karma* (action) due to its experiencing of duality (like-dislike, attraction-repulsion, good-bad, etc.).

- Physically, respiration stops, the person dies, and the *jīva* leaves the body with *prāṇa* (motility). The body is disposed and reverts to its primordial elements. The *prāṇa* in this situation is the *udāna-vāyu* (upward flowing motility).

- The *jīva* in this form is called *preta* (that which has gone to the nether world). At this time, the *jīva* is disoriented after having lost the body that it was used to and having experienced the brutality of death.

- *Para-loka-vidyā* espouses that the *jīva* does not wait for reconciliation, but moves to another body immediately. This contradicts the principle espoused by Śrī Kṛṣṇa in Chapter 8, 9 and other chapters, where he says that a person gets what he or she sows, which means that the process of rebirth is a clearly mapped reconciliation process.

- Let us look at the following quote from *Chāndogya-upaniṣad* - "Having become cloud, he rains down. Then he is born as rice, corn, herbs, tree, sesamum, and beans. From them, the escape is beset with most difficulties. For, whoever the person may be who eats the food and begets offspring, he henceforth becomes like unto them." *(Chāndogya-upaniṣad: 10.5)*[15].

- How can reconciliation happen if the *jīva* moves immediately to another body after expiration? There is simply no opportunity for all the players with whom one has debts *(ṛṇa),* to be available for *prārabdha-karma* to be reconciled.

- Another contradiction is the prevalence of other realms *(lokas)* such as abode of *Yama (yama-loka),* abode of the ancestors *(pitṛ-loka), brahma-loka, candra-loka* in the various *purāṇas* such as *Nāradīya-purāṇa,* etc. How can these

---

[14]https://prabhupadabooks.com/sb/2/5/40-41?d=1

[15]https://www.wisdomlib.org/hinduism/book/chandogya-upanishad-english/d/doc239196.html

realms exist outside of Viṣṇu since Śrī Kṛṣṇa says that everything is embedded in the *Brahmāṇḍa*. Again, this confusion needs to be resolved.

- Obviously, there is a great deal of confusion and reconciliation required as far as manifestation of reality is concerned. However, it is entirely possible that the ancient texts are using different terminologies to describe creation and re-creation. Also, it is possible that since the journey of Souls *(ātman)* is a subtle one, one needs greater perception of the subtle aspects of *prāṇa* to decipher the Truth.

Some contradictions to accepted positions:

- There is a discernible degree of confluence between the ancient texts on the origin of matter and the Universe and science. The confusion arises in the interpretation and reconciliation of points of convergence and divergence.

- An important conclusion is that all creation comes from one source, whether it is matter or energy. This is illusion *(māyā),* and the only thing outside this egg of matter *(hiraṇyagarbha)* is *Brahman*.

- *Pātāla-loka's* seems to represent *ṣaḍ-ripu* (six deluders)[16] which cover all aspects of *tamoguna* of *prakṛti*. Hence, it might be interpreted as aspects within the Self which prevent a person from achieving the design potential of becoming *sthita-prajña* (a person of steady awareness).

- The *kuṇḍalinī* is also a serpent that rests in null position until she emerges to move up from *Brahmadvāra* (door of Brahma) to *Brahmāṇḍa* (opening of Brahma). The *kuṇḍalinī,* a serpent, is *śakti* who emerges from the *mūlādhāra cakra* and merges with Śiva. Clearly, ancient Indian mythology and needs to be understood in the architectural framework of *yoga-vidyā*. So, it is possible that the *pātāla-loka* might be allegorically associated with the *cakras* and *kuṇḍlinī*.

- There are some differences between the different ancient texts and their various interpretations. For example, *Śrīmad-bhāgavad-purāṇa* suggests that *prakṛti* was creating matter by itself, but it burst out of its egg only when *Brahman* provided the motility in the form of *puruṣa*. Then, creation burst out of the egg as Viṣṇu. However, it does not violate the hypothesis that *puruṣa* and *prakṛti* weave together to create materiality. Another aspect is whether the egg, after the manifestation of Viṣṇu, remained an egg or just remained as Viṣṇu. The argument is irrelevant because we do know that the Universe expands, and the expanding boundary can be referred to as the perimeter of *hiraṇyagarbha*.

- Additionally, there is some confusion on the journey of souls *(ātman)* after expiration, but the subject is immensely vast, requiring greater research and personal experience.

---

[16]https://www.speakingtree.in/article/shadripu-six-enemies-of-the-human-mind

Lessons learned in Chapter 11:

- Śrī Kṛṣṇa is a manifestable state that controls creation and maintenance but does not participate in the operations.

- From the description of Arjuna's vision, one can conclude that birth, living, and death is brutal and without sentiment. So, one must stop attaching sentiment to action (like-dislike, good-bad, right-wrong etc.) and develop detachment *(vairāgyam)*.

The transliteration and translation of chapter 11 follows:

अर्जुन उवाच -

मदनुग्रहाय परमं गुह्यमध्यात्मसंज्ञितम् ।

यत्त्वयोक्तं वचस्तेन मोहोऽयं विगतो मम ॥ ११-१॥

भवाप्ययौ हि भूतानां श्रुतौ विस्तरशो मया ।

त्वत्तः कमलपत्राक्ष माहात्म्यमपि चाव्ययम् ॥ ११-२॥

Arjuna said (1-2) Out of compassion for me *(madanugrahāya)* this supreme secret called *adhyātma (paramaṃ guhyamadhyātmasaṃjñitam ।)* which you have spoken, by that word this delusion has left me *(yattvayoktaṃ vacastena moho'yaṃ vigato mama ॥ 11-1॥)*. Indeed, creation and dissolution of beings I have heard in great detail *(bhavāpyayau hi bhūtānāṃ śrutau vistaraśo mayā ।)*, from you, O Lotus-eyed, also supreme soul and imperishable *(tvattaḥ kamalapatrākṣa māhātmyamapi cāvyayam ॥ 11-2॥)*.

एवमेतद्यथात्थ त्वमात्मानं परमेश्वर ।

द्रष्टुमिच्छामि ते रूपमैश्वरं पुरुषोत्तम ॥ ११-३॥

मन्यसे यदि तच्छक्यं मया द्रष्टुमिति प्रभो ।

योगेश्वर ततो मे त्वं दर्शयात्मानमव्ययम् ॥ ११-४॥

(3-4) Thus, this you have declared yourself to be the Supreme Soul *(evametadyathāttha tvamātmānaṃ parameśvara ।)*, I wish to see you in your Sovereign Supreme Self form *(draṣṭumicchāmi te rūpamaiśvaraṃ puruṣottama ॥ 11-3॥)*. If you think that is possible for me to see it, O Lord! *(manyase yadi tacchakyaṃ mayā draṣṭumiti prabho ।)*, O Lord of Yogīs, then show me your imperishable Self *(yogeśvara tato me tvaṃ darśayātmānamavyayam ॥ 11-4॥)*.

श्रीभगवानुवाच -

पश्य मे पार्थ रूपाणि शतशोऽथ सहस्रशः ।

नानाविधानि दिव्यानि नानावर्णाकृतीनि च ॥ ११-५॥

पश्यादित्यान्वसून्रुद्रानश्विनौ मरुतस्तथा ।

बहून्यदृष्टपूर्वाणि पश्याश्चर्याणि भारत ॥ ११-६॥

Śrī Kṛṣṇa said (5-6) Behold my forms by the hundreds and thousands *(paśya me pārtha rūpāṇi śataśo 'tha sahasraśaḥ ǀ)* of different divine types, different colors, and shapes *(nānāvidhāni divyāni nānāvarṇākṛtīni ca ǁ 11-5ǁ)*. Behold Ādityas, Vasus, Rudraas, Aśvinis, Maruts, also, *(paśyādityānvasūnrudrānaśvinau marutastathā ǀ)*, many previously unseen wonders *(bahūnyadṛṣṭapūrvāṇi paśyāścaryāṇi bhārata ǁ 11-6ǁ)*.

इहैकस्थं जगत्कृत्स्नं पश्याद्य सचराचरम् ।

मम देहे गुडाकेश यच्चान्यद् द्रष्टुमिच्छसि ॥ ११-७॥

न तु मां शक्यसे द्रष्टुमनेनैव स्वचक्षुषा ।

दिव्यं ददामि ते चक्षुः पश्य मे योगमैश्वरम् ॥ ११-८॥

(7-8) Here, behold, centered in one place, the whole universe *(ihaikastham jagatkṛtsnam)*, now moving-unmoving *(paśyādya sacarācaram ǀ)*, in my body, that and other visions you with to see *(mama dehe guḍākeśa yaccānyad draṣṭumicchasi ǁ 11-7ǁ)*. But you cannot see me even with these eyes of yours *(na tu māṃ śakyase draṣṭumanenaiva svacakṣuṣā ǀ)*, I give you divine vision to behold my Powerful Yoga *(divyaṃ dadāmi te cakṣuḥ paśya me yogamaiśvaram ǁ 11-8ǁ)*.

संजय उवाच -

एवमुक्त्वा ततो राजन्महायोगेश्वरो हरिः ।

दर्शयामास पार्थाय परमं रूपमैश्वरम् ॥ ११-९॥

अनेकवक्त्रनयनमनेकाद्भुतदर्शनम् ।

अनेकदिव्याभरणं दिव्यानेकोद्यतायुधम् ॥ ११-१०॥

Sañjaya said (9-10) Rāja (Dṛtarāṣṭra), having thus spoken, the Great Yogī Hari, *(evamuktvā tato rājanmahāyogeśvaro hariḥ ǀ)* showed Partha the Supreme Sovereign form *(darśayāmāsa pārthāya paramaṃ rūpamaiśvaram ǁ 11-9ǁ)*. With multiple muzzles and eyes, numerous unique visions *(anekavaktranayanamanekādbhutadarśanam ǀ)*, with multiple divine ornaments *(anekadivyābharaṇam)*, many divine weapons lifted *(divyānekodyatāyudham ǁ 11-10ǁ)*.

दिव्यमाल्याम्बरधरं दिव्यगन्धानुलेपनम् ।

सर्वाश्चर्यमयं देवमनन्तं विश्वतोमुखम् ॥ ११-११॥

दिवि सूर्यसहस्रस्य भवेद्युगपदुत्थिता ।

यदि भाः सदृशी सा स्याद्भासस्तस्य महात्मनः ॥ ११-१२॥

(11-12) Wearing divine apparel and garlands *(divyamālyāmbaradharaṃ)* anointed with divine scents *(divyagandhānulepanam ।)*, everywhere astonishing visions *(sarvāścaryamayam)*, divine endless faces on all sides *(devamanantaṃ viśvatomukham ॥ 11-11॥)*. In a sky a thousand Suns were rising simultaneously *(divi sūryasahasrasya bhavedyugapadutthitā ।)*, if splendor like that were possible, such would be of a mighty Soul *(yadi bhāḥ sadṛśī sā syādbhāsastasya mahātmanaḥ ॥ 11-12॥)*.

तत्रैकस्थं जगत्कृत्स्नं प्रविभक्तमनेकधा ।

अपश्यद्देवदेवस्य शरीरे पाण्डवस्तदा ॥ ११-१३॥

ततः स विस्मयाविष्टो हृष्टरोमा धनञ्जयः ।

प्रणम्य शिरसा देवं कृताञ्जलिरभाषत ॥ ११-१४॥

(13-14) There, in one place, the whole universe divided in many parts *(tatraikasthaṃ jagatkṛtsnaṃ pravibhaktamanekadhā ।)* Pandava saw then in the body of the God of Gods *(apaśyaddevadevasya śarīre pāṇḍavastadā ॥ 11-13॥)*. Then he, filled with wonder, hair standing on end, Arjuna prostrated the Daiva with joined hands and spoke *(tataḥ sa vismayāviṣṭo hṛṣṭaromā dhanañjayaḥ । praṇamya śirasā devaṃ kṛtāñjalirabhāṣata ॥ 11-14॥)*.

अर्जुन उवाच -

पश्यामि देवांस्तव देव देहे

सर्वांस्तथा भूतविशेषसङ्घान् ।

ब्रह्माणमीशं कमलासनस्थ-

मृषींश्च सर्वानुरगांश्च दिव्यान् ॥ ११-१५॥

अनेकबाहूदरवक्त्रनेत्रं

पश्यामि त्वां सर्वतोऽनन्तरूपम् ।

नान्तं न मध्यं न पुनस्तवादिं

पश्यामि विश्वेश्वर विश्वरूप ॥ ११-१६॥

Arjuna said (15-16) I see all deities in your divine body *(paśyāmi devāṃstava deva dehe)*, also communities of various types of creatures *(sarvāṃstathā bhūtaviśeṣasaṅghān ।)*, Lord Brahmā seated on a Lotus *(brahmāṇamīśam kamalāsanastha)*, Ṛṣis, and all types of divine serpents *(mṛṣīṃśca sarvānuragāṃśca divyān ॥ 11-15॥)*. I see many arms, stomachs, mouths, and eyes in every part of your endless body *(anekabāhūdaravaktranetraṃ- paśyāmi tvāṃ sarvato'nantarūpam ।)*, I can see no end, no middle, not even you're beginning in your Universal form, Viśveśvara *(nāntaṃ na madhyaṃ na punastavādiṃ-paśyāmi viśveśvara viśvarūpa ॥ 11-16॥)*.

किरीटिनं गदिनं चक्रिणं च

    तेजोराशिं सर्वतो दीप्तिमन्तम् ।

पश्यामि त्वां दुर्निरीक्ष्यं समन्ताद्

    दीप्तानलार्कद्युतिमप्रमेयम् ॥ ११-१७॥

त्वमक्षरं परमं वेदितव्यं

    त्वमस्य विश्वस्य परं निधानम् ।

त्वमव्ययः शाश्वतधर्मगोप्ता

    सनातनस्त्वं पुरुषो मतो मे ॥ ११-१८॥

(17-18) Decorated with a diadem, club, discuss and filled with radiance everywhere and shining *(kirīṭinaṃ gadinaṃ cakriṇaṃ ca- tejorāśiṃ sarvato dīptimantam ।)*, I see you very hard to look at all around blazing hot like the immeasurable Sun *(paśyāmi tvāṃ durnirīkṣyaṃ samantād-dīptānalārkadyutimaprameyam ॥ 11-17॥)*. You are Supreme Indestructible worthy of cognisance *(tvamakṣaraṃ paramaṃ veditavyaṃ)*, you are the Supreme Universal treasure house *(tvamasya viśvasya paraṃ nidhānam ।)*, you are imperishable, the eternal preserver of Dharma *(tvamavyayaḥ śāśvatadharmagoptā)* that is universal, I think that you are *puruṣa (sanātanastvaṃ puruṣo mato me ॥ 11-18॥)*.

अनादिमध्यान्तमनन्तवीर्य-

    मनन्तबाहुं शशिसूर्यनेत्रम् ।

पश्यामि त्वां दीप्तहुताशवक्त्रं

    स्वतेजसा विश्वमिदं तपन्तम् ॥ ११-१९॥

द्यावापृथिव्योरिदमन्तरं हि

    व्याप्तं त्वयैकेन दिशश्च सर्वाः ।

दृष्ट्वाद्भुतं रूपमुग्रं तवेदं

    लोकत्रयं प्रव्यथितं महात्मन् ॥ ११-२०॥

(19-20) Without beginning, middle, or end, of infinite virility, having infinite arms, having the Sun and Moon for eyes *(anādimadhyāntamanantavīrya manantabāhuṃ śaśisūryanetram ।)*, I see you with flaming mouth, your own radiance heating this universe *(paśyāmi tvāṃ dīptahutāśavaktraṃ svatejasā viśvamidaṃ tapantam ॥ 11-19॥)*. Indeed, all quarters and interspace of this Earth and Heavens are filled by you alone *(dyāvāpṛthivyoridamantaraṃ hi vyāptaṃ tvayaikena diśaśca sarvāḥ ।)*, I am seeing this unique ferocious form of yours with the three worlds trembling in fear, Great Soul *(dṛṣṭvādbhutaṃ rūpamugraṃ tavedaṃ lokatrayaṃ pravyathitaṃ mahātman ॥ 11-20॥)*.

अमी हि त्वां सुरसङ्घा विशन्ति

केचिद्धीताः प्राञ्जलयो गृणन्ति ।

स्वस्तीत्युक्त्वा महर्षिसिद्धसङ्घाः

स्तुवन्ति त्वां स्तुतिभिः पुष्कलाभिः ॥ ११-२१॥

रुद्रादित्या वसवो ये च साध्या

विश्वेऽश्विनौ मरुतश्चोष्मपाश्च ।

गन्धर्वयक्षासुरसिद्धसङ्घा

वीक्षन्ते त्वां विस्मिताश्चैव सर्वे ॥ ११-२२॥

(21-22) In fact, communities of Devas enter you, some in fear, with joined palms, after uttering a prayer that all may be well (*amī hi tvāṃ surasaṅghā viśanti- kecidbhītāḥ prāñjalayo gṛṇanti ǀ svastītyuktvā*), communities or seers and sages praise you, glorifying hymns (*maharṣisiddhasaṅghāḥ stuvanti tvāṃ stutibhiḥ puṣkalābhiḥ ǁ 11-21ǁ*). The Rudras, ādityas, Vasus, and Sādhyās, Viśvadevas, Aśvinis, Maruts, and Pitrus, also communities of Gandharva, Yakṣa, Asura, Siddhas, and all others look at you in astonishment (*rudrādityā vasavo ye ca sādhyā viśve'śvinau marutaścoṣmapāśca ǀ gandharvayakṣāsurasiddhasaṅghā- vīkṣante tvāṃ vismitāścaiva sarve ǁ 11-22ǁ*).

रूपं महत्ते बहुवक्त्रनेत्रं

महाबाहो बहुबाहूरुपादम् ।

बहूदरं बहुदंष्ट्राकरालं

दृष्ट्वा लोकाः प्रव्यथितास्तथाहम् ॥ ११-२३॥

नभःस्पृशं दीप्तमनेकवर्णं

व्यात्ताननं दीप्तविशालनेत्रम् ।

दृष्ट्वा हि त्वां प्रव्यथितान्तरात्मा

धृतिं न विन्दामि शमं च विष्णो ॥ ११-२४॥

(23-24) Your form is huge with multiple mouths and eyes, many arms, thighs, and feet (*rūpaṃ mahatte bahuvaktranetram- mahābāho bahubāhūrupādam ǀ*), many stomachs, fearful with multiple tusks, seeing this world, I am indeed distressed (*bahūdaraṃ bahudaṃṣṭrākarālam- dṛṣṭvā lokāḥ pravyathitāstathāham ǁ 11-23ǁ*). Touching the sky, blazing in many colors, with mouths wide open, with inflamed large eyes (*nabhaḥspṛśaṃ dīptamanekavarṇam- vyāttānanaṃ dīptaviśālanetram ǀ*), having seen the true you, I am terrified within my soul, lose my courage, and find no peace, Vishno! (*dṛṣṭvā hi tvāṃ pravyathitāntarātmā- dhṛtiṃ na vindāmi śamaṃ ca viṣṇo ǁ 11-24ǁ*).

दंष्ट्राकरालानि च ते मुखानि

दृष्ट्वैव कालानलसन्निभानि ।

दिशो न जाने न लभे च शर्म

प्रसीद देवेश जगन्निवास ॥ ११-२५॥

अमी च त्वां धृतराष्ट्रस्य पुत्राः

सर्वे सहैवावनिपालसङ्घैः ।

भीष्मो द्रोणः सूतपुत्रस्तथासौ

सहास्मदीयैरपि योधमुख्यैः ॥ ११-२६॥

वक्त्राणि ते त्वरमाणा विशन्ति

दंष्ट्राकरालानि भयानकानि ।

केचिद्विलग्ना दशनान्तरेषु

सन्दृश्यन्ते चूर्णितैरुत्तमाङ्गैः ॥ ११-२७॥

(25-27) Having seen your mouth with terrifying tusks and blazing like pralaya fires (*daṃṣṭrākarālāni ca te mukhāni- dṛṣṭvaiva kālānalasannibhāni ।*), I lose orientation, purpose, and am unable to be calm. Have mercy, Lord of the Devas, in whom the Universe resides (*diśo na jāne na labhe ca śarma- prasīda deveśa jagannivāsa ॥ 11-25॥*). These and all the sons of Dhṛtarāṣṭra, along groups of kings, Bhīṣma, Droṇa, Sūtaputra, also with warrior chiefs from our side (*amī ca tvāṃ dhṛtarāṣṭrasya putrāḥ- sarve sahaivāvanipālasaṅghaiḥ । bhīṣmo droṇaḥ sūtaputrastathāsau- sahāsmadīyairapi yodhamukhyaiḥ ॥ 11-26॥*). They hurry and enter your terrible toothed mouth that is fear inspiring, some are seen sticking between the teeth, their heads crushed to powder (*vaktrāṇi te tvaramāṇā viśanti- daṃṣṭrākarālāni bhayānakāni । kecidvilagnā daśanāntareṣu- sandṛśyante cūrṇitairuttamāṅgaiḥ ॥ 11-27॥*).

यथा नदीनां बहवोऽम्बुवेगाः

समुद्रमेवाभिमुखा द्रवन्ति ।

तथा तवामी नरलोकवीरा

विशन्ति वक्त्राण्यभिविज्वलन्ति ॥ ११-२८॥

यथा प्रदीप्तं ज्वलनं पतङ्गा

विशन्ति नाशाय समृद्धवेगाः ।

तथैव नाशाय विशन्ति लोका-

स्तवापि वक्त्राणि समृद्धवेगाः ॥ ११-२९॥

(28-29) Just as torrents of many rivers are truly directed towards the sea (*yathā nadīnāṃ bahavo'mbuvegāḥ samudramevābhimukhā dravanti ।*), similarly, these worldly heroes enter your flaming mouths *(tathā tavāmī naralokavīrā viśanti vaktrāṇyabhivijvalanti ॥ 11-28॥)*. Just as moths enter a blazing fire to destruction with increased speed *(yathā pradīptaṃ jvalanaṃ pataṅgā viśanti nāśāya samṛddhavegāḥ ॥)*, similarly, earthlings also enter your mouths with increased speed only *(tathaiva nāśāya viśanti loka stavāpi vaktrāṇi samṛddhavegāḥ ॥ 11-29॥)*.

लेलिह्यसे ग्रसमानः समन्ताल्-

   लोकान्समग्रान्वदनैर्ज्वलद्भिः ।

तेजोभिरापूर्य जगत्समग्रं

   भासस्तवोग्राः प्रतपन्ति विष्णो ॥ ११-३०॥

आख्याहि मे को भवानुग्ररूपो

   नमोऽस्तु ते देववर प्रसीद ।

विज्ञातुमिच्छामि भवन्तमाद्यं

   न हि प्रजानामि तव प्रवृत्तिम् ॥ ११-३१॥

(30-31) Frequently licking you swallow all in every side of the world with flaming mouths, *(lelihyase grasamānaḥ samantāl lokānsamagrānvadanairjvaladbhiḥ ॥)*, your fierce radiant brightness fills the whole universe by its heat, Viṣṇu *(tejobhirāpūrya jagatsamagram- bhāsastavograḥ pratapanti viṣṇo ॥ 11-30॥)*. Tell me who you are, I salute your fearsome form, supreme deity, show mercy *(ākhyāhi me ko bhavānugrarūpo-namo'stu te devavara prasīda ॥)*, I wish to know your primal state, indeed, I cannot understand your purpose *(vijñātumicchāmi bhavantamādyaṃ-na hi prajānāmi tava pravṛttim ॥ 11-31॥)*.

श्रीभगवानुवाच -

कालोऽस्मि लोकक्षयकृत्प्रवृद्धो

   लोकान्समाहर्तुमिह प्रवृत्तः ।

ऋतेऽपि त्वां न भविष्यन्ति सर्वे

   येऽवस्थिताः प्रत्यनीकेषु योधाः ॥ ११-३२॥

तस्मात्त्वमुत्तिष्ठ यशो लभस्व

   जित्वा शत्रून् भुङ्क्ष्व राज्यं समृद्धम् ।

मयैवैते निहताः पूर्वमेव

   निमित्तमात्रं भव सव्यसाचिन् ॥ ११-३३॥

द्रोणं च भीष्मं च जयद्रथं च

   कर्णं तथान्यानपि योधवीरान् ।

मया हतांस्त्वं जहि मा व्यथिष्ठा

   युध्यस्व जेतासि रणे सपत्नान् ॥ ११-३४॥

Śrī Kṛṣṇa replied (32-34) I am the mighty world destroying Time, now destroying the world *(kālo'smi lokakṣayakṛtpravṛddho lokānsamāhartumiha pravṛttaḥ ।)*, even without you none of the entire arrayed hostile armies shall live *(ṛte'pi tvāṃ na bhaviṣyanti sarve ye'vasthitāḥ pratyanīkeṣu yodhāḥ ॥ 11-32॥)*. Therefore, stand up and achieve fame of having conquered your enemies and enjoy unparalleled power *(tasmāttvamuttiṣṭha yaśo labhasva jitvā śatrūn bhuṅkṣva rājyaṃ samṛddham ।)*, these have already been killed by me, you will be a mere instrument, left-handed one *(mayaivaite nihatāḥ pūrvameva nimittamātraṃ bhava savyasācin ॥ 11-33॥)*. Drona and Bhishma and Jayadratha and Karna and other valiant warriors have been slain by me. Do not vacillate, fight, and you shall conquer your opponents in battle *(droṇaṃ ca bhīṣmaṃ ca jayadrathaṃ ca karṇaṃ tathānyānapi yodhavīrān । mayā hatāṃstvaṃ jahi mā vyathiṣṭhā yudhyasva jetāsi raṇe sapatnān ॥ 11-34॥)*.

सञ्जय उवाच -

एतच्छुत्वा वचनं केशवस्य

कृताञ्जलिर्वेपमानः किरीटी ।

नमस्कृत्वा भूय एवाह कृष्णं

सगद्गदं भीतभीतः प्रणम्य ॥ ११-३५॥

Sañjaya said (35) having heard Keśava's speech, with joined palms, trembling, he with a diadem prostrated again and again, even addressed Kṛṣṇa in a choked voice overwhelmed with fear and deep respect *(etacchrutvā vacanaṃ keśavasya-kṛtāñjalirvepamānaḥ kirīṭī । namaskṛtvā bhūya evāha kṛṣṇaṃ- sagadgadaṃ bhītabhītaḥ praṇamya ॥ 11-35॥)*.

अर्जुन उवाच -

स्थाने हृषीकेश तव प्रकीर्त्या

जगत्प्रहृष्यत्यनुरज्यते च ।

रक्षांसि भीतानि दिशो द्रवन्ति

सर्वे नमस्यन्ति च सिद्धसङ्घाः ॥ ११-३६॥

कस्माच्च ते न नमेरन्महात्मन्

गरीयसे ब्रह्मणोऽप्यादिकर्त्रे ।

अनन्त देवेश जगन्निवास

त्वमक्षरं सदसत्तत्परं यत् ॥ ११-३७॥

Arjuna said (36-37) In their place, Hṛṣīkeśa, in praising you, the world is delighted and rejoices and Rākṣasas are afraid and run everywhere and the entire community of Siddhas bow to you *(sthāne hṛṣīkeśa tava prakīrtyā jagatprahṛṣyatyanurajyate ca । rakṣāṃsi bhītāni diśo dravanti sarve namasyanti ca siddhasaṅghāḥ ॥ 11-36॥)*. And why should they not, Great Soul, you are superior to Brahma also, the primal creator, infinite, Lord of the deities, abode of the Universe, you are the imperishable being, which is also the supreme non-being *(kasmācca te na nameranmahātman garīyase brahmaṇo'pyādikartre ı ananta deveśa jagannivāsa tvamakṣaraṃ sadasattatparaṃ yat ॥ 11-37॥).*

त्वमादिदेवः पुरुषः पुराण-

स्त्वमस्य विश्वस्य परं निधानम् ।

वेत्तासि वेद्यं च परं च धाम

त्वया ततं विश्वमनन्तरूप ॥ ११-३८॥

वायुर्यमोऽग्निर्वरुणः शशाङ्कः

प्रजापतिस्त्वं प्रपितामहश्च ।

नमो नमस्तेऽस्तु सहस्रकृत्वः

पुनश्च भूयोऽपि नमो नमस्ते ॥ ११-३९॥

नमः पुरस्तादथ पृष्ठतस्ते

नमोऽस्तु ते सर्वत एव सर्व ।

अनन्तवीर्यामितविक्रमस्त्वं

सर्वं समाप्नोषि ततोऽसि सर्वः ॥ ११-४०॥

(38-40) You are the primordial Deity, ancient *puruṣa*, you are Supreme refuge of this Universe, you know everything and are the supreme abode, and you pervade the Universe, you are of infinite forms *(tvamādidevaḥ puruṣaḥ purāṇa- stvamasya viśvasya paraṃ nidhānam ı vettāsi vedyaṃ ca paraṃ ca dhāma- tvayā tataṃ viśvamanantarūpa ॥ 11-38॥).* You are Vāyu, Yama, Agni, Varuṇa, Moon, Prajāpati, you are the great-grandfather and a thousand salutations, salutations to you, again and again also, salutations, salutation to you *(vāyuryamo'gnirvaruṇaḥ śaśāṅkaḥ prajāpatistvaṃ prapitāmahaśca ı namo namaste'stu sahasrakṛtvaḥ punaśca bhūyo'pi namo namaste ॥ 11-39॥).* Salutations in front also behind you, also do it on every side, even everywhere, encompassing all infinite virility, immeasurable power, you pervade everything, wherever there is anything *(namaḥ purastādatha pṛṣṭhataste namo'stu te sarvata eva sarva ı anantavīryāmitavikramastvaṃ sarvaṃ samāpnoṣi tato'si sarvaḥ ॥ 11-40॥).*

सखेति मत्वा प्रसभं यदुक्तं

हे कृष्ण हे यादव हे सखेति ।

अजानता महिमानं तवेदं

मया प्रमादात्प्रणयेन वापि ॥ ११-४१॥

यच्चावहासार्थमसत्कृतोऽसि
विहारशय्यासनभोजनेषु।
एकोऽथवाप्यच्युत तत्समक्षं
तत्क्षामये त्वामहमप्रमेयम्॥ ११-४२॥

(41-42) If I have been presumptuous in regarding you as a friend and saying "O Kṛṣṇa", "O Yādava", "O Companion", these were due to ignorance of your greatness by me, from carelessness, even due to affection. *(sakheti matvā prasabhaṃ yaduktaṃ he kṛṣṇa he yādava he sakheti ǀ ajānatā mahimānaṃ tavedaṃ mayā pramādātpraṇayena vāpi ǁ 11-41ǁ).* If and for the sake of in jest I have been disrespectful to you while at play, during rest, sitting or eating or when by myself, Achyuta, or in company, for this I ask your forgiveness without restraint *(yaccāvahāsārthamasatkṛto'si vihāraśayyāsanabhojaneṣu ǀ eko'thavāpyacyuta tatsamakṣaṃ tatkṣāmaye tvāmahamaprameyam ǁ 11-42ǁ).*

पितासि लोकस्य चराचरस्य
त्वमस्य पूज्यश्च गुरुर्गरीयान्।
न त्वत्समोऽस्त्यभ्यधिकः कुतोऽन्यो
लोकत्रयेऽप्यप्रतिमप्रभाव॥ ११-४३॥
तस्मात्प्रणम्य प्रणिधाय कायं
प्रसादये त्वामहमीशमीड्यम्।
पितेव पुत्रस्य सखेव सख्युः
प्रियः प्रियायार्हसि देव सोढुम्॥ ११-४४॥

(43-44) You are the father of the people, of the moving and unmoving, thou are to be revered, and Guru, none is weightier or equal to you. Where can anyone in the three worlds also be of your unmatched prowess? *(pitāsi lokasya carācarasya tvamasya pūjyaśca gururgarīyān ǀ na tvatsamo'styabhyadhikaḥ kuto'nyolokatraye'pyapratimaprabhāva ǁ 11-43ǁ).* Therefore, having respectfully bowed the body, I propitiate you, the Lord who is adorable, like a father to a son, friend to a friend, like a beloved should to the beloved, bear me, my deity *(tasmātpraṇamya praṇidhāya kāyaṃ prasādaye tvāmahamīśamīḍyam ǀ piteva putrasya sakheva sakhyuḥ priyaḥ priyāyārhasi deva soḍhum ǁ 11-44ǁ).*

अदृष्टपूर्वं हृषितोऽस्मि दृष्ट्वा
भयेन च प्रव्यथितं मनो मे।
तदेव मे दर्शय देव रूपं
प्रसीद देवेश जगन्निवास॥ ११-४५॥

किरीटिनं गदिनं चक्रहस्तं
    इच्छामि त्वां द्रष्टुमहं तथैव ।
तेनैव रूपेण चतुर्भुजेन
    सहस्रबाहो भव विश्वमूर्ते ॥ ११-४६॥

(45-46) I have delighted in what has never been seen, my cognition is frightened and distressed, show to me, my deity, that merciful form, Lord of deities, abode of the Universe (*adṛṣṭapūrvaṃ hṛṣito'smi dṛṣṭvā bhayena ca pravyathitaṃ mano me | tadeva me darśaya deva rūpam prasīda deveśa jagannivāsa ॥ 11-45॥*). Crowned, bearing a mace, bearing a discuss in the hand, I wish to see you just as before, as the same four-armed form, instead of thousand-armed Universal form (*kirīṭinaṃ gadinam cakrahastam icchāmi tvāṃ drastumaham tathaiva | tenaiva rūpeṇa caturbhujena sahasrabāho bhava viśvamūrte ॥ 11-46॥*).

श्रीभगवानुवाच -
मया प्रसन्नेन तवार्जुनेदं
    रूपं परं दर्शितमात्मयोगात् ।
तेजोमयं विश्वमनन्तमाद्यं
    यन्मे त्वदन्येन न दृष्टपूर्वम् ॥ ११-४७॥
न वेदयज्ञाध्ययनैर्न दानै-
    र्न च क्रियाभिर्न तपोभिरुग्रैः ।
एवंरूपः शक्य अहं नृलोके
    द्रष्टुं त्वदन्येन कुरुप्रवीर ॥ ११-४८॥
मा ते व्यथा मा च विमूढभावो
    दृष्ट्वा रूपं घोरमीदृङ्ममेदम् ।
व्यपेतभीः प्रीतमनाः पुनस्त्वं
    तदेव मे रूपमिदं प्रपश्य ॥ ११-४९॥

Śrī Kṛṣṇa said (47-49) I am pleased with you, so I showed you this Supreme form, by the Yoga of my soul, full of Universal splendor, endless, primordial, this that I have shown you has not been seen before (*mayā prasannena tavārjunedam rūpam param darśitamātmayogāt | tejomayam viśvamanantamādyam yanme tvadanyena na dṛṣṭapūrvam ॥ 11-47॥*). Not by the study of Vedas, *yajña*, not by gifts and not by actions either, nor by severe tapas either, such a form that I showed you, is possible to be seen by any other in the world of men (*na vedayajñādhyayanairna dānai rna ca kriyābhirna tapobhirugraiḥ | evaṃrūpaḥ śakya aham nṛloke drastum tvadanyena kurupravīra ॥ 11-48॥*). Be not alarmed, do not be perplexed by my form with qualities like this (*mā te vyathā mā ca vimūḍhabhāvo- dṛṣṭvā rūpam ghoramīdṛṅmamedam |*), with your fear dispelled, with peaceful cognition, again behold that form you truly had of me *(vyapetabhīḥ prītamanāḥ punastvaṃ tadeva me rūpamidaṃ prapaśya ॥ 11-49॥)*.

इत्यर्जुनं वासुदेवस्तथोक्त्वा

स्वकं रूपं दर्शयामास भूयः ।

आश्वासयामास च भीतमेनं

भूत्वा पुनः सौम्यवपुर्महात्मा ॥ ११-५०॥

Sañjaya said (50) Thus, to Arjuna, Vāsudeva, so having spoken, his own form showed again and consoled him who was terrified by becoming once again the pleasant-bodied great soul. *(ityarjunaṃ vāsudevastathoktvā- svakaṃ rūpaṃ darśayāmāsa bhūyaḥ । āśvāsayāmāsa ca bhītamenaṃ- bhūtvā punaḥ saumyavapurmahātmā ॥ 11-50॥)*.

दृष्ट्वेदं मानुषं रूपं तव सौम्यं जनार्दन ।

इदानीमस्मि संवृत्तः सचेताः प्रकृतिं गतः ॥ ११-५१॥

Arjuna said (51) After seeing this gentle human form of yours, Janārdana, now I am composed in my consciousness, and my normal nature is restored *(dṛṣṭvedaṃ mānuṣaṃ rūpaṃ tava saumyaṃ janārdana । idānīmasmi saṃvṛttaḥ sacetāḥ prakṛtiṃ gataḥ ॥ 11-51॥)*.

सुदुर्दर्शमिदं रूपं दृष्ट्वानसि यन्मम ।

देवा अप्यस्य रूपस्य नित्यं दर्शनकाङ्क्षिणः ॥ ११-५२॥

नाहं वेदैर्न तपसा न दानेन न चेज्यया ।

शक्य एवंविधो द्रष्टुं दृष्ट्वानसि मां यथा ॥ ११-५३॥

भक्त्या त्वनन्यया शक्य अहमेवंविधोऽर्जुन ।

ज्ञातुं द्रष्टुं च तत्त्वेन प्रवेष्टुं च परन्तप ॥ ११-५४॥

मत्कर्मकृन्मत्परमो मद्भक्तः सङ्गवर्जितः ।

निर्वैरः सर्वभूतेषु यः स मामेति पाण्डव ॥ ११-५५॥

Śrī Kṛṣṇa said (52-55) Very hard to behold this form of mine you have seen *(sudurdarśamidaṃ rūpaṃ dṛṣṭavānasi yanmama ।)*, deities always desire to behold this form *(devā apyasya rūpasya nityaṃ darśanakāṅkṣiṇaḥ ॥ 11-52॥)*. I am not accessible for vision as you have seen of me by Vedas, nor austerities, nor charities, nor sacrifices *(nāhaṃ vedairna tapasā na dānena na cejyayā । śakya evaṃvidho* *drasṭuṃ dṛṣṭavānasi māṃ yathā* ॥ *11-53*॥). By single-minded devotion only can you cognize this form of mine, understand, and experience the subtlety *(bhaktyā tvananyayā śakya ahamevaṃvidho 'rjuna ׀ jñātuṃ drasṭuṃ ca tattvena praveṣṭuṃ ca parantapa* ॥ *11-54*॥). Perform actions for me, regards me as Supreme, is devoted to me, is detached from society, without aggression *(vaira=* virility) to all creation, he who does this, comes to me *(matkarmakṛnmatparamo madbhaktaḥ saṅgavarjitaḥ ׀ nirvairaḥ sarvabhūteṣu yaḥ sa māmeti pāṇḍava* ॥ *11-55*॥).

◆——— · ● ◆ ● · ——— ◆

Chapter 12

Bhakti-yoga (yoga of surrender) [1]

Introduction – *bhakti-yoga* is a yoga method where the identity of Self is transferred to a deity or role model such as a *Guru*.

Some terms that need to be understood:

- *Śraddhā* – *Śraddhā* is a combination of intent, dedication, patience, sincerity, enterprise, focus, and effort. It is quality of input into any activity and is not dependent on capability, and is independent of outcome or result.

Consequently, a person may not have the requisite capability or be successful in a particular activity, but because of *śraddhā,* his success is considered as assured.

- Renunciation of action *(karma-tyāga)* – here, the practitioner sacrifices his or her action to the owner of sacrifice (Śrī Kṛṣṇa). This nullifies all outcomes of action, making sacrifice into sacrifice akin to adding null to null, which is null.

कर्मात्मनां च देवानां सोऽसृजत् प्राणिनां प्रभुः ।
साध्यानां च गणं सूक्ष्मं यज्ञं चैव सनातनम् ॥ २२ ॥

karmātmanāṃ ca devānāṃ so'sṛjat prāṇināṃ prabhuḥ ।
sādhyānāṃ ca gaṇaṃ sūkṣmaṃ yajñaṃ caiva sanātanam ॥ 22 ॥

For the sake of living being's intent upon action, he created the eternal sacrifice; as also the host of Gods and the subtle multitude of the lesser divinities, the *sādhyas* (22).

Arjuna said – which is better? Worshiping you or the imperishable *Brahman?*

---

[1] https://www.bhagavad-gita.org/Gita/chapter-12.html

Śrī Kṛṣṇa said – those that worship me with sincerity and devotion (śraddhā), I consider perfect in *Yoga,* but even those that worship the *Brahman* – living with restrained senses, even in their dealings and working for the welfare of all, they too come to me. The problem of worshipping the *Brahman* is that it is very difficult to visualize and focus on the unmanifest.

- However, by renouncing all actions into me and regarding me as the supreme goal is easier.

- So, focus on me as the supreme goal and I will deliver you from the cycle of life and death *(saṃsāra)*. Fix your consciousness on me and make me the source of your intellect. Thereafter, you will live in me.

- If you are unable to steadily focus your awareness on me, then reach me with *abhyāsa-yoga* (Yoga of rigorous practice). In case you are unable to practice *abhyāsa-yoga*, sacrifice the intent of your actions to me. If you are unable to do even that, just renounce the fruit of your action to me and attain perfection.

- Verse 12 – This is an important verse where Śrī Kṛṣṇa explain the meditation process with a solution. Wisdom of the Self *(jñāna)* is better than practice of surrender to the deity *(iṣṭa-deiva),* in this case Śrī Kṛṣṇa *(abhyāsa).* In the process of acquisition of wisdom *(jñāna)* meditation *(dhyāna)* ensures success. However, during meditation, when a person practices renunciation of the fruits of action *(karma-phala-tyāga),* there is immediate peace. This quickens the process of achieving perfection.

- In the above verse, Śrī Kṛṣṇa is suggesting hybrid solutions where one element from one path acts as a catalyst to another path. This is a method which can be seen throughout *Śrīmad-bhagavad-gītā.* Śrī Kṛṣṇa is not a purist, but a pragmatist who tries to increase the number of options for the *yogī* by suggesting solutions that fit individual capability and capacity.

Śrī Kṛṣṇa explains the qualities of the *bhakti-yogī,* verse 13 to 19:

- Hating none, friendly and compassionate; with no feeling of being the doer *(nirahaṅkāra),* content in whatever comes and living without expectations *(santoṣa);* steady in yoga, with cognition *(manas)* and intelligence *(buddhi)* under control the practitioner becomes dear to me.

- Dear to me is also one who does not get agitated at the world or does not spread agitation; who is free from exuberance, envy, fear, or anxiety. Also, dear is also one who has no expectations, is pure, dexterous, untroubled, without ambition, and renounces all undertaking. He who neither rejoices nor rejects, grieves, or desires, renounces superstition, and devoted to me is dear to me.

- He who treats friend and foe alike, also honor or dishonor, heat or cold, pleasure or pain, and is free from attachment; to whom praise or censure is the same, content with anything, homeless, and steady in mind, he is dear to me. Practitioners who practice this conditioning with sincerity and devotion are dear to me.

Śrīmad-bhāgavad-purāṇa propounds nine primary tools of _bhakti_:

- _Śravana_ (listening to achievements of the deity) – practitioners view the deity as a role model, analyze the deity's life, and try to emulate those qualities in their own life.

- _Kīrtana_ (praising the achievements of the deity) – the practitioner extols the virtues mythological life and qualities of their favorite deity _(iṣṭa-daiva)_ in great detail through music and bhajans.

- _Smaraṇa_ (retaining an image of the deity at all time) – practitioners try to retain the deity in an external form in pictures and then internalize it.

- _Pada-sevana (pada_ = feet + _sevana_ = service) – means service at the feet, doing whatever is possible to support the _guru_. Since _bhakti_ can also be to a living entity like a Guru, country or system like Yoga, service before Self becomes a critical experiential exercise in subduing the Self.

- _Suracanā_ (worshipping the deity with hyperbole) – when a practitioner extols using hyperbole, there is the natural ambition to reach for the same outcomes. A vision is created for oneself and effort gets aligned to those goals. Also, such prayers keep the deity at a high position, thus motivating one to surrender one's Self.

- _Vandanā_ (worshipping the deity) – integration of the self with the deity.

- _Dāsya_ (servitude) – negating the sense of Self by serving as a servant.

- _Sākhya_ (retaining a base of friendship) – maintaining company of like-minded individuals allows the yogi to stay integrated with the deity 24 x 7.

- _Ātmanivedana (ātma_ = soul + _nivedana_ = state of no schism) or state where there is no difference between the yogi and the deity. This is achieved when the practitioner practices all the above steps and constantly views him or herself as an extension of the deity.

Example of _bhakti-yoga_:

At the end of the _Rāmāyana_, Hanumān returned to Ayodhyā with Rāma, who was now the king. One day, while Rāma was performing a sacrifice, a relative shot a bird which fell into the sacrificial fire, defiling it. An angry Rāma ordered that the miscreant be put to death. The terrified relative surrendered to Hanumān and sought shelter. When Hanumān refused to surrender the relative, stating that rules of *dharma* required that he protect anyone who surrendered to him, Rāma challenged him to a duel. At the appointed hour, Hanumān took the relative to the site of the duel, encircled him with his tail and sitting on top of the hive like structure, went into *samādhi*. When Rāma came out and saw Hanumān, he prepared for battle. Knowing the quality of Hanumān's chivalry, Rāma sent his most powerful missile – the Rāma-bāṅ, instructing it to destroy Hanumān. The missile went towards

12.1 - Hanumān, the epitome of *bhakti-yoga.*

Hanumān, circled him, and returned to Rāma without doing anything. A perplexed Rāma kept shooting the missile with no change in result. When he meditated on why the missile was malfunctioning, he intuited that the missile was unable to find Hanumān, there was only Rāma!

Hanumān had subsumed his identity into Rāma; this is the highest form of *bhakti-yoga-samādhi.*

Some contradictions to accepted positions:

- There is considerable difference between *bhakti-yoga* and religion as practiced in the Abrahamic tradition.

- In religion, the individual accepts a subordinate position to that of a deity, there is supplication of the devotee to the deity. However, since the person does not lose his or her identity and remains separated from the deity, there is a subtle filter between the practitioner and deity, which hinders complete merger with the deity.

- In Yoga, the deity is worshipped as a role model but maintained as equal in Identity. So, there is no supplication. There is only surrender. This means that the yogī does everything to transfer his or her sense of identity on to the target identity (deity).

- Consequently, when the practitioner applies Śrī Kṛṣṇa's *bhakti-yoga* advise and surrenders completely, then the yogī's identity slowly gets subsumed into the deity.

- When this happens, the yogī's *puruṣa* becomes zero, which brings *prakṛti* to *nirguṇa* state, resulting in merger with the deity and Brahman at the same time.

- Finally, *bhakti-yoga* is not confined to Śrī Kṛṣṇa. It can be to any deity, Guru or teacher, subject, thought, country, or even task.

Lessons learned:

Complete merger is not easy, the sense of identity *(asmitā)* will not allow it's own destruction. So, *bhakti-yoga* is not easy.

The yogī will need to be steadfast in the attitude of surrender and removal of *asmita*. This quality of restraint subdues the *asmita* and elevates the yogī in *bhakti-yoga*.

The transliteration and translation of chapter 12 follows:

अर्जुन उवाच -

एवं सततयुक्ता ये भक्तास्त्वां पर्युपासते ।

ये चाप्यक्षरमव्यक्तं तेषां के योगवित्तमाः ॥ १२-१॥

Arjuna said (1) Between those that worship you and those that worship the imperishable, unmanifested *Brahman*, who is likely to succeed *(evaṃ satatayuktā ye bhaktāstvāṃ paryupāsate । ye cāpyakṣaramavyaktaṃ teṣāṃ ke yogavittamāḥ ॥ 12-1॥)*.

श्रीभगवानुवाच -

मय्यावेश्य मनो ये मां नित्ययुक्ता उपासते ।

श्रद्धया परयोपेताः ते मे युक्ततमा मताः ॥ १२-२॥

ये त्वक्षरमनिर्देश्यमव्यक्तं पर्युपासते ।

सर्वत्रगमचिन्त्यञ्च कूटस्थमचलन्ध्रुवम् ॥ १२-३॥

सन्नियम्येन्द्रियग्रामं सर्वत्र समबुद्धयः ।

ते प्राप्नुवन्ति मामेव सर्वभूतहिते रताः ॥ १२-४॥

Śrī Kṛṣṇa said (2-4) Those that fix their cognition on me with steadfast focus and serve me with dedication and sincerity, these are endowed with qualities to become realized souls, in my opinion *(mayyāveśya mano ye māṃ nityayuktā upāsate । śraddhāyā parayopetāḥ te me yuktatamā matāḥ ॥ 12-2॥)*. Those who worship the indestructible, indefinable, omnipresent, unthinkable, immovable, eternal *(ye tvakṣaramanirdeśyamavyaktaṃ paryupāsate । sarvatragamacintyañca kūṭasthamacalandhruvam ॥ 12-3॥)*. Having restrained the multitude of senses, even minded everywhere, they obtain me only, those that rejoice in the welfare of all creation *(sanniyamyendriyagrāmaṃ sarvatra samabuddhayaḥ । te prāpnuvanti māmeva sarvabhūtahite ratāḥ ॥ 12-4॥)*.

क्लेशोऽधिकतरस्तेषामव्यक्तासक्तचेतसाम् ।

अव्यक्ता हि गतिर्दुःखं देहवद्भिरवाप्यते ॥ १२-५॥

ये तु सर्वाणि कर्माणि मयि संन्यस्य मत्पराः ।

अनन्येनैव योगेन मां ध्यायन्त उपासते ॥ १२-६॥

(5-6) The struggle is greater for those whose consciousness is focused on the indistinct unmanifested *Brahman* as a goal, it is a painful journey for the embodied *(kleśo'dhikatarasteṣāmavyaktāsaktacetasām ı avyaktā hi gatirduḥkhaṃ dehavadbhiravāpyate ॥ 12-5॥)*. But those that renounce all actions to me, regard me as the supreme goal, meditation in calmness with undistracted union *(ye tu sarvāṇi karmāṇi mayi saṃnyasya matparāḥ ı ananyenaiva yogena māṃ dhyāyanta upāsate ॥ 12-6॥)*.

तेषामहं समुद्धर्ता मृत्युसंसारसागरात् ।

भवामि नचिरात्पार्थ मय्यावेशितचेतसाम् ॥ १२-७॥

मय्येव मन आधत्स्व मयि बुद्धिं निवेशय ।

निवसिष्यसि मय्येव अत ऊर्ध्वं न संशयः ॥ १२-८॥

(7-8) For those with a focused consciousness, I am the navigator who ultimately brings them out of the sea of cycle of rebirth *(teṣāmahaṃ samuddhartā mṛtyusaṃsārasāgarāt ı bhavāmi nacirātpārtha mayyāveśitacetasām ॥ 12-7॥)*. Fix your cognition on me only, let your intellect be placed on me, you will live in me alone hereafter, without doubt *(mayyeva mana ādhatsva mayi buddhiṃ niveśaya ı nivasiṣyasi mayyeva ata ūrdhvaṃ na saṃśayaḥ ॥ 12-8॥)*.

अथ चित्तं समाधातुं न शक्नोषि मयि स्थिरम् ।

अभ्यासयोगेन ततो मामिच्छाप्तुं धनञ्जय ॥ १२-९॥

अभ्यासेऽप्यसमर्थोऽसि मत्कर्मपरमो भव ।

मदर्थमपि कर्माणि कुर्वन्सिद्धिमवाप्स्यसि ॥ १२-१०॥

(9-10) If you are unable to fix the consciousness steadily on me by practice of Yoga, then just wish to reach me *(atha cittaṃ samādhātuṃ na śaknoṣi mayi sthiram ı abhyāsayogena tato māmicchāptuṃ dhanañjaya ॥ 12-9॥)*. If also by practice you are unable, then let the focus of your actions, and also action be for my sake, and in this process, you will attain perfection *(abhyāse'pyasamartho'si matkarmaparamo bhava ı madarthamapi karmāṇi kurvansiddhimavāpsyasi ॥ 12-10॥)*.

अथैतदप्यशक्तोऽसि कर्तुं मद्योगमाश्रितः ।

सर्वकर्मफलत्यागं ततः कुरु यतात्मवान् ॥ १२-११॥

श्रेयो हि ज्ञानमभ्यासाज्ज्ञानाद्ध्यानं विशिष्यते ।

ध्यानात्कर्मफलत्यागस्त्यागाच्छान्तिरनन्तरम् ॥ १२-१२॥

(11-12) If you are unable to do even this, take refuge in my Yoga by renouncing all the fruits of your action with a self-restrained Soul *(athaitadapyaśakto'si kartuṃ madyogamāśritaḥ | sarvakarmaphalatyāgaṃ tataḥ kuru yatātmavān || 12-11||)*. Indeed, wisdom of the Self is better than practice, in wisdom meditation excels, in meditation renunciation of the fruits of action, in renunciation there is immediate peace *(śreyo hi jñānamabhyāsājjñānāddhyānaṃ viśiṣyate | dhyānātkarmaphalatyāgastyāgācchāntiranantaram || 12-12||)*.

अद्वेष्टा सर्वभूतानां मैत्रः करुण एव च ।

निर्ममो निरहङ्कारः समदुःखसुखः क्षमी ॥ १२-१३॥

सन्तुष्टः सततं योगी यतात्मा दृढनिश्चयः ।

मय्यर्पितमनोबुद्धिर्यो मद्भक्तः स मे प्रियः ॥ १२-१४॥

(13-14) Without rejecting any of creation, friendly, kind, and also without the feeling of the Self, without feeling of being the doer, same in adversity and gain. *(adveṣṭā sarvabhūtānāṃ maitraḥ karuṇa eva ca | nirmamo nirahaṅkāraḥ samaduḥkhasukhaḥ kṣamī || 12-13||)*. Always content, the yogī is self-restrained, having firm conviction, who offers cognition and logic to me, this devotee is dear to me *(santuṣṭaḥ satataṃ yogī yatātmā dṛḍhaniścayaḥ | mayyarpitamanobuddhiryo madbhaktaḥ sa me priyaḥ || 12-14||)*.

यस्मान्नोद्विजते लोको लोकान्नोद्विजते च यः ।

हर्षामर्षभयोद्वेगैर्मुक्तो यः स च मे प्रियः ॥ १२-१५॥

अनपेक्षः शुचिर्दक्ष उदासीनो गतव्यथः ।

सर्वारम्भपरित्यागी यो मद्भक्तः स मे प्रियः ॥ १२-१६॥

(15-16) He who is not agitated by the world and who does not agitate the world and who is free from joy, impatience, fear, and agitation, he is dear to me *(yasmānnodvijate loko lokānnodvijate ca yaḥ | harṣāmarṣabhayodvegairmukto yaḥ sa ca me priyaḥ || 12-15||)*. One is free from need, clean, diligent, unconcerned, who has renounced all new ventures, such a devotee is dear to me *(anapekṣaḥ śucirdakṣa udāsīno gatavyathaḥ | sarvārambhaparityāgī yo madbhaktaḥ sa me priyaḥ || 12-16||)*.

यो न हृष्यति न द्वेष्टि न शोचति न काङ्क्षति ।

शुभाशुभपरित्यागी भक्तिमान्यः स मे प्रियः ॥ १२-१७॥

समः शत्रौ च मित्रे च तथा मानापमानयोः ।

शीतोष्णसुखदुःखेषु समः सङ्गविवर्जितः ॥ १२-१८॥

(17-18) He who neither rejoices nor rejects, does not grieve nor hankers, who has renounced auspicious and inauspicious, he who is completely devoted to me is dear to me *(yo na hṛṣyati na dveṣṭi na śocati na kāṅkṣati ǀ śubhāśubhaparityāgī bhaktimānyaḥ sa me priyaḥ ǁ 12-17ǁ)*. He who treats friend and foe alike and is the same when respected or insulted, in cold or heat, same in happiness or sadness and free from attachment *(samaḥ śatrau ca mitre ca tathā mānāpamānayoḥ ǀ śītoṣṇasukhaduḥkheṣu samaḥ saṅgavivarjitaḥ ǁ 12-18ǁ)*.

तुल्यनिन्दास्तुतिमौंनी सन्तुष्टो येन केनचित् ।
अनिकेतः स्थिरमतिर्भक्तिमान्मे प्रियो नरः ॥ १२-१९॥
ये तु धर्म्यामृतमिदं यथोक्तं पर्युपासते ।
श्रद्धाना मत्परमा भक्तास्तेऽतीव मे प्रियाः ॥ १२-२०॥

(19-20) Who is modulated in praise or criticism, silent, content in all situations, homeless, steadfast in devotion to me, that human is dear to me *(tulyanindāstutirmaunī santuṣṭo yena kenacit ǀ aniketaḥ sthiramatirbhaktimānme priyo naraḥ ǁ 12-19ǁ)*. Whoever devotee follows this immortal dharma as declared here, with sincerity and dedication, regarding me as supreme, they are exceedingly dear to me *(ye tu dharmyāmṛtamidaṃ yathoktaṃ paryupāsate ǀ śraddadhānā matparamā bhaktāste'tīva me priyāḥ ǁ 12-20ǁ)*.

◆——— • ● ◆ • • ——— ◆

Chapter 13[1]

Kṣetra-kṣetrajña-vibhāga-yoga (yoga of discrimination between *kṣetra* (region/field) and *kṣetrajña* (awareness of the region/field

Introduction

- In chapters 9 and 10, Śrī Kṛṣṇa shows Arjuna his actual Self. This obviously confuses as well as amazes and scares Arjuna, making him circumspect with respect to his relationship with Śrī Kṛṣṇa, just like a soldier who is confronted with the fact that the person he thought was a friend is actually the Head of State.

- In chapter 13, he moves to the next step, and explains how sentience and awareness allow a person to cognize beyond the visible or gross. *(sthūla)* To evolve to the next level, a person should be able to cognize the subtle *(sūkṣma)* state as well as the causal *(kāraṇa)* state.

- What are these states? How does one evolve to the next level of personal development?

- Before starting this chapter, we recommend that you review,

    o   Chapter 2 *(śaṅkha-yoga)* [2].

    o   Chapter 11 *(viśvarūpadarśana-yoga)* [3].

- Importantly, one must recognize that development in Yoga is experiential, and everything that is said in *Śrīmad-bhagavad-gītā* can only create value when there is introspection and practice.

---

[1]https://www.bhagavad-gita.org/Gita/chapter-13.html

[2]https://schoolofyoga.in/yoga-social-system/bhagawat-geeta-chapter-2

[3]https://www.schoolofyoga.in/yoga-social-system/bhagavad-geeta-chapter-11

What are *puruṣa, prakṛti, kṣetra,* and *kṣetrajña*? (verse 1-12)

Arjuna said – educate me on *prakṛti* and *puruṣa, kṣetra,* and *kṣetrajña*.

Śrī Kṛṣṇa said – this body is the *kṣetra* (region/field) and anyone who is wise to its functioning is a *kṣetrajña*. In fact, many consider me to be the knowledge of the *kṣetra*. Hence, I will explain the features and functions of the *kṣetra*.

- The cardinal elements *(mahābhūta)*, the sense of being the doer *(ahankāra)*, logic *(buddhi),* and those unmanifested *(avyakta)*, the ten senses *(indriya)* and five objects of the senses *(indriyagocara)*. Also, desire, repulsion, happiness, pain, intelligence, fortitude, and their amalgamations form the *kṣetra*.

- To increase knowledge of the *kṣetra (kṣetrajña),* cultivate selflessness (humility), unpretentiousness, non-violence, peacefulness, straightforwardness, service to teacher, cleanliness, steadiness, and controlling/restraining the soul *(ātma-vinigraha)*.

- Cultivate dispassion towards sense objects, eschew the sense of doer-ship *(ahankāra)*, and negativity towards birth, death, old age, sickness, and pain. Also, be detached from everything, without intense attachment to the wife, son, home, or society. Finally, treat everything with equal demeanor, whether they are desirable or undesirable.

- By meditating on the soul (self), some can experience the soul in others; others achieve this through knowledge of the Self through *jñāna-yoga*, yet others by *karma-yoga*. Also, others who may have no conceptual knowledge, follow paths that others speak of and reach perfection by practicing what they have heard.

The concept of *kṣetra* (region/field) and *kṣetrajña* (awareness of the region/ field):

- Our body is a *kṣetra* (region/field). It has an Identity and we identify ourselves with it. So, when we act, *karma* occurs, and debt *(ṛṇa or āgāmi-karma)* is created. This debt *(ṛṇa)* is stored as *sañcita-karma* (overall debt) by the *jīva* (soul) and manifests as *prārabdha-karma* when the time for repayment/ reconciliation fructifies.

- Just as the body may be considered as an entity with a soul *(jīva)*, entities such as heart, liver, kidneys, and lungs as well as red blood corpuscle (RBC) elements within the body that operate independently can also be considered as minor souls *(jīva)* who also perform *karma* in their own way and create and reconcile their own debt *(ṛṇa)*.

- All matter is made up of the cardinal elements *(pañca-mahābhūta* - earth, water, fire, air, and ether) in various c o m b i n a t i o n s and its properties come from its combinations. For example - the heart can be considered as

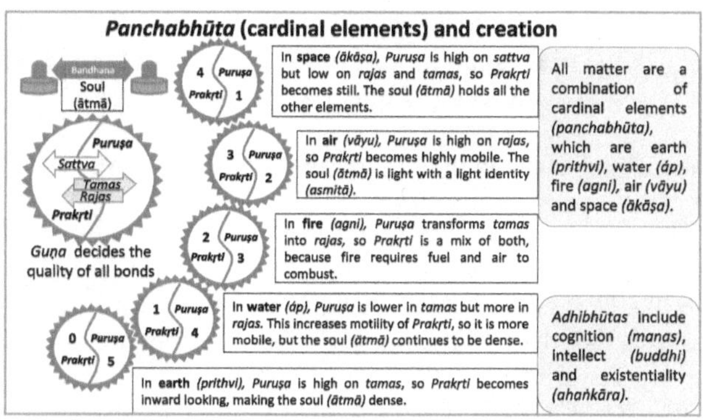

13.1 - Elements of *pañca-mahābhūta*

a combination of earth, water, and fire; lungs may be considered to comprise of a combination of earth, water, and air, and so on.

- Hence, it can be assumed that the relationship between various entities within a system will remain for as long as there is debt between them. When debt is reconciled, the relationship ceases to exist. For example - the kidneys will function for as long as they have a debt *(ṛṇa)* with the body and other organs within the body but will fail naturally when their debt has been reconciled. However, when we force the kidneys to function after their debt has been cleared through medication, dialysis, or replacement, we are re-enacting the cycle of action *(karma)*. When our identity *(asmitā)* experiences fear of loss of identity (death), it forces us to incur fresh *karma,* as the old debt *(ṛṇa)* has been discharged. This insecurity of self-worth *(asmitā)* is the reason why some people continue treatment and others stop fighting. Also, kidneys will fail when they are abused, and if the abuse is on account of free will, then fresh karma is generated.

What is the *Brahman* (verse 12-13):

- Yoke yourself to me with no differentiation between us, seek seclusion. Also, be constant in the awareness of the self, staying focused on understanding the concept of the Self, for this is the most exalted knowledge.

- Now, I will describe the supreme *Brahman* which neither exists nor not-exists. *Brahman* envelops all, with hands feet, eyes, and mouths everywhere. Also, while *Brahman* defines attributes of the senses, it has no senses. Though it is unattached, supporting all, with no attributes *(guṇas),* yet defines the experience of all attributes.

- *Brahman* exists outside and inside all beings, neither dynamic or static because of its subtlety incomprehensible, far, and near. Also, *Brahman* is undivided; yet appears as different in beings that are supported by it, generating, and destroying.

- It is the essence behind light, beyond darkness, knowledge which is to be known, its goal, its seat in the heart of all beings. Thus, *kṣetra* (region) and that which is to be known is described.

- Finally, those that know this can merge with me.

The concept of *Brahman* (source):

What is the *Brahman*? *Bṛhadāraṇyakopaniṣad* states "*aham-brahmāsmi*". This means that the *Brahman* and the Self or Soul are one and the same.

In *Śrīmad-bhagavad-gītā* - chapter 2 *(sāṅkhya-yoga)*, Śrī Kṛṣṇa, states that the *Brahman* is indestructible without calling it by name.

Also, *Taittirīyopaniṣad* states[4],

ॐ पूर्णमदः पूर्णमिदं पूर्णात्पुर्णमुदच्यते
पूर्णश्य पूर्णमादाय पूर्णमेवावशिष्यते ॥
ॐ शान्तिः ॥

oṃ pūrṇamadaḥ pūrṇamidaṃ pūrṇātpurṇamudacyate
pūrṇaśya pūrṇamādāya pūrṇamevāvaśiṣyate ॥
oṃ śāntiḥ ॥

Meaning:

Aum! That (Brahman) is infinite, and This (Self/Soul) is infinite. Infinite (soul) proceeds from the infinite (Brahman). From infinity, when infinity is removed, infinity is the balance (infinity remains). Aum! Peace! Peace! Peace!

- The above means that the *Brahman* is infinite and indestructible, because no matter what is added or removed, its quality remains unchanged.

- Similarly, since the *ātmā*, Soul or Self emerges from the same infinity *(Brahman)*, it is infinite and indestructible.

- As a result, since both are indestructible and infinite, there is no difference between the two *(Brahman* and the *ātmā*, Self or Soul).

Brahman is more than the source. It is the source, that which sustains everything and motility. Importantly, it is undivided, which means that it is continuous and everywhere. Also, it is the essence of everything - the energy of the sun, the lighting capability of light, burning capability of fire, enveloping capability of a building, protection capability of a constitution, patriotic capability of a flag, etc.

---

[4]https://www.templepurohit.com/mantras-slokas-stotras/shanti-mantra/om-purnamadah-purnamidam

Direct explanation of *Brahman* is impossible; one can only describe *Brahman* using correlations and qualities. For example, to experience an approximation of *Brahman,* stand in the middle of railway tracks and look at the tracks. They seem to merge somewhere in the distance, which we know is not true. This feeling of merger at a distance can be approximated as *Brahman.*

Śrī Kṛṣṇa explains *prakṛti* and *puruṣa* (verse 13-28):

- Both, *prakṛti* and *puruṣa* emerge from the *Brahman.* From *puruṣa* emerges consciousness *(citta)* and attributes *(guṇa)* are created by *prakṛti.*

- *Puruṣa* experiences the actions that are caused by *prakṛti,* this is done through the medium of consciousness *(citta).* So, experience of pleasure and pain are caused by *puruṣa* who, seated in *prakṛti* experiences the *guṇa-s* born of *prakṛti.*

Verse 22.

पुरुष: प्रकृतिस्थो हि भुङ्क्ते प्रकृतिजान्गुणान् ।
कारणं गुणसङ्गोऽस्य सदसद्योनिजन्मसु ॥ 22॥

puruṣaḥ prakṛtistho hi bhuṅkte prakṛtijāngunān ।
kāraṇaṃ guṇasaṅgo 'sya sadasadyonijanmasu ॥ 13-22॥

puruṣa, seated in *prakṛti* experiences the *guṇa-s* born of *prakṛti.*

Example - You are strolling down a street and suddenly meet an acquaintance. Happily, you smile, but the other person ignores you and walks away.

Let us review the above transaction:

- When you are walking down the road with no specific purpose, your mind is generally empty. This is the state of *Brahman,* a state of peace without any disturbance. While, the actual *Brahman* is infinite sublime peace, this allusion is for the purpose of explaining the situation.

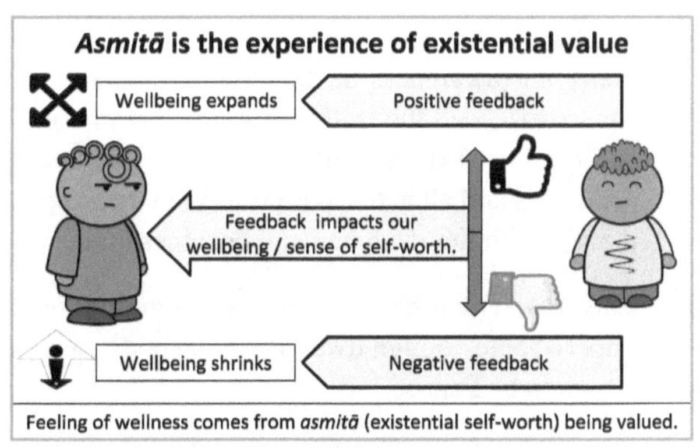

13.2 - *Asmitā* is our sense of self-worth

- You meet a friend – Your consciousness *(citta)* recognises another *puruṣa* (identity). So, you manifest. Here, your *puruṣa* and *prakṛti* weave and energizing the *citta* (consciousness) to reach out to the other *puruṣa.* As a result of the weave, *prāṇa* flows in the various channels or *nāḍīs,* increasing your *prāṇa-vāyu* (incoming motility) and *vyāna-vāyu* (personality projection motility/aura).

- The acquaintance ignores you – The feedback comes through the *citta* (consciousness) to the *puruṣa.* Consequently, *puruṣa* experiences loss of existence/ self-worth (shrinking *asmitā* or self-esteem) and it shrinks. This changes the *guṇa* (attribute) balance to predominantly *tamas* (inertia/delusion, despondence, melancholy, or shrinkage).

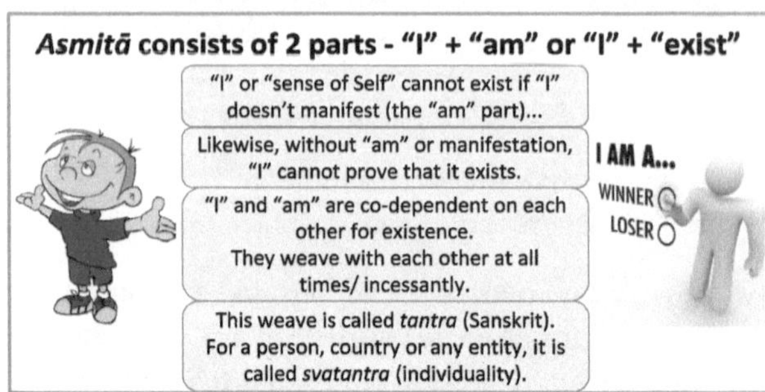

13.3 - *Asmitā* arises from the weave of our sense of identity and behaviour

Here, *puruṣa* is the experiencer, *prakṛti* is the manifestation of *puruṣa,* and their weave is *svatantra* or individuality. *Prakṛti* and *puruṣa* manifest from *Brahman.* *Citta* is the cognitive transmitter of identity which enables both identities *(puruṣa)* to transact. The *ātmā* (Self or that unit which represents the weave of *puruṣa* with *prakṛti* as *svatantra)* experiences the situation through the *citta* (consciousness). *Prāṇa* is the motility that flows from the transaction of the two entities and the foundation of materiality.

Śrī Kṛṣṇa explains *kṣetra* and *kṣetrajña* verse 29 onwards:

- All that is created, comes from the union of the *kṣetra* (region) with the *kṣetrajña* (awareness of the identity of the region). Thus, the *jñanī* (one who has experienced the truth) sees the *Brahman* in everything – those that perish and those that do not. Also, such a person recognizes that the *ātmā* (Self) is actionless and all activity is performed by *prakṛti.* Consequently, such a person merges with the *Brahman* and becomes that.

- This *ātmā* (Identity/Self), has no beginning, possesses no *guṇa* (attributes), is imperishable, though dwelling in the body, neither acts nor is tainted just as the all-pervading space.

- Just as the Sun illuminates the world, the Lord of the *kṣetra* illuminates the *kṣetra.* So, those that can perceive the distinction between *kṣetra* (region) and *kṣetrajña* (controller of the *kṣetra),* thus they get liberated from *prakṛti,* and merge with the *Brahman.*

How *puruṣa* and *prakṛti* are connected to life, living, and awareness:

- We can see that *Brahman* is an integral part in every aspect of the experience, but it is not the experiencer.

- *Puruṣa* is the experiencer that uses consciousness *(citta)* to transmit and receive information.

- *Prakṛti* manifests as the expression of *puruṣa,* and their weave changes according to the feedback as attributes *(guṇa).*

- Next, *prāṇa* is the motility that results from the weave of *śiva* (quanta identity) and *śakti* (quanta manifestation), which is the building block of *puruṣa* and *prakṛti,* and moves in the direction of *guṇa.*

- Also, consciousness *(citta)* participates like a postman, transmitting *puruṣa's* message to the object and receiving feedback, which it passes on to *puruṣa.* It is also inert, not experiencing anything!

- Importantly, *puruṣa* the experiencer cannot express its experience without *prakṛti.*

- The weave of *puruṣa* and *prakṛti* gives rise to creation and existence of a primary self-sustaining unit called *ātmā* (soul, Identity or Self).

- Also, *ātmā* (soul), by virtue of being the primary unit of Identity, is the repository of debt *(ṛṇa),* but it cannot act without the motility factor *(prāṇa).*

- With *prāṇa,* the *ātmā* expands by integrating many more *ātmā-s* to form a body *(kṣetra)* and interacts with its environment. Importantly, each of these new entities is also an identity/experiencer *(puruṣa).*

- The repository of all *karma* of a *kṣetra* resides in the *ātmā.* So, when *prāṇa-vāyu* leaves, the body *(kṣetra)* loses its ability to perform *karma* and the *ātmā* must reconcile its debts *(ṛṇa)* and get another body *(kṣetra).*

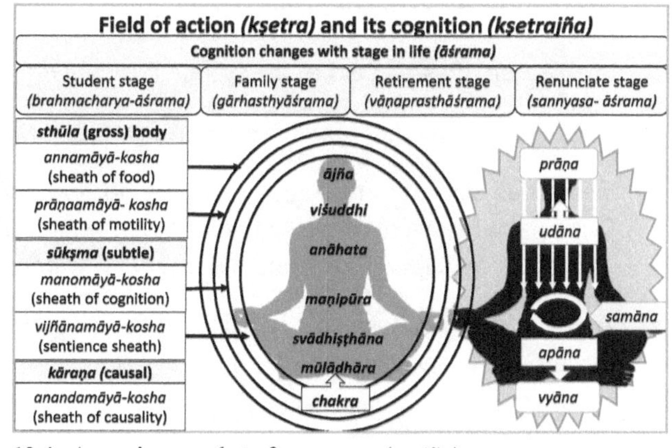

13.4 - A concise snapshot of awareness *(prajña)*

- The experiencer, YOU, are acting on the foundation of *Brahman*, but not engaging with *Brahman* (That). *Brahman* is in YOU, but YOU are not in the *Brahman*. This must be understood.

- Since *Brahman* is an unchanging, infinite cognitive state of peace; it is called the absolute truth *(paramarth-sathya)*. Everything else is conditional Truth, *saguṇa Brahman, samvritti-sathya* or *maya*.

- So, all of us are an infinite, inexhaustible, unrelenting, continuous field of a weave of *puruṣa* and *prakṛti*. This infinite creation of individual expressiveness is called *svatantra (sva* = self + *tantra* = weave of *puruṣa* and *prakṛti)* or individuality.

- All entities, *prāṇa* (motility) moves in the form of a motility -stream or *vāyu*. These are

  - *prāṇa-vāyu* (incoming/ life generation motility),

  - *apāna-vāyu* (outgoing/ excretion motility),

  - *vyāna-vāyu* (ethereal or aural motility),

  - *udāna-vāyu* (upward moving/ communication or expression motility),

  - *samāna-vāyu* (digestion or circulatory motility).

- The above five motilities *(prāṇa)* combine with the five primordial elements *(pañca-bhūta)* to form five sheaths *(kośas)* around the body. These are:

  - Sheath made by food *(annamaya-kośa)*,

  - Sheath of *prāṇa (prāṇamaya-kośa)*,

  - Sheath of cognition *(manomaya-kośa)*,

  - Sheath of awareness of the system *(vijñānamaya-kośa)*,

  - Sheath of merger *(ānandamaya-kośa)*.

- Whenever, one tries to cognize any region, one must recognize each of the factors and be aware of the state of the Self *(ātmā)* of the region/field *(kṣetra)*. This awareness *(prajñā)* is called *kṣetrajña* (awareness of the region).

- Anyone who is constantly in this state of awareness is called *sthita-prajña* (person of steady awareness).

We can dissect awareness *(prajñā)* further into three levels:

- Gross *(sthūla)* - This covers all aspects that can be cognized by the senses *(indriya)*, cognitive apparatus *(manas)*, and logic *(buddhi)*.

o   For example: the world we see around us is made of the primordial elements, such as earth, water, fire, air, and space *(pañcabhūta)*.

o   All these elements can be sensed by the sensory system and decoded into what they represent by the cognitive and logical apparatus.

For example, when we shop for vegetables, we look at the gross aspects of the vegetable - its color, texture, and feel to ascertain its health through our sensory apparatus, and this is decoded by our cognitive and logical apparatus.

o   Within our bodies, this translates to awareness of the sheath made by food *(annamaya-kośa)* and sheath of *prāṇa (prāṇamaya-kośa)*.

o   In the body, this is called *sthūla-śarīra* or cognition of the gross body, which covers awareness of the material aspect of the human body driven by diet *(annamaya)* and motility *(prāṇamaya)*.

- Subtle *(sūkṣma)*- The awareness of gross elements is driven by an underlying principle, which is the consciousness *(citta)*.

For example – the internal combustion engine works on the principle of "Ideal gas law" [5] which says that increasing the temperature of a gas increases the pressure that makes it expand.

The gross *(sthūla)* element is the physical internal combustion engine, which is available to the senses in the form of earth, water, fire, air, and space *(pañcabhūta)*.

- The subtle element *(sūkṣma)* is the cognition of the principle of "Ideal gas law" *(manomaya)* and adapting it to build a system *(vijñānamaya)* that uses fuel to drive the engine. In real terms, this translates to the Internal Combustion Engine (ICE) or, more popularly, the petrol/diesel engine.

- The awareness of this subtle principle *(sūkṣma-śarīra)* is driven by the consciousness *(citta)* which takes the principle *(vijñānamaya)* and visualizes it *(manomaya)* into a gross body *(sthūla-śarīra)*. Any engine designer must be conscious of the variables that form the design basis, such as where and how it will be used, its various limits, fuels (petrol, diesel, CNG, etc) and others.

- In the body, this is the awareness of the movement of consciousness within the body is called sheath of cognition *(manomaya-kośa)* and sheath of awareness of the system *(vijñānamaya-kośa)*,

For instance, when you read this sentence, the primary information you see is derived through its physical attributes *(sthūla-śarīra),* of alphabets and words

---

[5] https://energyeducation.ca/encyclopedia/Internal_combustion_engine#:~:text=Internal%20 combustion%20heat%20engines%20work,the%20temperature%20of%20the%20gas.

that are transmitted through a device or book. However, your experience of the underlying principles *(sūkṣma-śarīra)* comes from the quality of your awareness as you decipher the information *(manomaya)* relating to the subject *(vijñānamaya)*.

- Causal *(kāraṇa)* – this is the state from which all materiality *(māyā)* is caused.

  - While the base is the *Brahman,* it is the launch point of *puruṣa* and *prakṛti* and also the point where joy of cognitive infinity is experienced. So, this is called the sheath of joy *(ānandamaya-kośa)*.

For example – we know that Archimedes[6] was bathing *(sthūla)* in a bathtub in a state of null *(Brahman)* watching his body bobbing and bath-waters sloshing over the tub. Suddenly, an inspiration occurred *(ānandamaya),* and he cracked the problem of buoyancy *(sūkṣma)*. The same can be applied to Newton sitting under a tree watching the apple fall, August Kekule[7] imagining the Benzene ring to be a snake chasing its own tail, or Watson to discover the ATGC (adenine-thyamine-guanine-cystocine) model of DNA. This can roughly be approximated as the inspiration that results in a cognition of the causal state *(kāraṇa-śarīra)*.

Union of the *kṣetra* (region/field) and *kṣetrajña* (awareness of the region/field):

Field or region can also refer to an entity, such as a building, society, office, company, country, region, world, solar system, and even the Universe. How would it work?

Let us look at a company and country:

A country is a *kṣetra*, its understanding and management is *kṣetrajña*.

Earth	prithvi
prāṇa	Land use balance
apāna	Solid waste management
vyāna	Border control, Customs
udāna	Export, currency mgmt.
samāna	Infrastructure, factories

Water	áp
prāṇa	All liquid resource mgmt.
apāna	Liquid waste management
vyāna	Coast guard, Customs
udāna	Weather and climate
samāna	Fishing, water use mgmt.

Fire	agni
prāṇa	Energy security
apāna	Manage energy waste
vyāna	Kinetic forces
udāna	Hard power
samāna	Industry/ infrastructure

Air	vāyu
prāṇa	Increased forestry
apāna	Air pollution control
vyāna	National soft-power
udāna	Communication
samāna	Weather mgmt.

Space	ākāṣa
prāṇa	Education/ literacy
apāna	Removal of chaos/ order
vyāna	Air-space control
udāna	GDP, Indices management
samāna	Knowledge management

13.5 - How awareness *(prajña)* translates for a country

---

[6] https://en.wikipedia.org/wiki/Archimedes

[7] https://www.nature.com/articles/465036a#:~:text=Most%20organic%20chemical%20compounds%20contain,snake%20eating%20its%20own%20tail.

- A company or country is just an idea... first, there is nothing! This is the *Brahman*.

- In the case of a company, someone gets an idea or desire to start one. Similarly, in the case of a country people unite in a desire for a country! This is *icchā-śakti*.

- Next, people make sacrifices necessary for creation of their country. In the case of a company, the promoter sacrifices time, resources, and energy to get the requisite technology, funding, people, and systems. This is *ādhiyajña*.

- From the sacrifice emerges a national identity *(puruṣa)*. When it weaves with its own manifestation *(prakṛti)*, a national soul *(ātmā)* is formed, and this is represented by the Government, National Flag, and Constitution. In the case of a company, the identity *(puruṣa)* is established by the articles of association, vision, mission, and brand. *Puruṣa* and *prakṛti* weave to form and market a product. *Vijñāna* is market feedback/ intelligence/awareness.

- *Prakṛti* manifests as *guṇa* (attributes). Legislature represents the people; hence, their identity, fears, aspirations, and delusions, is predominantly *tāmasika*. Judiciary, which represents equality, balance, and harmony must be *sāttvika* and Executive, which runs the country must be *rājasika,* since effort and energy are required to keep all systems functioning. In the case of the company, these *guṇa-s* are embedded in each department and the way each department functions. For example, a well-run manufacturing department will have quality systems, low wastage and rejection, optimized use of manpower, etc. Thus, a good manufacturing department should be low on *tamas,* but high on *rajas* and *sattva.* However, a branding department would need to understand Identity, which is intrinsically *tāmasika* but must be balanced by *sattva* so that the brand does not become narcissistic! Quality department would have a mix of *rajas* and *sattva,* while accounts would need to be a mix of *tamas* and *sattva* owing to the intrinsic need for integrity, ability to say no, and accuracy.

- *Kṣetra* is defined by the borders of the country. In a company, this depends on the product line and markets as can be seen in the case of Amazon, Microsoft, Indian Railways, or Ford!

- The Head of the country is its *kṣetrajña* (soul of the *kṣetra).* So, the ability of any Head to understand and define the country's goals determines how the *guṇa-s* will mix in its operation. The board, in a company would ideally be the *kṣetrajña,* but often, it might be the department heads if functions are compartmentalized.

- If the Head of Government were to be delusional, then all actions by the Government will be predominantly *tāmasika.* Next, if the Head were to be ambitious, then the Governments actions will be *rājasika* and aggressive.

Finally, a *sāttvika* Government will adopt a balanced and harmonic approach to all issues, mixing reconciliation, aggression, and passivity appropriately. This applies to companies as well.

- The country's awareness of its position in the external environment is *vijñāna* and its understanding of itself, its strengths and weaknesses is *jñāna*. In the case of a company, it would be the strategic as well as competitive environment.

- Also, the motility that flows through the country which makes the *guṇa-s* function is *prāṇa* and encompassing foundation of all experience within the *kṣetra* (country) is an undefinable state of nothing. Indeed, this applies to companies as well.

- Finally, the degree to which the leader and people of a company or country are yoked to their country's identity will determine the seamlessness with which their actions will mirror the requirements of their country. This forms the base on which decisions are made, this is *dharma*.

- The yoking of people to their company or country is Yoga, and the outcome is determined by the mix of situational awareness *(prajñā)*, conditioning/order, and harmony *(dharma)*, sincerity and dedication *(śraddhā)*, knowledge *(jñāna)* and sacrifice *(yajña)*, which includes effort *(karma)*.

- It is amazing, how this ancient philosophy is so universally applicable *(sanātana)* in every situation as a manual of life and living.

Some contradictions to accepted positions:

Are *Brahman* and God one and the same? We pray to God, which means that we adopt a subordinate attitude when dealing with God. However, since the Self and *Brahman* are the same, we adopt an attitude of equalness with the *Brahman (ahaṃ brahmāsmi)*. Hence, equating *Brahman* with God may not be appropriate.

Lessons learned:

- Cognition of the *kṣetra* in its gross *(sthūla)* and subtle *(sūkṣma)* aspects is *kṣetrajña. Brahman* is the causal state *(kāraṇa)*.

- *Puruṣa* is the spectator, that which experiences the Self. Consequently, those with knowledge of the *puruṣa* and *prakṛti* along with the *guṇa-s* are able to isolate experience from the Self and are never born again.

- So, anyone who is attached to these material outcomes will be unable to move from the gross state to the subtle and finally causal state. To achieve this, one needs to move beyond the material by avoiding duality of like/dislike, discrimination between permanent and impermanent *(vivekam)*, dispassion to all objects *(vairāgya)*, and adopt an equal gaze *(sama-dṛṣṭi)* to everything.

The transliteration and translation of chapter 13 follows:

अर्जुन उवाच -
प्रकृतिं पुरुषं चैव क्षेत्रं क्षेत्रज्ञमेव च ।
एतद्वेदितुमिच्छामि ज्ञानं ज्ञेयं च केशव ॥ १३-१॥

Arjuna asked (1) primordial manifestation and primordial Identity as well as battle field and knowledge of the field *(prakṛtiṃ puruṣaṃ caiva kṣetraṃ kṣetrajñameva ca I)*, this I wish to know whatever is necessary to know *(etadveditumicchāmi jñānaṃ jñeyaṃ ca keśava ॥ 13-1॥)*.

श्रीभगवानुवाच -
इदं शरीरं कौन्तेय क्षेत्रमित्यभिधीयते ।
एतद्यो वेत्ति तं प्राहुः क्षेत्रज्ञ इति तद्विदः ॥ १३-२॥
क्षेत्रज्ञं चापि मां विद्धि सर्वक्षेत्रेषु भारत ।
क्षेत्रक्षेत्रज्ञयोर्ज्ञानं यत्तज्ज्ञानं मतं मम ॥ १३-३॥

Śrī Kṛṣṇa replied (2-3) this body is called the field, he that understands it is called knower of the field *(idaṃ śarīraṃ kaunteya kṣetramityabhidhīyate I etadyo vetti taṃ prāhuḥ kṣetrajña iti tadvidaḥ ॥ 13-2॥)*. Know me to be the knower of all fields, the field and knowledge of the field is cognition of me *(kṣetrajñaṃ cāpi māṃ viddhi sarvakṣetreṣu bhārata I kṣetrakṣetrajñayorjñānaṃ yattajjñānaṃ mataṃ mama ॥ 13-3॥)*.

तत्क्षेत्रं यच्च यादृक्च यद्विकारि यतश्च यत् ।
स च यो यत्प्रभावश्च तत्समासेन मे शृणु ॥ १३-४॥
ऋषिभिर्बहुधा गीतं छन्दोभिर्विविधैः पृथक् ।
ब्रह्मसूत्रपदैश्चैव हेतुमद्भिर्विनिश्चितैः ॥ १३-५॥

(4-5) What is the field, what is it like, what changes occur to in and in what circumstances, what are its powers, in brief, hear *(tatkṣetraṃ yacca yādṛkca yadvikāri yataśca yat I sa ca yo yatprabhāvaśca tatsamāsena me śarṇu ॥ 13-4॥)*. Many seers have chanted various distinct descriptions about *Brahman* which are decisive and full of reasoning *(ṛṣibhirbahudhā gītaṃ chandobhirvividhaiḥ pṛthak I brahmasūtrapadaiścaiva hetumadbhirviniścitaiḥ ॥ 13-5॥)*.

महाभूतान्यहङ्कारो बुद्धिरव्यक्तमेव च ।
इन्द्रियाणि दशैकं च पञ्च चेन्द्रियगोचराः ॥ १३-६॥
इच्छा द्वेषः सुखं दुःखं सङ्घातश्चेतना धृतिः ।
एतत्क्षेत्रं समासेन सविकारमुदाहृतम् ॥ १३-७॥

(6-7) Great elements, feeling that I am the doer, intellect, the one unmanifested and even the ten senses and the five objects of the senses *(mahābhūtānyahaṅkāro buddhiravyaktameva ca ǀ indriyāṇi daśaikaṃ ca pañca cendriyagocarāḥ ǁ 13-6ǁ)*. Desire, dislike, pleasure, pain, the steady aggregate consciousness, this field with its modifications has been described *(icchā dveṣaḥ sukhaṃ duḥkhaṃ saṅghātaścetanā dhṛtiḥ ǀ etatkṣetraṃ samāsena savikāramudāhṛtam ǁ 13-7ǁ)*.

अमानित्वमदम्भित्वमहिंसा क्षान्तिरार्जवम् ।
आचार्योपासनं शौचं स्थैर्यमात्मविनिग्रहः ॥ १३-८॥
इन्द्रियार्थेषु वैराग्यमनहङ्कार एव च ।
जन्ममृत्युजराव्याधिदुःखदोषानुदर्शनम् ॥ १३-९॥

(8-9) Humility, unpretentiousness, non-injury, tranquility, uprightness, service to the teacher, purity, steadiness, and subduing the Self *(amānitvamadambhitvamahiṃsā kṣāntirārjavam ǀ ācāryopāsanaṃ śaucaṃ sthairyamātmavinigrahaḥ ǁ 13-8ǁ)*. Dispassion towards materiality, absence of doer-ship, and even disregard for the affliction of birth-death, old age, infirmity, and suffering *(indriyārtheṣu vairāgyamanahaṅkāra eva ca ǀ janmamṛtyujarāvyādhiduḥkhadoṣānudarśanam ǁ 13-9ǁ)*.

असक्तिरनभिष्वङ्गः पुत्रदारगृहादिषु ।
नित्यं च समचित्तत्वमिष्टानिष्टोपपत्तिषु ॥ १३-१०॥
मयि चानन्ययोगेन भक्तिरव्यभिचारिणी ।
विविक्तदेशसेवित्वमरतिर्जनसंसदि ॥ १३-११॥
अध्यात्मज्ञाननित्यत्वं तत्त्वज्ञानार्थदर्शनम् ।
एतज्ज्ञानमिति प्रोक्तमज्ञानं यदतोऽन्यथा ॥ १३-१२॥

(10-12) Non-attachment, non-identification of the Self with son, wife, and family, having constant and even consciousness in the justification of the desirable and undesirable *(asaktiranabhiṣvaṅgaḥ putradāragṛhādiṣu ǀ nityaṃ ca samacittatvamiṣṭāniṣṭopapattiṣu ǁ 13-10ǁ)*. To me, with unswerving focused yoga of devotion, resort to lonely places, and avoid people *(mayi cānanyayogena bhaktiravyabhicāriṇī ǀ viviktadeśasevitvamaratirjanasaṃsadi ǁ 13-11ǁ)*. Constantly seeking cognition of the primordial Self, the subtle wisdom seen in materiality, this wisdom which is thus declared is the opposite of ignorance *(adhyātmajñānanityatvaṃ tattvajñānārthadarśanam ǀ etajjñānamiti proktamajñānaṃ yadato 'nyathā ǁ 13-12ǁ)*.

ज्ञेयं यत्तत्प्रवक्ष्यामि यज्ज्ञात्वामृतमश्नुते ।
अनादिमत्परं ब्रह्म न सत्तन्नासदुच्यते ॥ १३-१३॥
सर्वतः पाणिपादं तत्सर्वतोऽक्षिशिरोमुखम् ।
सर्वतः श्रुतिमल्लोके सर्वमावृत्य तिष्ठति ॥ १३-१४॥

(13-14) That which should be cognized, I will declare, which on cognizing one will attain immortality by merging with the beginningless supreme *Brahman,* which is said not to have value nor not have value *(jñeyaṃ yattatpravakṣyāmi yajjñātvāmṛtamaśnute ı anādimatparaṃ brahma na sattannāsaducyate ॥13-13॥).* With hands and feet that are everywhere, everywhere with eyes, head, and mouth, everywhere with ears, it exists covering everything in the world *(sarvataḥ pāṇipādam tatsarvato 'kṣiśiromukham ı sarvataḥ śrutimalloke sarvamāvṛtya tiṣṭhati ॥ 13-14॥).*

सर्वेन्द्रियगुणाभासं सर्वेन्द्रियविवर्जितम् ।

असक्तं सर्वभृच्चैव निर्गुणं गुणभोक्तृ च ॥ १३-१५॥

बहिरन्तश्च भूतानामचरं चरमेव च ।

सूक्ष्मत्वात्तदविज्ञेयं दूरस्थं चान्तिके च तत् ॥ १३-१६॥

15-16) Bringing clarity to all senses driven by attributes, all senses removed and unattached, supporting all and even devoid of attributes and still the user of attributes *(sarvendriyaguṇābhāsaṃ sarvendriyavivarjitam ı asaktam sarvabhṛccaiva nirguṇam guṇabhoktṛ ca ॥ 13-15॥).* Outside and within creation, unmoving yet moving also and because of its subtlety, that incognizable is far and near *(bahirantaśca bhūtānāmacaraṃ carameva ca ı sūkṣmatvāttadavijñeyaṃ dūrastham cāntike ca tat ॥ 13-16॥).*

अविभक्तं च भूतेषु विभक्तमिव च स्थितम् ।

भूतभर्तृ च तज्ज्ञेयं ग्रसिष्णु प्रभविष्णु च ॥ १३-१७॥

ज्योतिषामपि तज्ज्योतिस्तमसः परमुच्यते ।

ज्ञानं ज्ञेयं ज्ञानगम्यं हृदि सर्वस्य विष्ठितम् ॥ १३-१८॥

(17-18) Undivided and in creation existing as if divided, existing as well as supporting creation and know that to be devouring and generating *(avibhaktam ca bhūteṣu vibhaktamiva ca sthitam ı bhūtabhartṛ ca tajjñeyaṃ grasiṣṇu prabhaviṣṇu ca ॥ 13-17॥).* That which is the light that lights complete darkness it is said, wisdom that is cognized, the goal of wisdom, seated in the heart of all *(jyotiṣāmapi tajjyotistamasaḥ paramucyate ı jñānaṃ jñeyaṃ jñānagamyaṃ hṛdi sarvasya viṣṭhitam ॥ 13-18॥).*

इति क्षेत्रं तथा ज्ञानं ज्ञेयं चोक्तं समासतः ।

मद्भक्त एतद्विज्ञाय मद्भावायोपपद्यते ॥ १३-१९॥

प्रकृतिं पुरुषं चैव विद्ध्यनादी उभावपि ।

विकारांश्च गुणांश्चैव विद्धि प्रकृतिसम्भवान् ॥ १३-२०॥

(19-20) Thus, the field as well as wisdom as well as the knowable have been stated briefly. Knowing this, my devotee merges with my essence *(iti kṣetraṃ tathā jñānaṃ jñeyaṃ coktaṃ samāsataḥ | madbhakta etadvijñāya madbhāvāyopapadyate || 13-19||)*. Know that both *prakṛti* and *puruṣa* are also without beginning, know that all changes and *guṇa-s* are born out of *prakṛti (prakṛtiṃ puruṣaṃ caiva viddhyanādī ubhāvapi | vikārāṃśca guṇāṃścaiva viddhi prakṛtisambhavān || 13-20||)*.

कार्यकारणकर्तृत्वे हेतुः प्रकृतिरुच्यते ।

पुरुषः सुखदुःखानां भोक्तृत्वे हेतुरुच्यते ॥ १३-२१॥

पुरुषः प्रकृतिस्थो हि भुङ्क्ते प्रकृतिजान्गुणान् ।

कारणं गुणसङ्गोऽस्य सदसद्योनिजन्मसु ॥ १३-२२॥

(21-22) The act, reason for the act, the actor is caused by *prakṛti,* it is said. *Puruṣa* is the cause of the experience of pleasure and pain, it is said *(kāryakāraṇakartṛtve hetuḥ prakṛtirucyate | puruṣaḥ sukhaduḥkhānāṃ bhoktṛtve heturucyate || 13-21||)*. Indeed, *puruṣa* embedded in *prakṛti* experiences *guṇa* that emerge from *prakṛti,* which include cause, attachment to the attributes, of one's value, lack of value, of birth from various wombs *(puruṣaḥ prakṛtistho hi bhuṅkte prakṛtijāṅguṇān | kāraṇaṃ guṇasaṅgo'sya sadasadyonijanmasu || 13-22||)*.

उपद्रष्टानुमन्ता च भर्ता भोक्ता महेश्वरः ।

परमात्मेति चाप्युक्तो देहेऽस्मिन्पुरुषः परः ॥ १३-२३॥

य एवं वेत्ति पुरुषं प्रकृतिं च गुणैः सह ।

सर्वथा वर्तमानोऽपि न स भूयोऽभिजायते ॥ १३-२४॥

(23-24) The spectator, permitter, and husband, the experiencer is the great *īśvara,* who is the supreme Soul, and so the body is also called supreme *puruṣa (upadraṣṭānumantā ca bhartā bhoktā maheśvaraḥ | paramātmeti cāpyukto dehe'sminpuruṣaḥ paraḥ || 13-23||)*. He who this cognizes *puruṣa, prakṛti,* and *guṇa-s* in all combinations in the state of the present; also, he is not born again *(ya evaṃ vetti puruṣaṃ prakṛtiṃ ca guṇaiḥ saha | sarvathā vartamāno'pi na sa bhūyo'bhijāyate || 13-24||)*.

ध्यानेनात्मनि पश्यन्ति केचिदात्मानमात्मना ।

अन्ये साङ्ख्येन योगेन कर्मयोगेन चापरे ॥ १३-२५॥

अन्ये त्वेवमजानन्तः श्रुत्वान्येभ्य उपासते ।

तेऽपि चातितरन्त्येव मृत्युं श्रुतिपरायणाः ॥ १३-२६॥

(25-26) By meditating into the Self, some can cognize the Self in the Self, others use yoga of knowledge and yet others *karma-yoga (dhyānenātmani paśyanti kecidātmānamātmanā ǀ anye sāṅkhyena yogena karmayogena cāpare ǁ 13-25ǁ).* Others, even though not knowing, worship as they have heard from others, and even they also cross beyond death due to their devotion to what they have heard *(anye tvevamajānantaḥ śrutvānyebhya upāsate ǀ te'pi cātitarantyeva mṛtyuṃ śrutiparāyaṇāḥ ǁ 13-26ǁ).*

यावत्सञ्जायते किञ्चित्सत्त्वं स्थावरजङ्गमम् ।
क्षेत्रक्षेत्रज्ञसंयोगात्तद्विद्धि भरतर्षभ ॥ १३-२७॥
समं सर्वेषु भूतेषु तिष्ठन्तं परमेश्वरम् ।
विनश्यत्स्वविनश्यन्तं यः पश्यति स पश्यति ॥ १३-२८॥

(27-28) Anything that comes into existence, the static and mobile, the confluence of the field and knowledge of the field must be cognized *(yāvatsañjāyate kiñcitsattvaṃ sthāvarajaṅgamam ǀ kṣetrakṣetrajñasamyogāttadviddhi bharatarṣabha ǁ 13-27ǁ).* Equally in all creation exists the supreme Being, he is the accrual seer who sees the non-perishable among the perishable *(samaṃ sarveṣu bhūteṣu tiṣṭhantaṃ parameśvaram ǀ vinaśyatsvavinaśyantaṃ yaḥ paśyati sa paśyati ǁ 13-28ǁ).*

समं पश्यन्हि सर्वत्र समवस्थितमीश्वरम् ।
न हिनस्त्यात्मनात्मानं ततो याति परां गतिम् ॥ १३-२९॥
प्रकृत्यैव च कर्माणि क्रियमाणानि सर्वशः ।
यः पश्यति तथात्मानमकर्तारं स पश्यति ॥ १३-३०॥

(29-30) Indeed, he that sees equally everywhere, as the baseline the Being, that Self is not destroyed, the self then goes to the supreme goal *(samaṃ paśyanhi sarvatra samavasthitamīśvaram ǀ na hinastyātmanātmānaṃ tato yāti parāṃ gatim ǁ 13-29ǁ).* He who cognizes that all actions are performed by *prakṛti* alone, that seer also is a Self which becomes actionless *(prakṛtyaiva ca karmāṇi kriyamāṇāni sarvaśaḥ ǀ yaḥ paśyati tathātmānamakartāraṃ sa paśyati ǁ 13-30ǁ).*

यदा भूतपृथग्भावमेकस्थमनुपश्यति ।
तत एव च विस्तारं ब्रह्म सम्पद्यते तदा ॥ १३-३१॥
अनादित्वान्निर्गुणत्वात्परमात्मायमव्ययः ।
शरीरस्थोऽपि कौन्तेय न करोति न लिप्यते ॥ १३-३२॥

(31-32) When one sees all creation is as the same entity, from that development onward, he becomes *Brahman (yadā bhūtapṛthagbhāvamekasthamanupaśyati ǀ tata eva ca vistāraṃ brahma sampadyate tadā ǁ 13-31ǁ).* Without beginning, without attributes, this imperishable supreme Self, though in the body, does not act, nor is it tainted *(anāditvānnirguṇatvātparamātmāyamavyayaḥ ǀ śarīrastho'pi kaunteya na karoti na lipyate ǁ 13-32ǁ).*

यथा सर्वगतं सौक्ष्म्यादाकाशं नोपलिप्यते ।

सर्वत्रावस्थितो देहे तथात्मा नोपलिप्यते ॥ १३-३३॥

यथा प्रकाशयत्येकः कृत्स्नं लोकमिमं रविः ।

क्षेत्रं क्षेत्री तथा कृत्स्नं प्रकाशयति भारत ॥ १३-३४॥

क्षेत्रक्षेत्रज्ञयोरेवमन्तरं ज्ञानचक्षुषा ।

भूतप्रकृतिमोक्षं च ये विदुर्यान्ति ते परम् ॥ १३-३५॥

(33-35) Just as ether exists everywhere in a subtle manner but does not get tainted, the Self exists everywhere in the body but is not tainted *(yathā sarvagatam sauksmyādākāśam nopalipyate । sarvatrāvasthito dehe tathātmā nopalipyate ॥ 13-33॥)*. Just as this one Sun lights the whole field, similarly, the *Brahman* illuminates everything *(yathā prakāsayatyekaḥ krtsnam lokamimam raviḥ । kṣetram kṣetrī tathā krtsnam prakāśayati bhārata ॥ 13-34॥)*. So, the distinction between the field and knower of the field is by cognition of wisdom that liberation of creation from *prakṛti* and those that know go to the Supreme *(kṣetrakṣetrajñayorevamantaram jñānacakṣuṣā । bhūtaprakṛtimokṣam ca ye viduryānti te param ॥ 13-35॥)*.

◆———·●◆●·———◆

Chapter 14

Guṇatraya-vibhāga-yoga
(yoga of differentiation of the three guṇa-s) [1]

Introduction

- Starting with chapter 9, Śrī Kṛṣṇa moves from explaining the basics to implementation of concepts. To do this, he speaks about his Absolute *(virāt)* Self in chapter 9 and finally shows him his Universal form *(viśva-rūpa)* in chapter 10. This obviously confuses as well as amazes and scares Arjuna.

- In chapter 13, he moves to the next step and explains cognition of the body and environment. In terms of daily living, it is all about *vijñāna* or cognition of the body and environment in the visible or gross *(sthūla),* subtle *(sūkṣma)* state as well as the causal *(kāraṇa)* state.

- In chapter 14, though he seems to repeat the same concepts, he is actually applying those concepts to various situations, so that the *yogī* understands the myriad opportunities for implementation of the Yoga of *Śrīmad-bhagavad-gītā* in normal life.

- In this chapter, Śrī Kṛṣṇa speaks about how attributes affect behavior. Let us examine how this concept affects various aspects of living.

Śrī Kṛṣṇa explains the three attributes *(triguṇa-s)* [2], verse 1-20:

Śrī Kṛṣṇa said – I will now teach you that knowledge of the Self *(jñāna)* which will enable you to merge with the source *(Brahman).*

- I am the seed, the womb, and the placer of the seed of all creation.

---

[1] https://www.bhagavad-gita.org/Gita/chapter-14.html

[2] https://www.sivanandaonline.org//?cmd=displaysection§ion_id=866

- From me is born the (three *guna-s)* *triguna-s* – *sattva, rajas,* and *tamas,* the qualities which are common to all entities.

- Of these, *sattva* is spotless, luminescent, and free from faults. Also, it binds one to the knowledge of the self which is sourced from contentment.

- *Rajas* is the embodiment of passion, the source of thirst and attachment. Consequently, it binds one to action.

- Finally, *tamas* is born out of ignorance and delusion. As a result, it binds one to heedlessness, indolence, and sleep.

- *Sattva* binds one to peace, *rajas* to action, and by shrouding one from the knowledge of oneself, *tamas* binds one to heedlessness.

- There is a constant struggle for ascendancy, with *sattva, rajas,* and *tamas* competing to overpower the other two. Firstly, when every sense is filled with awareness, this is the state of *sattva.* Next, when greed drives any undertaking, and there is restlessness and longing, *rajas* predominates. Lastly, when darkness, inertness, heedlessness, and delusion manifest, then *tamas* is predominant.

- In fact, if one dies when *sattva* is predominant, then he goes to the world of the pure. Next, if he dies in *rajas,* then he is born again attached to action. Finally, if one dies when *tamas* is predominant, then he is born into a deluded home.

- *Sattva* is born out of good action; *rajas* results in pain, and *tamas* results in ignorance. From *sattva* emerges knowledge of the Self, from *rajas* arises greed, and from *tamas* arises heedlessness, ignorance, and error. Those whose awareness of the Self is fixed in *sattva* rise. In *rajas,* there is stagnation, and in *tamas,* there is deterioration of one's progress.

- When a practitioner recognizes all action as arising out of *gunas*, and transcends it, he will merge with the *Brahman.*

Example: A person is using an ATM (Automatic Teller Machine) for the first time after the bank issued an ATM card to him. Let us imagine the person's state of anxiety when he/she stands in front of the ATM.

- Initially, there is confusion – "How am I going to do this?" or anxiety/fear "What will happen if…?" This is *tamas.*

- Next, comes anger or irritation – "This is ridiculous! How do they expect me to operate this machine without training?" Then, there is effort… "Let's see what we can do." This is *rajas.*

- Finally, there is acceptance, ownership, and finally peace. Here, the person hacks around and finds a solution, either by doing it himself or by asking someone. This is *sattva.*

Consequently, an awareness of having found a solution builds in the person. This is *vijñāna*. This results in increased confidence in the Self, an increase in *asmitā* (I am this or self-esteem) which is called *jñāna*.

Qualities of *guṇa* (attributes)

Tamas (Inertia): This aspect is characterized by fear, laziness, indolence, confusion, delusion, etc. A person with a predominance of this state is generally vacillatory, lethargic, prone to giving excuses, and indecisive.

Rajas (Passion): This state governs nearly all forms of passion and is driven primarily by desire. As a result, a person in this state would typically focus on personal achievement and gratification, be result oriented, dominating, aggressive, impatient, etc.

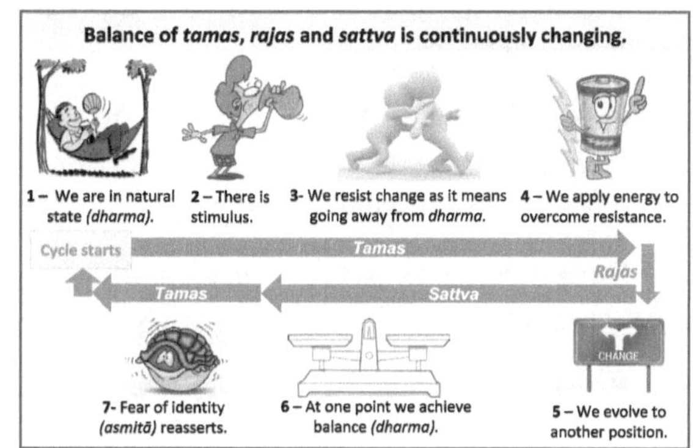

14.1 - The three *guṇa-s* are changing continuously

Sattva (Harmony): This state is characterized by harmony. It is demonstrated when a person tries to balance result with resource or process, task with quality and relationships, etc. A person in this state avoids confrontation, but in a conflict situation is calm, absorbs emotional outburst, and remains objective.

Obviously, no one is endowed with one attribute only. The mix of attributes changes according to the situation, desires, perception of threat, and this changes continuously as the situation unfolds. This means that the three attributes constantly change in composition with each other, with each attribute trying to gain ascendancy over the other, depending on the quality of change and its impact on one's self-worth *(asmitā)*.

How does one rise above the *guṇa-s*? (verse 21 onwards)

Arjuna said: What are the characteristics of him who has transcended the *guṇa-s*? How does one rise above the *guṇa-s*?

Śrī Kṛṣṇa said: The qualities of a person who has transcended the *guṇa-s* are:

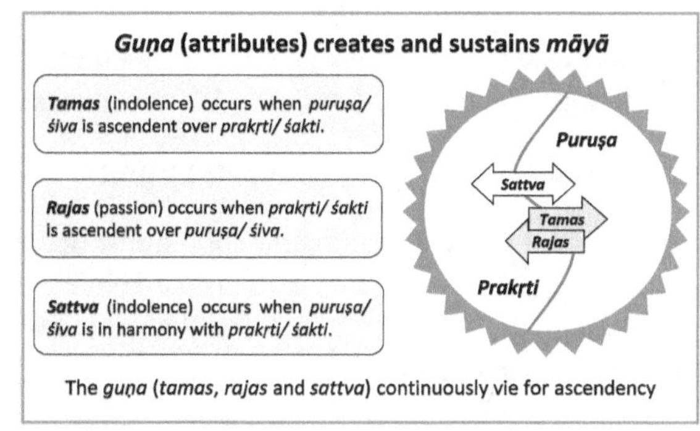

14.2 - What are the *guṇa-s*?

- He who does not hate light, activity, or delusion when it occurs, nor longs for them when they are absent (is free from opposites such as like-dislike, good-bad, right-wrong).

- Also, he who is unaffected by the *guna-s,* for he knows how they operate. Therefore, this person is centered in the Self and does not get swerved by the actions of the *guna-s.*

- Balanced in peace, centered in the Self, viewing earth, stone, and gold alike, treating loved ones and strangers in the same manner, firm in all situations and treating censure and praise with equal importance/indifference.

- Same in honor or dishonor, treating friend or foe equally, and abandoning all undertakings.

- He who is devoted to me, merges with me reaches the Brahman.

Concept of *samādhi* (transcending of the Self):

From first principles, we know that;

- *Guna* rises from the weave of *puruṣa* and *prakṛti.*

- *Puruṣa* is the experiencer, and *prakṛti* is the manifestation of *puruṣa.*

- *Puruṣa* and *prakṛti* combine to form the Self *(ātmā)*

- Hence, when the *puruṣa* ceases to experience, *prakṛti* has no impact on the *ātmā* (Self).

How can we stop our *puruṣa* from experiencing?

- Stop dealing in dualities such as like-dislike, love-hate, etc. That stops judgmental responses, which is possible only if the person is secure within his or her identity *(asmitā).*

- Be even-handed. Treat everything and every situation without bias.

- Let go/stop living in the past and do not dream about the future. Be aware of the present. Become a *sthitha-prajñā* (one of steady awareness)

Concept of *sva-tantra* (individuality) using India as an example:

Since Yoga is from India, it seems appropriate that one should explore the possibility of applying Śrī Kṛṣṇa's advice in all the above chapters to India. Obviously, once this is done, the litmus test for *Śrīmad-bhagavad-gītā* would be its applicability to humanity as *sanātana-dharma.*

What is a country? What would constitute the personality of a country? How would the principles of *guṇa* apply to a collective society of people such as a country?

To start, a country is established by a group of people with a common culture and purpose. The individuality/personality *(sva-tantra)* of a country is the way it is perceived by its people, other peoples, and countries. However, this perception is an outcome of the way people perceive their own country which would be reflected in the way they carry themselves and behave.

For example, if the people had a balanced view of themselves and behaved in a responsible manner, that country would be considered to be in harmony with its own nature *(sāttvika)*. Next, if the people of a country behaved in an aggressive manner and bullied others, they would be considered as a volatile or greedy country *(rājasika)*. Finally, if the people of a country were deluded, confused, and weary or if the people did not resonate with their government, it would be a deluded country *(tāmasika)*. Obviously, no single *guṇa* would dominate public discourse, but people's conditioning *(dharma)* would determine their individuality *(sva-tantra)* which would get reflected in the way the citizens and the country behaved in the environment*(sāttvika)*.

Since people live in the country for betterment and harmonic living, is there a template on which a country's development could be based? Ancient texts from the sub-continent talk about *puruṣārtha-s (puruṣa* = human + *artha* = reason) which means reason-for-living or raison d'etre of human existence.

Puruṣārtha principle states that people live for *artha* = material gain, *kāma* = sensual pleasure, *dharma* = order and harmony, *mokṣa* = freedom from seeking. Importantly, for balanced living, *dharma* must be resident in *artha* = material gain and *kāma* = sensual pleasure.

The question that needs answering is, does freedom-from-seeking *(mokṣa)* fit? Absolutely! After people have achieved material *(artha)* enjoyment and sensual pleasure *(kāma)* in harmony *(dharma),* they begin to look for an answer to the question, "What is life?", "Why am I alive?", "Does life have a purpose?" etc. This takes them into an esoteric world that culminates with absolute freedom from materiality *(māyā)*. This freedom comes when the person has cognized the Self and results in the person having no further desire-to-seek *(mokṣa)*.

Therefore, any country that wishes to exist as a balanced individual *(sātvika-sva-tantra)* must be able to create, for its citizens, circumstances for them to comprehend their Self, the reason they are alive. Not encouraging people to seek freedom from materiality *(mokṣa)* would condition people into viewing materiality as life's sole objective. Also, the practice of *mokṣa* brings with it finer altruistic sentiments *(bhāva)* of charity *(dāna),* tolerance *(kṣamā),* non-violence *(ahiṃsā),* etc.

So, any society that wishes to develop its personality must develop the finer qualities of behavior control *(yama)* and self-restraint *(niyama)* of its people, as detailed in *rāja-yoga* [3] on *yama* and *niyama)*.

Obviously, behavior control *(yama)* and self-restraint *(niyama)* cannot be taught overnight, so they need to be inculcated in children when they are young. This means

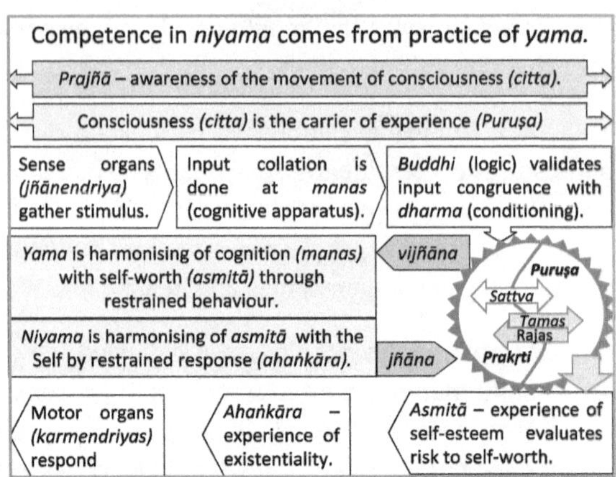

14.3 - *yama* and *niyama* are the bedrock of stable societies

that the education system of the country must systematically teach *yama* (behavior control) and *niyama* (self-restraint) and encourage its citizens to discuss its values as well as practice the concept in civic life. This will condition people to live a life of natural peace *(dharma)* while they are enjoying material *(artha)* and sensual *(kāma)* pleasures and prepare them for absolute freedom *(mokṣa)* later.

How can the principles of *puruṣārtha-s* (reason for human existence) be applied to the management of the country? *Artha* is obviously material well-being, availability of food, shelter, clothing, and infrastructure, such as transport, electricity, availability of water, etc., *kāma* is the softer aspects of *artha*. For example, while shelter might be available, if it is designed and constructed in a haphazard manner, badly designed or dilapidated, there can be no positivity about the place and residents would be unhappy. If food is spoiled, cold, unappetizing or lacking in nutrition, then there is no pleasure derived in eating. This means that both hardware *(artha)* and software *(kāma)* are required for a society to be a functional and happy place. So, we can see that material aspects *(artha)* and sensual aspect *(kāma)* of a country cannot function independently.

Additionally, material aspects *(artha)* and sensual aspect *(kāma)* cannot be independent of order and harmony *(dharma)*. For example, even if food and shelter were to be made available in a country, if there is no order, harmony or peace, then material aspects *(artha)* and sensual aspect *(kāma)* become irrelevant.

So, we can also see that for a country *(kṣetra)* to experience it individuality *(sva-tantra)* with complete awareness *(prajñā)*, its society *(kṣetra)* must be conditioned for a life of harmony *(dharma)* which must be a weave of its material *(artha)* and sensual *(kāma)* aspects in the gross/visible/overt *(sthūla)* as well as subtle *(sūkṣma)* states. This knowledge of how to manage a country is called *(kṣetrajña)* and is completely dependent on sincere and diligent application *(śraddhā)* of the policies, systems, processes, and rules *(dharma)* by its rulers as well as citizens.

---

[3] https://schoolofyoga.in/yoga-concept/raja-hatha-yoga

Prāṇa (motility)

If we accept that the principles of *kṣetra* as espoused by Śrī Kṛṣṇa in chapter 12 can be applied to an individual as well as a country, then we can apply the principles of individuality *(sva-tantra)* to a country because the individual is the unit of a country. To begin, the person and country are both living entities, and both have *prāṇa*. Consequently, this means that a country can die, just like a person. For example – Czechoslovakia split into Czech and Slovakia while North and South Vietnam merged into Vietnam. All these countries displayed different personalities *(sva-tantra)* before and after their change in composition. So, countries can die, and when they do, the personality dies with them. Similarly, when countries are born, they get a new personality *(svatantra)* as defined by their region *(kṣetra)* and citizens *(jana)*.

We also know that all entities have five vital airs *(vāyus):*

- *Prāṇa-vāyu,* which controls all incoming value *(sat),*

- *Apāna-vāyu,* which controls all excretory value,

- *Vyāna-vāyu,* which determines the quality of motility or aura that governs the projection of individuality *(sva-tantra)* of the country,

- *Udāna-vāyu,* which determines how the country communicates with the outside world, and

- *Samāna-vāyu,* which determines how it digests all the resources that it ingests.

Let us detail this further

A country is a *kṣetra*, its understanding and management is *kṣetrajña*.

Earth	*prithvi*		Water	*áp*
prāṇa	Land use balance		*prāṇa*	All liquid resource mgmt.
apāna	Solid waste management		*apāna*	Liquid waste management
vyāna	Border control, Customs		*vyāna*	Coast guard, Customs
udāna	Export, currency mgmt.		*udāna*	Weather and climate
samāna	Infrastructure, factories		*samāna*	Fishing, water use mgmt.

Fire	*agni*	Air	*vāyu*	Space	*ākāṣa*
prāṇa	Energy security	*prāṇa*	Increased forestry	*prāṇa*	Education/ literacy
apāna	Manage energy waste	*apāna*	Air pollution control	*apāna*	Removal of chaos/ order
vyāna	Kinetic forces	*vyāna*	National soft-power	*vyāna*	Air-space control
udāna	Hard power	*udāna*	Communication	*udāna*	GDP, Indices management
samāna	Industry/ infrastructure	*samāna*	Weather mgmt.	*samāna*	Knowledge management

14.4 - How personalities of societies and countries evolve

- *Prāṇa-vāyu* is incoming motility, which includes material, ideas, and resources. The key discriminator is *ṛṇa* (debt). When a country is not in debt and adds value in all its actions, it can enjoy material *(artha)* and sensual *(kāma)* prosperity, but when it borrows beyond its means of repayment and lives without adding value, there is loss of *dharma,* and the country lapses into delusion and depression *(tamas).*

- *Apāna-vāyu* can be viewed in the light of the primordial elements *(pañṭca-bhūta).* For as long as solid *(prithvi)* and liquid *(áp)* waste management ensures betterment of the community, when air *(vāyu)* and space *(ākāśa)* are pure and energy/fire *(agni)* used is adequate to transform raw materials into products of value *(sat), apāna-vāyu* will not become destructive *(tāmasika)* but ensure that the country is harmonized, clean, and in peace *(sāttvika).*

- *Vyāna-vāyu* - when people of a land *(kṣetra)* use their energies in constructive development of themselves and their neighborhood, the overall aura of the country becomes one of a people that can be called civilized and developed. Example – both Germany and Japan ended World War II with a terrible reputation and in servitude. However, over the years, they used their energies to transform themselves in a holistic manner (increased *dharma),* so much so that today their World War II reputation has become insignificant.

- *Udāna-vāyu* is how the country communicates and represents itself. Some countries like India become multilateral, while others punch above their weight, become bullies, struggle to keep their composure, turn docile, or become rebellious. We can see examples of the above qualities in countries in the neighborhood of *Bhārat,* in Asia itself. The quality of attributes *(guṇa)* is evident in the manifestation of self-worth *(asmitā)* in the individuality *(sva-tantra).*

- *Samāna-vāyu* is the motility that circulates within a country. For example, Germany and Japan were able to acquire reputations as countries that add value *(sat)* on account of their hard work and harmonious societal ethics.

So, how does *samāna-vāyu* work?

In the body *(kṣetra), samāna-vāyu* is centered around the abdomen. Resources such as food, water, and air enter the body. Air goes to the lungs, after which oxygen-impregnated blood is brought to the abdomen. Food and water enter the stomach, where they are broken down, digested, and absorbed into the blood for transportation to organs as nourishment for work or waste for disposal.

Similarly, in country *(kṣetra),* resources come into a country in the form of goods, services, and ideas where they are converted by citizens of the country. What do people need to convert resources into goods?

Dharma, good constitution, governance, law and order, and a citizenry that understand as well as follow *dharma.* Conditioning *(dharma)* is determined by the quality of attributes *(guṇa)* that are encouraged and practiced by the people of the country *(kṣetra),* which is also known as culture *(saṃskriti),* life-event management *(saṃskāra),* and practices *(sampradāya)* of a people.

Additionally, we need to cycle back to the definition of individuality *(sva-tantra)* and knowledge of the region *(kṣetrajña).*

Some situations

- When indolence, delusion, and laziness *(tamas)* are the predominant attributes of the people, then the country is likely to remain poor, living on hand-outs/aid, and blaming others for its situation.

- Next, when the people of a country are full of passion *(rajas),* then one will see a high level of energy, passion, and ambition. If this *rājasika* energy is tempered by indolence *(tamas),* then growth will be haphazard, with frequent conflicts. In many countries, there will be a disconnect between the people and their governments.

- However, when *rājasika* energy is tempered by balance and harmony *(sattva),* then one will see an attempt by the government to make each person stand on his or her own feet and be independent.

For example - when passion *(rajas)* is tempered with indolence *(tamas),* every citizen will be given fish to eat. However, when passion *(rajas)* is tempered by balance *(sattva),* citizens will be taught and encouraged to fish so that they stop being dependent on others for free fish, as this makes them vulnerable to power, pressure, and influence and weakens their individuality *(svatantra).* The latter method is harder and more painful, but leads to a self-reliant and stronger country.

- The difference between the above two situations is the quantum of sacrifice *(yajña)* that is required.

- In the former, the citizen merely needs to convince his leaders that giving fish freely will lead to harmony and easier governing of the country *(kṣetra).* However, in the latter case it becomes incumbent on the leader to convince citizen that free fish is not in their interest and they must learn to fish.

- There is a big difference in the input required to condition *(dharma)* the citizens in the latter situation and the way the citizens *(jana)* and leaders *(rā-jana)* relate will determine whether the country comes out with a strong and resilient personality *(sva-tantra).*

***Samāna-vāyu* and the four *āśrama* (stages of existence):**

How does *samāna-vāyu* affect people in various stages of their existence *(āśrama)?*

- There are four stages of existence *(āśramas)*,

    o *Brahmacaryāśrama* (stage of youth),

    o *Gṛhasthāśrama* (stage of a house-holder),

    o *Vānaprasthāśrama* (stage of retirement),

    o *Sannyāsāśrama* (stage of renunciation).

- *Brahmacaryāśrama* (stage of youth) is a phase of learning and formation of conditioning *(dharma)*. This is the most critical stage of a country and effort that society invests in teaching its youth to work with dedication *(śraddhā)*, to sacrifice *(yajña)*, act *(karma-yoga)* and align sacrifice *(yajña)* with Truth *(satya)* and live in order/harmony *(dharma)* will determine the country's individuality *(svatantra)*.

- *Gṛhasthāśrama* (stage of a householder) is that stage where maximum consumption occurs. Here, awareness *(prajñā)* is the quality that needs to be developed. The householder *(gṛhastha)* implements everything that was learned in *brahmacaryāśrama* and begin to understand

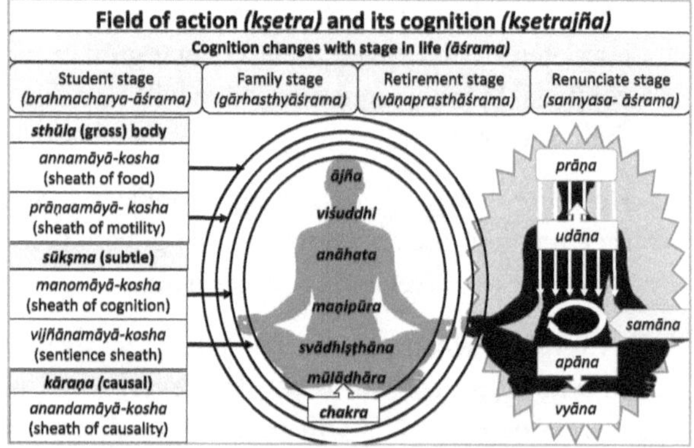

14.5 - The impact of awareness and control on living

the value or shortcoming of everything that was taught. They become alert to income, expenses, waste, and its disposal. They learn discrimination *(viveka)* and dispassion *(vairāgya)*. Only then do householders understand and contribute to all aspects of the country's development *(kṣetrajña)*.

- *Vānaprasthāśrama* (stage of retirement) is a stage when the person steps back from activity and reflect on the learnings of his or her *gṛhasthāśrama*. The key requirement of this stage is having enough resources to face the remainder of life and not be dependent on anyone as well as *svādishtāna* (ability to view the Self dispassionately *(vairāgya)*.

- *Sannyāsāśrama* (stage of renunciation) is the last stage, where a person is expected to focus on the nature of the Soul *(ātma-vichāra)*, absolute freedom *(mokṣa)*, and nature of death. However, people often baulk at any suggestion that they should reflect on the nature of death and after-life. As a result of ignoring this major life-event, there is loneliness, anxiety, and fear of death as one ages. Every individual must practice this to some extent after 65.

The universality of the *Śrīmad-bhagavad-gītā* and *sanātana-dharma*:

- Lastly, for universal application of the principles of *Śrīmad-bhagavad-gītā*, every creature or vegetation gets included with a right to exist in its own state of natural state *(dharma)*. Only then can a country become truly universal *(sanātana)* and secular.

- This is not a plea against animal slaughter or meat consumption. The natural food pyramid is universal and inviolable *(sanātana-dharma)*.

- However, humans sit on top of this pyramid, thus having the ability to control how the rest of the ecosphere functions.

- So, it becomes the responsibility of humans to ensure that the balance between the various flora and fauna that inhibit Earth is maintained and not interfere with it.

- For Bhārat, this means balancing consumption with resource and environment (increasing forest cover, reducing pollution and carbon footprint, and stabilizing usage of resources).

- This also means managing population, for as India increases in prosperity and consumes more resources, it will need to ensure that the per capita utilization of resource is kept constant and ultimately brought down to a sustainable level such that all its resident Souls *(ātmā)*, sentient, and insentient exist in peace *(śānti)*.

Conclusion - the principles in *Śrīmad-bhagavad-gītā* can be extended to a country, where each citizen contributes to build an orderly, harmonic, strong, and resilient *dhārmika* society which ultimately becomes recognized as its individuality *(sva-tantra)*.

Some contradictions to accepted positions:

There is no other world, everything is here, on this Earth. There is no past or future, there's only the present, and this is situational awareness *(sthita-prajñā)*. Total situational awareness *(sthita-prajñā)* gives control over all variables that affect a person, thereby ensuring complete free will.

In India, *apāna-vāyu* (the force of excretion and waste management) has always been casually managed.

- Be it personal hygiene, disposal of solid and liquid waste of a town/city, management of waste at the various ship breaking yards, disposal of effluence from leather tanneries or from washing of petroleum tankers, even plastic, garbage or harvest waste, Indians have low awareness and integrity.

- The integrity factor is important because, waste management is personal. How we deal with plastic, how we dispose household garbage, what detergents do we use to clean our toilets and clothes, whether we spit on the road or drop empty bags of eats and bottles of drinks in public places. The list is endless and defines how we integrate with the Earth. Both self-awareness and integrity are required, and urgently. As consumption increases, disposal of waste becomes a critical requirement which needs to be addressed by every citizen.

- This lack of integrity and awareness extends to larger entities. All the requisite knowledge, laws and procedures exist, but companies, users, and regulators choose to undermine the country's future for today's profit. There is no one else, only us, we have to be responsible.

- This is not to say that development is bad, but right of development and growth must weave with responsibility to maintaining the *panchabhūtas* (five primordial elements) and *pancaprāṇa* (five motilities). Growth cannot be sacrificed for environment because both protecting and abusing have a price tag at the end.

- We can either pay up-front, install waste management hardware and software, have clean earth, water and air or pay later with bad health, medical costs, and large clean-up costs. India must address this critical issue quickly or the cost of neglect will be paid for by future generations.

- Another aspect of India's waste management narrative is a tendency to compare India with the rest of the world. It is important for Indians to realize that while the outside world's consumption and waste issues are important in the larger scheme of environmental sustainability, controlling India's own waste by individuals, companies, and civic authorities is a clear and present danger.

Lessons learned in Chapter 14:

Principles of *Śrīmad-bhagavad-gītā* are universal, like *sanātana-dharma*. It can be applied to any society, company, region, or country also.

The transliteration and translation of chapter 14 follows:

श्रीभगवानुवाच -

परं भूयः प्रवक्ष्यामि ज्ञानानां ज्ञानमुत्तमम् ।

यज्ज्ञात्वा मुनयः सर्वे परां सिद्धिमितो गताः ॥ १४-१॥

इदं ज्ञानमुपाश्रित्य मम साधर्म्यमागताः ।

सर्गेऽपि नोपजायन्ते प्रलये न व्यथन्ति च ॥ १४-२॥

Śrī Kṛṣṇa said (1-2) Again I will declare the supreme of all wisdom, the knowledge of the highest degree, which after cognizing, all sages have attained supreme perfection after leaving life (*paraṃ bhūyaḥ pravakṣyāmi jñānānāṃ jñānamuttamam*

| *yajñātvā munayaḥ sarve parāṃ siddhimito gatāḥ* || *14-1*||). Having taken refuge in this wisdom and having attained one-ness with me, one is not born at creation, nor disturbed at dissolution (*idaṃ jñānamupāśritya mama sādharmyamāgatāḥ* | *sarge'pi nopajāyante pralaye na vyathanti ca* || *14-2*||).

मम योनिर्महद् ब्रह्म तस्मिन्गर्भं दधाम्यहम् ।
सम्भवः सर्वभूतानां ततो भवति भारत ॥ १४-३॥
सर्वयोनिषु कौन्तेय मूर्तयः सम्भवन्ति याः ।
तासां ब्रह्म महद्योनिरहं बीजप्रदः पिता ॥ १४-४॥

(3-4) In my womb is the great *Brahma* in whose womb, I place at his birth creation of all beings thereafter (*mama yonirmahad brahma tasmingarbhaṃ dadhāmyaham* | *sambhavaḥ sarvabhūtānāṃ tato bhavati bhārata* || *14-3*||). In all wombs where creation occurs embedded in the womb of great *Brahma*, I am the seed-giving father (*sarvayoniṣu kaunteya mūrtayaḥ sambhavanti yāḥ* | *tāsāṃ brahma mahadyonirahaṃ bījapradaḥ pitā* || *14-4*||).

सत्त्वं रजस्तम इति गुणाः प्रकृतिसम्भवाः ।
निबध्नन्ति महाबाहो देहे देहिनमव्ययम् ॥ १४-५॥
तत्र सत्त्वं निर्मलत्वात्प्रकाशकमनामयम् ।
सुखसङ्गेन बध्नाति ज्ञानसङ्गेन चानघ ॥ १४-६॥

(5-6) *Satva, rajas, tamas,* these attributes which are born out of *prakṛti* bind within the body, the indestructible embodiment (*sattvaṃ rajastama iti guṇāḥ prakṛtisambhavāḥ* | *nibadhnanti mahābāho dehe dehinamavyayam* || *14-5*||). Of these, *sattva* displays stainlessness, luminosity, health, bias towards happiness, and binding to wisdom (*tatra sattvaṃ nirmalatvātprakāśakamanāmayam* | *sukhasaṅgena badhnāti jñānasaṅgena cānagha* || *14-6*||).

रजो रागात्मकं विद्धि तृष्णासङ्गसमुद्भवम् ।
तन्निबध्नाति कौन्तेय कर्मसङ्गेन देहिनम् ॥ १४-७॥
तमस्त्वज्ञानजं विद्धि मोहनं सर्वदेहिनाम् ।
प्रमादालस्यनिद्राभिस्तन्निबध्नाति भारत ॥ १४-८॥

(7-8) Cognize *rajas* to be the nature of passion, the source of attachment, which binds the embodied to action (*rajo rāgātmakaṃ viddhi tṛṣṇāsaṅgasamudbhavam* | *tannibadhnāti kaunteya karmasaṅgena dehinam* || *14-7*||). But cognize *tamas* to be born out of ignorance, with stronghold of being confused when dealing with others, negligent, lazy, and somnolent (*tamastvajñānajaṃ viddhi mohanaṃ sarvadehinām* | *pramādālasyanidrābhistannibadhnāti bhārata* || *14-8*||).

सत्त्वं सुखे सञ्जयति रजः कर्मणि भारत ।

ज्ञानमावृत्य तु तमः प्रमादे सञ्जयत्युत ॥ १४-९॥

रजस्तमश्चाभिभूय सत्त्वं भवति भारत ।

रजः सत्त्वं तमश्चैव तमः सत्त्वं रजस्तथा ॥ १४-१०॥

(9-10) *Sattva* attaches one to happiness, *rajas* to action by truly shrouding wisdom, but *tamas* attaches one to heedlessness *(sattvam sukhe sañjayati rajaḥ karmaṇi bhārata | jñānamāvṛtya tu tamaḥ pramāde sañjayatyuta || 14-9||)*. Overpowering *rajas* and *tamas, sattva* rises; similarly *rajas* rises over *sattva* and *tamas;* and *tamas* over *rajas* and *sattva (rajastamaścābhibhūya sattvam bhavati bhārata | rajaḥ sattvam tamaścaiva tamaḥ sattvam rajastathā || 14-10||)*.

सर्वद्वारेषु देहेऽस्मिन्प्रकाश उपजायते ।

ज्ञानं यदा तदा विद्याद्विवृद्धं सत्त्वमित्युत ॥ १४-११॥

लोभः प्रवृत्तिरारम्भः कर्मणामशमः स्पृहा ।

रजस्येतानि जायन्ते विवृद्धे भरतर्षभ ॥ १४-१२॥

(11-12) When every sensory aperture in the body shines with the light of wisdom then this wisdom is predominantly *sattva* indeed *(sarvadvāreṣu dehe'sminprakāśa upajāyate | jñānaṃ yadā tadā vidyādvivṛddhaṃ sattvamityuta || 14-11||)*. When greed, restlessness and longing predominate in any undertaking of action, these arise from *rajas (lobhaḥ pravṛttirārambhaḥ karmaṇāmaśamaḥ spṛhā | rajasyetāni jāyante vivṛddhe bharatarṣabha || 14-12||)*.

अप्रकाशोऽप्रवृत्तिश्च प्रमादो मोह एव च ।

तमस्येतानि जायन्ते विवृद्धे कुरुनन्दन ॥ १४-१३॥

यदा सत्त्वे प्रवृद्धे तु प्रलयं याति देहभृत् ।

तदोत्तमविदां लोकानमलान्प्रतिपद्यते ॥ १४-१४॥

(13-14) No clarity, inertness, and heedlessness, even delusion, these arise when *tamas* becomes prominent *(aprakāśo 'pravṛttiśca pramādo moha eva ca | tamasyetāni jāyante vivṛddhe kurunandana || 14-13||)*. In fact, if *sattva* becomes prominent at time of dissolution, the spotless embodied then attains the highest world *(yadā sattve pravṛddhe tu pralayaṃ yāti dehabhṛt | tadottamavidāṃ lokānamalānpratipadyate || 14-14||)*.

रजसि प्रलयं गत्वा कर्मसङ्गिषु जायते ।

तथा प्रलीनस्तमसि मूढयोनिषु जायते ॥ १४-१५॥

कर्मणः सुकृतस्याहुः सात्त्विकं निर्मलं फलम् ।

रजसस्तु फलं दुःखमज्ञानं तमसः फलम् ॥ १४-१६॥

(15-16) At dissolution in *rajas,* the person is born among those attached to action, those dying in *tamas* are born in the womb of the deluded *(rajasi pralayaṃ gatvā karmasaṅgiṣu jāyate ı tathā pralīnastamasi mūḍhayoniṣu jāyate ıı 14-15ıı).* The outcome of *sāttvika* action is pure, the fruit of *rājasika* action is pain, and ignorance is the fruit of *tāmasika* action *(karmaṇaḥ sukṛtasyāhuḥ sāttvikaṃ nirmalaṃ phalam ı rajasastu phalaṃ duḥkhamajñānaṃ tamasaḥ phalam ıı 14-16ıı).*

सत्त्वात्सञ्जायते ज्ञानं रजसो लोभ एव च ।

प्रमादमोहौ तमसो भवतोऽज्ञानमेव च ॥ १४-१७॥

ऊर्ध्वं गच्छन्ति सत्त्वस्था मध्ये तिष्ठन्ति राजसाः ।

जघन्यगुणवृत्तिस्था अधो गच्छन्ति तामसाः ॥ १४-१८॥

(17-18) From *sattva* rises wisdom, from *rajas* it's surely greed, heedlessness, and delusion rise from *tamas* and also gives rise to ignorance *(sattvātsañjāyate jñānaṃ rajaso lobha eva ca ı pramādamohau tamaso bhavato'jñānameva ca ıı 14-17ıı).* Upward go those seated in *sattva,* those of *rajas* remain in the middle, those abiding in the lowest of attributes which is *tamas,* go downward *(ūrdhvaṃ gacchanti sattvasthā madhye tiṣṭhanti rājasāḥ ı jaghanyaguṇavṛttisthā adho gacchanti tāmasāḥ ıı 14-18ıı).*

नान्यं गुणेभ्यः कर्तारं यदा द्रष्टानुपश्यति ।

गुणेभ्यश्च परं वेत्ति मद्भावं सोऽधिगच्छति ॥ १४-१९॥

गुणानेतानतीत्य त्रीन्देही देहसमुद्भवान् ।

जन्ममृत्युजरादुःखैर्विमुक्तोऽमृतमश्नुते ॥ १४-२०॥

(19-20) When the seer beholds no agent higher than the attributes, and goes beyond the qualities of the attributes, he attains my state *(nānyaṃ guṇebhyaḥ kartāraṃ yadā drastānupaśyati ı guṇebhyaśca paraṃ vetti madbhāvaṃ so'dhigacchati ıı 14-19ıı).* The embodied that has transcended the three attributes out of which the body is evolved is freed from birth, death, ageing and pain, and attains immortality *(guṇānetānatītya trīndehī dehasamudbhavān ı janmamṛtyujarāduḥkhairvimukto'mṛtamaśnute ıı 14-20ıı).*

अर्जुन उवाच ।

कैर्लिङ्गैस्त्रीन्गुणानेतानतीतो भवति प्रभो ।

किमाचारः कथं चैतांस्त्रीन्गुणानतिवर्तते ॥ १४-२१॥

Arjuna asked (21) what are the indicators of one who has transcended these three attributes? What is the conduct, and how can one go beyond the three attributes *(kairliṅgaistriṅguṇānetānatīto bhavati prabho ı kimācāraḥ kathaṃ caitaṃstriṅguṇānativartate ıı 14-21ıı).*

श्रीभगवानुवाच -

प्रकाशं च प्रवृत्तिं च मोहमेव च पाण्डव ।

न द्वेष्टि सम्प्रवृत्तानि न निवृत्तानि काङ्क्षति ॥ १४-२२॥

उदासीनवदासीनो गुणैर्यो न विचाल्यते ।

गुणा वर्तन्त इत्येवं योऽवतिष्ठति नेङ्गते ॥ १४-२३॥

Śrī Kṛṣṇa replied (22-23) He neither hates nor longs for light or activity or even delusion. He does not dislike it when it is available or long for it when it is absent *(prakāśaṃ ca pravṛttiṃ ca mohameva ca pāṇḍava ǀ na dveṣṭi sampravṛttāni na nivṛttāni kāṅkṣati ǁ 14-22ǁ)*. Sitting indifferent among attributes, who operates unmoved by attributes, who is centered within and not shaky *(udāsīnavadāsīno guṇairyo na vicālyate ǀ guṇā vartanta ityevam yo 'vatiṣṭhati neṅgate ǁ 14-23ǁ)*.

समदुःखसुखः स्वस्थः समलोष्टाश्मकाञ्चनः ।

तुल्यप्रियाप्रियो धीरस्तुल्यनिन्दात्मसंस्तुतिः ॥ १४-२४॥

मानापमानयोस्तुल्यस्तुल्यो मित्रारिपक्षयोः ।

सर्वारम्भपरित्यागी गुणातीतः स उच्यते ॥ १४-२५॥

(24-25) Alike in pain and pleasure, secured in the Self, regarding mud, stone, and gold alike, balanced with liked and disliked, steadily balanced Self in censure and praise *(samaduḥkhasukhaḥ svasthaḥ samaloṣṭāśmakāñcanaḥ ǀ tulyapriyāpriyo dhīrastulyanindātmasaṃstutiḥ ǁ 14-24ǁ)*. Balanced in honor and dishonor, balanced with friend and foe, abandoning motivation of starting anything, such a person is said to have transcended attributes *(mānāpamānayostulyastulyo mitrāripakṣayoḥ ǀ sarvārambhaparityāgī guṇātītaḥ sa ucyate ǁ 14-25ǁ)*.

मां च योऽव्यभिचारेण भक्तियोगेन सेवते ।

स गुणान्समतीत्यैतान्ब्रह्मभूयाय कल्पते ॥ १४-२६॥

ब्रह्मणो हि प्रतिष्ठाहममृतस्याव्ययस्य च ।

शाश्वतस्य च धर्मस्य सुखस्यैकान्तिकस्य च ॥ १४-२७॥

(26-27) He that unswervingly practices yoga of dedication and serves me, he crosses beyond the attributes and becomes fit to become *Brahman (māṃ ca yo 'vyabhicāreṇa bhaktiyogena sevate ǀ sa guṇānsamatītyaitānbrahmabhūyāya kalpate ǁ 14-26ǁ)*. Indeed, *Brahman* is the abode, I exist in immortal, immutable, and everlasting natural state of absolute bliss *(brahmaṇo hi pratiṣṭhāhamamṛtasyāvyayasya ca ǀ śāśvatasya ca dharmasya sukhasyaikāntikasya ca ǁ 14-27ǁ)*.

◆———•◆◆•◆——◆

Chapter 15

Puruṣottama yoga
(yoga of the supreme *puruṣa* or supreme Self) [1]

Introduction

- In chapters 13, Śrī Kṛṣṇa speaks about the body being a field and understanding the field as *kṣetrajña*. However, it is evident that the *kṣetra* and *kṣetrajña* concepts have wider application than the body and that the conceptual underpinning is the same for all creation.

- In chapter 14, he takes this concept into personal development, speaking about how attributes *(guṇa)* drive behavior.

- In chapter 15, he speaks about how a person of excellence *(puruṣottama)* should live, using himself as a role model.

- Excellence has always fascinated us, and today's progress is a result adherence to perfection and excellence. But what is it? How does science view it, and is there any correlation between today's understanding of excellence and the way ancient culture of Bhārat encouraged it?

- This chapter looks at some of management and manufacturing science's accepted theories and compares it to that which was practiced in Bhārat, the results are quite astonishing.

Śrī Kṛṣṇa explains *aśvattha* (fig tree) - the tree of life [2]:

If one were to compare with the indestructible *aśvattha* tree with its roots above and branches below, the metering hymns are the leaves and one who knows the Vedas

---

[1]https://www.bhagavad-gita.org/Gita/chapter-15.html
[2]https://en.wikipedia.org/wiki/Ficus_religiosa

comprehends this. Also, below and above are its branches, nourished by the *guṇa-s;* sense-objects are its buds rooted in action and stretching its branches in the world of humans.

Thus, this fig tree *(aśvattha)* has no beginning, middle, or end and needs to be cut with the axe of non-attachment. This goal should be sought, for reaching this condition, one merges with the Supreme Self.

Competency requirement for reaching this state:

- Such people are free from pride and delusion, victorious over attachment, constant in the Supreme Self, passion under control, freed from opposites, such as peace or pain.

- A part of me (Śrī Kṛṣṇa) is embedded in the world of beings as a being driving the six senses which abide in *prakṛti,* enabling the person to be sentient.

- When the person dies, he leaves the body but this part of me (Śrī Kṛṣṇa) stays with the soul and moves to another body.

- The departure of the soul cannot be seen if one is mired in the activities of the *guṇa,* but if a person is able to transcend this, then one can see the soul depart.

- To reach this stage, one should strive, endured by yoga to cognize the Supreme Identity *(puruṣa)* within the soul. It is this Identity which drives motivation to relate to the world.

  I am the light in the Sun, Moon, and the fire. Also, I am the *vaiśvānara-agni* (the warmth of the body), residing in *prāṇa* and *āpaṇa* where I digest food.

- Finally, I am memory, knowledge of the identity, and lack of it; the author of Vedanta and the knower of the Vedas.

- There are two *puruṣa-s* – those that perish and those that are imperishable. All creation is perishable, the Supreme Identity *(kūṭastha)* is imperishable and it supports everything. Since, I transcend the perishable as well as the imperishable, I am called *puruṣottama.*

- Know this, that when a man becomes enlightened, all his duties are accomplished.

How does cognition function?

- *Brahman* experiences existential crisis and a desire to express/project itself *(icchā-śakti* or strength of desire).

- Effort to manifest requires sacrifice to overcome inhibition or fear of loss of Identity *(adhiyajña* or primordial sacrifice).

- From this sacrifice arises *puruṣa* (primordial Soul, experiencer, or identity) and *prakṛti* (primordial manifestation) of *puruṣa.*

- *Prakṛti* manifests as attributes *(guṇa).*

- The motility interface between *puruṣa* and *prakṛti* is *prāṇa* (primordial motility).

- The unit of the weave of *prakṛti* and *puruṣa* is the Soul *(ātmā).*

- *Citta* (consciousness) emerges from *puruṣa* and becomes the medium of transmitting the expression of the Soul *(ātmā),* which is seen by all as *asmitā* (self-esteem or self-worth).

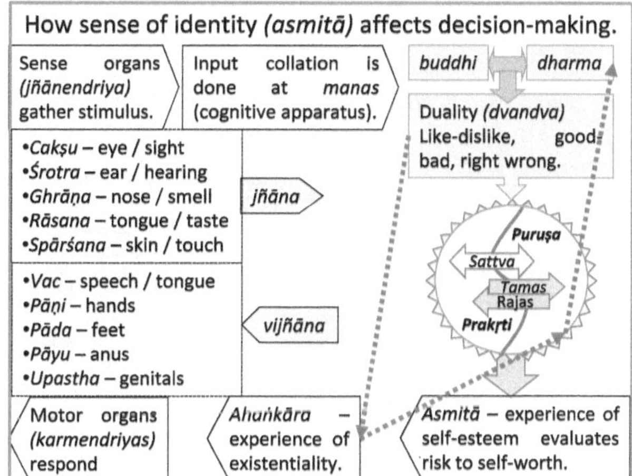

15.1 - How cognition works

- Impressions carried by the consciousness *(citta)* enter through the senses *(indriyas).* First, they go to the center of cognition *(manas)* for collation of stimulus. Then, the collated information is carried by the consciousness *(citta)* to the centers of logic *(buddhi).* Here, the incoming stimulus is compared with conditioning *(dharma)* and a response is formulated. Since conditioning *(dharma)* is the foundation of self-worth *(asmitā),* the response is called *ahaṅkāra* (I am the doer).

- If there is congruence between the incoming stimulus and *dharma, asmitā* (self-worth) pulls the entity towards itself because it wants continued engagement. If there is dissonance, *asmitā* pushes the object away to avoid discomfort. Consequently, there is a transaction which results in give or take which is called action *(karma)* [3].

- Since all give-take transactions are always unequal, there is an imbalance between giver and taker.

- This imbalance creates debt *(ṛṇa)* which must be repaid, even if it means taking another birth *(janma).*

- The ensuing cycle of birth and death is called *saṃsāra.*

- Lastly, the objective of life is to break this cycle of birth and death *(saṃsāra)* and merge with the *Brahman.*

Puruṣottama

Puruṣottama is a compound word of *puruṣa* (experiencer or identity) + *uttama* (supreme). This word can be rearranged as *uttama-puruṣa* or a person who has complete control of the experience or response to stimuli in any situation. This means that the person has an awareness that does not change under any circumstances. Consequently, this person can be called a *"sthitaprajñā"* or a person with steady situational awareness as described in *Śrīmad-bhagavad-gītā* Chapter 2 *(śaṅkha-yoga)* [4].

What are the qualities of such a person?

- We know that *puruṣa* (primordial Self or experiencer) weaves with *prakṛti* which manifests as *guṇa* (attribute).

- There are two types of *puruṣa-s,* one that perishes and one that is imperishable. The imperishable *puruṣa* is Śrī Kṛṣṇa and the role model. All creation is perishable *puruṣa* that needs to be optimized and brought to a state of congruence that is close to that of Śrī Kṛṣṇa.

Sthithaprajñā –the 4 stage evolution to perfection

Jāgrat – awakened or living state.	*Svapna –* dream, imagination, or play back state.	*Suṣupti –* all become equal *(samasti),* we transcend form.	*Turīya –* where we transcend *guṇa* (attributes)

Combination of state of awareness (the first one is the dominant state)

Jāgrat – Jāgrat	Svapna – Jāgrat	Suṣupti – Jāgrat	Turīya – Jāgrat
Jāgrat – Svapna	Svapna – Svapna	Suṣupti – Svapna	Turīya – Svapna
Jāgrat – Suṣupti	Svapna – Suṣupti	Suṣupti – Suṣupti	Turīya – Suṣupti
Jāgrat – Turīya	Svapna – Turīya	Suṣupti – Turīya	Turīya – Turīya

15.2 - The stages in awareness

- This means that when *prakṛti* is in a *nirguṇa* state *(nir =* without + *guṇa =* attributes), *puruṣa* will not experience anything. But, is that the only way?

- We know that when *puruṣa* projects its consciousness *(citta)* into the environment for confirmation of existence. So, when consciousness *(citta)* is not allowed to project itself, *puruṣa* remains steady is its own awareness.

- This can also happen, if *puruṣa* engages and acts without any attachment to the outcome. When this happens, there is no feedback, hence *puruṣa* has no experience.

Concept of individuality *(sva-tantra)* over the ages:

Until now, mankind has always enquired into the meaning of existence. This has mainly taken the form of trying to understand the Universe and a hierarchy for

---

[3] https://schoolofyoga.in/yoga-concept/action-karma
[4] https://schoolofyoga.in/yoga-social-system/bhagawat-geeta-chapter-2

everything that exists within the Self *(kṣetrajña)*. This enquiry can be broadly split into Western thought, which is based on Greek logic as well as Abrahamic thought, and Oriental thought, which has two major branches, Bhārat's philosophy of Sanatana-dharma, Buddhism, Jainism and Sikhism, along with the Chinese philosophy of Tao and Confucianism and Japanese Shinto. There are other schools of thought, but most of today's peoples are covered by the above schools.

An important difference between the two streams of thought is that while the base of Western thought has been molded heavily by shifting power and conquests, the fundamentals of Oriental thought have largely remained unaffected by conquest and remained unchanged over the centuries with some modification dictated by societal development.

Though *Śrīmad-bhagavad-gītā* is very lucid in its explanation of concept and clarity of personal goals, it is a high-level document and not an easy starter kit! So, some DIY (do it yourself) solutions are required while the person works out the larger goals espoused by Śrī Kṛṣṇa.

So, it seems appropriate that one seeks an intermediate solution which can act as springboard to higher development. One place that one could search is the developments that became popular post World War 2 because the current world is largely shaped by that period and all of us subscribe to it, directly or indirectly.

Some convergence of concepts:

Ivan Pavlov (1849-1936)[5] - The journey into conditioning *(dharma)* is incomplete without Pavlov and his work on classical conditioning and reflex. Almost all conclusions of Pavlov reinforce the *sanātana-dharma* hypothesis that conditioning *(dharma)* determines personality *(svabhāva)*.

However, *dharma* takes the concept further in two areas,

- *Dharma* says that all creation, sentient *(jīva)* or insentient *(jadam)*, have a natural state and

- The natural state of an individual entity is *svadharma* and this translates to conditioning.

Sigmund Freud (1856-1939)[6] – Freud is often considered the father of psychoanalysis, using concepts such as free-association, transference, sexuality, and id-ego-super ego, etc., in the framework of psychoanalysis. The interesting aspect of psychoanalysis is its congruence with ancient *yoga-vidyā*.

---

[5]https://www.verywellmind.com/ivan-pavlov-biography-1849-1936-2795548
[6]https://iep.utm.edu/freud/

- Id is considered to be the desire that drives behavior and in control of the person. In *yoga-vidyā*, these impulses are called *vāsanā-s* which are indelible-impressions arising from unpaid debts *(prārabdha-karma)*. So, even when people seem to be acting out of control, they are actually driven by unpaid debts. Consequently, the control of the individual is nominal and ends when the debt is reconciled.

- The super-ego is considered to be the moral and critical side of the individual that acts like a counterbalance to the Id. In *yoga-vidyā,* this is *dharma* (conditioning). *Dharma* is also considered to be a product of debt that has come up for resolution *(prārabdha-karma)* and determines where a person is born as well as how he or she will be conditioned. Our incomplete and unfulfilled desires *(vāsanā-s)* are constantly struggling with our conditioning *(dharma).*

- The ego is the one that plays mediator between Id and Super-ego to moderate behavior. In *yoga-vidyā,* this is called *asmitā* (I am this or self-worth). While in psychoanalytic theory the ego is a completely internal function, in *yoga-vidyā*, the self-worth *(asmitā)* is entirely dependent on feedback that the Self receives to its manifestation as well as stimulus through the consciousness *(citta)* which carries the impression of the situation through the senses *(indriyas)* to the cognitive apparatus *(manas),* after which intellect *(buddhi)* compares the information with conditioning/super-ego *(dharma).* However, in some situations, even self-worth *(asmitā)* gets hijacked by unfulfilled desires *(vāsanā-s),* this is the power of unfulfilled impressions of unresolved debts *(prārabdha-karma).*

- Also, while in psychoanalysis free will is considered available to the individual, in *yoga-vidyā*, this is considered a product of awareness *(prajñā)* and increases only with sacrifice *(yajña).*

Abraham Maslow (1908-1970)[7] – in 1943, Abraham Maslow published his paper "Theory of Human Motivation" where he postulated that humans have a hierarchy with which they approach any need. He said that there are five stages of Motivation. It is a hierarchy because a person will need to be complete in one need to be able to go to the next need. The hierarchy is,

- o Physiological – food, safety, rest, and shelter,

- o Safety – the feeling of not being threatened,

- o Social needs – relationships and social validation,

- o Esteem Needs – need for accomplishment and prestige,

- o Self-actualization – the ability to achieve complete potential.

---

[7]https://www.verywellmind.com/biography-of-abraham-maslow-1908-1970-2795524

Interestingly, it is possible to correlate the psychological state as propounded by Abraham Maslow in his 1943 paper "Theory of Motivation" with motility vortices *(cakra)* in *yoga-vidyā*. It is known in *yoga-vidyā* and other forms of Oriental healing that rate of energy flow through these centers affects the behavior of the person. As a matter of

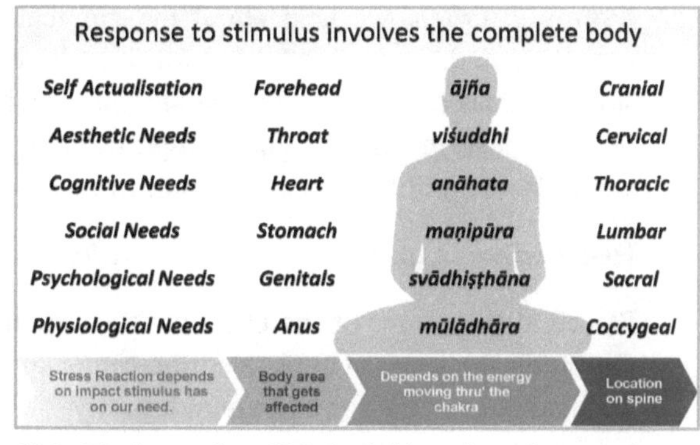

15.3 - The integration of Maslow's hierarchy and *yoga-vidyā*

fact, ancient Oriental texts on this subject from India, China, Korea, and Japan speak of multiple motility vortices *(cakra)* [8], but all agree that there are six major vortice locations in the human body which control all major organs.

- **Base *cakra (mūladhāra)* - (*mūla* = base + *ādhāra* = foundation or source)**
  The first of the motility vortices aligns itself with the perineum, a flat region above the coccyx and between the anus and genitals. This center affects the physiological aspects of the individual, that is, the overall energy levels, feeling of safety and health.

  Example: People in difficult situations squirm in their seats. When fears for personal safety overwhelm us, there is acute discomfort at the region of the anus. There is an urge to shift in the seat, and the need to relieve ourselves when fear is very great. The rocking action energizes the *mūladhāra-cakra*.

- **Self-evolution *cakra (svādhiṣṭhāna)* - (*sva* = self + *adhiṣṭhāna* = evolved place)**

  This motility vortex corresponds to the sacral region around the genital area. It affects sexuality, social, and communications skills of the individual. Control of this center results in strong response control and emotional stability.

  Example: After a heated argument, often there is an ache in the lower back. This occurs on account of our need to communicate effectively and to be able to convince the other person about our point of view and reinforce our sense of self-worth *(asmitā)*. This strains the lumbar arch and often results in stress.

- **Stomach *cakra (maṇipūra)* - (*maṇipūra* = navel)**

  This motility vortex is placed around the navel and corresponds to the lumbar area of the spine. This is a center that controls situational and management skills.

---

[8]https://www.yogapedia.com/definition/4964/chakra

Example: Often, we hear about the gut feel or taking a decision from the gut! How is that possible? After all, it is the brain that decides. Or is it? The stomach does have a role, for the *maṇipūra,* with its acids and bile, is affected by blood flow in case of fight or flight stimulus. Consequently, this impacts the *maṇipūra*'s motility vortex and comfort in a social environment.

- **Heart *cakra (anāhata)* - *(ana* = not + *ahat* = touched)**

Placed at the center of the chest at the sternum, this responds to the thoracic region on the spine. This is also the center of emotional balance. A balanced *anāhata* is essential for emotional stability.

Example: Blood pressure is directly related to anger and speech. Generally, doctors advise a person to reduce speaking after a heart attack. Why? Because when a person gets excited, the release of adrenaline has a direct impact on the heart and lungs.

- **Throat *cakra (viśuddha)* - *(viśuddha* = extraordinarily pure)**

This motility vortex is placed around the Adam's apple and corresponds to the cervical region in the spine. The thyroid, parathyroid, and lymphatic systems, which control metabolic activity reside here. Since metabolism is the ability of the body to convert food into usable energy and rebuilding of tissue, seamless motility flow here is critical.

This is also the area which controls breathing and food intake, so any disruption in our stress levels will immediately impact the quality of our breathing and digestion.

Example: When we are afraid, we often feel choked! Why? Because the *prāṇa* flow at the *viśuddha* gets congested. The chocking action impacts the thyroid & parathyroid. Consequently, disruption of this center can lead to various illnesses.

- **Forehead *cakra (ājñā)* - *(ājñā* = that which commands)**

This motility vortex is placed between the eyebrows in the front of the cranium. It controls the functioning of the other motility vortices. It energizes the amygdala, pituitary, hypothalamus, and endocrine/adrenaline glands etc., and controls both primary and secondary response. Consequently, this motility vortex is the primary input center for "fight or flight" stimulus.

One can see that the *cakra* system of *yoga-vidyā* is highly evolved and can be used in therapy. Another important aspect is that *yoga-vidyā* recognizes that each of these vortices may be activated, depleted, or congested to varying degrees and that this is an actively changing parameter. This makes the *yoga-vidyā* system personal, subtle and sophisticated.

The only problem is that this system is not completely understood and its subtlety makes it hard to quantify or systematize. However, at an individual level, it is possible for a practitioner to intuit this cognitive-science.

Hans Seyle (1907-1982)[9] - Hans Seyle, an endocrinologist, propounded the theory of stress where he described stress as "the non-specific response of the body to any demand made upon it". He postulated that when there is stimulus which moves the person away

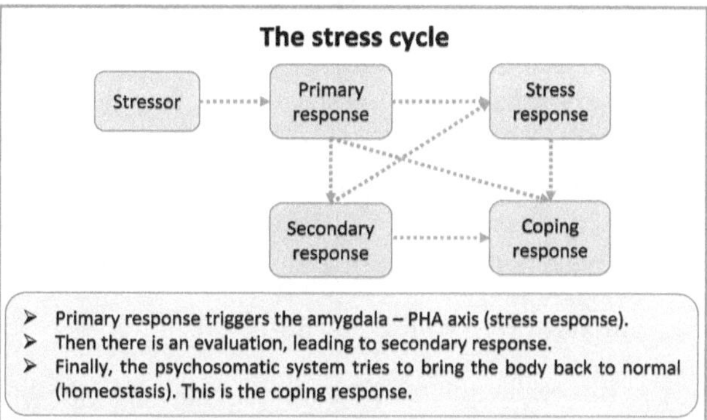

15.4 - How we respond to stimulus

from homeostasis (natural state of peace/order/harmony or *dharma)*, the PTA axis (pituitary-hypothalamus-adrenal axis) is activated depending on the impact to the person's self-worth *(asmitā)*. As a result, the person experiences eustress/motivation *(rāga)* or distress/misery *(dveṣa)* and this triggers an internal as well as external (fight or flight) response *(karma)*.

It is clear that there are many theories which are evolving in modern scientific space and that many of these "discoveries" are reinforcing concepts already embedded in *sanātana-dharma* and Yoga.

Can we use concepts from modern science and engineering for self-improvement and development?

It might sound silly, but some of the best personality development concepts actually come from TQM (Total Quality Management) and Manufacturing Engineering principles. These principles are generic and full of common sense, so they can be adapted by us for personal development to become *puruṣottama* (people of high caliber).

We can define a perfect person *(puruṣottama)* as one who can solve problems, find solutions, and generate minimum waste. So, what steps would a typical problem-solving technique have?

- Identification of the problem and its root cause

- Implementing a solution and

- Ensure minimum waste/minimum utilization of resource.

---

[9] https://www.ncbi.nlm.nih.gov/pmc/articles/PMC5915631

Identification of the problem and its root cause:

Two interesting root cause identification techniques can be used in daily life also.

- **The first is called "5-Why technique" where a person asks himself "Why is there a problem?" five times** [10]

  For example - If you missed a flight, then the first question would be - Why did I miss the flight. Let us say, the answer is - I got up late. The second question would be - Why did I get up late? The answer might be - I slept late. The third question would be - Why did I sleep late... and this question-answer will continue until a root cause and solution is identified.

- **The second technique is "Is-Is not"** [11]:

  In this technique the practitioner looks at both, that which is occurring as well as that which is not occurring. So, a matrix of what is working and what is not working gets constructed. This leads the person to identifying the root cause.

  Example 1 - Start by asking, what is the problem? Say, water is not draining from the kitchen sink. Is there obstruction? There is no debris in the sink. There is accumulated waste in the line.

  Example 2 - Project getting delayed! Is - people are submitting reports late. Is not - project resources not available. Then ask - Is there review? Review is done every month. Review is not adequate. So, change review frequency.

  Both practices have their uses in various situations and increase situational awareness *(prajñā)*.

Finding a solution:

Once the root cause is identified, we need to find ways to improve and this means change! Since, change is not easy, the best path of change seems to be gradual and systematic effort *(abhyāsa)*. Let us look at some of the concepts that come out of manufacturing.

1- Kaizen [12] - Kai means change and Zen means good, so Kaizen means continuous improvement. While, this concept was designed primarily for manufacturing, it is applicable for personal development also because it allows people to change in a planned and structured manner that ensures risk to self-worth *(asmitā)* is minimized.

Since Kaizen focuses on continuous improvement in an iterative manner, it becomes a useful tool in *puruṣottama-yoga,* because yoga is all about increasing situational awareness *(sthitaprajñā),* and this effort requires constant application on oneself.

---

[10] https://kanbanize.com/lean-management/improvement/5-whys-analysis-tool
[11] https://sigmamagic.com/help/SM16/Is%20-%20Is%20Not/index.php
[12] https://kaizen.com/what-is-kaizen

Kaizen is based on three major pillars:

- **Gemba (situation)** – The starting point is self-empowerment, which means that the responsibility for building a solution that fits you belongs to you. So, taking cues from what Śrī Kṛṣṇa says in *Śrīmad-bhagavad-gītā* on free will.

  o Each is his own friend or enemy. Take responsibility for your actions.

  o It is important to have a vision of where one is going *(satya),* otherwise the journey cannot be planned.

  o Stop worrying about the outcome *(karma-phala),* perform the action as a sacrifice *(yajña).*

  o Keep an attitude of discrimination *(viveka)* and dispassion *(vairāgya)* so that the activity is constantly kept in focus *(ekāgratā).*

  o Perform the action with complete dedication *(śraddhā).*

  o Be balanced in success and failure (avoid duality of like-dislike, good-bad etc.).

- **Organize your life with 5S** [13] – 5S has been used as a critical tool to organize the workplace. However, it is incredibly useful as a personal development tool and consists of (Japanese word has been placed first):

  o **Seiri (Sort)** – discriminate that which adds value from that which is extraneous from the incoming information and discard that which does not add value *(viveka).*

  o **Seiton (Organize logically)** – a place for everything and everything in its place. Once you align your information logically, retrieval becomes easy and one expends less energy in searching. This is somewhat like defragging your hard-disk, only it is an individual's personal defrag!

  o **Seiso (Clean)** – in *yoga-vidyā,* this is called *śauca* or cleanliness. While 5S focuses primarily on cleanliness of the workplace, *śauca* has two components - *antara-śauca* (internal cleanliness) and *bāhira-śauca* (external cleanliness). Clean your cognitive *(manas)* and logical *(buddhi)* apparatus continuously. Dump baggage. This ensures that sentimentality *(bhāva)* is separated from rationality *(vairāgya).*

  o **Seiketsu (Perfect it)** – practice it *(abhyāsa).* Make it a habit, a part of yourself.

---

[13]https://www.creativesafetysupply.com/content/education-research/5S/index.html#:~:text=The%20
5S%20system%20of%20visual%20management%20has%20improved%20organization%20
and,good%20condition%20a%20visual%20process.

- o **Shitsuke (Self-discipline)** – ensure that you do not veer from what you have started unless you address the gap areas. When you do identify a drop in your standard, rectify yourself. This will increase situational awareness *(prajñā)* and free will. As Michelangelo is reputed to have said – trifles make perfection and perfection is no trifle.

- **Change** – how can we change? this is by building success daily, with each effort *(karma)*. Change principle calls for Plan/Do/Check/Act - this means;

  - o plan how you wish to change,

  - o institute change,

  - o check the outcome and reaction, and

  - o recalibrate your actions to suit the situation and your vision.

2- Quality Circles *(satsaṅga)* [14] – Quality Circles or Cross-functional teams (CFT) are teams that comprise specialists and generalists who discuss a subject by bringing their unique experience and perspective. This develops everyone's awareness *(prajñā)* since everyone is discussing the same subject with a specific objective *(ekāgratā)*. So, when we are in the company of like-minded people, there is sharing of ideas, concepts, encouragement, and maybe even resources and kaizen (systematic improvement).

For example, if one has an interest in aeromodelling, then ideally, one should join an aeromodelling club. Since people who come there have similar interests and have varying levels of expertise, experience, interest, and capability, one will find opportunities to increase knowledge, capability, skills, find resources and occasions to practice, thus perfect the craft and become a *puruṣottama*.

Similarly, in *bhajagovindam* - 9, Śrī Ādi Śaṅkara says [15]:

सत्सङ्गत्वे निस्सङ्गत्वं निसङ्गत्वे निर्मोहत्वम् ।
निर्मोहत्वे निश्चलतत्वं निश्चलतत्वे जीवन्मुक्तिः ॥ ९॥

satsaṅgatve nissaṅgatvaṃ nisaṅgatve nirmohatvam ।
nirmohatve niścalatatvaṃ niścalatatve jīvanmuktiḥ ॥ *9*॥

Through the company of the wise or the good, there arises non-attachment; from non-attachment comes freedom from delusion; where there is freedom from delusion, there is abidance in self-knowledge, which leads to freedom while alive.

---

[14]https://www.businessmanagementideas.com/management/quality-circles/quality-circles-q-c-meaning-objectives-and-benefits/6302
[15]https://ahambrahmasmi4.wordpress.com/2016/09/21/bhajagovindamverse9/#:~:text=Satsangatve%20nissangatvam%20%E2%80%93%20The%20sanga%20or,as%20a%20little%20plant%20does.

What does this verse mean? To become a *puruṣottama* (perfect person) is not easy. One requires extreme dedication *(śraddhā)* and commitment to salvation *(mumukṣutvam)* but that does not come easily. So, when the practitioner joins a group of like-minded people where they discuss and motivate each other, slowly the person is able to overcome inertia and delusion *(tamas)* with group support and encouragement *(rajas)*, build capability, and strive for perfection.

Eliminating waste

This is a part of lean manufacturing, and the key aspect is to maximize outcome by ensuring minimum resources are used in the conversion.

- **Muda** – means identifying aspects that waste our resources (time is a resource) and eliminate it.

  For example – when we water a garden with a hose-pipe, if there is a kink in the pipe, if the pipe has holes in it, or if the water is not being directed properly, the water flow is not going to be effective for its designed purpose. Muda is identifying anything that does not add value and eliminating it.

- **Mura** – means removing unevenness and irregularity from activity.

  For example – if we were to run a restaurant, then obviously there would be peak and lean utilization periods. If the restaurant was over or under designed, then we would end up having more capacity or making customers wait, which results in a waste of time and resources on account of poor planning.

Is there any ancient indigenous Bhārat *(sanātana-dharma)* practice that uses the above concepts?

The ancient Bhārat lean manufacturing system is called queue *(paṅkti)* in Saṃskṛta, pangat in Hindi, and panthi in Tamil.

Introduction – *paṅktis* occur whenever there is a sacrifice *(yajña)*. All sacrifices have a fire because fire is a transforming agent. For instance, ore is converted to steel by fire, crude becomes diesel and petrol by application of fire. So, fire *(agni)* is used in a sacrifice *(yajña)* to transform intent to outcome *(saṅkalpa)*. Details of the sacrifice process *(yajña)* are given in *Śrīmad-bhagavad-gītā*, Chapter 16.

A queue *(paṅkti)* occurs at the end of a sacrifice *(yajña)* because any sacrifice requires offering *(naivedya)* which becomes an outcome of peace *(prasādam)*. This food is offered to all participants of the sacrifice *(yajña)* by the initiator of the *yajña (yajamāna)* in a set-up called queue *(paṅkti)*.

Paṅkti follows batch-process business rules in any setting where people congregate for a sit-down meal. In *yoga-vidyā*, food is considered central to awareness *(prajñā)* – "we are what we eat." This makes the *paṅkti* a very important set-up. Let us look at some of the parameters:

Quality Standards *(ācāra)* – The food must conform to the following standards.

- It must be served hot and fresh so that it is nutritious and there are no bacteria.

- It must bring awareness to all the senses (touch, smell, taste, sight, and be consumed in an environment that is peaceful).

- It must be tasty *(rasāya)* cover all the tastes (salt, sweet, sour, and astringent).

- It must be served in sufficient quantity but without wastage. Everyone who eats must depart satisfied *(karma)*. Positivity and contentment are considered a benediction *(āśīrvāda)*.

Optimization of effort and output *(yajña)* – This means that the chef of any *paṅkti* must cover the following factors;

- The chef must understand food, the customer *(yajamāna)* and his requirements.

- He must plan a menu that is healthy, nutritious, has no dishes that people may dislike because that will spoil the atmosphere in the entire eating hall, and be able to control a team.

- Since this is food which impacts health, and also the *yajamāna's karma*, the chef must ensure that his team is healthy and enters the kitchen or serving area only after a head-bath *(snānam)*. Also, should the team members go to the toilet, they must clean themselves thoroughly.

- The chef must have experts who know how to make certain dishes as well as generalists who can support any station.

- The chef must know how many people will eat in a sitting and ensure that at any time during the serving process no one has an empty plate. So, he must have serving people moving at the right time, serving the right dish (Just-in-time) in portion sizes that are appropriate.

- He must also ensure that wastage is minimized. Waste is considered *abhiśāpa* (curse) because the intended outcome has not been reached. Also, the sponsor's *(yajamāna)* resources have been wasted and natures' resources which should be put to constructive purpose have been vitiated, so some other entity that might have needed it will not get it. This leads to imbalance and chaos *(adharma)*.

- This calls for line-balancing, resource management, constraint/emergency management skills among other management capabilities, but yes, ancient Bhārat has a lean manufacturing philosophy and process which can be compared with modern manufacturing techniques.

Some contradictions to accepted positions:

Much of "discoveries" of today existed in the ancient oriental world, maybe under a different guise. Also, it is clear that *Bhārat's* ancient *ṛṣis* were wise and full of common sense because, in addition to cognizing the principles of effective-life science, they integrated it into the person, household, clan, society and Bhārat, thereby making *dharma* a harmonious, scalable, and sustainable philosophy.

Lessons learned in Chapter 15: There is a discernible degree of confluence between the concepts embedded in *yoga-vidyā* and management science. However, what is most important is that a person chooses those values from the many schools of thought that exist today *(sat)* that help in increasing awareness and help in becoming a perfect person *(puruṣottama)*.

The transliteration and translation of chapter 15 follows:

श्रीभगवानुवाच -

ऊर्ध्वमूलमधःशाखमश्वत्थं प्राहुरव्ययम् ।

छन्दांसि यस्य पर्णानि यस्तं वेद स वेदवित् ॥ १५-१॥

अधश्चोर्ध्वं प्रसृतास्तस्य शाखा

गुणप्रवृद्धा विषयप्रवालाः ।

अधश्च मूलान्यनुसन्ततानि

कर्मानुबन्धीनि मनुष्यलोके ॥ १५-२॥

Śrī Kṛṣṇa said (1-2) Rooted above, branches below, the fig tree, they say is indestructible. Its leaves are the Vedas and he that knows this knows the Vedas *(ūrdhvamūlamadhaḥśākhamaśvattham prāhuravyayam | chandāṃsi yasya parṇāni yastaṃ veda sa vedavit ॥ 15-1॥)*. Below and above spread its branches, nourished by attributes, objects are its new shoots, below and roots continue the binding of action in the world *(adhaścordhvaṃ prasṛtāstasya śākhā guṇapravṛddhā viṣayapravālāḥ | adhaśca mūlānyanusantatāni karmānubandhīni manuṣyaloke ॥ 15-2॥)*.

न रूपमस्येह तथोपलभ्यते

नान्तो न चादिर्न च सम्प्रतिष्ठा ।

अश्वत्थमेनं सुविरूढमूलं

असङ्गशस्त्रेण दृढेन छित्त्वा ॥ १५-३॥

ततः पदं तत्परिमार्गितव्यं

यस्मिन्गता न निवर्तन्ति भूयः ।

तमेव चाद्यं पुरुषं प्रपद्ये

यतः प्रवृत्तिः प्रसृता पुराणी ॥ १५-४॥

(3-4) This has no form as such, as such cannot be perceived, it has no end or origin, nor foundation. This *ashvattam* is cut by well-rooted people with the strong axe of non-attachment *(na rūpamasyeha tathopalabhyate nānto na cādirna ca sampratiṣṭhā | aśvatthamenaṃ suvirūḍhamūlam asaṅgaśastreṇa dṛḍhena chittvā || 15-3||).* Then the goal that should be sought to go forth and not return again is by seeking refuge in the ancient primordial *puruṣa* when performing activity *(tataḥ padaṃ tatparimārgitavyaṃ yasmingatā na nivartanti bhūyaḥ | tameva cādyaṃ puruṣaṃ prapadye yataḥ pravṛttiḥ prasṛtā purāṇī || 15-4||).*

निर्मानमोहा जितसङ्गदोषा

अध्यात्मनित्या विनिवृत्तकामाः ।

द्वन्द्वैर्विमुक्ताः सुखदुःखसंज्ञै-

गच्छन्त्यमूढाः पदमव्ययं तत् ॥ १५-५॥

न तद्भासयते सूर्यो न शशाङ्को न पावकः ।

यद्गत्वा न निवर्तन्ते तद्धाम परमं मम ॥ १५-६॥

(5-6) Free from pride and delusion, victorious over the affliction of attachment, dwelling constantly in the Self, turned away from passion and pairs of opposites, freed from what is known as pleasure and pain reach that undeluded eternal goal *(nirmānamohā jitasaṅgadoṣā adhyātmanityā vinivṛttakāmāḥ | dvandvairvimuktāḥ sukhaduḥkhasaṃjñai rgacchantyamūḍhāḥ padamavyayaṃ tat || 15-5||).* Sun does not illuminate it, nor does the Moon, nor fire. Once they reach, they do not return, that is my Supreme abode *(na tadbhāsayate sūryo na śaśāṅko na pāvakaḥ | yadgatvā na nivartante taddhāma paramaṃ mama || 15-6||).*

ममैवांशो जीवलोके जीवभूतः सनातनः ।

मनःषष्ठानीन्द्रियाणि प्रकृतिस्थानि कर्षति ॥ १५-७॥

शरीरं यदवाप्नोति यच्चाप्युत्क्रामतीश्वरः ।

गृहीत्वैतानि संयाति वायुर्गन्धानिवाशयात् ॥ १५-८॥

(7-8) Even my Eternal aspect that has become a material Soul and participates in this world with the sixth aspect of cognition and sensory apparatus due to the engagement with *prakṛti (mamaivāṃśo jīvaloke jīvabhūtaḥ sanātanaḥ | manaḥṣaṣṭhānīndriyāṇi prakṛtisthāni karṣati || 15-7||).* When *Īśvara* obtains or leaves a body, it takes these just as a wind takes scent from its source *(śarīraṃ yadavāpnoti yaccāpyutkrāmatīśvaraḥ | gṛhītvaitāni saṃyāti vāyurgandhānivāśayāt || 15-8||).*

श्रोत्रं चक्षुः स्पर्शनं च रसनं घ्राणमेव च ।

अधिष्ठाय मनश्चायं विषयानुपसेवते ॥ १५-९॥

उत्क्रामन्तं स्थितं वापि भुञ्जानं वा गुणान्वितम् ।

विमूढा नानुपश्यन्ति पश्यन्ति ज्ञानचक्षुषः ॥ १५-१०॥

(9-10) With ear, eye, touch, taste, and smell and even presiding over the cognition he experiences materiality *(śrotraṃ cakṣuḥ sparśanaṃ ca rasanaṃ ghrāṇameva ca ǀ adhiṣṭhāya manaścāyaṃ viṣayānupasevate ǁ 15-9ǁ)*. Whether leaving, staying, or also enjoying, everything is based on the attribute. However, those that are deluded do not cognize this, only those of wisdom cognize *(utkrāmantaṃ sthitaṃ vāpi bhuñjānaṃ vā guṇānvitam ǀ vimūḍhā nānupaśyanti paśyanti jñānacakṣuṣaḥ ǁ 15-10ǁ)*.

यतन्तो योगिनश्चैनं पश्यन्त्यात्मन्यवस्थितम् ।

यतन्तोऽप्यकृतात्मानो नैनं पश्यन्त्यचेतसः ॥ १५-११॥

यदादित्यगतं तेजो जगद्भासयतेऽखिलम् ।

यच्चन्द्रमसि यच्चाग्नौ तत्तेजो विद्धि मामकम् ॥ १५-१२॥

(11-12) Yogis who strive see this dwelling in the Self; however, immature Souls and those with low consciousness cannot cognize even with effort *(yatanto yoginaścainam paśyantyātmanyavasthitam ǀ yatanto'pyakṛtātmāno nainaṃ paśyantyacetasaḥ ǁ 15-11ǁ)*. That light residing in the Sun which illuminates the whole world, which is also there in the Moon and Fire, know that light to come from my state *(yadādityagataṃ tejo jagadbhāsayate'khilam ǀ yaccandramasi yaccāgnau tattejo viddhi māmakam ǁ 15-12ǁ)*.

गामाविश्य च भूतानि धारयाम्यहमोजसा ।

पुष्णामि चौषधीः सर्वाः सोमो भूत्वा रसात्मकः ॥ १५-१३॥

अहं वैश्वानरो भूत्वा प्राणिनां देहमाश्रितः ।

प्राणापानसमायुक्तः पचाम्यन्नं चतुर्विधम् ॥ १५-१४॥

(13-14) Permeating the Earth, I support all beings with my vitality and nourish all herbs by becoming the watery Moon *(gāmāviśya ca bhūtāni dhārayāmyahamojasā ǀ puṣṇāmi cauṣadhīḥ sarvāḥ somo bhūtvā rasātmakaḥ ǁ 15-13ǁ)*. Having become fire in the body I abide as *prāna* and *apāna* and digest the four kinds of food (sweet, salt, astringent, and sour) *(ahaṃ vaiśvānaro bhūtvā prāṇināṃ dehamāśritaḥ ǀ prāṇāpānasamāyuktaḥ pacāmyannaṃ caturvidham ǁ 15-14ǁ)*.

सर्वस्य चाहं हृदि सन्निविष्टो

मत्तः स्मृतिर्ज्ञानमपोहनञ्च ।

वेदैश्च सर्वैरहमेव वेद्यो

वेदान्तकृद्वेदविदेव चाहम् ॥ १५-१५॥

(15) And I am seated in the heart of all and from me comes memory and wisdom as well as their absence. And I am the wisdom of all the Vedas, even author of

Vedānta, and I am the knower of the Vedas *(sarvasya cāhaṃ hṛdi sanniviṣṭo mattaḥ smṛtirjñānamapohanañca ǀ vedaiśca sarvairahameva vedyo vedāntakṛdvedavideva cāham ǀǀ 15-15ǀǀ).*

द्वाविमौ पुरुषौ लोके क्षरश्चाक्षर एव च ।

क्षरः सर्वाणि भूतानि कूटस्थोऽक्षर उच्यते ॥ १५-१६॥

उत्तमः पुरुषस्त्वन्यः परमात्मेत्युदाहृतः ।

यो लोकत्रयमाविश्य बिभर्त्यव्यय ईश्वरः ॥ १५-१७॥

यस्मात्क्षरमतीतोऽहमक्षरादपि चोत्तमः ।

अतोऽस्मि लोके वेदे च प्रथितः पुरुषोत्तमः ॥ १५-१८॥

(16-18) There are two *puruṣa-s* in the world, the perishable and imperishable. All beings are perishable and the imperishable is called *kūṭastha* (supreme soul) *(dvāvimau puruṣau loke kṣaraścākṣara eva ca ǀ kṣaraḥ sarvāṇi bhūtāni kūṭastho'kṣara ucyate ǀǀ 15-16ǀǀ).* The supreme *puruṣa* is another name for supreme Soul, the indestructible, *Īśvara* who pervades and sustains the three worlds *(uttamaḥ puruṣastvanyaḥ paramātmetyudāhṛtaḥ ǀ yo lokatrayamāviśya bibhartyavyaya īśvaraḥ ǀǀ 15-17ǀǀ).* Since I transcend the perishable, am above the imperishable also and I am the highest, therefore in the world and the Vedas I am declared as the Supreme *puruṣa (yasmātkṣaramatīto'hamakṣarādapi cottamaḥ ǀ ato'smi loke vede ca prathitaḥ puruṣottamaḥ ǀǀ 15-18ǀǀ).*

यो मामेवमसम्मूढो जानाति पुरुषोत्तमम् ।

स सर्वविद्भजति मां सर्वभावेन भारत ॥ १५-१९॥

इति गुह्यतमं शास्त्रमिदमुक्तं मयानघ ।

एतद्बुद्ध्वा बुद्धिमान्स्यात्कृतकृत्यश्च भारत ॥ १५-२०॥

(19-20) He who is undeluded and knows me to be the Supreme Soul, he is completely wise and worships me with all sentiment *(yo māmevamasammūḍho jānāti puruṣottamam ǀ sa sarvavidbhajati māṃ sarvabhāvena bhārata ǀǀ 15-19ǀǀ).* Thus, this most secret scientific treatise has been taught by me and knowing this, the wise become accomplished in all activities *(iti guhyatamaṃ śāstramidamuktaṃ mayānagha ǀ etadbuddhvā buddhimānsyātkṛtakṛtyaśca bhārata ǀǀ 15-20ǀǀ).*

◆ —— · ◆ · —— ◆

Chapter 16

Daivāsura-samadvibhāga-yoga
(yoga of the difference between divine and demonical)[1]

Śrī Kṛṣṇa said that the divine *(daiva-guṇa)* traits are:

- Divinity is fearlessness, purity of heart, steadfast awareness of the Self and Yoga, being generous and keeping senses under control. It is also performing required sacrifices, studying scriptures, and being austere and straightforward.

- Also, such people avoid causing harm, are truthful, without anger, renunciate, peaceful, not crooked, and compassionate to all beings. They are not covetous. Contrarily, they are gentle, modest, and not fickle.

- Finally, they are filled with vigor *(tejas)*, are forgiving and with fortitude, clean, with enmity to none and without pride.

- These are those divine qualities.

- The divine nature is fit for liberation, the demoniacal leads to bondage.

The demoniac *(āsura-guṇa)* traits are:

- The qualities of the demoniacal are hypocrisy, arrogance, pride, anger, harshness, and ignorance. Also, the demoniacal do not know how to deal with people. They are unaware of what to do and what not to do. They know not purity or right conduct, and are neither truthful nor moral. Hence, they denounce the existence of God and claim that all creation is born out of lust.

- Their actions, petty and aggressive are generally destructive. In fact, they are filled with insatiable desires, hypocrisy, pride and arrogance and act with

---

[1]https://www.bhagavad-gita.org/Gita/chapter-16.html

malicious intent. Therefore, they regard lust as the highest gratification, their endless desires end only with death. Consequently, held by bonds of hope, passion and anger they strive to satiate their sensual desires through wealth obtained by unjust means.

- Their attitude is – This has been gained by me. I will fulfil this desire. This wealth shall be mine in future. I am rich and well-born, better than others. Hereafter, I will perform sacrifices give alms and rejoice.

- Such people are deluded by ignorance. Consequently, they chase fancies, are enmeshed in a snare of delusion, addicted to gratification of their passions and they go to hell.

- Also, they are beset by thoughts of achievement *(ahaṅkāra)*, obsessed with control and power, haughty, full of passion, anger and hate the thought of having any divinity in their body and in others.

How do divine and demonic traits manifest?

- First, there is nothing. This is the *Brahman.*

- Then, from *Brahman* emerges *puruṣa* (primordial Soul, experience, or identity) and *prakṛti* (primordial manifestation) of *puruṣa.*

- The experience of *puruṣa* is carried by the consciousness *(citta),* while *prakṛti* weaves with *puruṣa* to manifest as *guṇa* (attributes).

The three *guṇas* (attributes) revisited:

Tamas (inertia) – this aspect is characterized by fear, laziness, indolence, confusion, delusion, etc. A person with a predominance of this state is generally vacillatory, lethargic, prone to giving excuses and, indecisive.

Rajas (passion) – this state governs nearly all forms of passion and is driven primarily by desire. As a result, a person in this state would typically focus on personal achievement and gratification, be result oriented, dominating, aggressive, impatient, etc.

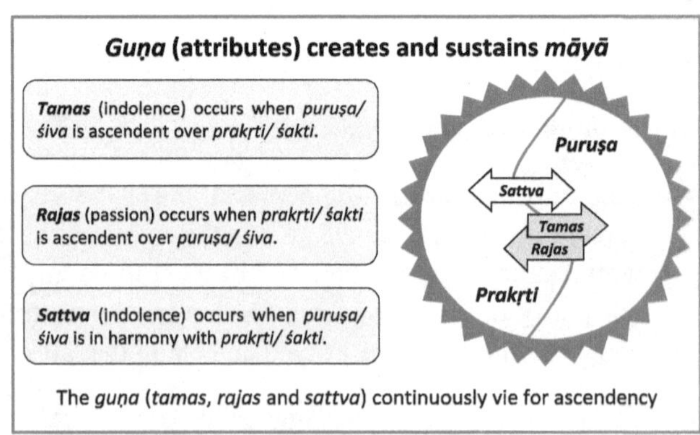

16.1 - the movement of guṇas determine behaviour

Sattva (harmony) – this state is characterized by harmony. It is demonstrated when a person tries to balance result with resource or process, task with quality and relationships, etc. A person in this state avoids confrontation, but in a conflict situation, is calm, absorbs emotional outburst, and remains objective.

Why is the concept of divine *(daiva)* and demonic *(āsura)* important?

- It is a reality that no one has any one trait. Each of us is a mix of these traits.

- But Śrī Kṛṣṇa is attempting to reinforce the need for a person to actively identify his or her demonic *(āsurika)* traits and try to either subdue or overcome it with divine *(daivika)* traits.

The characteristics of the divine *(daiva)* and demonic *(āsura)*:

- When *sattva* is predominant, the person demonstrates level-headedness, harmony, emotional intelligence, patience, and such divine qualities. In this quality, the balance between *puruṣa* and *prakṛti* is equal.

- While Śrī Kṛṣṇa has clubbed both *tamas* and *rajas* as *āsura-guṇa*, these can be subdivided into *āsura-guṇa* when *tamas* predominates over *sattva* or *rajas* and *rākṣasa-guṇa* when *rajas* predominates over the other two.

- In *āsura-guṇa*, where *tamas* (indolence, laziness, and confusion) predominates, this means that *puruṣa* (identity) predominates over *prakṛti* (manifestation). As a result, the person keeps reflecting on the consequence of his or her action on the sense of Identity/self-worth and becomes defensive as well as inward looking, narcissistic, unsure, indolent, and delusional.

- Consequently, the person exhibits behavior that is predominantly weak in self-esteem/worth, with a lust for sexual gratification, beset by anxiety, and filled with laziness/indolence.

- In *rākṣasa-guṇa*, *puruṣa* (identity) is weak as compared with *prakṛti* (manifestation). This makes the person outward looking with a need to gratify its sense of self-worth/identity *(puruṣa)*.

- Here, the person keeps reaching out to gratify *puruṣa* by material gain, possessions, passion, and power. So, where *rajas* overshadows the other two, desire, anger, ambition, jealousy and lust for power are predominant behavioural characteristics.

- Finally, it is important to remember that each of us exhibits all three *guṇas* *(daivika, āsura* and *rākṣasa)* in varying proportions depending on the situation and state of self-esteem/self-worth *(asmitā)*.

Can a person increase divine qualities and become a *puruṣottama* (perfect person)?

The performance code of ancient India was a simple but complete system which conditioned society and the individual into a cohesive lifestyle system called *"dharma"*. This was called *ṛta* or code of excellence.

Introduction to the performance code of India *(ṛta)*

During the Trojan wars (around 1000 BC), hero Achilles refused to fight in the early days, alleging that King Agamemnon had faulted the Law of arête, the ancient Greek law of excellence. Arête defined that men or women of Arête were people of the highest effectiveness, who used their capabilities to achieve tangible results.

Arête is the Greek cognate of *Saṃskṛta* word *"ṛta"*, Persian word "asa" which, in Avestan means righteousness and Latin word "ariete" which means battering ram – one that breaks down obstacles and ensures effectiveness of purpose.

Clearly, the ancient world lived by a well-defined, codified ideal of performance, which subsequent conquests subjugated and destroyed, especially in Greece, Italy, and Persia. In India, *ṛta* was woven into the fabric of ancient Indian society at a people and personal level, as *dharma*.

Concept of *ṛta* [2]

The basis of *ṛta* came from the assumption that performance comes from sacrifice or *yajña* [3].

Yajña was considered to have three components:

1. Truth or *satya* - the objective, vision, or focus of the sacrifice.

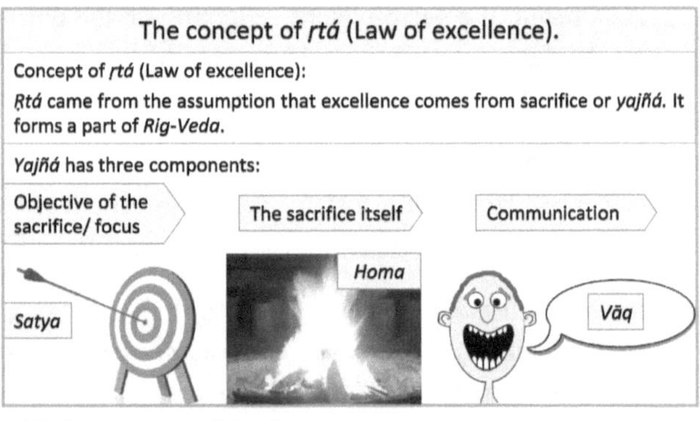

16.2 - The concept of *"ṛta"*

2. The sacrifice itself or *homa*.

3. Communication or *vāk* - that critical component, which kept the sacrifice together and enabled achievement of the objective.

---

[2] https://schoolofyoga.in/thought-leadership/performance-concept-india
[3] https://schoolofyoga.in/yoga-concept/action-karma

1- Truth, vision, or objective *(satya)*

The first component of *ṛta* is recognizing what needs to be done and why. Once a person is able to discriminate between truth and perception, clarity of goal is achieved and effort is maximized to achieve the goal.

First and foremost, all projects need a sponsor. A sponsor is one who determines the need, provides the resources, and defines the system. The sponsor is called *yajamāna* (the sponsor of the sacrifice) in *ṛta*.

Example - In the case of a football team, the *yajamāna* or sponsor is one who pays the bills and under whose colors the team plays. The *yajamāna* decides where the team shall play. Obviously, if the estimation is incorrect, the team will either lose or not play to its full potential.

2- The sacrifice itself *(homa)*

Once the *yajamāna* decides on the activity to be performed, the execution of the sacrifice can start.

- **Appointment of a manager *(guru)*:** Often, the sponsor or *yajamāna* would not have the capability or capacity to manage the activity directly. The sensible thing to do would be to appoint someone who has the requisite experience and expertise – a *guru* can be defined as "the weighty one or anchor" or "he that sheds light on darkness." Today, such an individual might be called SME (Subject Matter Expert).

Clearly, the quality of outcome would depend on the competence of the *guru* who would need to know how to manage a project or sacrifice *(yajña)*.

Example - Continuing with the above example, once the sponsor or *yajamāna* forms a football team, the key to its success of the team would be the quality and capability of the Team manager or Coach.

The *homa* process:

- **Making a commitment – *saṅkalpa* (taking the vow)**

    Firstly, the sponsor *(yajamāna)* and *guru* would need to bring the members together and explain to them the objectives of the activity *(yajña)*. This will bring the team members into alignment with the goal and enable focus for a successful completion of the activity.

- **Conversion from intent to outcome – *āgama* (conversion technique)**

    Once the team has been selected and aligned to the goal, the conversion of intent to outcome requires the following inputs;

1. Methodology, process, or skill-sets, *śāstra* (knowledge) – the coach of any football team should have knowledge on football rules, strategy, competitive assessment, weather, health, and fitness, etc. Obviously, all these skill-sets, including specialist skills, training, and development should also be resident in the team to make it effective. This is *kṣetrajña* (awareness of the region).

2. Resources *(dravyamaya)* – No activity can be completed without adequate resources, these are called *dravyamaya* (components) – right resource, tools, and capital required to perform the sacrifice. For a football team, this is - right players for each position, a practice location, administration facilities, technology support, etc.

3. The activity itself - *agni* (fire) – the moment of truth occurs when the activity is performing and the outcomes become visible. Fire *(agni)* is the transformation agent. In the case of football, this is the match, where energy is expended! The match decides whether integration of all the elements in the region *(kṣetra)* has worked. For instance, the match shows whether the sponsor has set the correct goals and provided proper resources as requested by the coach. Similarly, it demonstrates whether the coach has recruited and trained the correct team, estimated the opposition or coordinated the correct strategy. Most importantly, whether the assumptions and hard work lead to victory or achievement of the goals.

4. Sharing the prize – *prasāda* (fruits of the sacrifice) – the successful team shares the fruits of a successful completion of the activity. This could be credits, profits etc. In the case of the football match, this could mean bonuses, advertising contracts etc.

5. Thanksgiving or *kāyenavācha* – the activity is completed by the sponsor bringing the team together and thanking them for supporting the successful completion of the activity.

3- Communication or *vāk*

Communication is the lifeblood of any activity. Instructions cannot be passed and feedback cannot be received without communication. Clearly, no activity can be successful if there is a breakdown in communication between the team members. This consists of,

- Communication between the sponsor or *yajamāna* and the officiating manager or *guru* (officiator of the sacrifice) on the intent of the sacrifice and periodic appraisal of progress.

- Communication between manager or *guru* and various participants of the activity is critical for team effectiveness. This includes recruitment, training, performance monitoring and remuneration of team members.

Ṛta acts hierarchically. Firstly, the *yajamāna* becomes the initiator and employs the *guru*. Next, the *guru* becomes the *yajamāna* for the next level, but becomes a role model in addition to being a sponsor. This is then carried to the next level until finally, there was no one left to instruct. This is very similar to today's organizational structure where power flows from the Board, to the CEO, various department heads and finally to Team Leaders.

Integration of *ṛta* into society

The ancients realized that quality and motivation had to be conditioned into every activity and individual for ensuring performance. These elements had to be made the highest ideals worth aspiring for, the existential lifeblood or *dharma* of their society.

Ṛta is derived from the syllable *"hṛ"* which means dynamism, vibrancy, seasoning, and ownership. The derived noun *"hṛtam"* means order, rule, or divine law. To make *ṛta* an unassailable concept, the ancients equated it with divinity *(daivam)*.

They gave *ṛta* a mythical status and equated it with a role model of impeccable standing - the Sun. *Ṛta* was equated with the Sun's rays or *uṣas* to make it the part of their existence *dharma* (existential natural state) and made *savitṛ* (deity that signifies energy of the Sun) as the presiding deity.

Conclusion on *ṛta*

In conclusion, by codifying *ṛta,* ancient Bhārat institutionalized and integrated purpose, quality and commitment to every activity. Even today, 6000 years on, the principle of *ṛta* are valid, reinforcing the sagacity of the ancient ancestors of the land.

Some contradictions to accepted positions:

- There is some dissonance in Chapter 16. The logic is not completely in alignment with the rest of *Śrīmad-bhagavad-gītā*.

- To start, is there anything called divine and demonical at all? Is a person completely one or another, or are we all a mix of these qualities?

- Divine and demonical often depend on which side of the conditioning *(dharma)* fence one sits. For example - during the Cold War, the West portrayed the Soviets as demonical and themselves as divine while the Soviets narrated an opposite position. Neither side was either divine or demonical, so this chapter has unresolved structural issues.

- The next question is, can people and societies move from one state to another? The Soviets have gone, but Russia exists. Is there any change? If yes, then who has changed and to what extent? Is the West still the same or has it changed?

- The ability to change comes from awareness *(prajñā)*, which comes from conditioning *(dharma)*. Consequently, *dharma* drives our self-worth *(asmitā)* which crimps our ability to think freely and act without fear.

- The reality seems to be that *karma* is acting independent of individuals, we have the rise of China and a Covid-19 pandemic. Can anyone say that they have controlled reality?

- So, chapter 16 needs to be read more as an aspirational ideal than an instructional one.

- *Ṛta* is a concept that is part of *ṛgveda*. Over time, this concept has atrophied and is today no longer mainstream thought. Also, there is no direct linking between Truth *(satya)*, sacrifice *(yajña)* and communication *(vāk)*, but when one looks at various *śauryam* (Sun worship) practices, there are indications that *satya, yajña* and *ṛta* were intimate woven with each other. For example, in *ṛgveda179.3*, the *Ṛṣi* declare *"suśrātaṃ manye tadṛtaṃ navīyaḥ* which translates to "that which is well cooked is *ṛta*". Obviously, to cook, one must have a menu (Truth), there is sacrifice in terms of effort, resources, and motivation to be perfect and presentation/communication with the guests.

- The object of the above example on *ṛta* is not to prove the veracity of *ṛta,* but to try and bring out the subtlety in thought of the ancient people of Bhārat and try to bring out divine qualities in behavior.

Lessons learned:

- Three elements which destroy the Self are passion, anger, and greed, and these should be avoided. Once avoided, the practitioner begins walking the path of development

- Scriptures guide the person to self-development, and one should follow them, not cast them aside.

The transliteration and translation of chapter 16 follows:

श्रीभगवानुवाच ।

अभयं सत्त्वसंशुद्धिर्ज्ञानयोगव्यवस्थितिः ।

दानं दमश्च यज्ञश्च स्वाध्यायस्तप आर्जवम् ॥ १६-१॥

अहिंसा सत्यमक्रोधस्त्यागः शान्तिरपैशुनम् ।

दया भूतेष्वलोलुप्त्वं मार्दवं ह्रीरचापलम् ॥ १६-२॥

तेजः क्षमा धृतिः शौचमद्रोहो नातिमानिता ।

भवन्ति सम्पदं दैवीमभिजातस्य भारत ॥ १६-३॥

Śrī Kṛṣṇa said (1-3) Fearlessness, balanced internal purity, steadfast in yoga of wisdom, charity, control of the senses, sacrifice and introspection, austerity, and straightforwardness *(abhayaṃ sattvasaṃśuddhirjñānayogavyavasthitiḥ ǀ dānaṃ damaśca yajñaśca svādhyāyastapa ārjavam ǁ 16-1ǁ)*. Non-injury, truth, non-anger, renunciation, tranquility, absence of crookedness, compassion towards creation, non-covetousness, gentleness, modesty, absence of fickleness *(ahiṃsā satyamakrodhastyāgaḥ śāntirapaiśunam ǀ dayā bhūteṣvaloluptvaṃ mārdavaṃ hrīracāpalam ǁ 16-2ǁ)*. Vigor, forgiveness, fortitude, purity, absence of hatred, not too much pride are the qualities of divine born *(tejaḥ kṣamā dhṛtiḥ śaucamadroho nātimānitā ǀ bhavanti sampadaṃ daivīmabhijātasya bhārata ǁ 16-3ǁ)*.

दम्भो दर्पोऽभिमानश्च क्रोधः पारुष्यमेव च ।

अज्ञानं चाभिजातस्य पार्थ सम्पदमासुरीम् ॥ १६-४॥

(4) Hypocrisy, arrogance, self-conceit and wrath, harshness also and ignorance are the qualities of the demonic born *(dambho darpo 'bhimānaśca krodhaḥ pāruṣyameva ca ǀ ajñānaṃ cābhijātasya pārtha sampadamāsurīm ǁ 16-4ǁ)*.

दैवी सम्पद्विमोक्षाय निबन्धायासुरी मता ।

मा शुचः सम्पदं दैवीमभिजातोऽसि पाण्डव ॥ १६-५॥

द्वौ भूतसर्गौ लोकेऽस्मिन्दैव आसुर एव च ।

दैवो विस्तरशः प्रोक्त आसुरं पार्थ मे शृणु ॥ १६-६॥

(5-6) Divine state is deemed for liberation; the demonical state is deemed fit for bondage *(daivī sampadvimokṣāya nibandhāyāsurī matā ǀ mā śucaḥ sampadaṃ daivīmabhijāto'si pāṇḍava ǁ 16-5ǁ)*. Two types of creations in this world are divine and demonical, and divine has been described at length, hear from me about demonical *(dvau bhūtasargau loke'smindaiva āsura eva ca ǀ daivo vistaraśaḥ prokta āsuraṃ pārtha me śaṛṇu ǁ 16-6ǁ)*.

प्रवृत्तिं च निवृत्तिं च जना न विदुरासुराः ।

न शौचं नापि चाचारो न सत्यं तेषु विद्यते ॥ १६-७॥

असत्यमप्रतिष्ठं ते जगदाहुरनीश्वरम् ।

अपरस्परसम्भूतं किमन्यत्कामहैतुकम् ॥ १६-८॥

(7-8) Action and inaction and people the demonical do not cognize, not purity also, right conduct or truth is in them *(pravṛttiṃ ca nivṛttiṃ ca janā na vidurāsurāḥ ǀ na śaucaṃ nāpi cācāro na satyaṃ teṣu vidyate ǁ 16-7ǁ)*. Without Truth, without value, they say that there is no *īśvara* and the world was brought about by mutual union with desire as the cause *(asatyamapratiṣṭhaṃ te jagadāhuranīśvaram ǀ aparasparasambhūtaṃ kimanyatkāmahaitukam ǁ 16-8ǁ)*.

एतां दृष्टिमवष्टभ्य नष्टात्मानोऽल्पबुद्धयः ।
प्रभवन्त्युग्रकर्माणः क्षयाय जगतोऽहिताः ॥ १६-९॥

काममाश्रित्य दुष्पूरं दम्भमानमदान्विताः ।
मोहाद्गृहीत्वासद्ग्राहान्प्रवर्तन्तेऽशुचिव्रताः ॥ १६-१०॥

(9-10) Holding this view, ruined soul of fickle intellect come forth with fierce deeds of destruction as enemies of the world (*etāṃ dṛṣṭimavaṣṭabhya naṣṭātmāno'lpabuddhayaḥ | prabhavantyugrakarmāṇaḥ kṣayāya jagato'hitāḥ || 16-9||*). Holding insatiable desires, full of hypocrisy, pride, arrogance, delusion, holding malicious ideas they work with impure resolve (*kāmamāśritya duṣpūraṃ dambhamānamadānvitāḥ | mohādgṛhītvāsadgrāhānpravartante'śucivratāḥ || 16-10||*).

चिन्तामपरिमेयां च प्रलयान्तामुपाश्रिताः ।
कामोपभोगपरमा एतावदिति निश्चिताः ॥ १६-११॥

आशापाशशतैर्बद्धाः कामक्रोधपरायणाः ।
ईहन्ते कामभोगार्थमन्यायेनार्थसञ्चयान् ॥ १६-१२॥

(11-12) With immeasurable cares that end only in death, regarding gratification of desire as the highest goal, that is all that they are sure of (*cintāmaparimeyāṃ ca pralayāntāmupāśritāḥ | kāmopabhogaparamā etāvaditi niścitāḥ || 16-11||*). Bound by hundred expectations, bound completely by desire and anger, they strive for materiality of desire by unjust hoarding of material (*āśāpāśaśatairbaddhāḥ kāmakrodhaparāyaṇāḥ | īhante kāmabhogārthamanyāyenārthasañcayān || 16-12||*).

इदमद्य मया लब्धमिमं प्राप्स्ये मनोरथम् ।
इदमस्तीदमपि मे भविष्यति पुनर्धनम् ॥ १६-१३॥

असौ मया हतः शत्रुर्हनिष्ये चापरानपि ।
ईश्वरोऽहमहं भोगी सिद्धोऽहं बलवान्सुखी ॥ १६-१४॥

(13-14) Today, by me this has been gained, I shall fulfil this desire. This is mine; this wealth shall also be mine (*idamadya mayā labdhamimaṃ prāpsye manoratham | idamastīdamapi me bhaviṣyati punardhanam || 16-13||*). That enemy has been slain by me; I shall slay others also. I am *īśvara*, I am the enjoyer, I am perfect, powerful, and happy (*asau mayā hataḥ śatrurhaniṣye cāparānapi | īśvaro'hamahaṃ bhogī siddho'haṃ balavānsukhī || 16-14||*).

आढ्योऽभिजनवानस्मि कोऽन्योऽस्ति सदृशो मया ।
यक्ष्ये दास्यामि मोदिष्य इत्यज्ञानविमोहिताः ॥ १६-१५॥

अनेकचित्तविभ्रान्ता मोहजालसमावृताः ।
प्रसक्ताः कामभोगेषु पतन्ति नरकेऽशुचौ ॥ १६-१६॥

(15-16) I am rich and wellborn, who else is equal to me? I will sacrifice, I will give charity, I will rejoice, thus deluded by ignorance *(āḍhyo'bhijanavānasmi ko'nyo'sti sadṛśo mayā । yakṣye dāsyāmi modiṣya ityajñānavimohitāḥ ॥ 16-15॥).* Bewildered by many options, caught in the web of delusions, addicted to gratification of desire, they into foul torment *(anekacittavibhrāntā mohajālasamāvṛtāḥ । prasaktāḥ kāmabhogeṣu patanti narake'śucau ॥ 16-16॥).*

आत्मसम्भाविताः स्तब्धा धनमानमदान्विताः ।
यजन्ते नामयज्ञैस्ते दम्भेनाविधिपूर्वकम् ॥ १६-१७॥
अहङ्कारं बलं दर्पं कामं क्रोधं च संश्रिताः ।
मामात्मपरदेहेषु प्रद्विषन्तोऽभ्यसूयकाः ॥ १६-१८॥

(17-18) Absorbed in themselves, stubborn, intoxicated by wealth, full of arrogance, they perform sacrifices out of hypocrisy without understanding of the concepts *(ātmasambhāvitāḥ stabdhā dhanamānamadānvitāḥ । yajante nāmayajñaiste dambhenāvidhipūrvakam ॥ 16-17॥).* Thoughts of being the doer, addicted to power, haughtiness, desire, wrath, and obsessed with "me" and others, constantly judging and envious *(ahaṅkāraṃ balaṃ darpaṃ kāmaṃ krodhaṃ ca saṃśritāḥ । māmātmaparadeheṣu pradviṣanto'bhyasūyakāḥ ॥16-18॥).*

तानहं द्विषतः क्रूरान्संसारेषु नराधमान् ।
क्षिपाम्यजस्रमशुभानासुरीष्वेव योनिषु ॥ १६-१९॥
आसुरीं योनिमापन्ना मूढा जन्मनि ।
मामप्राप्यैव कौन्तेय ततो यान्त्यधमां गतिम् ॥ १६-२०॥
त्रिविधं नरकस्येदं द्वारं नाशनमात्मनः ।
कामः क्रोधस्तथा लोभस्तस्मादेतत्त्रयं त्यजेत् ॥ १६-२१॥

(19-21) Those that hate, are cruel in society, wretched, I throw them in perpetuity only in the vicious wombs of demons *(tānahaṃ dviṣataḥ krūrānsaṃsāreṣu narādhamān । kṣipāmyajasramaśubhānāsuriṣveva yoniṣu ॥ 16-19॥).* Entering into demonical wombs, deluded birth after birth, not attaining me ever, thereafter they fall into lower states *(āsurīṃ yonimāpannā mūḍhā janmani । māmaprāpyaiva kaunteya tato yāntyadhamāṃ gatim ॥ 16-20॥).* These three gates of hell destroy the Self, desire, anger, and greed, and these three should be abandoned *(trividhaṃ narakasyedaṃ dvāraṃ nāśanamātmanaḥ । kāmaḥ krodhastathā lobhastasmādetattrayaṃ tyajet ॥ 16-21॥).*

एतैर्विमुक्तः कौन्तेय तमोद्वारैस्त्रिभिर्नरः ।
आचरत्यात्मनः श्रेयस्ततो याति परां गतिम् ॥ १६-२२॥
यः शास्त्रविधिमुत्सृज्य वर्तते कामकारतः ।
न स सिद्धिमवाप्नोति न सुखं न परां गतिम् ॥ १६-२३॥

तस्माच्छास्त्रं प्रमाणं ते कार्याकार्यव्यवस्थितौ ।
ज्ञात्वा शास्त्रविधानोक्तं कर्म कर्तुमिहार्हसि ॥ १६-२४॥

(22-24) When a person gets freed from the gates of darkness by practice of these three that are good, then he goes to the supreme goal *(etairvimuktaḥ kaunteya tamodvāraistribhirnaraḥ ı ācaratyātmanaḥ śreyastato yāti parāṃ gatim ॥ 16-22॥).* He that acts without understanding of process but is driven by impulsive desires, he does not attain perfection or happiness or the supreme goal *(yaḥ śāstravidhimutsṛjya vartate kāmakārataḥ ı na sa siddhimavāpnoti na sukhaṃ na parāṃ gatim ॥ 16-23॥).* Therefore, follow standard operating procedures to know what should be done and ought not to be done. After understanding the standard operating procedures, perform all your actions *(tasmācchāstram pramāṇam te kāryākāryavyavasthitau ı jñātvā śāstravidhānoktam karma kartumihārhasi ॥ 16-24॥).*

◆———•◆•———◆

Chapter 17

Śraddhā-traya-vibhāga-yoga[1]
(yoga delineating the three types of *śraddhā*)

Introduction to *śraddhā*

Śraddhā is the quality of dedication, sincerity, steadfastness, and desire for perfection that a person exhibits when performing any action *(karma)*. Also, Śrī Kṛṣṇa clarifies that *śraddhā* is the ability to focus on the task at hand with all attention, without worrying excessively about the outcome of the sacrifice.

Another critical aspect of *śraddhā* that Śrī Kṛṣṇa clarifies, is that capability or quality of outcome are not key drivers in any activity. It is *śraddhā* that matters. Hence, Śrī Kṛṣṇa delinks quality of outcome from quality of input, clearly asserting the ascendancy of effort over outcome.

Relationship between attributes *(guṇa)*, sacrifice *(yajña)* and *śraddhā*, verse (1-15)

Arjuna said: What is the nature of those that do not follow the scriptures, but perform sacrifice with devotion and sincerity? Is it *sāttvika, rājasika,* or *tāmasika?* The devotion and sincerity of any person is determined by his innate nature *(svabhāva* - sva = self + *bhāva* = expression), which could be *sāttvika, rājasika,* or *tāmasika.*

- *Sāttvika* people worship the divine, *rājasika* people worship the greedy *(yakṣa* and *rākṣasa),* and *tāmasika* people worship decadence *(pretas* or spirits and hosts of the *bhūtas).*

- Those that practice extreme austerities not authorized by scripture, are attached to hypocrisy, and feeling of doer-ship, lust, and ownership. So, when people

---

[1]https://www.bhagavad-gita.org/Gita/chapter-17.html

subject themselves to unauthorized austerities, they punish not just themselves, but the divine that resides therein.

- *Sāttvika* people maintain a balanced diet which increases vitality, strength, health, joy, and cheerfulness; one which is full of taste, having a marrow, substantial and agreeable.

- *Rājasika* people prefer food which is bitter, sour, saline, pungent, dry, and acrid.

- *Tāmasika* people like stale, tasteless, stinking, cooked overnight, refuse and impure.

- When performing a sacrifice *sāttvika* people desire no fruit and perform the *yajña* for its sake only; however, *rājasika* people perform *yajña* for selfish reason and reward; finally, *yajña* where there is no discipline, sincerity or sharing is *tāmasika*.

- Ideal persons are those who worship the divine, twice born, teachers, and those with awareness *(prajñā)*. Also, these people are upright, practice continence and non-injury to themselves and others. This is the highest possible austerity or self-restraint *(tapas)*.

- Also, their way of speaking is calm and causes no excitement, are truthful, pleasant, seeking win-win, constantly practicing self-improvement *(svādhyāya-abhyāsanam)* and controlled speech.

Svabhāva (personality traits)

- When we meet someone, we either like or dislike the person.

- If there is congruence between *atmas* (souls), *puruṣa* (experiencer) pulls the object towards itself because it wants continued engagement *(rāga)*. If there is dissonance, *puruṣa* pushes the object away to avoid discomfort *(dveṣa)*. This results in a give-take movement or a transaction, which is *karma* (action).

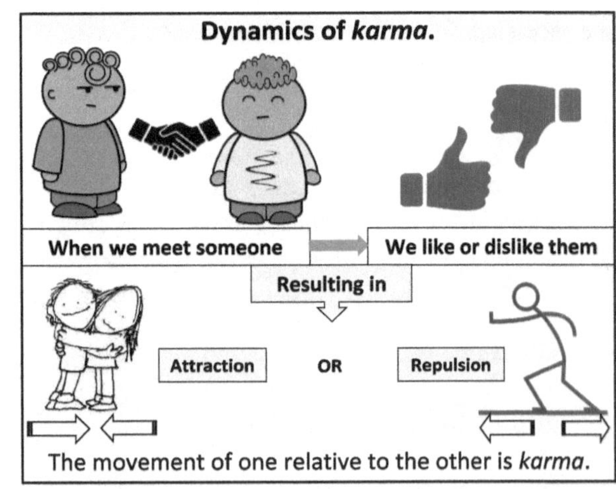

17.1 - How *karma* occurs

- But, how do we decide that we like or dislike the object? What is the standard by which we compare stimulus from any object?

- We compare the behavior of the other person *(svabhāva - sva* = self + *bhāva* = expression) with our *svadharma (sva* = self + *dharma* = natural state) to decide our position of like or dislike.

- *Dharma* is our natural state, where we experience a sense of peace. This state occurs when the proportion of the three *guṇa's (tamas* = delusion/*rajas* = passion/*satva* = harmony) reside harmoniously within our self-worth *(asmitā).*

- When fresh stimulus comes in through the senses *(indriyas)*, it is collated by the center of cognition *(manas)* and compared with *svadharma* (our personal natural state). This changes *puruṣa* (experiencer) which expands in happiness or contracts in anxiety and fear. Consequently, this disturbs the *guṇa* proportion and balance.

- So, our behaviour *(svabhāva)* emerges from our conditioning *(svadharma).* We behave in our own unique manner because of our natural state which conditions our responses to stimuli.

The underlying principle driving *svadharma* and *svabhāva* in the human body

- The human body consists of many sub-systems such as the circulatory system, digestive system, musculo-skeletal system etc. Also, each of these systems are unique and have specific characteristics and functions with are independent of other systems, but related with each other.

- Next, within each system are specific organs which have specific functions, such as the heart, lungs, stomach, liver etc. These are also independent and their function cannot be interchanged.

- Also, each of these systems and entities have their own operational range and they operate best within this range. This is called homeostasis or *dharma* (natural state).

- Hence, each of these systems as well as organs can be considered as an independent entity functioning within a macro-system, the human body which has its own natural state.

- Since each of these systems and organs is unique, each has a unique identity *(puruṣa),* which functions in a specific manner *(prakṛti)* and responds to stimulus in a particular manner indicating that each has an independent soul *(ātman)* which is driven by the availability of a consciousness *(citta)* and has a unique debt account *(karma* or *ṛṇa).*

- There is movement of nutrients in and out of the body due to the movement of *prāṇa* (motility), which results in the weave of *puruṣa* and *prakṛti.*

- Since each of these entities such as heart, lungs etc have a Soul *(ātman)*, it stands to reason that these organs get diseased and die on account of fulfilment of debt *(ṛṇa)* with the body.

- One can force continuation of functioning by use of medicines, but there comes a point when even this is exhausted and the system fails. There is no other logical explanation for ageing.

Is there a way in which we can act without creating *karma*?

Of course! That is the essence of *Śrīmad-bhagavad-gītā* and everything Śrī Kṛṣṇa is trying to say. Let us look at *karma* from first principles.

- *Karma* occurs on account of *puruṣa/Śiva* experiencing existential anxiety (do I exist? How do I prove that I exist?).

- So, *puruṣa/Śiva* establishes a bond with another *puruṣa/ Śiva* to confirm and ensure confirmation of existence.

- However, since the awareness of each of the two entities is different, there is an awareness imbalance which results in congruence/lack of congruence between the two entities.

- Consequently, the two entities experience like *(rāga)* or dislike *(dveṣa)* of each other, and this results in an unbalanced give-take relationship and debt *(ṛṇa)* which becomes *prārabdha-karma*.

- This debt which comes as *prārabdha-karma* has to be liquidated. This is why we have *saṃsāra* or the cycle of birth and death, to enable debt to be liquidated.

- This means that, for as long as *puruṣa/Śiva* experiences existential anxiety, this cycle will continue.

- For this cycle to be disrupted, the *yogī* must reduce and finally eliminate existential primordial anxiety of identity of *puruṣa/Śiva* which manifests as self-worth *(asmitā)* in the person.

- When this happens, even when *prārabdha-karma* or debt is being liquidated, *puruṣa/Śiva* continue to act in the situation but does not experience existential anxiety, so there is no fresh accumulation of debt *(ṛṇa)*.

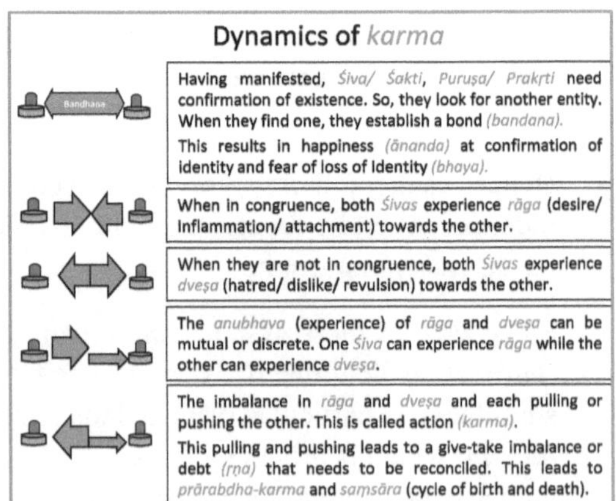

17.2 - How *karma* results in debt

- The starting point for the *yogī* to stop experiencing existential anxiety is awareness of existence and identity *(jñāna)*.

- Then, as the *yogī* increases span of control over response, the *asmitā* reduces and finally merges into nothing, so there is no identity in the experience. With the elimination of the identity, the experience will cease to exist as well.

- This effort is free-will *(saṅkalpa)* and also the crux of Śrī Kṛṣṇa's message throughout *Śrīmad-bhagavad-gītā*.

What are the steps that we need to understand so that we avoid creation of *karma* when acting?

1. First, do not react. Do not give in to impulse. Your reflex is your *svabhāva*. Stop! take a deep breath and allow the urge to react to pass.

2. Recognize the temporary nature of all situations. This is *viveka* (the ability to discriminate temporary from permanent/value and loss of value).

3. Next, view the situation dispassionately. This capability is called *vairāgya*.

4. Then, think win-win. Negotiate with *śraddhā* and *vairāgya*. Avoid dualities such as like-dislike, good-bad, right-wrong etc.

5. Sacrifice without expecting credit. Practice *sama-dṛṣṭi* (equal sightedness - treating everything equally and without bias).

Quality of austerity *(tapas)*, sacrifice *(yajña)* and *śraddhā*, verse (16-28)

- Finally, serenity of mind, gentleness, silence, self-control, and purity of disposition is cognitive austerity. Thus, the above austerity *(tapas)* when practiced with no desire for fruit is called *sāttvika*.

- Next, austerity which is ostentatious and practiced with the intent of gaining respect, honor or reverence is called *rājasika*.

- Lastly, austerity practiced with foolish and obstinate intentions, with torture to the self or another is *tāmasika*.

- A gift *(dāna)* given with the pure intent of giving, with a feeling that it is a duty to give, given at the right time, place, and to the right person is *sāttvika;* however, a gift given grudgingly and with a view of return is *rājasika;* a gift given at the wrong time or place, without respect, or with insult is *tāmasika*.

- However, no matter what the sacrifice, if a person were to utter "*om-tat-sat*", meaning that all actions reside in the reality of *Brahman* and perform the sacrifice with *śraddhā,* that would be a complete sacrifice.

The three types of dedication *(śraddhā-traya-vibhāga):*

- Śrī Kṛṣṇa says that a person's behavior is influenced by his innate nature or personality trait *(svabhāva).*

- This innate nature is a combination *śraddhā* (sincerity, dedication, patience, and focus) and *yajña* (their sacrifice for the cause). *Yajña* is possible only when a person has the ability control yearning *(tapas),* hence this is an important yardstick.

- Śrī Kṛṣṇa delineates *śraddhā, tapas* and *yajña* by *guṇa* (attributes). Importantly, the *guṇa* mix changes continuously depending on our insecurities, desires, and delusion. Hence, qualities given below are based on the *guṇa* that is predominant.

- It is important to realize *guṇa* is a manifestation of *puruṣa* (identity or experiencer) as *prakṛti.*

- Both *prakṛti* and *puruṣa* weave with each other, without *puruṣa* there is no *prakṛti,* and without *prakṛti, puruṣa* cannot manifest or experience.

What are the qualities of *śraddhā, yajña* and *tapas* of people with different guṇas? verse (16-28)

Sāttvika **people**

- Generally, *sāttvika* people are matured and do not feel the need to prove themselves.

- A *sāttvika* person likes the company of people who are honest, level-headed, calm, forgiving, solution-seeking, and peaceful.

- *Sāttvika* people generally prefer the company of teachers, wise, learned, and level-headed people.

- When performing any activity, they do it without selfish intent, they do it because it is right. They are straight-forward, honest, diplomatic, and seek a win-win solution.

- *Sāttvika* people exhibit enormous self-restraint and give without expectation of return. They speak in a calm manner and do not excite others.

- Also, they generally prefer fresh food and eat moderately.

Rājasika and tāmasika **people**

- Generally, *rājasika* people are passionate, ambitious, aggressive, and enjoy power. For example, in an office, these are people who constantly update their resume, discuss office politics, and are sensitive to power equations, etc.

Typically, they are Type A personalities.

- They like the company of passionate people and always seek to win in any negotiation. Also, they love the spotlight and will try to ensure that they get credit for anything they do.

- *Rājasika* people can go into extremes when they get passionate. They have enormous lust for life, food, sex, and possessions.

- *Rājasika* people prefer acting for personal gain. They get satisfaction from material gain such as wealth, property, promotions etc.

- Lastly, they like heavy and pungent food like meats. Susceptible to high alcohol usage.

- *Tāmasika* people are those that do not act. They have excuses for everything; why something should not be done or was not done, is not being done right, that too much is being spent, process is incorrect and that everyone is against them.

- Such people do not choose their friends. They will listen to anyone who is able to control them at the moment. When they give anything, it tends to be inappropriate because they do not empathize or understand.

- Their decision making tends to be vacillatory, they waver and change direction without reason.

- *Tāmasika* people do not understand sacrifice. Hence, their effort in any situation is without reason, understanding or reverence. As a result, their expectation of outcome also becomes one of chance and hope due to which they adopt different kinds of superstitious and occult practices.

- They eat without restraint or control and are unable to differentiate between what they eat. Also, they are susceptible to substance abuse.

Self-improvement suggestions:

- It is very important for us to reflect on our own *svabhāva* (personality traits) and recognize those of others in various situations.

- To develop and evolve, we need to improve our capabilities in the following areas - discrimination between permanent and impermanent *(viveka)*, dispassion *(vairāgya)*, sincerity and dedication *(śraddhā)*, austerity *(tapas)*, and ability to sacrifice *(yajña)*.

- When we begin the practice, we begin to experience resistance from *puruṣa* (experiencer) because *asmitā* (self-worth) becomes threatened by non-existence. The weakest link is our *vāsanās* (memories of past knowledge) which force us to behave in particular manner.

- When we evolve in this practice,

  - Slowly, a stillness begins to set in. This stillness brings *prāṇayama* (control over *prāṇa).*

  - There is increased control over reaction to stimulus *(pratyāhāra).*

  - *Dhyāna* (meditation) becomes steady.

  - We become non-threatening and get a steady awareness *(sthitaprajña).*

Does yoga have an easy method for implementation of Śrī Kṛṣṇa's instructions in Chapter 17?

Rāja-yoga is a stream of yoga that tries to allow a person to live in the world while trying to improve his or her capability to live *Śrīmad-bhagavad-gītā.* The first two steps of *Rāja-yoga* are *yama* (behavior control) and *niyama* (self-control or internal discipline) which are very useful in improving the

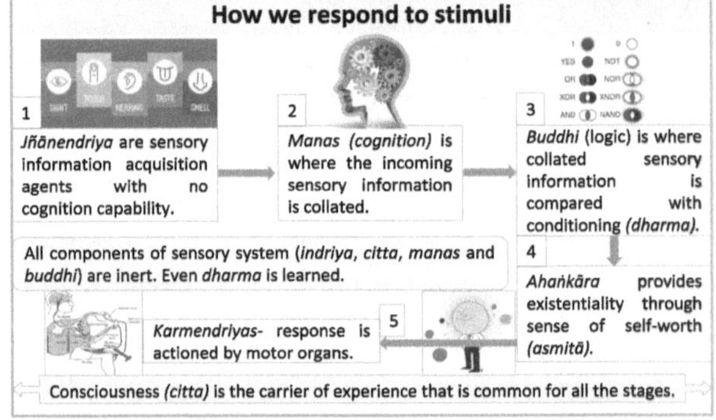

17.3 - The stimulus-response cycle

qualities of sincerity and dedication *(śraddhā)* in a person. What are these methods?

Yama: Generally, stimulus comes from more than one source; hence, it is rare that the stimulus is received with complete attention *(ekāgratā).* The state of awareness, called *vijñāna* (cognition of sentience in any situation) covers reception, comparison with conditioning and response. Any drop of awareness creates error in estimation and expectation or *māyā*, in both, the manifesting and receiving individual *(puruṣa).*

Yama is response or behaviour control					
Yama has different meanings, "rein, curb, or bridle, discipline or restraints".					
ahiṃsā	*satya*	*asteya*	*aparigrāhya*	*brahmacaryam*	*mitāhāra*
Non-harm	Truth	Non Stealing	Renouncing possessions	Sexual continence	Diet Control
Meaning					

This can generate stress, especially if the situation calls for a high degree of adjustment and is difficult to cope. Also, one gets stressed if the situation results in confrontation, or there is an insensitive or irrelevant response. Ones reactions to stimulus and ability to work with others in harmony or bring balance into his or her tasks and relationships are fundamental building blocks for a sustainable solution to stress.

Yama can mean "rein, curb, or bridle, discipline or restraint" when dealing with the environment. Therefore, *yama* means exercising restraint or ethical reaction to stimulus.

Patañjali-yoga-sūtra recommends six key elements in *yama* that cover most aspects of behavior with the external environment, these being non-violence *(ahiṃsa)*, truth or integrity *(satya)*, sexual continence *(brahmacaryam)*, non-stealing *(asteya)*, equanimity *(aparigraha)*, and diet control *(mitāhāra)*.

Haṭha-yoga-pradīpikā recommends – non-violence *(ahiṃsa)*, truth or integrity *(satya)*, sexual continence *(brahmacarya)*, forgiveness *(kṣamā)*, self-discipline *(drīti)*, compassion *(dayā)*, frankness or being straightforward *(ārjava)*, diet control *(mitāhāra)* and cleanliness *(śauca)*.

Let us look at some of the elements of behaviour control *(yama)*:

Non-Violence *(ahiṃsā)* – To understand non-violence, one must understand violence and its relationship to anger, fear, frustration, sexuality, ambition, and power.

Yama can be defined as the ability to react in a non-threatening manner to stimulus contrary to one's *dharma* (conditioning), controlling anger, frustration, and giving positive feedback.

We know that violence covers a vast spectrum – from internet abuse and bullying to genocide, where entire populations are exterminated. There are three types of violence *(hiṃsā)* – *tāmasika* (confused/delusional), *rājasika* (passionate), and *sāttvika* (balanced).

Tāmasika violence comes out of lack of knowledge and is driven primarily by inertia, fear, and confusion. *Rājasika* violence primarily out of passion and is driven by emotions such as anger, lust, greed, ambition etc. *Sāttvika* violence is very difficult to achieve and is characterized by high levels of discrimination *(vivekam)* dispassion *(vairāgyam)*, communication and patience.

Example: A case of a parent scolding a truant child. When the parent scolds the child because he or she is afraid of what society will say (not the real reason), it is *tāmasika*. However, when the parent tries to superimpose his or her own expectations/ambitions on the child, it is *rājasika*. Finally, when the parent scolds the child for deviation of a value that has been explained often, then the reason is *sāttvika*, this is characterized by the parent trying to separate the person from the problem.

Truth or *satya* – Truth or *satya* is one of the most difficult but vital elements of behavior control or *yama*.

There is only one truth, the imperishable *Brahman* or *(paramarth-sathya)*. Everything else is materiality *(māyā)* or *(samvritti-sathya)*, which is driven by the senses *(indriyas)* and shrouds the intellect *(buddhi)* as well as cognition *(manas)*, constantly impacting sense of self-worth *(asmitā)* and conditioning *(dharma)*.

But, absolute truth *(paramarth-sathya)*, while being the ultimate goal of yoga is hard to understand, cognize, and experience. So, a more easily implementable derivative of absolute truth, called conditional truth *(samvritti-sathya)* is better suited for daily use. *Samvritti-sathya* comprises empirical/transactional truth *(vyāvahārika-satya)* or truth that is supported by evidence, and perceptual truth *(prātibhāsika-satya)*, one that is not backed by evidence, illusionary or hear-say.

Consequently, we can see that truth in this world of illusion is difficult to define and easy to deflect. It is also hard to understand, interpret, experience, and perform due the shroud of perceptions always surrounding it which emanates from our sense of self-worth *(asmitā)*, which is based on our conditioning *(dharma)*. So, truth requires the foundation of discrimination *(vivekam)* as well as dispassion *(vairāgyam)*.

Non-stealing *(asteya)* – stealing or theft is taking anything which does not belong to us, without permission. This can be expanded to include effort. Some examples might be:

- Taking stationery from the office for personal work.

- Not paying taxes.

- Ticketless travel.

- Not contributing to household chores.

- Not sharing an inheritance.

Sexual continence or control *(brahmacarya)* is the ability to control seminal discharge. However, it does not mean stoppage of sexual activity. Therefore, one can conclude that *brahmacarya* is the responsible management of sexual activity with no wastage of seminal discharge.

Procreation is deeply embedded in our psyche and need for sexual activity is natural. However, it is easily possible for one to lose control and engage in indiscriminate activity, thus losing seminal fluid.

Especially today, as more people and business cross countries and continents, sensitivity and awareness needs to be integrated with removal of sexual bias to each other's cultural and racial background in all relationships.

Controlled diet *(mitāhāra)* – The traditional adage is that we are what we eat. Food is a major source of nutrition. Nutrients that nourish the body can only come from diet. Therefore, it is important that we not only eat the right foods but also adopt correct eating habits. Poor food habits lead to ill-heath and stress.

Some suggestions on eating right:

- Food is broken down into manageable pieces in the mouth and mixed with enzymes for digestion. This is why chewing of the food and mixing it with saliva is so important. The food is then swallowed and goes into the stomach. As the food enters the stomach, signals are sent so that more enzymes are released into the stomach.

- Additional blood is sent to the stomach muscles to enable it to churn and mix the food and enzymes completely. So, the stomach should not be overloaded with food. There should be adequate space for the stomach to squeeze the gases out. Also, there should be sufficient water in the stomach to ensure elastic movement of the stomach muscles to squeeze, churn and break up the food.

- The half-digested food then moves into the intestines where the nutrients are absorbed while food breaks up and churn continues. Food with adequate roughage ensures that food does not stick to the walls of the intestines but moves forward for absorption and evacuation.

- Expulsion of waste is a very important element of digestion and often determines the health of the person. We should ensure that we keep this requirement in view when we eat.

- Stay within the recommended weight range. It is the starting point for good health.

- Most religions prescribe a benediction before a meal is started. In Bhārat, the benediction translates to "let food optimize motility in ingestion *(prāṇāya-svāhā)*, let food optimize motility in excretion *(apānāya-svāhā)*, let food optimize motility in personality and aura *(vyānāya-svāhā)*, let food optimize motility in good demeanor *(udānāya-svāhā)*, let food optimize motility in assimilation and circulation of resources *(samānāya-svāhā)* and let food optimize motility in alignment with the source *(brahmane-svāhā)*." Very pragmatic benediction, covering the role of food in every aspect of existence.

Niyama **(self-control)** is the process of increasing our internal discipline and self-control. While *yama* is the process of harmonizing our relationship with our environment, *niyama* is the practice of harmonizing and assimilating the impact of stimulus with our sense of self-worth *(asmitā)*. So, *niyama* and *yama* increase harmony between our sense of self-worth *(asmitā)* and awareness of the Self *(jñāna)* within the stimuli-response cycle.

<table>
<tr><td colspan="6" align="center">Niyama is internal discipline or self-control</td></tr>
<tr><td colspan="6" align="center">Niyama has different meanings, "rules, discipline, convention, taming, etc."</td></tr>
<tr><td align="center">Śaucam</td><td align="center">Santoṣam</td><td align="center">Svādhyāyam</td><td align="center">Tapas</td><td align="center">Śraddhā</td><td align="center">Dāna</td></tr>
<tr><td align="center">Hygiene</td><td align="center">Contentment</td><td align="center">Introspection</td><td align="center">Austerity</td><td align="center">Dedication</td><td align="center">Charity</td></tr>
<tr><td colspan="6" align="center">Meaning</td></tr>
</table>

Hatha Yoga Pradeepika (Chapter 1) - the 10 rules of *niyama* are – austerity *(tapas)*, contentment *(santoṣa)*, belief in the Vedas *(āstikya)*, charity *(dāna)*, prayer to God *(īśvara-pūjana)*, listening to spiritual teaching *(siddhānta-vākya)*, modesty *(hrī)*, repetition of sacred word *(japa)*, and sacrifice with fire *(hūta)*.

Patañjali-yoga-sūtra (Chapter 2) - recommends cleanliness, *(śauca)*, contentment *(santoṣam)*, introspection *(svādhyāyam)*, austerity *(tapas)*, surrender to a God *(īśvarapraṇidhānam)*.

Let's look at the six most suitable *niyama* elements - hygiene *(śauca)*, contentment *(santoṣam)*, introspection *(svādhyāya)*, austerity *(tapas)*, sincerity and dedication *(śraddhā)*, and charity *(dāna)*.

Śauca consists of *bāhya-śauca* (external hygiene) and *āntara-śauca* (internal hygiene)

- **External Hygiene** *(bāhya-śauca)* – This aspect consists of performance of ablutions regularly, maintaining a clean body and environment. For example, In India – *snānam* (head-bath) requires wetting the body completely so that the nine apertures on the body (mouth, eyes, ears, nostrils, anus and genitals) are thoroughly cleaned. The act of water falling on the body + rubbing action of the hands on the body increases blood flow to the skin resulting in a feeling of increased freshness and awareness.

Environmental hygiene is also very important – Almost all major illnesses which result in lost time and cost come from lack of awareness of the criticality of hygiene. In fact, public spitting, defecation, urination, and other practices, such as smoking chewing tobacco, etc., result in water-borne diseases such as cholera, typhoid, leptospirosis, and air-borne diseases, such as throat infection, etc. Clearly, an individual is responsible, not just for his own health, but also for the health of his neighbor and society at large.

Example - In 1330s, a plague hit China and spread to Europe in 1347 and by 1351 had reached all corners of Europe and the Middle East. It had the effect of killing around 35% of Europe's population (35 million people in 2 years). Overall, it reduced the world's population from 450 million to between 350 and 375 million.

During this time, it was noticed that Jews, living in ghettos away from the village, suffered lower deaths. This was on account of strict Rabbinical Laws on cleanliness followed by them. The water that they used was from wells in their backyard, and not community wells, leading to greater control over bacterial infection. Also, injunctions on personal hygiene and disposal of waste ensured that the carriers, such as rats were less likely to infect the community. Clearly, this ritual practice protected Jews long before antiseptics and understanding of germs.

Similarly, in Bharat, there are strict rules for cleanliness, especially when eating. Indians eat only with the right hand. Eating from another person's plate, something that has encountered one's mouth, saliva, or plate is not allowed and called *'jootha'* (in North India), *'ushth'* (in Western India), *'etho'* (in Bengal), *'aitha'* (in Orissa), *'echal'* (in Tamil Nadu), *'enjulu'* (in Karnataka), or *'engili'* (in Andhra Pradesh).

In many parts of Bhārat, one is not allowed to touch lacto-based ghee, milk, curds, etc., after touching any food that has been cooked, unless hands have been washed, to avoid contamination of vegetable-based dishes with animal products and vice-versa.

It is also normal for people of Bhārat to use separate utensils for cooking, serving, eating, and also to clean and keep them separately. Unfortunately, these practices are diluting and since poor practice could impact public health, they should be practiced with sincerity.

- **Internal cleanliness** *(āntara-śauca)* is continuous discarding of baggage so that the person feels light, clear-headed, and free from anxiety of self-worth *(asmitā)*. This is also called soul-cleaning *(ātma-śuddhi)*.

Contentment *(santoṣa)* - Any feeling of happiness is fleeting, but the sense of peace is more lasting. Also, contentment increases calmness, resulting in increased clarity of thought and reduced conflict. This leads to greater productivity without agitation within, and in the environment. Finally, contentment increases positive energy in us. But, how does one recognize this & more importantly, imbibe it?

- We accept that which comes to us - this means that we do not resist change.

- We avoiding opposites, such as happy/sad, good/bad, like/dislike, right/wrong with any outcome. We get our gratification from quality of input (that which we are supposed to do in that situation).

Self-inquiry or examination *(svādhyāya)* – literally means, "to get close to something." Consequently, it means to study oneself through meditation or contemplation *(mīmāṃsā)*.

Learning has two components – an inflexible and a flexible component. So, when we review any situation, both inflexible and flexible components are reviewed, resulting in learning. This is reflection *(mīmāṃsā)* and is an element of introspection.

Austerity *(tapas)* is the exercise of increasing awareness of the Self by practice of austerities. Austerities come from self-denial of wants and suppression of desire. *Tapas* requires two qualities: denial and internal cleaning.

- **Denial** – The world has the ability to continuously engage us. However, to increase self-control, material interactions need control. This includes,

  - Reducing interactions with the world, including social media. This reduces distraction/mental clutter and allows one to engage in greater analysis of oneself.

  - Reducing personal possessions such as clothes, jewelry, etc. As a result, this reduces attraction to impermanent or ephemeral possessions.

- **Internal cleansing** *(āntara-śauca)* – continuously cleaning the self-worth of baggage ensures that we are able to deal with fear, anxiety and frustration that the practice of austerity *(tapas)*

Charity *(dāna)* – means giving without expectation of return.

There are many types of sacrifices or selfless giving and the most important, in order of significance are;

- *Anna-dāna*   (giving food as charity)
- *Vastra-dāna*   (giving clothes as charity)
- *Vidyā-dāna*   (giving knowledge as charity)
- *Kriyā-dāna*   (giving effort as charity)
- *Lakṣmī-dāna*   (giving money as charity)

Of all forms of charity *(dāna)*, those where there is direct benefit to another such as *anna-dāna* (feeding others) are considered higher forms of charity *(dāna)*, especially because food is life. This is followed by any charity which requires sacrifice of one's personal time or energy such as *kriyā* (effort), *vidyā* (knowledge sharing), and *vastra-dāna* (giving clothes to the needy). Finally, on the list of charities that increase altruistic sensitivities are those that have no direct involvement and there is no control over the outcome, such as *lakṣmī-dāna* (money).

But this is not to take the sheen away from any form of sacrifice or giving. All forms of giving and sacrifice result in a feeling of goodness and altruism which opens the sense of identity to awareness and introspection *(jñāna)*.

Dedication *(śraddhā)* – is the ability to complete a chosen task to the best of one's ability with sincerity, focus on result, patience, dedication, and willingness subsume personal preferences to complete the task. Often, this may mean working with severe constraints, with no assistance or support, maybe in adverse conditions, with no recognition or resources - including money and having to overcome failure as well as frustration. The qualities that one requires in these circumstances are;

- **Patience** *(sahāna)* – The ability to start and maintain an activity till its logical conclusion despite the obstacles, delays, stumbles, and constraints.

- **Modesty** *(hrī)* – Modesty and humility allow us to accept other people's suggestion and reach the goal. This also applies to the quality of giving credit to others and keeping *asmitā* in check.

Taiichi Ohno,[2] the father of the Toyota Production System penned "The 10 precepts to think, act and win". These are simple and valuable rules for implementing *śraddhā*.

- You are your own resource, reduce waste and optimize yourself. Resource is time, energy, ideas, capability, creativity, self-worth etc. These are the constraints that impede us from perfection. Yogacharya Sundaram used to say "only a busy man finds time." This is true for everything; you generally find the resource when you optimize yourself and stop waste.

- Do not be pessimistic. Adopt a "can-do" spirit and try to complete the activity. Practice Śrī Kṛṣṇa's advice in Chapters 3 & 4, act with focus on the goal, but without hankering for the fruits.

- Your environment is your teacher. You can learn from every situation if you are open to change.

- Start any activity immediately. This is *rajo-guṇa*. Procrastination is not doing that which needs doing. When you linger, one of two things happen; another urgent activity comes up which pushes this activity down. As a result, this activity festers and suddenly becomes a crisis when you are unprepared.

- When you start the activity, persevere. It is the nature of activity *(karma)* that you will encounter obstacles. Consequently, when you persevere and overcome it you will experience *sattva-guṇa* (harmony).

- Explain things in an easy-to-understand manner. Also, confirm that people have understood what you are saying by repeating it and seeking confirmation. Seek to understand before trying to be understood.

---

[2]https://opscombinator.com/2020/08/28/taiichi-ohnos-ten-precepts-broken-down

This is something many people forget, to tell the most important thing first and give details later. For example - after Hanuman and team visited Lanka and met Sītā, they returned to Sugrīva to inform him. However, they did not come in immediately, but wasted an orchard. This distracted Rama, Lakshmana, and Sugrīva from the anxiety they would have experienced when waiting for Hanuman to come in from the time the forward posts reported that Hanuman was sighted. When angry Sugrīva ordered Hanuman to be brought in, the first words that he uttered to Rama were "I saw Sītā"; not how they went, how they overcame obstacles etc., just the most critical information! How often people beat around the bush and forget to impart the most important information first.

- Waste is hidden, be transparent. We hoard information, possessions, and ideas. The tragedy is that as a result, none of these ideas are used, only wasted. So, share, because when you share, you grow as well.

- Valueless motion is equal to shortening one's life. In Bhārat, people say *"OM-tat-sat"*, meaning in sacrifice *(yajñá)*, there is value (sat). When a person performs non value adding activity, he not only destroys intrinsic value of the activity, but also increases *tamas* within and forces others to waste their time and energy on the same activity. This is equivalent to reducing one's life. In the words of Northcote Parkinson[3] - work expands to fill the time available, don't do that!

- Improve everything, including that which has already been improved - perfection is an iterative process. it is not necessary that this be achieved in one go. For example – the story goes, once a friend visited Michelangelo when he was sculpting and found him sculpting a nose. When he visited the famous artist a few weeks later, he found him working on the same nose! Surprised, he remarked "But Michael, 'tis but a trifle" to which Michelangelo replied "Aye, 'tis but a trifle, but trifles make perfection"! One does not know if the story is true, but the moral is worth adopting.

- Everyone has wisdom, it is in the usage that the differences emerge. This is what Śrī Kṛṣṇa speaks throughout *Śrīmad-bhagavad-gītā*, when he refers to a person acquiring steady awareness *(sthitaprajña)*, a person of high experience *(puruṣottama)*, one who cognizes his physical state *(kṣetrajña)* or one who has optimized his *guṇa* Everyone has the capability to add value, but only those that use it and change emerge as valuable. For example – In Bhārat, there is a common practice of younger people touching the feet of older people. This show of respect is not for the age of the person, it is for the wisdom acquired through experience by the person, which makes the elder a *(mahānubhava - mahā* = great + *anubhavu* = those with experience). So, the person bows to the knowledge of the Self *(kṣetrajña)* acquired by the person through experience, which wisdom.

---

[3] https://en.wikipedia.org/wiki/Parkinson%27s_law#:~:text=Parkinson's%20law%20is%20the%20 adage,of%20bureaucracy%20in%20an%20organization.

Some contradictions to accepted positions:

- *Śraddhā* has often been termed as faith. *Śraddhā* is not faith; in fact, it has no direct translation in English. *Śraddhā* is a mix of dedication, patience, and perseverance, all of which are real and measurable *(sat)*. In fact, faith is considered an affliction because it is a state of *svapna-avasthā* (dream state), a state that is not real and should be transcended *(asat)*.

- Do *guṇa* ratios change over time? What makes them change? Is it your *karma?* Once a debt *(ṛṇa)* has been paid off, the identity no longer has that load to carry. Also, once a debt is paid off, other debts may not immediately come up for repayment because the framework and players for repayment may not be available. This lightens the Self. This also allows awareness *(prajñā)* the freedom to increase discrimination *(viveka)* and dispassion *(vairāgya)*. So, this is an opportunity for the Soul to increase awareness, reduce creation of fresh debt and merge with *brahma*

Lessons learned:

- There are two primary states, permanent and impermanent.

- *Prārabdha-karma* drives personality traits *(svabhāva),* and these manifest through attributes *(guṇa)*.

- From awareness *(prajñā)* comes the ability to increase discrimination *(viveka)* and dispassion *(vairāgya)*. When this happens, there is a reduction in the creation of fresh debt, and this allows the Soul to merge with *brahman*.

- *Om-tat-sat* means the *brahmān (Om)* is cognized every time sacrifice *(yajña)* is performed *(tat)* with the sole intention of adding value *(sat)*.

- To achieve *Om-tat-sat, śraddhā* is required.

The transliteration and translation of chapter 17 follows:

अर्जुन उवाच -

ये शास्त्रविधिमुत्सृज्य यजन्ते श्रद्धयान्विताः ।

तेषां निष्ठा तु का कृष्ण सत्त्वमाहो रजस्तमः ॥ १७-१॥

Arjuna said (1) What about those that abandon operating procedures and simply perform sacrifices with dedication? What becomes of them? What are the conditions of *sattva, rajas* and *tamas (ye śāstravidhimutsṛjya yajante śraddhāyānvitāḥ ı teṣāṃ niṣṭhā tu kā kṛṣṇa sattvamāho rajastamaḥ ıı 17-1ıı).*

श्रीभगवानुवाच -

त्रिविधा भवति श्रद्धा देहिनां सा स्वभावजा ।

सात्त्विकी राजसी चैव तामसी चेति तां शृणु ॥ १७-२॥

सत्त्वानुरूपा सर्वस्य श्रद्धा भवति भारत ।

श्रद्धामयोऽयं पुरुषो यो यच्छ्रद्धः स एव सः ॥ १७-३॥

Śrī Kṛṣṇa replied (2-3) Now, hear the threefold dedication of the embodied which is inherent in *sāttvika, rājasika,* and even *tāmasika (trividhā bhavati śraddhā dehināṃ sā svabhāvajā | sāttvikī rājasī caiva tāmasī ceti tāṃ śaṛṇu ॥ 17-2॥)*. Conformance of nature in everyone is as per his dedication. *Śraddhā* determines the person; truly, he is what his dedication is *(sattvānurūpā sarvasya śraddhā bhavati bhārata | śraddhāmayo'yaṃ puruṣo yo yacchraddhaḥ sa eva saḥ ॥ 17-3॥)*.

यजन्ते सात्त्विका देवान्यक्षरक्षांसि राजसाः ।

प्रेतान्भूतगणांश्चान्ये यजन्ते तामसा जनाः ॥ १७-४॥

(4) Those of *sāttvika* qualities worship the deities, *rājasika* people worship demigods and demons, and *tāmasika* people worship ghosts and myriad nature spirits *(yajante sāttvikā devānyakṣarakṣāṃsi rājasāḥ | pretānbhūtagaṇāṃścānye yajante tāmasā janāḥ ॥ 17-4॥)*.

अशास्त्रविहितं घोरं तप्यन्ते ये तपो जनाः ।

दम्भाहङ्कारसंयुक्ताः कामरागबलान्विताः ॥ १७-५॥

कर्षयन्तः शरीरस्थं भूतग्राममचेतसः ।

मां चैवान्तःशरीरस्थं तान्विद्ध्यासुरनिश्चयान् ॥ १७-६॥

(5-6) Those people not following proper procedures, practicing terrible austerity, given to feeling of doer-ship, hypocrisy, desire, attachment, and power *(aśāstravihitaṃ ghoraṃ tapyante ye tapo janāḥ |dambhāhaṅkārasamyuktāḥ kāmarāgabalānvitāḥ ॥ 17-5॥)*. Senselessly torturing all the elements in the body and me who dwells in the body, these are known to be of demonic resolve *(karṣayantaḥ śarīrastham bhūtagrāmamacetasaḥ | māṃ caivāntaḥśarīrasthaṃ tānviddhyāsuraniścayān ॥ 17-6॥)*.

आहारस्त्वपि सर्वस्य त्रिविधो भवति प्रियः ।

यज्ञस्तपस्तथा दानं तेषां भेदमिमं शृणु ॥ १७-७॥

आयुःसत्त्वबलारोग्यसुखप्रीतिविवर्धनाः ।

रस्याः स्निग्धाः स्थिरा हृद्या आहाराः सात्त्विकप्रियाः ॥ १७-८॥

(7-8) Indeed, of all, food is critical in the three paths of sacrifice, austerity, and charity, hear the distinction between them (*āhārastvapi sarvasya trividho bhavati priyaḥ ǀ yajñastapastathā dānaṃ teṣāṃ bhedamimaṃ śaṛṇu ǁ 17-7ǁ*). Those that promote life, value, strength, health, happiness, amicability, are tasty, viscous, substantial, agreeable foods are dear to *sāttvika* people (*āyuḥsattvabalārogyasukhaprītivivardhanāḥ ǀ rasyāḥ snigdhāḥ sthirā hṛdyā āhārāḥ sāttvikapriyāḥ ǁ 17-8ǁ*).

कट्वम्ललवणात्युष्णतीक्ष्णरूक्षविदाहिनः ǀ
आहारा राजसस्येष्टा दुःखशोकामयप्रदाः ǁ १७-९ǁ
यातयामं गतरसं पूति पर्युषितं च यत् ǀ
उच्छिष्टमपि चामेध्यं भोजनं तामसप्रियम् ǁ १७-१०ǁ

(9-10) Food that is bitter, sour, salty, very pungent and fiery, dry, burning are liked by *rājasika* people and bring pain, grief, and disease (*kaṭvamlalavaṇātyuṣṇatīkṣṇarūkṣavidāhinaḥ ǀ āhārā rājasasyeṣṭā duḥkhaśokāmayapradāḥ ǁ 17-9ǁ*). That which is stale, tasteless, putrid, rotten, left-overs, and also impure foods are liked by *tāmasika* (*yātayāmaṃ gatarasaṃ pūti paryuṣitaṃ ca yat ǀ ucchiṣṭamapi cāmedhyaṃ bhojanaṃ tāmasapriyam ǁ 17-10ǁ*).

अफलाकाङ्क्षिभिर्यज्ञो विधिदृष्टो य इज्यते ǀ
यष्टव्यमेवेति मनः समाधाय स सात्त्विकः ǁ १७-११ǁ
अभिसन्धाय तु फलं दम्भार्थमपि चैव यत् ǀ
इज्यते भरतश्रेष्ठ तं यज्ञं विद्धि राजसम् ǁ १७-१२ǁ
विधिहीनमसृष्टान्नं मन्त्रहीनमदक्षिणम् ǀ
श्रद्धाविरहितं यज्ञं तामसं परिचक्षते ǁ १७-१३ǁ

(11-13) Those not longing for fruits of sacrifice that is performed as per process, which is offered as it should be, with their cognition steady is *sāttvika* (*aphalākāṅkṣibhiryajño vidhidṛṣṭo ya ijyate ǀ yaṣṭavyameveti manaḥ samādhāya sa sāttvikaḥ ǁ 17-11ǁ*). Those seeking fruits by fraudulent means and also which is offered as sacrifice, that is *rājasika* (*abhisandhāya tu phalaṃ dambhārthamapi caiva yat ǀ ijyate bharataśreṣṭha taṃ yajñaṃ viddhi rājasam ǁ 17-12ǁ*). Any effort that does not follow process, food is not shared, no mantras are chanted, no emoluments are made and there is no dedication, that sacrifice is called *tāmasika* (*vidhihīnamasṛṣṭānnaṃ mantrahīnamadakṣiṇam ǀ śraddhāvirahitaṃ yajñaṃ tāmasaṃ paricakṣate ǁ 17-13ǁ*).

देवद्विजगुरुप्राज्ञपूजनं शौचमार्जवम् ǀ
ब्रह्मचर्यमहिंसा च शारीरं तप उच्यते ǁ १७-१४ǁ

अनुद्वेगकरं वाक्यं सत्यं प्रियहितं च यत् ।
स्वाध्यायाभ्यसनं चैव वाङ्मयं तप उच्यते ॥ १७-१५॥
मनः प्रसादः सौम्यत्वं मौनमात्मविनिग्रहः ।
भावसंशुद्धिरित्येतत्तपो मानसमुच्यते ॥ १७-१६॥

(14-16) Those that worship the deities, twice-born, teachers, awareness, purity, straight-forwardness, celibacy, and non-injury is called austerity of the body *(devadvijaguruprājñapūjanaṃ śaucamārjavam | brahmacaryamahiṃsā ca śārīraṃ tapa ucyate || 17-14||)*. Causing no excitement in speech, truthful, pleasant, and beneficial, which comes from self-study is austerity of speech *(anudvegakaraṃ vākyam satyaṃ priyahitaṃ ca yat | svādhyāyābhyasanaṃ caiva vāṅmayaṃ tapa ucyate || 17-15||)*. Serenity of cognition, good-heartedness, silence, self-control, clean sentiment, this is called *tapas* of the cognition *(manaḥ prasādaḥ saumyatvaṃ maunamātmavinigrahaḥ | bhāvasaṃśuddhirityetattapo mānasamucyate || 17-16||)*.

श्रद्धया परया तप्तं तपस्तत्त्रिविधं नरैः ।
अफलाकाङ्क्षिभिर्युक्तैः सात्त्विकं परिचक्षते ॥ १७-१७॥
सत्कारमानपूजार्थं तपो दम्भेन चैव यत् ।
क्रियते तदिह प्रोक्तं राजसं चलमध्रुवम् ॥ १७-१८॥
मूढग्राहेणात्मनो यत्पीडया क्रियते तपः ।
परस्योत्सादनार्थं वा तत्तामसमुदाहृतम् ॥ १७-१९॥

(17-19) These threefold austerity, when practiced with dedication my men united with no desire for the fruit are called *sāttvika (śraddhāyā parayā taptaṃ tapastattrividhaṃ naraiḥ | aphalākāṅkṣibhiryuktaiḥ sāttvikaṃ paricakṣate || 17-17||)*. When hypocrisy is practiced in austerity with the object of gaining praise, honor, or wealth, that is said to be *rājasa,* and this is unstable and transient *(satkāramānapūjārthaṃ tapo dambhena caiva yat | kriyate tadiha proktaṃ rājasaṃ calamadhruvam || 17-18||)*. When the self is encased in delusion and includes practice of torture in the austerity or is for destroying another, that is declared as *tāmasika (mūḍhagrāheṇātmano yatpīḍayā kriyate tapaḥ | parasyotsādanārthaṃ vā tattāmasamudāhṛtam || 17-19||)*.

दातव्यमिति यद्दानं दीयतेऽनुपकारिणे ।
देशे काले च पात्रे च तद्दानं सात्त्विकं स्मृतम् ॥ १७-२०॥
यत्तु प्रत्युपकारार्थं फलमुद्दिश्य वा पुनः ।
दीयते च परिक्लिष्टं तद्दानं राजसं स्मृतम् ॥ १७-२१॥
अदेशकाले यद्दानमपात्रेभ्यश्च दीयते ।
असत्कृतमवज्ञातं तत्तामसमुदाहृतम् ॥ १७-२२॥

(20-22) When charity is given without expectation of return, in a proper place, at the correct time and to a worthy person, that charity is deemed *sāttvika* (*dātavyamiti yaddānaṃ dīyate'nupakāriṇe ǀ deśe kāle ca pātre ca taddānaṃ sāttvikaṃ smṛtam ǁ 17-20ǁ*). Indeed, when it is given with an expectation of return favor and reluctantly, that charity is called *rājasika* (*yattu pratyupakārārthaṃ phalamuddiśya vā punaḥ ǀ dīyate ca parikliṣṭaṃ taddānaṃ rājasaṃ smṛtam ǁ 17-21ǁ*). A gift that is given without heeding place or time and given without respect, even insult, that charity is called *tāmasika* (*adeśakāle yaddānamapātrebhyaśca dīyate ǀ asatkṛtamavajñātaṃ tattāmasamudāhṛtam ǁ 17-22ǁ*).

ॐतत्सदिति निर्देशो ब्रह्मणस्त्रिविधः स्मृतः ।
ब्राह्मणास्तेन वेदाश्च यज्ञाश्च विहिताः पुरा ॥ १७-२३॥
तस्मादोमित्युदाहृत्य यज्ञदानतपःक्रियाः ।
प्रवर्तन्ते विधानोक्ताः सततं ब्रह्मवादिनाम् ॥ १७-२४॥

(23-24) *Om-tat-sat* (*pranava-brahman*-value creation), thus is the designation for *brahman*, the threefold *brahman*, Veda and sacrifices have been created by the ancients (*omtatsaditi nirdeśo brahmaṇastrividhaḥ smṛtaḥ ǀ brāhmaṇāstena vedāśca yajñāśca vihitāḥ purā ǁ 17-23ǁ*). So, as enjoined in the scriptures, OM is thus uttered every time by the students of *brahman* when acts of sacrifice, charity, and austerity are begun (*tasmādomityudāhṛtya yajñadānatapaḥkriyāḥ ǀ pravartante vidhānoktāḥ satataṃ brahmavādinām ǁ 17-24ǁ*).

तदित्यनभिसन्धाय फलं यज्ञतपःक्रियाः ।
दानक्रियाश्च विविधाः क्रियन्ते मोक्षकाङ्क्षिभिः ॥ १७-२५॥
सद्भावे साधुभावे च सदित्येतत्प्रयुज्यते ।
प्रशस्ते कर्मणि तथा सच्छब्दः पार्थ युज्यते ॥ १७-२६॥

(25-26) *Tat* is the act of sacrifice, austerity, and charity without desire for fruits in any action generated by seekers of liberation (*tadityanabhisandhāya phalaṃ yajñatapaḥkriyāḥ ǀ dānakriyāśca vividhāḥ kriyante mokṣakāṅkṣibhiḥ ǁ 17-25ǁ*). *Sat* is the sentiment of reality, sentiment of goodness, and thus, *sat* word is thus used in auspicious acts also (*sadbhāve sādhubhāve ca sadityetatprayujyate ǀ praśaste karmaṇi tathā sacchabdaḥ pārtha yujyate ǁ 17-26ǁ*).

यज्ञे तपसि दाने च स्थितिः सदिति चोच्यते ।
कर्म चैव तदर्थीयं सदित्येवाभिधीयते ॥ १७-२७॥
अश्रद्धया हुतं दत्तं तपस्तसं कृतं च यत् ।
असदित्युच्यते पार्थ न च तत्प्रेत्य नो इह ॥ १७-२८॥

(27-28) In sacrifice, in austerity, in charity and steadfastness, *sat* is thus called, and action undertaken for anything is called *sat (yajñe tapasi dāne ca sthitiḥ saditi cocyate । karma caiva tadarthīyaṃ sadityevābhidhīyate ॥ 17-27॥)*. Without dedication, when sacrifice is given, austerity is performed, and the outcome is called *asat* and has no value here or hereafter *(aśraddhāyā hutaṃ dattaṃ tapastaptaṃ kṛtaṃ ca yat । asadityucyate pārtha na ca tatpretya no iha ॥ 17-28॥)*.

Chapter 18

Mokṣa-sannyāsa-yoga **(yoga of liberation by renunciation)** [1]

Introduction

The last chapter is mostly a recap of chapters 1-17. Some of the important aspects that are covered are,

- Difference between *sannyāsa* and *tyāga.*

- Delineation of *yajña* - sacrifice, *dāna* – donate without expectation of return and *tapas* - self-restraint.

- Description of attributes *(guṇa)* – *tamas* (attitude of indolence), *rajas* (attitude of passion) and *sattva* - (attitude of balance or harmony).

- Constitution of action *(saṃgraha).*

- How attributes affect people in action and contribution in society *(varna).* Importance of understanding that *varna* does not affect personal development.

- Recap of natural state *(dharma)* and its impact on excellence in action *(karma).*

- His own (Śrī Kṛṣṇa's) ability to affect the outcome of any effort in Yoga.

Mokṣa-sannyāsa-yoga

Arjuna said – I wish to know the truth about *sannyāsa* and *tyāga* (renunciation).

Śrī Kṛṣṇa said:

- *Sannyāsa* is renunciation of action motivated by desire *(kāma).*

- Abandonment of fruits of action is called *tyāga.*

[1] https://www.bhagavad-gita.org/Gita/chapter-18.html

- Difference between *sannyāsa* and *tyāga* - *sannyāsa* is renunciation of desire *(kāma)* for an outcome in an act. For example - a soldier charging an enemy position does not know whether he will succeed. However, *tyāga* is the renunciation of all fruits from the action. The soldier charging an enemy position can have 3 possible outcomes; he may die, in which case all further discussion ends; he may succeed in overcoming the enemy or he may be defeated and captured. *Tyāga* is acceptance of both, success, and defeat with same attitude, one of indifference. (Ch 18 verse 12)

- One must treat desire *(kāma)* like an affliction *(doṣa)*.

- Relinquish all action except,

  - *Yajña* – sacrifice,

  - *Dāna* – donate without expectation of return,

  - *Tapas* – self-restraint,

- Even when performing *yajña, dāna,* and *tapas,* do not expect any return.

- Recognize that behavior is driven by attributes *(guṇa),*

  - *Tamas* (attitude of indolence) – when action is abandoned due to ignorance.

  - *Rajas* (attitude of passion) – when action is abandoned because of fear.

  - *Sattva* - (attitude of balance) – when action is performed because it must be done, not for fruits.

- It is impossible to renounce action entirely. However, it is possible to renounce fruits of one's action.

- But any person can free himself from the effects of *karma* by discarding the attitude of being the doer *(ahaṅkāra).*

Śrī Kṛṣṇa explains *mokṣa-sannyāsa-yoga*, verse 1-18:

Śrī Kṛṣṇa's explanation on *karma* in this chapter gives the best understanding on the subject. This chapter is almost completely devoted to action in its various forms. Therefore, one could conclude that Śrī Kṛṣṇa in a subtle manner, indicates that everything related to existence is action *(karma).*

- In this chapter, Śrī Kṛṣṇa explains the gross components of any act. There are five:

  - *adhiṣṭhāna* – place or body – this is any place where action is being performed, within or outside the body.

- o   *kartṛ* – the doer. Since multiple entities may be impacted, this can include the person, team members and others as well. Also, when the team is integrated, it is considered a single unit.

  - o   *kāraṇa* – causation or reason – reason for the action (mission, strategy, and tactics).

  - o   *pāṭhaka-ceṣṭā* – discrete aspect – all action can be split into discrete stages, systems, or processes.

  - o   *daiva* - presiding deity – all action has a presiding deity that personifies its identity (like a brand).

- Subtle components of action consist of three aspects *(saṃgraha):*

  - o   *karmacodanā* – motivators of action comprising of three sub-elements

    - *jñāna* – wisdom – knowledge of the subject, including integration of resources and processes.

    - *jñeya* – the unknown aspects of the action such as various assumptions and forecast.

    - *parijñeyatā* – data, evidence on which decisions are based.

  - o   Action *(karma)* itself – here it is important to realize that action should be performed as a sacrifice *(yajña)*, the person should perform the sacrifice without expectation and accept any outcome without duality (like-dislike, good-bad, right-wrong etc.).

  - o   *kartṛ* – doer and team members.

- What is the difference between gross *(sthūla)* and subtle *(sūkṣma)* aspects of action or *karma*? We can compare these two aspects to the hardware (gross) and software (subtle) of any action! The gross aspect covers all visible components of action, while the subtle aspect covers logic and the drivers *(kāraṇa)* of action as well as Identity *(Śiva)*. The subtle elements drive both, cognition of the system *(vijñāna)* and cognition of the Self *(jñāna)*.

- Another important aspect which Śrī Kṛṣṇa highlights is the difference between *prārabdha-karma* (action that is occurring on account of previous debt or destiny) and free-will *(svatantra)*. The question that is never clearly answered is to what extent do we control our own actions? Some of the points made by Śrī Kṛṣṇa are,

  - o   No one can stop *karma* from occurring, *prakṛti* (nature's own instinct) will force action. (Ch 18 verse 59).

o   Next, *karma* or action manifests as natural instincts *(svabhāva),* but these are driven by conditioning *(dharma).*

o   This means that events occur due to repayment of debt *(prārabdha-karma)* and response to stimulus occurs in conformance with one's conditioning *(sva-dharma).*

o   *Dharma* occurs at various levels. For example, humans eat food, but unlike other creatures, humans also eat when they are not hungry; this is conditioning *(svadharma).* Next, humans eat a variety of foods and in various ways, called cuisines. Animals eat without variation; a cow will eat grass and some vegetation, a lion will eat a cow. Humans wear clothing and follow cultures which they protect very assiduously. This type of existence that exists on earth is unique to Earth because the natural conditioning *(dharma)* of the earth allows it.

o   The important aspect of all the above examples is that no entity has a choice of the positions they occupy – not the human, animal, Earth, Solar system, nor the fire, snow, or rain, all manifest according to their natural states with no control.

o   Then, how does Śrī Kṛṣṇa say, renounce desire and fruit of your action? All this indicates free will! The root and span of control can be found in the *citta* or consciousness.

From first principles:

o   *Brahman* is an infinite, unchanging, immutable sea of peace.

o   From *brahman* emerges *puruṣa* and *prakṛti.*

o   From the weave of *puruṣa* and *prakṛti* comes *karma* (action).

o   The common thread in this process is the consciousness *(citta).*

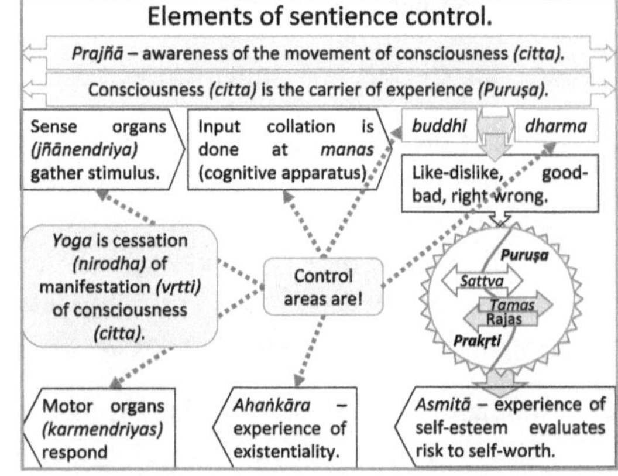

18.1 - How can one control sentience?

Citta plays the role of a messenger, carrying the projection of *puruṣa* through *prakṛti* to the object, bringing feedback. The mechanical components of the transaction are the senses *(indriya),* cognition *(manas)* where the intellect *(buddhi)* compares data with conditioning *(dharma)* before initiation of reaction and the action *(karma)* itself.

o   *Citta* is a projection of *puruṣa* through *prakṛti*. When it is not projecting, it is in turmoil because the *puruṣa* (experiencer) is constantly anxious about losing its Identity.

o   The *citta* can be quietened when one becomes aware of its movement as an agency external to the Self *(ātman)*. This awareness is called *prajñā*.

o   When awareness *(prajñā)* quietens consciousness *(citta)*, reactions become independent of self-worth *(asmitā)* and free-will or ability to control response increases.

o   When *prajñā* is combined with sacrifice *(yajña)*, which requires acting for a selfless purpose, *(dāna)* donating without expectation of return and self-restraint *(tapas)* which is possible only if the consciousness *(citta)* has been quietened, self-will is exerted to ensure that the Self is removed from the action.

o   This is *"Om-tat-sat"*. *Brahmān* exists in any sacrifice *(tat)* that adds value *(sat)*, and this requires dedication, sincerity and focus on contribution *(śraddhā)*.

o   To achieve this, one must follow the law of *ṛta* (excellence), which has been explained in Chapter 16.

Karma-sannyāsa:

- First, to achieve *karma-sannyāsa*, stop applying logic to everything. When acting, sacrifice to add value *(Om-tat-sat)*.

- Next, ensure that logic is consistently discriminating between permanent-impermanent *(vivekam)*.

- Also, to practice dispassion *(vairāgya)*, avoid arrogance, passion, anger, and greed. Abandon feelings of being a doer *(ahaṅkāra)* and dualities such as *rāga-dveṣa* (like-dislike).

- To reach the above state, live in solitude eat sparingly and control speech, body, and cognitive apparatus through meditation.

- Finally, when the *yogī* has no attachments and has reached a state of sublime peace, that person becomes fit to merge with the *Brahman*.

- On merging with the *Brahman,* this serene soul neither grieves nor has expectations.

- Also, the person treats all alike and sees *Brahman* is all creation *(samaḥ-sarveṣu-bhūteṣu)*. As a result, the *yogī* realizes that "I" and "Truth" are the same and attains indestructible, everlasting bliss.

- So, consciously surrender all actions unto the *guru* (in this case, Śrī Kṛṣṇa) with complete devotion and follow the Yoga of discrimination. Then, when acting, fix your consciousness on the *guru* to overcome all obstacles, by his grace.

- However, if anyone retains the attitude of being the doer *(ahaṅkāra),* then they will lose everything.

Mokṣa-sannyāsa **follows** ***karma-sannyāsa*** **(verse 20-40)***:*

- No one can escape the power of *guṇas* (attributes).

- *Jñāna, karma* and *kartṛ* can be further sub-classified according to the three *guṇas (guṇabhedataḥ).* Verses 20 to 40 cover this sub-classification.

- Duties of a *brāhmaṇa, kṣatriya, vaiśya,* or *śūdra* can be attributed to their *guṇa.*

- However, no matter what *varṇa* one is, that person can realize the Self by performing work with an attitude that is in congruence with his personality trait and being consciously aware of the *Brahman.*

Importantly, one should act in accordance with one's own conditioning or *dharma,* rather than try to satisfy someone else's. So, one must not convert to another *dharma,* nor ask anyone to convert from his or her *dharma.*

Conclusion – There is a clear understanding that *jāti* (community) is different from *varṇa* (classification), and neither is an impediment to the *yogī* who seeks the Truth.

Dharma, guṇa, **and human stratification:**

- *Karma* acts continuously. In fact, action, inaction, and inappropriate action are all *karma.*

- Also, even if a person were to exercise free will to avoid action *(karma), prakṛti* (creation) will force the person to act through his or her *svabhāva* which are driven by the *guṇas,* to ensure an outcome.

- All activities look daunting at the start, like smoke envelopes fire. Let go your fear, control yourself, abandon duality such as like-dislike, stop judging and take one step at a time (verse 48).

- *Guṇa* comes out of *prakṛti* and drives conditioning *(dharma).*

- Everyone has a competence that aligns with one's own natural state *(dharma). Dharma* drives behavior *(svabhāva).* So, it is always better for one to act in congruence with one's own competence in a bad situation that try to function on someone else's conditioning or state of harmony *(dharma).* The outcome will never be satisfactory. (verse 47).

- The mix of *guṇas* determines the personality and behavior *(svabhāva)* of individuals and consequently, duties that they are expected to perform in society. There are 4 categories *(varṇa)* of people - *brāhmaṇa* (one who has cognized *brahma-vidya, kṣatriya* (warrior and leader in any situation requiring honor and virility), *vaiśya* (trader, businessman, farmer or arbitrator), and *śūdra* (workman).

- An examination of the definition will confirm that these structures are defined by capability, so generally people who act according to their *dharma* would acquire specific competencies and become SME's (Subject Matter Experts).

- Since *varṇa* comes from *dharma* which is driven by *guṇa,* one can conclude that everyone's behavior *(svabhāva)* is driven by *guṇa.*

- Also, anyone acquiring a particular specialization would require an ecosystem as well as conditioning *(dharma)* and oftentimes, this comes from DNA and upbringing during childhood, which makes family and community living important.

- Consequently, specific communities end up specializing in particular tasks. These are called *jāti* (community). It is important to note that *jāti* is not caste but community, because caste has a hierarchy, which *jāti* does not have.

- Finally, anyone from any community can reach *Brahman* by focused application in performance of duties (verse 49). For example: Shri Sant Gora Kumbhar (1236 to 1317 A.D) [2] was a potter by profession who merged with the *Brahman.*

- So, no matter what activity a person may perform, everyone should be respected for their competence and contribution and not personality or position *(samaḥ-sarveṣu-bhūteṣu)* (verse 45-46).

Dharma, mokṣa-sannyāsa, and surrender to Śrī Kṛṣṇa:

Renounce all conditioning *(dharma)* and surrender unto me. Then, I shall liberate you from all sins. This verse is critical in understanding the process of Yoga. (verse 65-66).

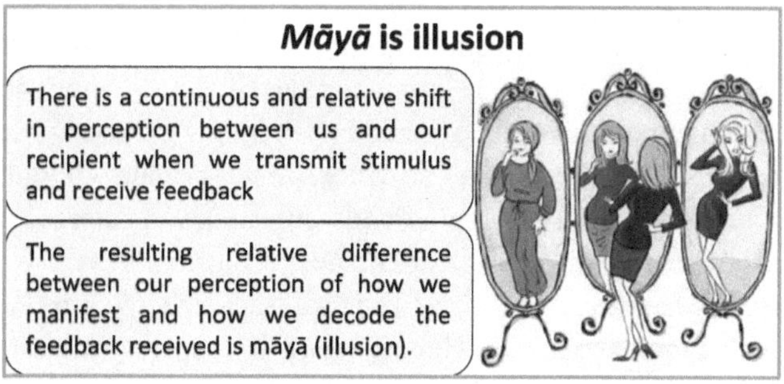

18.2 - *Māyā* is conditional Truth or illusion

------

[2] https://www.hindujagruti.org/hinduism-for-kids/335.html

- All yoga is about transcending the material Self and merging with *Brahman*.

- The material Self is *māyā* and created and operationalized by *puruṣa* and *prakṛti* that drive *karma*.

- *Karma* has a circular relationship with *dharma* (natural state), it creates *dharma* and in turn, gets governed by rules of *sanātana-dharma*.

Hence, to transcend the Self, one would need to transcend *dharma*. What are the types of *dharma* that a person needs to transcend?

- *Sva-dharma* (personal conditioning) - here a person will need to overcome all inhibitions and influences of DNA, education, upbringing, conditioning arising from employment, life experiences etc., truly a formidable challenge!

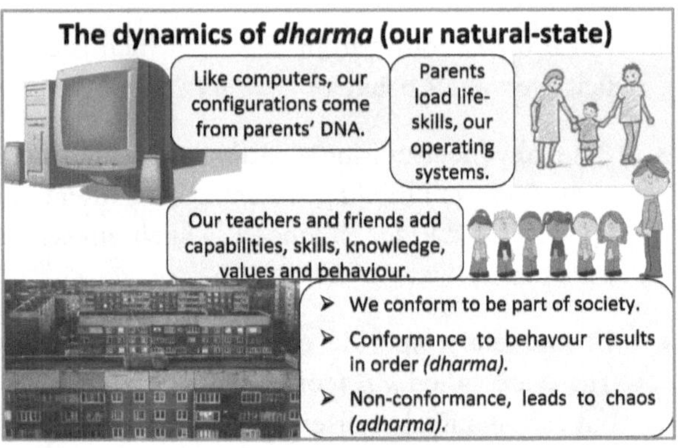

18.3 - *Dharma* is natural state

- *Viśeṣa-dharma* (specific *dharma)* or conditioning of society,

- *Sāmānya-dharma* (generic *dharma* of a genus) or instincts of being human,

- *Sanātana-dharma* (universal *dharma)* or state, such a *dharma* of creation.

Obviously, transcending *sva-dharma* should allow a person to overcome all existence *(māyā)* because all macrocosm *dharma* is embedded in the microcosm *(sva-dharma)*.

How does one transcend *dharma?* Śrī Kṛṣṇa answers this in the opening verses, by *sannyāsa* which is renunciation of action motivated by desire *(kāma)* or abandonment of fruits of action *(tyāga)*. At an activity level, there are three main actions. These are *yajña* - sacrifice, *dāna* - donate without expectation of return and *tapas* - self-restraint. *Dāna* adds advantage to internal development, but without sacrifice *(yajña), dāna* cannot be performed. *Tapas* is self-control and integral to development, but *tapas* requires sacrifice *(yajña)*. Also, *sannyāsa* and *tyāga*, both require sacrifice. Hence, *yajña* is the most important of all, without which transcending *māyā* and merger with *Brahman* is not possible.

---

[3] https://schoolofyoga.in/yoga-concept/bhakti-yoga

All sacrifice *(yajña)* **creates debt** *(ṛṇa)* **and we take many for granted. Some examples are as follows:**

- Parents sacrifice for us; we incur two debts to them - debt of birth and debt of upbringing. Debt of birth, we can repay by ensuring a decent funeral and appropriate remembrance ritual. Next, to reconcile debt of upbringing, we can repay them by looking after them when they are old and infirm in a manner that ensures grace and dignity.

- We take our teachers for granted. We think that paying fees is adequate repayment of debt, an incorrect assumption. Also, we forget that we learn from many people whom we never even acknowledge. Education without knowledge has no value because only knowledge prepares us for life, hence repayment to teachers has to extend beyond school and monetary elements.

- The earth sacrifices everything so that we may live well, but we take the Earth for granted, thereby incurring a debt. We pollute the five cardinal elements *(panchabhūtas* = earth *(prithvi)*, water *(āp)*, fire *(agni)*, air *(vāyu)*, space *(ākāṣa))* unthinkingly. This debt has to be repaid.

While there is no doubt that much of *karma* is out of personal control, but repayment cannot be denied, and this should be done to the extent free will permits. That, in itself is sacrifice *(yajña)*.

Conclusion of *Śrīmad-bhagavad-gītā*, verse 63-78:

Śrī Kṛṣṇa said - Thus, I have declared to you the profound wisdom. Hereafter, reflect and decide what you wish to do. Also, you are beloved to me and steadfast of heart. So, fix your cognition on the *Brahman* or on Me. Them, be devoted to me, sacrifice to me, prostate to me, you will then merge with me. This is my pledge to you.

Renounce all conditioning *(dharma)* and surrender unto me. Then, I shall liberate you from all delusions and debt.

This information should not be shared with one who is not disciplined or one who does not perform service. But if you teach this to the deserving, you will surely reach the Brahman, and such a person will understand the meaning of sacrifice of his identity. Also, one who learns with an open mind shall also attain liberation. So, Arjuna, has your delusion been destroyed?

Arjuna said - my delusion has been destroyed. Also, I have regained my awareness through your *māyā*. Consequently, I am firm and free from doubt and will do as you say.

Sanjaya said – I heard the wonderful dialogue between Arjuna and Śrī Kṛṣṇa, causing my hair to stand on end. Also, I have heard, through the grace of Vyasa, the secret of the supreme yoga espoused by the Lord of Yoga himself. Indeed, I rejoice again and again at the dialogue. Consequently, when I recall the wondrous form of Hari, I continue to remain astonished and rejoice again and again. Now, I am convinced that where there is Arjuna and Śrī Kṛṣṇa, there will be victory, prosperity, wealth, and correct policy.

Some contradictions to accepted positions:

From verses 64 onwards, Śrī Kṛṣṇa advises Arjuna to surrender to him (Śrī Kṛṣṇa) for liberation.

Herein lies the problem of existence and availability of free will; whether a person will be able to surrender out of personal volition and whether there will be any results. Will conditioning *(dharma)* or *prārabdha-karma* allow such a surrender? If *prakṛti* forces action, it stands to reason that in all situations, action and reaction is pre-ordained, so surrender may not be in the individual's control.

Next comes the question as to whether a person should surrender to Śrī Kṛṣṇa - the person, or Śrī Kṛṣṇa - the primordial sacrifice *(ādi-yajña)*.

- If surrender is to Śrī Kṛṣṇa the person, then obviously one should be able to surrender to any favorite deity *(iṣṭa-daivatā)* and results should be the same *(bhakti-yoga)* [3].

- However, if the surrender is to Śrī Kṛṣṇa as primordial sacrifice, then the surrender becomes process driven, one of systematic destruction of personal sense of Identity through *jñāna-yoga* [4], *rāja-yoga, haṭha-yoga* [5] etc.

Lessons learned:

- *Sannyāsa* is expectation management; it is renunciation of action motivated by desire. This means - perform action because you need to, not because you want to.

- *Tyāga* is renunciation of fruits of action. This means letting go the fruits once the results come in, whether good or bad, and being content with the result and using the outcome to move forward to the next goal post. It is the attachment to an expected outcome that brings pain.

- When we perform action as a sacrifice *(yajña),* charity *(dāna)* or austerity/self-denial *(tapas),* then selfishness reduces and selflessness increases, this ensures that we are not dependent on others for our self-worth *(asmitā).* This increases our individuality *(svatantra)* as well as thought that action occurs because of our own effort *(ahaṅkāra).*

---

[4]https://schoolofyoga.in/yoga-concept/jnana-yoga

[5]https://schoolofyoga.in/yoga-concept/raja-hatha-yoga

- This increases discrimination between value/non-value *(viveka)* and dispassion *(vairāgya)*.

- Segregation of people according to their attributes *(guṇa)* is natural and occurs everywhere because each person has a natural state *(sva-dharma)* which is a result of *prārabdha-karma*. This endows people with different attributes *(guṇa)*, and each adds different values to society and each other.

- However, it is essential that all people and creation are treated in the same manner, *Brahman* does not discriminate *(samaḥ-sarveṣu-bhūteṣu)*.

- The only requirement to reach *Brahman* is dedication *(śraddhā)*.

The transliteration and translation of chapter 18 follows:

अर्जुन उवाच -

सन्न्यासस्य महाबाहो तत्त्वमिच्छामि वेदितुम् ।

त्यागस्य च हृषीकेश पृथक्केशिनिषूदन ॥ १८-१॥

Arjuna said (1) I wish to know the truth about renunciation and abandonment *(sannyāsasya mahābāho tattvamicchāmi veditum ǀ tyāgasya ca hṛṣīkeśa pṛthakkeśiniṣūdana ǁ 18-1ǁ)*.

श्रीभगवानुवाच -

काम्यानां कर्मणां न्यासं सन्न्यासं कवयो विदुः ।

सर्वकर्मफलत्यागं प्राहुस्त्यागं विचक्षणाः ॥ १८-२॥

त्याज्यं दोषवदित्येके कर्म प्राहुर्मनीषिणः ।

यज्ञदानतपःकर्म न त्याज्यमिति चापरे ॥ १८-३॥

Śrī Kṛṣṇa said (2-3) Sages understand *sannyāsa* as renunciation of actions motivated by desire *(kāma)*. Similarly, abandonment of fruits of all activity is declared abandonment *(tyāga)* by the wise *(kāmyānāṃ karmaṇāṃ nyāsaṃ sannyāsaṃ kavayo viduḥ ǀ sarvakarmaphalatyāgaṃ prāhustyāgaṃ vicakṣaṇāḥ ǁ 18-2ǁ)*. Abandon some types of actions as noxious but sacrifice *(yajna)*, gifting without expectation *(dāna)* and self-restraint *(tapas)* should not be relinquished *(tyājyaṃ doṣavadityeke karma prāhurmanīṣiṇaḥ ǀ yajñadānatapaḥkarma na tyājyamiti cāpare ǁ 18-3ǁ)*.

निश्चयं शृणु मे तत्र त्यागे भरतसत्तम ।

त्यागो हि पुरुषव्याघ्र त्रिविधः सम्प्रकीर्तितः ॥ १८-४॥

यज्ञदानतपःकर्म न त्याज्यं कार्यमेव तत् ।

यज्ञो दानं तपश्चैव पावनानि मनीषिणाम् ॥ १८-५॥

एतान्यपि तु कर्माणि सङ्गं त्यक्त्वा फलानि च ।
कर्तव्यानीति मे पार्थ निश्चितं मतमुत्तमम् ॥ १८-६॥

(4-6) With certainty, it has been declared that there are 3 types of abandonment *(niścayaṃ śarṇu me tatra tyāge bharatasattama । tyāgo hi puruṣavyāghra trividhaḥ samprakīrtitaḥ ॥ 18-4॥)*. Sacrifice, donation, and austerity should not be abandoned when performing action. Indeed, *yajnya, dana,* and *tapas* are purification acts of the wise *(yajñadānatapaḥkarma na tyājyaṃ kāryameva tat । yajño dānaṃ tapaścaiva pāvanāni manīṣiṇām॥ 18-5॥)*. Even these, when these actions are performed, it is my best belief that one should abandon the fruits of such actions also *(etānyapi tu karmāṇi saṅgaṃ tyaktvā phalāni ca । kartavyānīti me pārtha niścitaṃ matamuttamam ॥ 18-6॥)*.

नियतस्य तु सन्न्यासः कर्मणो नोपपद्यते ।
मोहात्तस्य परित्यागस्तामसः परिकीर्तितः ॥ १८-७॥
दुःखमित्येव यत्कर्म कायक्लेशभयात्त्यजेत् ।
स कृत्वा राजसं त्यागं नैव त्यागफलं लभेत् ॥ १८-८॥
कार्यमित्येव यत्कर्म नियतं क्रियतेऽर्जुन ।
सङ्गं त्यक्त्वा फलं चैव स त्यागः सात्त्विको मतः ॥ १८-९॥
न द्वेष्ट्यकुशलं कर्म कुशले नानुषज्जते ।
त्यागी सत्त्वसमाविष्टो मेधावी छिन्नसंशयः ॥ १८-१०॥

(7-10) Importantly, abandoning obligatory duty is not proper. Abandonment arises out of ignorance, and is *tāmasika (niyatasya tu sannyāsaḥ karmaṇo nopapadyate । mohāttasya parityāgastāmasaḥ parikīrtitaḥ ॥ 18-7॥)*. When action is abandoned on account of fear of bodily harm or pain, it is *rājasika,* and when a person abandons it, he does not get the fruits of *tyāga (duḥkhamityeva yatkarma kāyakleśabhayāttyajet । sa kṛtvā rājasaṃ tyāgaṃ naiva tyāgaphalaṃ labhet ॥ 18-8॥)*. Thus, even when obligatory work is performed after abandoning the fruits of such action, such abandonment is known as *sāttvika (kāryamityeva yatkarma niyataṃ kriyate'rjuna । saṅgaṃ tyaktvā phalaṃ caiva sa tyāgaḥ sāttviko mataḥ ॥ 18-9॥)*. Such a person does not loathe disagreeable action, nor gets attached to that which is agreeable duty. Also, a person who is imbibed in *sattva* is self-contained, wise, with doubts torn asunder *(na dveṣṭyakuśalaṃ karma kuśale nānuṣajjate । tyāgī sattvasamāviṣṭo medhāvī chinnasaṃśayaḥ ॥ 18-10॥)*.

न हि देहभृता शक्यं त्यक्तुं कर्माण्यशेषतः ।
यस्तु कर्मफलत्यागी स त्यागीत्यभिधीयते ॥ १८-११॥
अनिष्टमिष्टं मिश्रं च त्रिविधं कर्मणः फलम् ।
भवत्यत्यागिनां प्रेत्य न तु सन्न्यासिनां क्वचित् ॥ १८-१२॥

(11-12) Without a doubt, it is impossible to renounce action. But he who renounces the fruits of one's action, can be regarded as one who has renounced action *(na hi dehabhṛtā śakyaṃ tyaktuṃ karmāṇyaśeṣataḥ ı yastu karmaphalatyāgī sa tyāgītyabhidhīyate ॥ 18-11॥)*. Disagreeable, agreeable, mixed, these threefold outcomes of *karma* accrue when not abandoned, on death, but not when renounced *(aniṣṭamiṣṭaṃ miśraṃ ca trividhaṃ karmaṇaḥ phalam ı bhavatyatyāgināṃ pretya na tu sannyāsinaṃ kvacit ॥ 18-12॥)*.

पञ्चैतानि महाबाहो कारणानि निबोध मे ।

साङ्ख्ये कृतान्ते प्रोक्तानि सिद्धये सर्वकर्मणाम् ॥ १८-१३॥

(13) Disagreeable, agreeable, mixed, these threefold outcomes of *karma* accrue when not abandoned, on death, but not when renounced *(pañcaitāni mahābāho kāraṇāni nibodha me ı sāṅkhye kṛtānte proktāni siddhaye sarvakarmaṇām ॥ 18-13॥)*.

अधिष्ठानं तथा कर्ता करणं च पृथग्विधम् ।

विविधाश्च पृथक्चेष्टा दैवं चैवात्र पञ्चमम् ॥ १८-१४॥

शरीरवाङ्मनोभिर्यत्कर्म प्रारभते नरः ।

न्याय्यं वा विपरीतं वा पञ्चैते तस्य हेतवः ॥ १८-१५॥

(14-15) Additionally, learn the 5 causation components of all actions which are declared as vital in philosophy *(adhiṣṭhānaṃ tathā kartā karaṇaṃ ca pṛthagvidham ı vividhāśca pṛthakceṣṭā daivaṃ caivātra pañcamam ॥ 18-14॥)*, *adhishtānaṃ* (place/body or *kṣetra*), *kartṛ* (doer), *karaṇam* (causation/operation), *prathagvidham* (various points of view), and *deivam* (deity). Whenever man in involved in dissolution of righteous or contrary *karma* involving body, cognition, and verbal skills, these 5 components will be used *(śarīravāṅmanobhiryatkarma prārabhate naraḥ ı nyāyyaṃ vā viparītaṃ vā pañcaite tasya hetavaḥ ॥ 18-15॥)*.

तत्रैवं सति कर्तारमात्मानं केवलं तु यः ।

पश्यत्यकृतबुद्धित्वान्न स पश्यति दुर्मतिः ॥ १८-१६॥

यस्य नाहङ्कृतो भावो बुद्धिर्यस्य न लिप्यते ।

हत्वाऽपि स इमाँल्लोकान्न हन्ति न निबध्यते ॥ १८-१७॥

(16-17) Thus, there the person sees the Self as the doer alone, truly he who does not see this owing to untrained intellect is ignorant *(tatraivaṃ sati kartāramātmānaṃ kevalaṃ tu yaḥ ı paśyatyakṛtabuddhivānna sa paśyati durmatiḥ ॥ 18-16॥)*. He who is free from the intellectual *(buddhihi)* sentiment *(bhāva)* of being the doer *(ahamkṛta)* is not bound *(nibhayate)* by his action, even if he slays other people *(hanti)*, *(yasya nāhaṅkṛto bhāvo buddhiryasya na lipyate ı hatvā 'pi sa imā~llokānna hanti na nibadhyate || 18-17||).*

ज्ञानं ज्ञेयं परिज्ञाता त्रिविधा कर्मचोदना ।

करणं कर्म कर्तेति त्रिविधः कर्मसङ्ग्रहः ॥ १८-१८॥

ज्ञानं कर्म च कर्ता च त्रिधैव गुणभेदतः ।

प्रोच्यते गुणसङ्ख्याने यथावच्छृणु तान्यपि ॥ १८-१९॥

jñānaṃ jñeyaṃ parijñātā trividhā karmacodanā |
karaṇaṃ karma karteti trividhaḥ karmasaṅgrahaḥ || 18-18||

(18-19) Wisdom *(jñānam)*, cognition of wisdom *(jñeyam)*, and knower of wisdom *(parijñātā)* are three-fold motivators for normal action *(karmacodanā)* *(jñānaṃ jñeyaṃ parijñātā trividhā karmacodanā |)*. Next, the organ, instrument, or equipment *(karaṇam)*, *karma* (act) and *kartṛ* (doer or performer) form the threefold constituents *(saṅgrahaḥ)* of action *(karaṇaṃ karma karteti trividhaḥ karmasaṅgrahaḥ || 18-18||)*. Wisdom *(jñānaṃ)*, action *(karma)* and doer *(kartā)* are split according to the mix of attributes *(guṇabhedataḥ - guṇa* = attribute + *bhedataḥ* = split into) are describes in the philosophy of attributes *(guṇasaṅkhyāne - guṇa* = attributes + *śaṅkhā* = philosophical enumeration), hear those also *(jñānaṃ karma ca kartā ca tridhaiva guṇabhedataḥ | procyate guṇasaṅkhyāne yathāvacchṛṇu tānyapi || 18-19||)*.

सर्वभूतेषु येनैकं भावमव्ययमीक्षते ।

अविभक्तं विभक्तेषु तज्ज्ञानं विद्धि सात्त्विकम् ॥ १८-२०॥

पृथक्त्वेन तु यज्ज्ञानं नानाभावान्पृथग्विधान् ।

वेत्ति सर्वेषु भूतेषु तज्ज्ञानं विद्धि राजसम् ॥ १८-२१॥

यत्तु कृत्स्नवदेकस्मिन्कार्ये सक्तमहैतुकम् ।

अतत्त्वार्थवदल्पं च तत्तामसमुदाहृतम् ॥ १८-२२॥

(20-22) First, when one sees the indestructible one-ness *(Brahman)* in all creation, not separated from each other; that wisdom is known is *sattvikam (sarvabhūteṣu yenaikaṃ bhāvamavyayamīkṣate | avibhaktaṃ vibhakteṣu tajjñānaṃ viddhi sāttvikam || 18-20||)*. Next, when one perceives distinct differences or variances in all creation, such wisdom is *rajas (pṛthaktvena tu yajjñānaṃ nānābhāvānpṛthagvidhān | vetti sarveṣu bhūteṣu tajjñānaṃ viddhi rājasam || 18-21||)*. When one extrapolates a single event into a phenomenon *(kṛtsnavat)*, is attached to anything without reason *(ahaitukam)*, does not look for evidence of reality *(athathvarthvath)* or is trivial/fickle *(alpam)*, that is declared to be *tāmasika (yattu kṛtsnavadekasminkārye saktamahaitukam | atattvārthavadalpaṃ ca tattāmasamudāhṛtam || 18-22||)*.

नियतं सङ्गरहितमरागद्वेषतः कृतम् ।

अफलप्रेप्सुना कर्म यत्तत्सात्त्विकमुच्यते ॥ १८-२३॥

यत्तु कामेप्सुना कर्म साहङ्कारेण वा पुनः ।

क्रियते बहुलायासं तद्राजसमुदाहृतम् ॥ १८-२४॥

अनुबन्धं क्षयं हिंसामनपेक्ष्य च पौरुषम् ।

मोहादारभ्यते कर्म यत्तत्तामसमुच्यते ॥ १८-२५॥

(23-25) Also, always indifferent, acting without longing or hatred, with no desire for the fruits of action, that action is *sāttvika (niyataṃ saṅgarahitamarāgadveṣataḥ kṛtam ׀ aphalaprepsunā karma yattatsāttvikamucyate ॥ 18-23॥)*. Action which is done due to craving or passion, a feeling of being the doer, lots of effort, that action is *rājasika (yattu kāmepsunā karma sāhaṅkāreṇa vā punaḥ ׀ kriyate bahulāyāsaṃ tadrājasamudāhṛtam ॥ 18-24॥)*. Lastly, action which is undertaken without heed to consequences, loss, or wastage, injury, with only virility, arises from delusion, is called *tāmasika (anubandhaṃ kṣayaṃ himsāmanapekṣya ca pauruṣam ׀ mohādārabhyate karma yattattāmasamucyate ॥ 18-25॥)*.

मुक्तसङ्गोऽनहंवादी धृत्युत्साहसमन्वितः ।

सिद्ध्यसिद्ध्योर्निर्विकारः कर्ता सात्त्विक उच्यते ॥ १८-२६॥

रागी कर्मफलप्रेप्सुर्लुब्धो हिंसात्मकोऽशुचिः ।

हर्षशोकान्वितः कर्ता राजसः परिकीर्तितः ॥ १८-२७॥

अयुक्तः प्राकृतः स्तब्धः शठो नैष्कृतिकोऽलसः ।

विषादी दीर्घसूत्री च कर्ता तामस उच्यते ॥ १८-२८॥

(26-28) Furthermore, anyone free from attachment, without self-doer-ship, with firm enthusiasm and resolve, unaffected by success or failure is called *sāttvika (siddhyasiddhyornirvikāraḥ)* is *sāttvika (muktasaṅgo'nahaṃvādī dhṛtyutsāhasamanvitaḥ ׀ siddhyasiddhyornirvikāraḥ kartā sāttvika ucyate ॥ 18-26॥)*. Passionate, attached to the fruits of effort, greedy, inclined towards violence, impure, full of joy and sorrow, is called *rājasika (rāgī karmaphalaprepsurlubdho himsātmako'śuciḥ ׀ harṣaśokānvitaḥ kartā rājasaḥ parikīrtitaḥ ॥ 18-27॥)*. Generating absurd positions, vulgar, stubborn, and arrogant, cheating, malicious, lazy, despondent, procrastinating, is called *tāmasika (ayuktaḥ prākṛtaḥ stabdhaḥ śaṭho naiṣkṛtiko'lasaḥ ׀ viṣādī dīrghasūtrī ca kartā tāmasa ucyate ॥ 18-28॥)*.

बुद्धेर्भेदं धृतेश्चैव गुणतस्त्रिविधं शृणु ।

प्रोच्यमानमशेषेण पृथक्त्वेन धनञ्जय ॥ १८-२९॥

प्रवृत्तिं च निवृत्तिं च कार्याकार्ये भयाभये ।

बन्धं मोक्षं च या वेत्ति बुद्धिः सा पार्थ सात्त्विकी ॥ १८-३०॥

यया धर्ममधर्मं च कार्यं चाकार्यमेव च ।

अयथावत्प्रजानाति बुद्धिः सा पार्थ राजसी ॥ १८-३१॥

अधर्मं धर्ममिति या मन्यते तमसावृता ।

सर्वार्थान्विपरीतांश्च बुद्धिः सा पार्थ तामसी ॥ १८-३२॥

(29-32) They have the intellect, ability to delineate, firmness to understand the threefold attributes that I declare to the granular level *(buddherbhedaṃ dhṛteścaiva guṇatastrividhaṃ śarṇu । procyamānamaśeṣeṇa pṛthaktvena dhanañjaya ॥ 18-29॥)*. They have the intellect to discriminate action from renunciation *(nivrittim)*, action which should be done from that which should be left alone, fear from fearlessness and bondage from liberation are *sāttvika (pravṛttiṃ ca nivṛttiṃ ca kāryākārye bhayābhaye । bandhaṃ mokṣaṃ ca yā vetti buddhiḥ sā pārtha sāttvikī ॥ 18-30॥)*. An intellect that is unable to discriminate between natural human state and chaos, correct and improper action is *rajasika (yayā dharmamadharmaṃ ca kāryaṃ cākāryameva ca । ayathāvatprajānāti buddhiḥ sā pārtha rājasī ॥ 18-31॥)*. That intellect which is confused by what constitutes natural state and what does not and views everything in a perverse or contrary manner is *tāmasika (adharmaṃ dharmamiti yā manyate tamasāvṛtā । sarvārthānviparītāṃśca buddhiḥ sā pārtha tāmasī ॥ 18-32॥)*.

धृत्या यया धारयते मनःप्राणेन्द्रियक्रियाः ।

योगेनाव्यभिचारिण्या धृतिः सा पार्थ सात्त्विकी ॥ १८-३३॥

यया तु धर्मकामार्थान्धृत्या धारयतेऽर्जुन ।

प्रसङ्गेन फलाकाङ्क्षी धृतिः सा पार्थ राजसी ॥ १८-३४॥

यया स्वप्नं भयं शोकं विषादं मदमेव च ।

न विमुञ्चति दुर्मेधा धृतिः सा पार्थ तामसी ॥ १८-३५॥

(33-35) He who has unswerving control over the functioning of cognition, life-force, and senses through practice of yoga is *sāttvika (dhṛtyā yayā dhārayate manaḥprāṇendriyakriyāḥ । yogenāvyabhicāriṇyā dhṛtiḥ sā pārtha sāttvikī ॥ 18-33॥)*. However, where control over the natural state desire and material possessions is exerted for fruits of one's action, that firmness is *rājasika (yayā tu dharmakāmārthāndhṛtyā dhārayate'rjuna । prasaṅgena phalākāṅkṣī dhṛtiḥ sā pārtha rājasī ॥ 18-34॥)*. When a person refuses to give up expectations, fear, grief, despair, arrogance, and firmly refuses to abandon delusion, such a person is *tāmasika (yayā svapnaṃ bhayaṃ śokaṃ viṣādaṃ madameva ca । na vimuñcati durmedhā dhṛtiḥ sā pārtha tāmasī ॥ 18-35॥)*.

सुखं त्विदानीं त्रिविधं शृणु मे भरतर्षभ ।

अभ्यासाद्रमते यत्र दुःखान्तं च निगच्छति ॥ १८-३६॥

यत्तदग्रे विषमिव परिणामेऽमृतोपमम् ।
तत्सुखं सात्त्विकं प्रोक्तमात्मबुद्धिप्रसादजम् ॥ १८-३७॥
विषयेन्द्रियसंयोगाद्यत्तदग्रेऽमृतोपमम् ।
परिणामे विषमिव तत्सुखं राजसं स्मृतम् ॥ १८-३८॥
यदग्रे चानुबन्धे च सुखं मोहनमात्मनः ।
निद्रालस्यप्रमादोत्थं तत्तामसमुदाहृतम् ॥ १८-३९॥

(36-39) Hear from me, the three kinds of happiness, the practice of which there is rejoicing from end of sorrow *(sukham tvidānīṃ trividhaṃ śaṛṇu me bharatarṣabha ı abhyāsādramate yatra duḥkhāntaṃ ca nigacchati ıı 18-36ıı)*. In that which is like poison at first but like nectar on reaching self-realization is *sāttvika (yattadagre viṣamiva pariṇāme'mṛtopamam ı tatsukhaṃ sāttvikaṃ proktamātmabuddhiprasādajam ıı 18-37ıı)*. That happiness which arises from the senses and sense-objects, and is like nectar at first but ends up like poison is *rājasika (viṣayendriyasaṃyogādyattadagre'mṛtopamam ı pariṇāme viṣamiva tatsukhaṃ rājasaṃ smṛtam ıı 18-38ıı)*. Finally, that delusive pleasure *(mohanam-atmanah)* which arises from excessive sleep, laziness and negligence *(nidra, alasya, pramada-uttam)* is *tāmasika (yadagre cānubandhe ca sukhaṃ mohanamātmanaḥ ı nidrālasyapramādotthaṃ tattāmasamudāhṛtam ıı 18-39ıı)*.

न तदस्ति पृथिव्यां वा दिवि देवेषु वा पुनः ।
सत्त्वं प्रकृतिजैर्मुक्तं यदेभिः स्यात्त्रिभिर्गुणैः ॥ १८-४०॥

(40) Nothing, not even the deities are free from the influence of the *gunas*, which is born from *prakṛti (na tadasti pṛthivyāṃ vā divi deveṣu vā punaḥ ı sattvaṃ prakṛtijairmuktaṃ yadebhiḥ syāttribhirguṇaiḥ ıı 18-40ıı)*.

ब्राह्मणक्षत्रियविशां शूद्राणां च परन्तप ।
कर्माणि प्रविभक्तानि स्वभावप्रभवैर्गुणैः ॥ १८-४१॥
शमो दमस्तपः शौचं क्षान्तिरार्जवमेव च ।
ज्ञानं विज्ञानमास्तिक्यं ब्रह्मकर्म स्वभावजम् ॥ १८-४२॥
शौर्यं तेजो धृतिर्दाक्ष्यं युद्धे चाप्यपलायनम् ।
दानमीश्वरभावश्च क्षात्रं कर्म स्वभावजम् ॥ १८-४३॥
कृषिगौरक्ष्यवाणिज्यं वैश्यकर्म स्वभावजम् ।
परिचर्यात्मकं कर्म शूद्रस्यापि स्वभावजम् ॥ १८-४४॥

(41-44) The duties of *brahmāṇas, kṣtriyas, vaiśyas* and *śūdras* are distributed according to their personality traits *(svabhava)* and these traits are driven by *gunas (brāhmaṇakṣatriyaviśāṃ śūdrāṇāṃ ca parantapa ı karmāṇi pravibhaktāni*

*svabhāvaprabhavairguṇaiḥ || 18-41||). Personality traits of *brahmāṇas* are –
serenity, subdued/restrained, self-restraint/denial, cleanliness, peacefulness,
uprightness, awareness of the Self, sentience of the environment or *kṣetra (vijñāna)*
and belief in the Vedas *(śamo damastapaḥ śaucaṃ kṣāntirārjavameva ca | jñānaṃ
vijñānamāstikyaṃ brahmakarma svabhāvajam || 18-42||).* Next, personality traits of
kṣtriyas – valor, virility, firmness, skill and cleverness, not flying in battle, generosity,
and behavior of a lord *(śauryaṃ tejo dhṛtirdākṣyaṃ yuddhe cāpyapalāyanam |
dānamīśvarabhāvaśca kṣātraṃ karma svabhāvajam || 18-43||).* Personality traits
of *vaiśyas* can be found in activities such as agriculture, taking care of cattle and
trade. *Sūdras* are born for service *(kṛṣigaurakṣyavāṇijyaṃ vaiśyakarma svabhāvajam
| paricaryātmakaṃ karma śūdrasyāpi svabhāvajam || 18-44||).*

स्वे स्वे कर्मण्यभिरतः संसिद्धिं लभते नरः ।

स्वकर्मनिरतः सिद्धिं यथा विन्दति तच्छृणु ॥ १८-४५॥

यतः प्रवृत्तिर्भूतानां येन सर्वमिदं ततम् ।

स्वकर्मणा तमभ्यर्च्य सिद्धिं विन्दति मानवः ॥ १८-४६॥

(45-46) Everyone has a zone of competence and when activity is performed in this
zone *(sva-karma-nirataha)* with dedication, person finds utopia *(samsiddhi) (sve
sve karmaṇyabhirataḥ saṃsiddhiṃ labhate naraḥ | svakarmanirataḥ siddhiṃ yathā
vindati tacchṛṇu || 18-45||).* When acting within one's competence *(sva=* self +
karmana = action), if dedication of the act is to the *Brahman, (sarva* = all + *idam* =
this + *tatam* = pervaded + *pravrittih* = evolution), mankind attains utopia *(siddhim)
(yataḥ pravṛttirbhūtānāṃ yena sarvamidaṃ tatam | svakarmaṇā tamabhyarcya
siddhiṃ vindati mānavaḥ || 18-46||).*

श्रेयान्स्वधर्मो विगुणः परधर्मात्स्वनुष्ठितात् ।

स्वभावनियतं कर्म कुर्वन्नाप्नोति किल्बिषम् ॥ १८-४७॥

सहजं कर्म कौन्तेय सदोषमपि न त्यजेत् ।

सर्वारम्भा हि दोषेण धूमेनाग्निरिवावृताः ॥ १८-४८॥

(47-48) It is better to act in conformance to one's conditioning even though it may
have fewer merits, rather than to perform good work which is the conditioning of
others. Action performed in conformance to one's own personality traits, no matter
how badly performed, incurs no negativity *(kilbhisham) (śreyānsvadharmo viguṇaḥ
paradharmātsvanuṣṭhitāt | svabhāvaniyataṃ karma kurvannāpnoti kilbiṣam || 18-
47||).* Innate nature is action. Even though action comes with its own challenges/
defects one should not abandon it, because when whenever activity is started,
each effort will have challenges, like smoke which covers the fire *(sahajaṃ karma
kaunteya sadoṣamapi na tyajet | sarvārambhā hi doṣeṇa dhūmenāgnirivāvṛtāḥ ||
18-48||).*

असक्तबुद्धिः सर्वत्र जितात्मा विगतस्पृहः ।
नैष्कर्म्यसिद्धिं परमां सन्न्यासेनाधिगच्छति ॥ १८-४९॥

सिद्धिं प्राप्तो यथा ब्रह्म तथाप्नोति निबोध मे ।
समासेनैव कौन्तेय निष्ठा ज्ञानस्य या परा ॥ १८-५०॥

बुद्ध्या विशुद्धया युक्तो धृत्यात्मानं नियम्य च ।
शब्दादीन्विषयांस्त्यक्त्वा रागद्वेषौ व्युदस्य च ॥ १८-५१॥

(49-51) A person whose logic is unattached at all times, has subdued the Self and is devoid of desire, who is completely without desire, that person attains supreme renunciate state *(asaktabuddhiḥ sarvatra jitātmā vigataspṛhaḥ ꠰ naiṣkarmyasiddhiṃ paramāṃ sannyāsenādhigacchati ꠰꠰ 18-49꠰꠰)*. Learn from me in brief, that supreme knowledge of how to reach the highest state of perfection and attain *Brahman* *(siddhiṃ prāpto yathā brahma tathāpnoti nibodha me ꠰ samāsenaiva kaunteya niṣṭhā jñānasya yā parā ꠰꠰ 18-50꠰꠰)*. Purify the intellect and join firmly to the Self through self-control. Then, relinquish sound related subjects and abandon duality such as like-dislike *(buddhyā viśuddhayā yukto dhṛtyātmānaṃ niyamya ca ꠰ śabdādīnviṣayāṃstyaktvā rāgadveṣau vyudasya ca ꠰꠰ 18-51꠰꠰)*.

विविक्तसेवी लघ्वाशी यतवाक्कायमानसः ।
ध्यानयोगपरो नित्यं वैराग्यं समुपाश्रितः ॥ १८-५२॥

अहङ्कारं बलं दर्पं कामं क्रोधं परिग्रहम् ।
विमुच्य निर्ममः शान्तो ब्रह्मभूयाय कल्पते ॥ १८-५३॥

(52-53) Live in solitude, eat sparingly, keep speech, body and cognition yoked by meditation, while constantly taking refuge in dispassion *(vairāgya)* *(viviktasevī laghvāśī yatavākkāyamānasaḥ ꠰ dhyānayogaparo nityaṃ vairāgyaṃ samupāśritaḥ ꠰꠰ 18-52꠰꠰)*. Abandon feeling of being the doer, all forms of power, arrogance, passion, anger, greed, then freed from non-possessiveness, peaceful *Brahman* transformation occurs *(ahaṅkāraṃ balaṃ darpaṃ kāmaṃ krodhaṃ parigraham꠰ vimucya nirmamaḥ śānto brahmabhūyāya kalpate ꠰꠰ 18-53꠰꠰)*.

ब्रह्मभूतः प्रसन्नात्मा न शोचति न काङ्क्षति ।
समः सर्वेषु भूतेषु मद्भक्तिं लभते पराम् ॥ १८-५४॥

भक्त्या मामभिजानाति यावान्यश्चास्मि तत्त्वतः ।
ततो मां तत्त्वतो ज्ञात्वा विशते तदनन्तरम् ॥ १८-५५॥

सर्वकर्माण्यपि सदा कुर्वाणो मद्व्यपाश्रयः ।
मत्प्रसादादवाप्नोति शाश्वतं पदमव्ययम् ॥ १८-५६॥

(54-56) On realizing *Brahman,* this serene soul neither grieves nor has expectations. Treating all alike my devotee attains supreme *(brahmabhūtaḥ prasannātmā na śocati na kāṅkṣati ǀ samaḥ sarveṣu bhūteṣu madbhaktim labhate parām ǀǀ 18-54ǀǀ).* Devoted to me, he perceives Truth in the Self. Then, recognizing that "I" and "Truth" are the same, thereafter there is merger *(bhaktyā māmabhijānāti yāvānyaścāsmi tattvataḥ ǀ tato mām tattvato jñātvā viśate tadanantaram ǀǀ 18-55ǀǀ).* Performing all actions always while taking refuge in me, by my grace, he attains, the indestructible, eternal abode *(sarvakarmāṇyapi sadā kurvāṇo madvyapāśrayaḥ ǀ matprasādādavāpnoti śāśvatam padamavyayam ǀǀ 18-56ǀǀ).*

चेतसा सर्वकर्माणि मयि सन्न्यस्य मत्परः ।

बुद्धियोगमुपाश्रित्य मच्चित्तः सततं भव ॥ १८-५७॥

मच्चित्तः सर्वदुर्गाणि मत्प्रसादात्तरिष्यसि ।

अथ चेत्त्वमहङ्कारान्न श्रोष्यसि विनङ्क्ष्यसि ॥ १८-५८॥

(57-58) Consciously renounce all actions in devotion to me, always be with the approach of joining the intellect with the consciousness on me *(cetasā sarvakarmāṇi mayi sannyasya matparaḥ ǀ buddhiyogamupāśritya maccittaḥ satatam bhava ǀǀ 18-57ǀǀ).* Devoted to me, you will overcome all obstacles, by my grace. However, if you listen to my words with the attitude of a doer, then you will lose everything *(maccittaḥ sarvadurgāṇi matprasādāttariṣyasi ǀ atha cettvamahaṅkārānna śroṣyasi vinaṅkṣyasi ǀǀ 18-58ǀǀ).*

यदहङ्कारमाश्रित्य न योत्स्य इति मन्यसे ।

मिथ्यैष व्यवसायस्ते प्रकृतिस्त्वां नियोक्ष्यति ॥ १८-५९॥

स्वभावजेन कौन्तेय निबद्धः स्वेन कर्मणा ।

कर्तुं नेच्छसि यन्मोहात्करिष्यस्यवशोऽपि तत् ॥ १८-६०॥

(59-60) In fact, even if you take refuge in your attitude of doer-ship and use your cognitive abilities in refusing to fight, *prakṛti* will compel you and your resolve will be in vain *(yadahaṅkāramāśritya na yotsya iti manyase ǀ mithyaiṣa vyavasāyaste prakṛtistvām niyokṣyati ǀǀ 18-59ǀǀ).* Despite your delusion, you are bound by *karma* which drives your own nature, and you cannot do as you wish. Indeed, you are helpless *(svabhāvajena kaunteya nibaddhaḥ svena karmaṇā ǀ kartum necchasi yanmohātkariṣyasyavaśo'pi tat ǀǀ 18-60ǀǀ).*

ईश्वरः सर्वभूतानां हृद्देशेऽर्जुन तिष्ठति ।

भ्रामयन्सर्वभूतानि यन्त्रारूढानि मायया ॥ १८-६१॥

तमेव शरणं गच्छ सर्वभावेन भारत ।

तत्प्रसादात्परां शान्तिं स्थानं प्राप्स्यसि शाश्वतम् ॥ १८-६२॥

(61-62) The *Brahman* is present in all beings. However, it is *Brahman's māyā* (*Brahmamaya*) which causes all beings to imagine that they are mounted on a machine *(īśvaraḥ sarvabhūtānāṃ hṛddeśe'rjuna tiṣṭhati ǀ bhrāmayansarvabhūtāni yantrārūḍhāni māyayā ǁ 18-61ǁ).* So, seek refuge in that, with all your faculties in the grace of *Brahman* you will gain supreme peace and obtain eternal abode *(tameva śaraṇaṃ gaccha sarvabhāvena bhārata ǀ tatprasādātparāṃ śāntiṃ sthānaṃ prāpsyasi śāśvatam ǁ 18-62ǁ).*

इति ते ज्ञानमाख्यातं गुह्याद्गुह्यतरं मया ।

विमृश्यैतदशेषेण यथेच्छसि तथा कुरु ॥ १८-६३॥

सर्वगुह्यतमं भूयः शृणु मे परमं वचः ।

इष्टोऽसि मे दृढमिति ततो वक्ष्यामि ते हितम् ॥ १८-६४॥

(63-64) Thus, an exclusive wisdom that is a secret has been declared by me to you. Reflect over it completely and take the course of action that you wish *(iti te jñānamākhyātaṃ guhyādguhyataraṃ mayā ǀ vimṛśyaitadaśeṣeṇa yathecchasi tathā kuru ǁ 18-63ǁ).* The biggest secret of all, hear my supreme word. Deeply beloved you are to me; therefore, I will tell you that which is favorable to you *(sarvaguhyatamam bhūyaḥ śaṛnu me paramaṃ vacaḥ ǀ iṣṭo'si me dṛḍhamiti tato vakṣyāmi te hitam ǁ 18-64ǁ).*

मन्मना भव मद्भक्तो मद्याजी मां नमस्कुरु ।

मामेवैष्यसि सत्यं ते प्रतिजाने प्रियोऽसि मे ॥ १८-६५॥

सर्वधर्मान्परित्यज्य मामेकं शरणं व्रज ।

अहं त्वा सर्वपापेभ्यो मोक्षयिष्यामि मा शुचः ॥ १८-६६॥

(65-66) With your cognition fixed on me, devoted to me, sacrifice to me, prostrate to me, verily you will come to me, this truth I confirm to you because you are beloved of me *(manmanā bhava madbhakto madyājī māṃ namaskuru ǀ māmevaiṣyasi satyaṃ te pratijāne priyo'si me ǁ 18-65ǁ).* Abandoning all conditioning *(sarva-dharma-parityajya)* to me alone, take surrender, I will liberate you from all wretchedness, do not grieve *(sarvadharmānparityajya māmekaṃ śaraṇaṃ vraja ǀ ahaṃ tvā sarvapāpebhyo mokṣayiṣyāmi mā śucaḥ ǁ 18-66ǁ).*

इदं ते नातपस्काय नाभक्ताय कदाचन ।

न चाशुश्रूषवे वाच्यं न च मां योऽभ्यसूयति ॥ १८-६७॥

य इदं परमं गुह्यं मद्भक्तेष्वभिधास्यति ।

भक्तिं मयि परां कृत्वा मामेवैष्यत्यसंशयः ॥ १८-६८॥

(67-68) You should not share this with anyone who does not practice austerities, never to one who is not devoted, one who does not pay attention or is can be blamed in his actions or one who is jealous *(idaṃ te nātapaskāya nābhaktāya kadācana ı na cāśuśrūṣave vācyaṃ na ca māṃ yo'bhyasūyati ıı 18-67ıı)*. This supreme secret shall be declared to those who are supremely devoted to me, who undoubtedly shall come to me *(ya idaṃ paramaṃ guhyaṃ madbhakteṣvabhidhāsyati ı bhaktiṃ mayi parāṃ kṛtvā māmevaiṣyatyasaṃśayaḥ ıı 18-68ıı)*.

न च तस्मान्मनुष्येषु कश्चिन्मे प्रियकृत्तमः ।

भविता न च मे तस्मादन्यः प्रियतरो भुवि ॥ १८-६९॥

अध्येष्यते च य इमं धर्म्यं संवादमावयोः ।

ज्ञानयज्ञेन तेनाहमिष्टः स्यामिति मे मतिः ॥ १८-७०॥

(69-70) And there is none dearer to me among men who works with affection, there shall be none dearer on Earth *(na ca tasmānmanuṣyeṣu kaścinme priyakṛttamaḥ ı bhavitā na ca me tasmādanyaḥ priyataro bhuvi ıı 18-69ıı)*. And who shall study this consensual conversation *(sam-vādam)* of ours on natural states through sacrifice of intellect *(jñānayajñena)*, him I shall like and this is my intuition *(adhyeṣyate ca ya imaṃ dharmyaṃ saṃvādamāvayoḥ ı jñānayajñena tenāhamiṣṭaḥ syāmiti me matiḥ ıı 18-70ıı)*.

श्रद्धावाननसूयश्च शृणुयादपि यो नरः ।

सोऽपि मुक्तः शुभाँल्लोकान्प्राप्नुयात्पुण्यकर्मणाम् ॥ १८-७१॥

कच्चिदेतच्छुतं पार्थ त्वयैकाग्रेण चेतसा ।

कच्चिदज्ञानसम्मोहः प्रनष्टस्ते धनञ्जय ॥ १८-७२॥

(71-72) Even that person who hears with integrity *(śraddhā)*, without envy *(anasooyah)* will also be liberated and be in a happy world, begetting the benefits of stain-free action *(puṇyakarmaṇām)* *(śraddhāvānanasūyaśca śaṛṇuyādapi yo naraḥ ı so'pi muktaḥ śubhā~llokānprāpnuyātpuṇyakarmaṇām ıı 18-71ıı)*. Have you heard this with a single pointed focussed consciousness, Arjuna? Have the delusions arising from ignorance been destroyed? *(kaccidetacchrutaṃ pārtha tvayaikāgreṇa cetasā ı kaccidajñānasammohaḥ pranaṣṭaste dhanañjaya ıı 18-72ıı)*

अर्जुन उवाच ।

नष्टो मोहः स्मृतिर्लब्धा त्वत्प्रसादान्मयाच्युत ।

स्थितोऽस्मि गतसन्देहः करिष्ये वचनं तव ॥ १८-७३॥

Arjuna said (73) My delusions have been destroyed, mindfulness has been gained through your grace, I am freed from doubts and firm. I will do as you say *(naṣṭo mohaḥ smṛtirlabdhā tvatprasādānmayācyuta ı sthito'smi gatasandehaḥ kariṣye vacanaṃ tava ıı 18-73ıı)*.

सञ्जय उवाच ।

इत्यहं वासुदेवस्य पार्थस्य च महात्मनः ।
संवादमिममश्रौषमद्भुतं रोमहर्षणम् ॥ १८-७४॥

व्यासप्रसादाच्छुतवानेतद्गुह्यमहं परम् ।
योगं योगेश्वरात्कृष्णात्साक्षात्कथयतः स्वयम् ॥ १८-७५॥

राजन्संस्मृत्य संस्मृत्य संवादमिममद्भुतम् ।
केशवार्जुनयोः पुण्यं हृष्यामि च मुहुर्मुहुः ॥ १८-७६॥

तच्च संस्मृत्य रूपमत्यद्भुतं हरेः ।
विस्मयो मे महान् राजन्हृष्यामि च पुनः ॥ १८-७७॥

यत्र योगेश्वरः कृष्णो यत्र पार्थो धनुर्धरः ।
तत्र श्रीर्विजयो भूतिर्ध्रुवा नीतिर्मतिर्मम ॥ १८-७८॥

Sanjaya said (74-78) Thus I heard this high-level dialogue between Vaasudeiva and Parth, this visionary, wonderful experience that causes my hair to stand on end *(ityaham vāsudevasya pārthasya ca mahātmanaḥ | samvādamimamaśrauṣamadbhutam romaharṣaṇam || 18-74||)*. Through the grace of Vyaasa, I have heard this supreme secret on Yoga from the Lord of Yoga, Krishna directly, declaring himself *(vyāsaprasādācchrutavānetadguhyamaham param | yogam yogeśvarātkṛṣṇātsākṣātkathayataḥ svayam || 18-75||)*. King, have remembered again and again, this wonderful and virtuous dialogue between Krishna and Arjuna, I rejoice again and again *(rājansamsmṛtya samsmṛtya samvādamimamadbhutam | keśavārjunayoḥ puṇyam hṛṣyāmi ca muhurmuhuḥ || 18-76||)*. And then having remembered again and again the most wonderful form of Hari I wonder, my great king, again and again *(tacca samsmṛtya rūpamatyadbhutam hareḥ | vismayo me mahān rājanhṛṣyāmi ca punaḥ || 18-77||)*. Wherever there is the Lord of Yoga Krishna, wherever there is Partha the archer, there will always be prosperity, victory, happiness, stable conduct is my conviction *(yatra yogeśvaraḥ kṛṣṇo yatra pārtho dhanurdharaḥ | tatra śrīrvijayo bhūtirdhruvā nītirmatirmama || 18-78||)*

With this, ends *Śimad-bhagavad-gītā*.
***Om-tat-sat* (hope that this effort adds value)**

Epilogue

What have I learned from this effort? I started translation and commentary in 2016 and tried to understand Śrī Kṛṣṇa and *Śrimad-Bhagavad-gītā*. But have I really achieved that?

I am still unclear on what to make of Śrī Kṛṣṇa. But I also think that it does not matter. An argument that plays in my head is that Śrī Kṛṣṇa and *Śrimad-Bhagavad-gītā* are the same; one is the artist, the other is the muse. So, why split hair?

As to *Śrimad-Bhagavad-gītā*, I can safely say that I have learned a lot, and my takeaways are as follows:

The business of living is a game of smoke and mirror, and there are no clear answers. This is the power of *māyā*. That is why we have *dharma*, a framework where everything is prescribed, and our sense of self-worth *(asmitā)* is undisturbed for as long as we follow the rules.

But *dharma* is a trap because it inhibits free thinking. So, a person must learn how to live within the rules of *dharma*, yet remain unentangled by *dharma's* chains. But how?

There is only one way that this can be done, and this is the essence of Śrī Kṛṣṇa's teachings, which is, remain in the present, because the present is the only place where there is no baggage of the past, no hope, dreams, or faith in the future, and, most importantly, it does not allow one to overthink anything.

But remaining in the present is very difficult, as one is always a little ahead or behind. So, one needs to practice yoga. This is where the practice of *kriya-yoga* (yoga of effort) aspect of *Rāja-yoga* comes in handy. The components of *kriya-yoga* are:

- *Yama* – harmonizing our consciousness with the external environment.

- *Niyama* – harmonizing stimulus so that our responses are synchronized with our conditioning *(svadharma)*.

- *Āsana* – physical fitness results in *prāṇa* flow that is unimpeded, resulting in a body that is fit to take on the rigors of yoga.

- *Prāṇāyāma* – controlling *prāṇa* so that internal harmony is complete.

- *Pratyāhāra* – stepping back from current state so that we are able to view everything in a detached manner (with *vairāgyam*), thereby increasing our ability to discriminate between the real and temporary (*vivekam*).

It's important to realize that maturity will come with age, and this will change our understanding of each aspect of *kriya-yoga*. As children, we will see each component literally. As married people *(gṛhastha)*, we get sucked into a maelstrom of action and often act on reflex, struggling to keep abreast of the stream of experiences. Retirement *(vānaprasthāśrama)* is a period of insecurity as we struggle to find new meaning in a life that has ceased to be materially productive. This is the most dangerous period of our life as we can easily become directionless. Finally, the last stage *(āśrama)*, and possibly the most important, is *sannyāsāśrama*, where we use our life experiences to transcend our sense of existence and prepare for death. But this last stage *(āśrama)* has not found takers in modern Bhārat; death has become a taboo subject, and so people are unable to outgrow *vānaprasthāśrama* as far as personal development is concerned.

The *puruṣārtha* and *āśrama* matrix has renunciate stage *(sannyāsāśrama)* in it for a reason. My recommendation is that we, who are around 65 must practice it. It does not have to be in the conventionally accepted or approved way. It can conform to one's capacity and capability, but it must be practiced for two reasons. First is for one's own evolution. Second, as this evolution manifests as silence, the austerity *(tapas)* manifests as effulgence *(tejas)*, and the *yogī* becomes a stabilizing role model in this society.

In conclusion, my recommendation to the reader is, do not view *Śrīmad-Bhagavad-Gītā* as a book of religion or Śrī Kṛṣṇa as a God! Because, neither is true and if you do, you will encase yourself in a non-existant chain that will prevent you from extracting the full potential of *Śrīmad-Bhagavad-Gītā*. Instead, view *Śrīmad-Bhagavad-Gītā* as a book of excellence and wisdom, and Śrī Kṛṣṇa as a wise elder/ *yogī* who has scaled the pinnacle of greatness, awareness and sagacity. If you do this, then you will be able to cast aside all your physical, psychological, physiological and psychosomatic limitations and achieve your full potential, a greatness that's your right, and become a role-model *(Puruṣottama)* that Bhārat desperately needs.

◆——— • ● ◆ ● • ———◆

www.ingramcontent.com/pod-product-compliance
Lightning Source LLC
Chambersburg PA
CBHW051133130726
47988CB00005B/1812